Contents

Foreword

1991 was an important landmark in British census taking; a question on ethnic group was included for the first time.

OPCS invited over 40 academic experts on ethnicity from a number of fields – including demography, social statistics, geography and sociology – to contribute chapters to four volumes of analyses of 1991 Census ethnic group data. Amongst these authors, five also acted as editors.

I am particularly grateful to the editors and the authors for their excellent work, and also to John Haskey who acted as the series coordinator.

PETER WORMALD
Registrar General
for England and Wales

February 1996

OFFICE OF POPULATION CENSUSES AND SURVEYS

7/91

D/002

Ethnicity in the 1991 Census

Volume One

Demographic characteristics of

the ethnic minority populations

Edited by David Coleman and John Salt

London: HMSO

Notice
On 1st April 1996 the Office of Population Censuses and Surveys (OPCS) and the Central Statistical Office (CSO) will merge to form the Office for National Statistics. The Office for National Statistics will be responsible for the full range of functions carried out by OPCS and CSO.

Front cover photograph: © Crispin Hughes/Photofusion

Printed in the United Kingdom for HMSO
Dd 0301925 C10 3/96 65862

Notes on contributors

Ann Berrington is a Lecturer in Population Studies at the University of Southampton. Her research interests lie in marriage and family formation and dissolution in Britain. Papers include 'Marriage and family formation patterns among the white and ethnic minority populations in Britain' *Ethnic and Racial Studies*, 17, 3, 517-46 (1994); 'Changes in the living arrangements of young adults in Britain during the 1980s' *European Sociological Review*, 10, 3, 235-257 (1994, with M. Murphy).

Martin Bulmer is Professor of Sociology at the University of Surrey and Academic Director of the Question Bank of the ESRC Centre for Applied Social Surveys. He is the editor of the academic journal *Ethnic and Racial Studies*. He has held teaching appointments at the University of Durham, the London School of Economics and Political Science, the University of Chicago and the University of Southampton. His research interests include the application of social science in public policy making, the history of sociology and the methodology of social research. His recent publications include *Citizenship Today: the contemporary relevance of T H Marshall* (edited, with A M Rees) (1996) and *Social Research in Developing Countries: Surveys and Censuses in the Third World* (edited, with D P Warwick) (1993).

David Coleman is the Lecturer in Demography at Oxford University. His research interests include the comparative demographic trends in the industrial world and their socio-economic consequences, immigration patterns and policies and the demography of ethnic minority populations. Publications include 'Does Europe Need Immigrants? Population and Workforce Projections'. *International Migration Review 26*, 2, (1992); 'International migrants in Europe: adjustment and integration processes and policies'. in *International Migration: regional processes and responses*. ed. M. Macura and D.A. Coleman. New York, United Nations, (1994); *'Europe's Population in the 1990s'* (editor; Oxford University Press, 1996). He is joint editor of the *European Journal of Population*.

Paul Compton, formerly Professor of Geography at Queen's University Belfast, is a free-lance writer and researcher, whose chief interests now lie outside academia. He has written on the politico-economic consequences of demographic differentials in Northern Ireland and has also researched minority questions in East-Central Europe. Publications include *Demographic Review Northern Ireland and Fertility and Family Planning in Northern Ireland* (with John Coward; Avebury, Aldershot 1989)

Mike Murphy is the Reader in Population Studies at the London School of Economics and Political Science, and is Chairman of the Royal Statistical Society Official Section. His main areas of research include: the demography of developed societies; family and household demography; investigating linkages between demographic and housing and labour markets; intergenerational relations and ageing. Publications include: 'Demographic and Socio-economic influences on recent British marital breakdown patterns'; *Population Studies 39*: 441-460 (1985); The onset of fertility transition, *Population and Development Review 11*: 399-440 (1985, with T. Dyson); The contraceptive pill and women's employment as factors in fertility change in Britain 1963-1980: a challenge to the conventional view, *Population Studies 47*: 221-243 (1993).

David Owen is a Senior Research Fellow at the Centre for Research in Ethnic Relations, University of Warwick. His research interests are in the analysis of the social and economic circumstances of minority ethnic groups in Britain, internal migration and population change and local labour market analysis. He is joint author of *Changing Places* (1987, with A. Champion, A. Green, D. Ellin and M. Coombes), and has recently had published a major research report for the Equal Opportunities Commission entitled *Ethnic Minority Women and the Labour Market: analysis of the 1991 Census*.

John Salt is Senior Lecturer in Geography and Director of the Migration Research Unit at University College London. He has worked as a consultant on migration to the OECD, Council of Europe, EU and UN. Publications include *The British Population: Demographic Patterns, Trends and Processes* (with D. A. Coleman, 1992, Oxford University Press) and *Europe's International Migrants: Data sources, patterns and trends* (with Singleton, A. and Hogarth, J., 1993, HMSO)

Stephen Simpson is a Principal Research Officer at the City of Bradford Metropolitan Council, and a Senior Research Associate at the University of Manchester's Centre for Census and Survey Research. His research interests include the quality and use of the census, needs assessment for resource distribution, and demographic methods. Papers include 'Those missing millions: implications for social statistics of non-response to the 1991 Census' (with Daniel Dorling), *Journal of Social Policy* 23 (4): 543-567

Tony Warnes is Professor of Social Gerontology in the University of Sheffield, and was formerly Professor of Human Geography at King's College London. He has held visiting research and teaching positions at the Universities of Michigan and South Florida. His research interests are in the demography of ageing societies, and migration and morbidity in later life. His books include *Movement in Cities* (with Peter Daniels, Methuen, 1980), *Geographical Perspectives on the Elderly* (Wiley, 1982), *Human Ageing and Later Life*, (Arnold, 1989) and *The Demography of Ageing in the United Kingdom*, (UN Institute on Aging, Malta 1993)

Chapter 1

The ethnic group question in the 1991 Census: a new landmark in British social statistics

David Coleman and John Salt

1.1 A new landmark

This volume is the first of four which record the results of a significant innovation in the British census — the introduction of a direct question on ethnic origin. That, in turn, is a belated response to one of the most striking new developments in British society since the census began in 1801 — the rise of substantial populations of non-European ethnic and racial origin through post-war immigration mostly from the New Commonwealth (that is, the Commonwealth excluding the old Dominions of Canada, Australia and New Zealand). The inclusion of the census question on ethnicity is the outcome of almost two decades of debate on the desirability of such a question and the form which it should take.

Its inclusion is significant for many reasons. One is the great volume of new and comprehensive data on the characteristics and conditions of the ethnic minority populations which it has yielded, to which the chapters in this and the other three volumes in this series bear witness. Another is the indication, given by the inclusion of the question, of the extent to which the multicultural nature of British society has become officially recognized, endorsed and in some respects institutionalized. Previous ethnic enquiries in surveys have been voluntary; this is a question in a compulsory census. In practical terms the census question will serve to facilitate public policy directed towards the ethnic minority populations: to redress inequalities and disadvantage, to meet their special needs and the requirements of race relations policies. It will give both a form of classification and a statistical basis for much more developed and refined forms of ethnic monitoring and targeting, already nearly universal in the public sector and becoming widespread in the voluntary and private sector of British life as well.

This introduction summarizes the chief findings of the chapters in the book. It explains why some topics connected with the demography of the ethnic minority populations have been omitted. More generally, it puts the ethnic question in the British census in a broader historical, statistical and international context. The history of people of non-European origin in the British Isles is briefly considered, to show that the innovation of the census ethnic question is a response to radical change in the composition of the British population. The form of the new census question is considered in relation to different forms of classification of ethnic origin, in particular those developed in connection with equal opportunities policies that the census ethnic question is intended to assist. Finally the ethnic question in the British census is compared with the practice on the enumeration or recognition of groups or people defined by ethnicity, race, language or religion in the censuses of other industrial countries in Europe, North America and the Old Commonwealth.

1.2   New findings from the census: a synopsis of chapters

It is clear from the chapters in this volume and its companion volumes that the ethnic question has materially added to our knowledge of the British population. That knowledge was not easily gained, as is evident from Bulmer's analysis of the history and development of the ethnic question in Chapter 2, and Simpson's discussion of non-response in Chapter 3.

Bulmer traces the emergence of a question on ethnic group, and discusses its effectiveness in identifying the main ethnic minority groups in the UK today. Perhaps more than any other census question, there was a complex and extended process of consultation, development and testing, leading to final ministerial and Parliamentary approval. But why was an ethnic question thought necessary? Bulmer puts the decision into its wider social context. During the period since the Second World War, not only has the ethnic minority population grown in size, it has become more complex, with migration streams from successively different source regions. Put simply, there was a need to enumerate a striking new element in the British population. There were also short and long-term policy considerations, namely the need for information to frame an increasingly restrictive immigration policy, and, in the longer term, deal with the issues of integration and discrimination that, if mishandled, might threaten national cohesion.

In view of the sensitive nature of the question, a number of practical issues had to be resolved. Bulmer identifies the problems of definition and terminology encountered, and reviews the various ways devised over the years for making the concept of an ethnic question operational. His conclusions indicate a broad balance of general overall success, tempered by the need to improve coverage and response. For the future, he identifies (as does Owen in Chapter 4) a need to deal better with those of mixed ethnic origin (a constituency growing in number), small ethnic minorities not separately identified, and (like Compton in Chapter 9) subgroups of the White population, notably the Irish.

The analyses in this and its companion volumes are affected by the degree of bias, introduced particularly by non-response to the ethnic question. This important topic is discussed by Simpson in Chapter 3. In the census as a whole it would appear that certain groups were undercounted, notably young children, young adults (especially men aged 20-34 living in city districts) and the very elderly. For ethnic minorities in these groups the undercount was greater. Simpson concludes that a larger proportion of each ethnic minority group than in the White population were missed, principally because of their location in areas and in age groups which proved difficult to enumerate fully.

There were also significant variations in non-response between ethnic groups. Overall, Black and Asian ethnic groups were relatively poorly enumerated in the country as a whole because of their concentration in low coverage areas of Britain. The proportion of ethnic minority children missed seems to have been particularly high, perhaps 17 per cent of children aged under 10 years of age born to New Commonwealth mothers. Why this under-enumeration occurred is unclear. One suggestion is the need for ethnographic studies of how people fill in census forms, in order to draw lessons for 2001. Whatever the reason, its existence needs to be borne in mind in the analyses that follow.

The purpose of Owen's chapter (4) is to provide a broad introduction to the remainder of the volume. He makes a frontal assault on the main characteristics and patterns of the ethnic minority populations. He reviews the size, structure, growth and geographical distribution of ethnic minority groups resident in Britain in 1991, comparing the characteristics of individual minority groups with those of the white population. His chapter provides a summary and context for the more detailed analyses in this and the other three volumes. He also echoes the warning of Bulmer on the inadequacy of the ethnic question in failing to distinguish the highly diverse range of ethnic groups, and especially the loss of specific information on the characteristics of people of mixed parentage, and that of Simpson on the uncertainties brought about by under-enumeration.

Using census birthplace data, and data from the Labour Force Survey, Owen shows the rapid growth, now slowing, in the ethnic minority population over the last 40 years. Ethnic composition has also changed, the initial domination of those of Caribbean origin giving way in stock size to South Asians, who will form an increasing proportion of the workforce and of students. These trends in composition have also been accompanied by changes in age structure. Earlier immigrant groups (Black Caribbean, Indian, Chinese) tend to be older than both more recent arrivals and those of mixed ethnic minorities whose members are predominantly UK-born.

Owen's analysis breaks new ground in its extensive treatment of the distributional aspects of ethnic minorities, themes picked up particularly in Volume 3 of this series. While the census broadly confirms the demographic patterns of ethnic minorities, it has the unique value of providing for the first time detailed demographic and socio-economic data on the structure of ethnic minority populations in small geographic areas. Owen shows the increasing relative concentration of ethnic minorities in larger cities and urban areas, and provides key insights into the processes of population change there. Subsequent censuses will allow these processes to be measured, including the degree to which ethnic minorities are undergoing suburbanisation and counter-urbanisation.

The relationship between the concepts of 'immigrants' and 'ethnic groups' is discussed by Salt in Chapter 5. He points out that the two are not synonymous, nor should it be assumed that all ethnic minority group immigration is necessarily for settlement purposes. His chapter focuses on immigration flows by ethnic minority groups, placing them within the broader statistical context of the UK's international migration patterns and trends. Analysis of birthplace information shows that nearly half of the non-White population was born in the UK, the proportions varying considerably: a large majority of Asians, especially, Chinese and Bangladeshis, were born outside the UK; the figure was less than half for Black–Caribbeans, while most Black–Other people, who include a high proportion of those of mixed parentage, were born in the UK.

About a quarter of immigrants, defined as those entering the UK during 1990–91, were from ethnic minority groups, the largest numbers being of Asians and Black Africans; numbers of Black–Caribbeans and Black–Others entering the UK were low. Non–White immigrants were more likely than White people to be young or elderly, less likely to be middle-aged. Geographically, the dominance of South-east England as a destination region was clear. The immigration rates of ethnic groups show wide variations, and there is a clear north-south gradient, reflecting particularly the recency of flows and the size of the existing ethnic minority populations.

The age structures of ethnic groups and the processes producing them are discussed in Chapter 6 by Warnes. He finds that without exception ethnic minority populations are presently young, but that all are showing a general tendency towards ageing, a trend associated with decreasing proportion of children in these populations brought about by falling fertility. The results of Warnes's analysis show variations in the common youthfulness of ethnic groups, sufficient to challenge suppositions of homogeneity among them: for example, the Black–Other group is youthfully distinctive, in contrast to the high average age of the Black–Caribbean population; the latter also has relatively few children, in contrast to Pakistani and Bangladeshi ethnic groups. How the ageing process will occur, and how its effects will vary, will depend upon immigration rates and fertility levels. There will be more elderly Black–Caribbeans and Indians, while among South Asians ageing will initially have the effect of 'curing' their under-representation in later working age-groups.

Household arrangements are broadly dichotomous. Asian groups are more associated than others with multi-generational households, often characterised by low incomes and recent immigration of kin. As material, housing and educational standards rise, family structures in Asian households may change quickly, perhaps leading to more multiply-deprived elderly people disadvantaged by histories of low pay, incomplete national insurance records, poor childhood nutritional standards, and poor English language ability.

Warnes suggests that as 'normalisation' of ethnic group age and sex structures continues, the social concerns and problems of ethnic minority groups will change. He argues that it is important not to encapsulate these problems in the simple concept of 'demographic ageing': age/sex structures of minority groups are sensitive to the process of self-ascription inherent in the census question and the cultural dynamics of changing identities. In other words, as people's views of their ethnicity evolve they may categorise themselves differently, presenting problems of comparison of age structures in future censuses.

The complexities of marriage patterns and inter-ethnic unions among ethnic groups are explored by Berrington (Chapter 7). She suggests a threefold rationale for understanding them, relating to assimilation, fertility and female status. Traditional marriage patterns in the origin societies of many ethnic minorities are often very different from those customary in the UK, so their study may give insights into the extent of assimilation. Marriage patterns also have important implications for family and household formation: in particular, entry into marriage is for many synonymous with the start of regular sexual intercourse. Finally, there is increasing interest, especially for South Asians, of the relationship between age at first marriage and changes in women's status.

Berrington's principal conclusions point to fundamental differences in marriage patterns, formation and dissolution between South Asian ethnic minorities and others. South Asians are characterised by earlier and near universal marriage, with age at marriage lowest among Pakistani and Bangladeshi men and women, but somewhat later for Indians. In contrast, age at marriage among Black–Caribbean and Black–Other groups was much higher. The dichotomy between South Asians and other groups was also apparent with respect to divorce, rates being low for the former, and for cohabiting unions, the incidence of which was low among South Asians, but common among White and Black groups.

The nature of ethnic households and families is discussed by Murphy in Chapter 8, where he also attempts to clarify some of the technical issues relating to the handling of information on the subject. Murphy's analysis highlights differences in living arrangements and family types between ethnic groups. He finds that ethnic minority groups generally, but particularly South Asians, have above average size households, mainly because of their younger age structures and larger numbers of children. After standardising for age, it appears that Black households have below average size, in contrast to all other ethnic minorities. Lone parenthood is also more common among Black groups. Overall, ethnic minority groups have more complex household arrangements than the White population, a trait especially of South Asians.

But there are a number of unresolved issues relating to household and family patterns: how far do they reflect socio-economic disadvantage or recency of arrival? How long are differences likely to persist as an increasing proportion of the ethnic minority population becomes British-born of British parents? Using evidence from the US, Murphy concludes that the distinctiveness of family patterns among ethnic minorities will continue into the foreseeable future, leading to a more vigorous debate on the issue than has so far occurred.

Unlike the others in the volume, the focus of Compton's chapter (9) is the White population. He discusses the heterogeneity of this group which includes a wide range of peoples from a variety of cultural backgrounds. He distinguishes three major groups. The first consists of the indigenous peoples of the four constituent parts of the United Kingdom, namely the English, Northern Irish, Scots and Welsh. These are characterised by relatively small demographic differences by international standards, but with deeply felt national, cultural and institutional structures. The second group consists of specific minorities within the four major indigenous groups, notably Roman Catholics and Protestants in Northern Ireland, and Jews. Thirdly come the white minorities stemming from outside the present UK. They include especially the Southern Irish, but also Europeans, Americans, and those from the Old and New Commonwealths (the latter including Cypriots and Maltese). There are problems in studying these groups. Because the census question fails to disaggregate the white population into its component groups, recourse to place of birth data is necessary. This presents particular problems for the study of long-established minorities.

Never the less, a number of substantive findings are reported. Most of the foreign-born white population has increased in recent years, especially those from the European Union, Old Commonwealth, USA and Turkey; the main decreases were among those from Central and Eastern Europe. The composition of the White population differs from the non-white: most white minorities are female dominated; often the child component of the age distribution is under-represented. Geographical distributions of the white minorities reflect patterns of long-term migration, especially among the indigenous minorities. Overall, however, the demographies of the different parts of the UK now show little variation, with the outstanding exception of Northern Ireland. Even here, though, there is evidence of demographic convergence, not only with the rest of the UK, but also between the two main minorities — with the important possibility that a Roman Catholic majority may no longer be inevitable.

Finally, a word on what is not presented in these chapters. This volume, and the others in this series, are primarily intended to report the findings of the census. They cannot pretend to offer a more comprehensive demographic account of the ethnic minority populations. That would require additional information, for example on births and deaths, from various sources (for more general accounts based on earlier data see, for example Coleman, 1982; Coleman and Salt, 1992 Chapter 12; Haskey, 1992). Data on vital events are not collected by the census itself (a retrospective question on fertility has not been asked since 1971, except in Northern Ireland in 1991). The incorporation of the ethnic data from the census into the Longitudinal Study, however, will eventually enable a more dynamic picture of the demography of the ethnic minority populations to be drawn. At present there is less prospect for marriage and divorce trends to be related to the ethnic group populations, as opposed to the cross-sectional marital status distributions revealed in the census.

Population projections of the ethnic minority population are needed, based on the new data from the census. New projections are long overdue, the latest official ones having been prepared in 1979 (OPCS, 1979). Simple projections based on the census and on the late 1980s Labour Force Survey have been published more recently (Ballard and Khalra, 1993; Coleman, 1995) along with detailed projections for London to 2011 (Storkey, 1995; London Research Centre, 1995). More substantial projections based upon the 1991 census must await the preparation of appropriate mortality and fertility and net immigration schedules based upon the 1991 ethnic categories, a final definition of undercount and the reconciliation of census ethnic population estimates with those defined on earlier criteria.

1.3 The novelty of non-European population

As a background to the chapters which follow, it is appropriate to begin with a brief look at what little is known about the size of non-European populations in Britain before the Second World War. That underlines the magnitude of recent changes in the ethnic and racial composition of the population and hence the importance of the first census question to attempt to measure it directly. There have been people of non-European origin in the British Isles since at least the 16th century. Systematic data on this early population are almost non-existent. King James IV of Scotland is reported to have had some Africans in his retinue as early as the 15th century. Five blacks — possibly the first to arrive from Africa — were brought to England from West Africa by John Lok's voyage of 1555. They returned to Africa, but slaves followed in sufficient numbers to provoke the Queen in Privy Council to order their removal in 1596 and in 1601.

Larger African populations developed in London, Bristol and Liverpool in the 18th century. A contemporary estimate by Lord Mansfield put the black population of Britain in the late 18th century at between 14,000 - 15,000 (Walvin, 1972; Shyllon, 1974). That represents about 0.2% of the English population, or about 2% of the population of London, if the majority was concentrated there. Most were male personal servants of African origin, brought to Britain from the West Indies as slaves (Fryer, 1984). While some were emancipated in service and other occupations (Scobie, 1972), their free legal status was not absolutely defined until as late as 1834. A small number rose to prominence in fashionable and literary society (Gerzina, 1995). By the end of the 18th century this population of slave or former slave origin had been supplemented by free seamen from Nelson's navy and from the merchant marine. From the early 19th century this black population disappears from public view and attention, and only partly because of repatriation to Sierra Leone or to the West Indies. The abolition of slavery, and the reduction of naval recruitment after the Napoleonic wars, ended new inflows. Many blacks living in Britain appear to have died without issue (there were few black women). Inter-racial cohabitations or marriages, however, attracted contemporary comment (Walvin, 1973).

Up to the early 20th century, relatively small black populations, always described in the absence of hard data as being ' a few thousand' in all, lived in London. Bristol, Cardiff, Liverpool and other ports, mostly West African seamen and their descendants rather than, it seems, the descendants of the earlier black population. Numbers increased during the First World War, following wartime demands for extra recruitment of seamen, including numbers of West Indians, who also served in the armed forces. Not all returned or were returned home after the war. A few hundred were returned in a subsidized repatriation scheme after the racial violence in 1919 and later in Liverpool, Bristol, Salford, Hull, the Tyne and elsewhere. (Jenkinson, 1993).

Asians in Britain in the 19th or earlier centuries from China or India seem to have attracted much less attention. Apart from a small number of Chinese and other Asian ('lascar') sailors mostly in London, some of whom later turned to itinerant peddling, most Asians were (free) servants, grandees or their children (Visram, 1986). By the end of the 19th century, small numbers of Chinese ex-sailors and others, had begun to specialise in particular trades such as laundries, especially in port towns (Jones, 1979). The 1921 census records only 4,382 persons born in China living in England and Wales, of whom 2,490 were British subjects (Registrar General 1923, Table 46). Indian aristocrats had been a familiar feature in British schools and universities by the late 19th century. After the 1920s they were joined by medical students and others from Africa and other parts of the then Empire. The non-European populations of Britain just after the Second World War are usually described as being of 'negligible proportions' (Peach *et al.* 1988, p 561). At the 1931 Census 86,963 persons born in the Indian Empire were enumerated in England and Wales, 5,232 born in the African colonies and 10,468 in the West Indies and other (South) American colonies. However almost all the first category, and a large but also unknown proportion of the latter two, would have been white people of British origin. By 1951 the return migration of British proconsuls and planters after independence had increased numbers of British residents born in India and Pakistan to 121,884. This was before the large-scale post-war immigration of persons of Indian origin to the United Kingdom: the 1971 Census makes it clear that almost all the persons in Britain in 1951 who were born in India were, as in 1931, White persons of British origin. Residents of England and Wales in 1951 born in African colonies rose to 13,638 and those born in the Caribbean and other South American colonies to 16,188 (Registrar-General 1934 Table LXXIV; Registrar-General 1954 Table 49). Much of the increase from 1931 to 1951 in those born in the Caribbean countries, probably represents the beginning of the post-war immigration. By 1954 it has been estimated that the 'Negro minority' in Britain, including the indigenous black populations, had risen to 43,000 (Banton, 1955 p. 69).

Large-scale post-war immigration to the UK from the New Commonwealth since the Second World War has produced populations of non-European origin about two orders of magnitude larger than those resident in the UK before 1939. This cultural and racial novelty, over and above the more familiar distinctions of social class and geography which have been charted by the census since the 19th century, is the starting-point for the justification of an additional question in a census directed towards establishing the condition of the people.

1.4 The need for the ethnic group question

Sociological or demographic curiosity is not in itself a justification for the addition of new questions in the census. Census questions are expected to serve some practical purpose. The rise of public and political interest in the new ethnic dimension in the British population has been paralleled by policy responses relating to equal opportunities, 'race relations' and special support for areas of immigrant concentration and for ethnic minority communities. Welfare considerations, in the broad sense, are behind the new question, particularly the need to establish the distribution and condition of the ethnic minority populations as a basis for policy making at local and national level. The concentration of disadvantage in many of the ethnic minority populations, documented in other volumes in this series, has aroused concern. The official justification for the inclusion of the ethnic question in the 1991 Census, set out in the Census White Paper of 1988, notes that the rectification of this disadvantage is a matter of general public welfare and is additionally important for the favourable development of race relations (Teague, 1993). The unique comprehensiveness and coverage of the census, it claims, are needed to provide data on the housing, employment, educational qualifications and age-structure of each group (analysed in this and other volumes in this series) so that resources can be appropriately allocated and special needs met. The information would help Government and local authorities carry out their responsibilities under the 1976 Race Relations Act and serve as a benchmark for employers to measure the success of 'equal opportunities' policies (HM Government, 1988).

These policies include various programmes targeted at Commonwealth immigrant and ethnic minority populations, to overcome difficulties in schools (Section 11; Cross, Johnson, and Cox, 1988; Home Office, 1990) to encourage training and enterprise and provide social and cultural facilities directed at specific immigrant communities (the former Urban Programme: Stewart and Whitting, 1983, Department of the Environment, 1991, and now elements of the new Single Regeneration Budget to renew urban areas) and many local authority multicultural initiatives aimed at specific ethnic minority communities. Comprehensive programmes directed at 'equal opportunities' depend upon ethnic 'targets' which will now use the 1991 Census data for their base.

The importance of culture or ethnicity, over and above birthplace, was first recognized in the 1971 Census which used parental birthplaces and surnames to try to identify populations of New Commonwealth ethnic origin irrespective of their birthplaces (Immigrant Statistics Unit, 1975, Immigrant Statistics Unit, 1977). That step took account of the emergence of potentially long-term or permanent ethnic group differences in preferences, behaviour and needs which were outlasting the first immigrant generation. Ethnic groups can be defined as groups of people with shared customs, values and beliefs, who regard themselves as being descended from at least nominal common ancestors. Ethnicity is usually defined by self-ascription; in censuses and surveys individuals are either presented with a choice of pre-coded groups or invited to write down the name of the group(s) to which they feel they belong. A direct question on ethnicity was first proposed for the 1981 Census (HM Government, 1978) on grounds similar to those, noted above, which were cited to justify its inclusion in 1991. But as Bulmer points out in Chapter 2, other counsels, including fears expressed by immigrant populations themselves, led to the plans for a direct ethnic question in the 1981 Census being dropped. Soon afterwards, however, arguments in favour of a question based on concerns about the problems of ethnic minority populations in Britain, and the apparent acceptability of such a question to ethnic minority groups (Sillitoe, 1987a, 1987b) had swayed a decision in favour of an ethnic question (Home Affairs Committee, 1983; HM Government, 1984). The census ethnic group question which has emerged uses a pragmatic, heterogeneous set of categories which pre-census tests showed that people were prepared to identify with and which fitted the reality of the differences between major groups derived from relatively recent post-war immigration from diverse third-world countries.

1.5 The census ethnic group question and the new pervasiveness of ethnic categorization

The 1991 Census ethnic group question is not just a demographic landmark. It is a major step forward in the more general ethnic categorization of the British population, of which it is both a notable symptom and, through the total population distribution which it gives, a potent facilitator. The practice of asking questions on ethnicity, rare even ten years ago, is now widespread and has become almost universal in the public sector. The census question, however, marks a new development. The coverage is universal, and it is linked at individual level to other characteristics. It is the first occasion that all the people in Britain have been obliged to identify for themselves an ethnic origin which only a few decades ago many would have been unaware that they even possessed. By 1995 all Whitehall departments, and most local authorities and local education authorities, monitor the ethnic composition of their workforces, and of new entrants and applicants to the civil service, according to ethnic origin. The 1988 Education Reform Act created the Higher Education Statistics Agency with powers to require universities to submit data on the ethnic origins of their employees. In April 1995 the Department of Health began its Ethnic Monitoring Initiative, whereby all persons admitted to hospitals will henceforth be asked to specify their ethnic origin according to the ethnic groups used in the census. Only rarely has the publication of ethnic statistics contracted; for example those on the ethnic origin of certain types of offender in the Metropolitan Police area ended in 1989.

The most important customers of census data are local authorities. The results of the ethnic group question in the 1991 Census will be used by all parts of local government, but will be of particular interest to race equality officers and others monitoring the condition of immigrant and ethnic minority populations in British cities. This is now a major activity. Its scale, and hence the demand for ethnic data, may be judged from the fact that the 1994 Local Authority Race Relations Information Exchange Directory of Race Equality Officers and related posts lists 1,370 officers in local government alone (LARRIE, 1994). Some local authorities employ substantial numbers of equality officers (20 in Islington LB, 29 in Hounslow LB, 42 in Leicester) to meet the varied needs of particular groups. All central government departments, their agencies and quangos now employ racial equality officers, as do most housing associations, universities, colleges and other organizations. It would be surprising if another 1,000 or so active professional consumers of census ethnic data could not be added from such sources.

1.6   The census ethnic group question and other schemes of ethnic or racial classification

As the White Paper notes, one of the aims of the census ethnic group question was to provide a sound and detailed basis for the establishment of numerical 'targets' for ethnic recruitment and promotion. Hitherto, these had been established based on simple demographic criteria derived from the Labour Force Survey. (These 'targets' are claimed to be different from 'quotas' in the US fashion, which remain illegal under UK law). Such targets are well developed in respect of the allocation of the 'social' housing managed by housing associations, but have also been established by such institutions as the Bar Council. Central government departments now use an ethnic classification identical with that used in the census. However local authorities and housing associations, student grant-giving bodies and others still use a variety of classifications (Table 1.1), not all of which can be made to correspond exactly with that in the census. No doubt as monitoring becomes universal, the census criteria will become more generally adopted. However, it is not yet certain that the exact 1991 classification will be adopted for any ethnic question posed in the next census.

The census ethnic question is officially justified, in part, because it may assist the rectification of disadvantage experienced by ethnic minority populations and more generally help in the improvement of what are still called 'race' relations. Despite this function, the census ethnic group question uses terminology which differ from much of that used in race relations law and procedure. The various usages noted above, including the census ethnic group question itself, employ colour, racial and national origin or ethnic categories. Race relations policy and legislation, which date from the Race Relations Acts of 1965 and 1968 (Lester and Bindman, 1972), use the terms 'race' and 'colour' more than 'ethnic and national' origin. The Race Relations Act 1976 is concerned ostensibly with 'racial', not 'ethnic' equality, to prohibit discrimination on 'racial' grounds. The term 'racial' , however, is used broadly to embrace race, colour, nationality or ethnic and national origin, as defined in general terms by Section 3 of the Act. 'Racial groups do not have to be 'racial' in the biological sense of coming from a

Table 1.1 *Some non-census ethnic and racial classifications*

Central government	Local government	Quango	University	Official survey
ESRC grant application, Application for entry to Civil Service CSSB 1991[1]	Application for planning permission Islington 1994[2]	Application for DipSW social work course CCETSW 1995[3]	Oxford University Staff survey questionnaire 1995	NDHS 1978
White	African	Racial origin	White	White
Asian	Caribbean	Black	Black (Caribbean)	West Indian
Indian	Other black	Black(African)		Indian
Pakistani	Indian	Other	Black(other)	Pakistani
Bangladeshi	Pakistani	Ethnic origin	Indian	Bangladeshi
East Afria	Bangladeshi	African	Bangladeshi	Chinese
Chinese	Chinese	Caribbean	Chinese	Turkish
Other	Asian other	Indian	Asian (other)	
Other Asian				
Black	Greek/Cypriot	Pakistani	Other	African
Caribbean	Turkish/Cypriot	Bangladeshi		Arab
African	Irish	Chinese		Other
Other	White	European (UK)		
Mixed		European (other)		
Other	Mixed/other	Other		
		Welsh speaking Religion (NI only)		

Notes:
1. Question is "I am of .... origin". The categories, but not the order, are identical to those used in the 1991 census ethnic question.
2. Question is "I would classify myself as ....".
3. Question is "How would you describe your .... origin?".

Sources:
   Civil Service Selection Board 1991, Economic and Social Science Research Council student grant application form.
   London Borough of Islington, Planning Control Section.
   Central Council for Education and Training in Social Work.
   Oxford University.
   Dept. of the Environment (1980) National Dwelling and Housing Survey 1978 p. 317.

common racial 'stock, as explicitly accepted by the courts in the case of the Gypsies. Discrimination on grounds of religion or culture alone is not forbidden unless it coincides with racial characteristics as broadly defined in the Act.

Complaints of racial discrimination can only be admitted if the plaintiff can demonstrate that he or she suffered that discrimination by virtue of being a member of a group deemed to fall under the protection of the Act. In most cases which relate to people of non-European origin, this poses no difficulty of definition. Following disputed cases, a small number of 'racial' groups have been specifically recognised by the Courts as definitely falling under the protection of the Act through the sporadic settlement of disputed situations through case law, not through any comprehensive *a priori* process of definition. There is no general or comprehensive 'list'. The law, as opposed to social scientists, apparently has little difficulty in deciding which individuals should be protected on grounds of the racial group from which they claim descent. More difficulty is encountered in defining the scope of 'ethnic' group. Following decisions in Industrial Tribunals , the Court of Appeal and in the House of Lords, these categories now include Jews (Seide v Gillette Industries), Gypsies (Commission for Racial Equality (CRE) v Dutton), Sikhs (Mandla v Dowell Lee) , Irish (Bogdeniec v Sauer-Sundstrand Ltd) and Welsh (Cameron v Arfon BC). Legal references are given in Appendix 1. In the case of the Sikhs the House of Lords decided that 'ethnic' should be construed widely in a broad cultural and historic sense. Above all, an ethnic group had to be a distinct community with a long shared history, of which the group was conscious, and a distinctive cultural tradition in family and social matters often but not necessarily associated with religion. Criteria might also include common geographical origin and descent, common language and literature and religion, and minority or oppressed status (Palmer, 1992). Religion by itself is not a sufficient criterion. The case made by Rastafarians, supported by the Commission for Racial Equality (CRE), eventually failed in the courts (Crown Suppliers (PSA) v Dawkins) on the grounds that they were not an ethnic group but a political-religious cult. Likewise Muslims as a group do not fall under the effects of the Act (Tariq v Young and others) as Islam is a religion.

Of the groups mentioned above none features in the census ethnic categories. For example, the Irish are not an 'ethnic ' group in the Census or in the Labour Force Survey classification, although they have become an 'honorary' ethnic group by being included in many of the ethnic volumes tabulations through birthplace (OPCS/GRO(S), 1993a) as described in detail in Chapters 4 and 9 by Owen and Compton. 11,000 people inserted 'Irish' in the ethnic question, along with possibly another 20,000 who wrote 'Irish' and also ticked the 'White' box. In 1991 there were 837,464 Irish-born residents of Great Britain (OPCS/GRO(S), 1993b).

This difference between census and race relations terminology arises in part from changes in language; race is an 1970s term, ethnicity has become the usage more favoured in the 1980s and 1990s. For example, the form of the ethnic question proposed for the 1981 Census was invariably headed 'Race or ethnic origin' (see Sillitoe, 1978), terminology dropped for 1991. Ethnicity is a concept residing clearly in the social sphere. While it may be a fuzzy concept generating ill defined categories, few social scientists have much difficulty with the concept, or in accepting that distinct ethnic groups may easily be identified in society. Racial characteristics, meaning biological, inherited characteristics such as skin colour and various biochemical polymorphisms, and the identification of racial groups or races defined on such criteria, are another matter. This volume is no place to discuss in detail the meaninglessness or otherwise of the notion of 'race'. (see Appendix note 3 in Chapter 2). Suffice to say that there is no necessary connection between ethnicity and race, although in practice there quite often is. Without denying the existence of biological or 'racial' differences between people, few social scientists accept distinct 'racial' groups as biological realities, only as social constructs. The opinions of biologists are more divided: the complexity of the topic is apparent in the genetical and biological anthropological literature, for example Harris, 1980; Lewontin, 1982; Cavalli-Sforza, Menozzi, and Piazza, 1988; Harrison, 1989; Sokal, Jacquez, and Oden, 1993, McKenzie and Crowcroft 1994; Bertranpetit *et al.* 1995.

1.7 Other statistical series relating to ethnic minority populations

The new census ethnic group classification has created a discontinuity between the 1991 Census ethnic population totals and those derived from previous statistical series of ethnic minority populations. These have not yet been entirely reconciled and possibly may never be. The earliest official estimates for the population of New Commonwealth ethnic origin were based upon the 1966 sample census (Registrar-General, 1970; Immigrant Statistics Unit, 1975). At that time there were few births to the new immigrant population. The major problem of estimation of numbers, necessarily based on census birthplace data, was the separation of the new immigrant ethnic population from the then large numbers of British people, mostly older, who had been born in India and other parts of the Empire and who had returned to the United Kingdom. Surnames were the most useful criterion. These tend to be distinctive among Asians, although not among West Indians. However, few people of white British origin were born in the West Indies. The 1971 Census did not ask a direct ethnic question but asked additional questions (unique to that census) on birthplace of parents, and date of entry into the UK, on which a new series of 'New Commonwealth and Pakistani Ethnic Group' (NCWP) population estimates were based. This generated a number of combinations of birthplace of individual with birthplace of parents. The proportion of persons in each combination assigned to the ethnic group populations was determined in part on the basis of surname analysis (Immigrant Statistics Unit, 1977). For a variety of reasons immigrant and ethnic minority populations are particularly prone to be under-counted in censuses and surveys. This applies to all sources and series; to the 1991 and earlier censuses (Simpson, Chapter 3; Peach, 1966; Peach and Winchester, 1974) and to the LFS and other surveys (Hollis, 1982; Brown, 1984). These NCWP estimates were updated each year from 1971 to 1981 through data on births to mothers born in the New Commonwealth and deaths of persons born there, together with the net immigration from the same national origins recorded by the International Passenger Survey (see Salt, Chapter 5). The annual birth and death data based on country of birth were first published for England and Wales and for Scotland in April 1969 (see OPCS, 1994b, Table 13; OPCS, 1994a, Tables 9.1 - 9.6; Registrar General for Scotland, 1995, Tables 3.8, 3.9, 5.3).

In constructing these series there were (and remain) obvious problems in making inferences from birthplace data concerning ethnic origin of mothers or of the deceased. In 1985, for example, 7,900 out of the 52,700 births to women who were born in the NCWP were estimated to be to white mothers, including 2,000 births to women born in the Mediterranean Commonwealth (mostly Cypriots)(OPCS, 1986; Shaw, 1988). A high proportion of deaths registered to persons born in the New Commonwealth are those of Whites, for reasons noted above. More important, an increasing proportion of mothers in the ethnic minority populations, especially Afro–Caribbean mothers, were themselves born in the UK and their babies are thus not recorded as contributing to the ethnic minority population. The 1971 Census could supply some of this deficit because it asked a retrospective question on children ever-born and on parental birthplace (Lomas, 1973). Subsequent censuses have omitted these valuable questions.

From 1981 to 1991 the Labour Force Survey (LFS) asked an ethnic question on national origin lines. From the estimates which it yields on population by age, overall ethnic minority birth totals can be estimated, for groups of years, although young children in censuses and surveys are usually under-counted, especially young children of ethnic minority populations (Owen, 1993). By 1981, these estimates from the LFS showed that between 10,000 and 20,000 children had been born in the UK with parents of NC ancestry but who had been born in the UK (OPCS, 1983). In 1984, 15% of the ethnic minority children aged 0–14 born in the UK had mothers also born in the UK, and therefore would not be included in the data reported by birthplace of mother (OPCS, 1985). Between 1982 and 1985 the OPCS estimated that the 'non-white' population of Great Britain was probably producing about 62,000 births per year, of which about 58,000 were to the population of New Commonwealth (NC) ethnic origin. That total included about 5,000 births to non-white mothers born in the UK and a further 5,000 births to non-white fathers, and excludes the 3,000 births to women born in the Mediterranean Commonwealth (Cyprus, Malta, Gibraltar) (Population Statistics Division, 1986).

After 1981, the NCWP ethnic group population estimates were replaced by ethnic minority population estimates derived directly from the Labour Force Survey, held annually from 1983 (OPCS, 1983; 1986). As noted by Bulmer, however, the LFS categories then in use did not exactly co-incide with the classification used in the 1991 Census. Neither do the numbers. The 1991 census, despite its undercount, revealed a larger overall ethnic minority population and a higher 'black' population than did the 1991 LFS (Teague, 1993). The LFS after 1991 has used the same ethnic categories as were used in the 1991 Census. This will make it more difficult to relate the ethnic population estimates to the births and deaths and immigration data derived from other systems, because of the creation of the 'black–other' category which cannot be related simply or directly to birthplace, or to ethnic categories based on national origins,. In order to make the categorization of vital events compatible with the ethnic group population denominator from the census and the LFS, the OPCS is reported to have pressed for ethnic origin to be asked at the registration of births and deaths. However, that would require new primary legislation.

In any case, further detailed statistics on the births and deaths to ethnic groups will soon become available from the Longitudinal Study (LS). The LS is a sample of 500,000 individuals (1 per cent of the population) taken from the 1971 Census (OPCS, 1982) and linked by the OPCS to subsequent censuses in 1981 and 1991(and, it is intended, in 2001). The record linkage is performed using the criteria of name and date of birth. Records of birth, death and cancer registration relating to people with the selectèd dates of birth have been routinely scanned since 1971. When these events occur to members of the LS cohort, the data can be linked to the data on their census schedules, including since 1991 ethnic origin data. However, records of marriage, divorce and International Passenger Survey movement, which lack date of birth data, cannot be linked to the LS. This process enables the comprehensive data on household, housing, employment , occupation and migration available uniquely from the census to be used in the analysis of the life course of individuals.

The LS has already been used for the analysis of the mortality of ethnic minority populations. Surnames analysis, in conjunction with the birthplace and parental birthplace data noted above, enabled an Asian cohort to be identified in the sample extracted from the 1971 Census to create the LS. This cohort has been followed through the 1981 Census (Balarajan, Bulusu, Adelstein, and Shukla, 1984). This is in addition to more straightforward analyses of immigrant mortality based upon the birthplace of the deceased (Benjamin, 1982; Marmot, Adelstein, and Bulusu, 1983; Balarajan and Bulusu, 1990) and of infant mortality based upon the birthplace of mother, through the conventional vital registration system and previous censuses (Adelstein, MacDonald Davies, and Weatherall, 1980; Balarajan, Raleigh, and Botting, 1989; Balarajan and Raleigh, 1990).

Thanks to the 1991 Census, the LS cohort can now be categorized by ethnic origin, retrospectively right back to 1971 for those individuals who were recorded in the 1991 Census LS sample and in the previous censuses. However, tracing has been more difficult with foreign-born groups. Births and deaths, past and future, occurring to members of the LS cohort are accordingly automatically categorized by ethnic origin, not thorough vital registration but because the ethnic origin of the mother and father, or of the deceased, is already known. However, because the numbers of the ethnic minority groups in the 1991 Census are relatively small, the OPCS believes that it will need five years' data on births before statistically acceptable fertility analyses can be carried out. Another new source of data, which may avert the need for primary legislation on vital registration, arises from the Ethnic Minority Initiative by the Department of Health (DH) in 1995. Under this initiative, all persons admitted to hospital are expected to provide information on their ethnic origin. As 98.6% of births occurred in hospital in 1992, and 73.8% of deaths, it follows that the ethnicity of many deceased persons and almost all mothers will automatically become known. This DH process will use the census ethnic classification.

1.8   The 1991 Census ethnic question in international context

The ethnic group question marks a new departure in the British census, in response to novel post-war immigration . However, most other countries in Western Europe, and the industrial countries overseas such as the United States and Australia, have also acquired substantial non-European populations through immigration since the 1950s. This final section compares the British innovation with the responses of censuses abroad to ethnic diversity. The aim is to see if Britain is following an established pattern in developing such a census question, and to contrast briefly the varied motivations and assumptions behind the questions related to ethnicity (or their absence) in censuses. Before doing so, however, it is worth noting that the United Nations (1987) refrained from recommending a standard classification for ethnic group or nationality for the 1990 round of censuses, stating that: 'the definitions and criteria applied by each country investigating ethnic characteristics of the population must .... be determined by the groups which it desires to identify. By the nature of the subject, these groups will vary widely from country to country, so that no internationally accepted criteria can be recommended.'[1].

Ethnicity and related topics in the censuses of Western European countries

In fact the United Kingdom is so far unique in Western Europe (with the minor exception of the Channel Islands) in posing a direct question in its census on ethnic origin. That reflects a divergence between Britain and most other European countries in policy towards immigrant and foreign populations and therefore in the form of enumeration which is thought to be appropriate. Many continental countries do not accept the notion of 'ethnic minorities', on which the GB census ethnic group question was based. Instead, some emphasise the constitutional ideal of a common and equal citizenship which immigrants of foreign nationality — mostly post-war immigrants — can attain through a process of naturalization, which is easy in some countries (e.g. France, Sweden) and more difficult in others (e.g. Germany). In continental Western Europe, it is under 'citizenship' categories, through foreign nationality, that data on populations of recent immigrant origin are usually collected. Once a foreigner has become naturalized, he or she disappears from statistical view. France, committed since the revolution to a concept of a strong secular state held together by equality under a single citizenship, a common language and a common identity, has developed this point of view most explicitly . There, notions of ethnicity are not officially countenanced. The use of ethnic minority categories in law or in statistical enumeration is contrary to official policy, which emphasises individual equality and the secular nature of the State and holds that the recognition of minorities is divisive and can lead to isolation and to conflict. A law of 1979 explicitly forbids the posing of questions on ethnic origin or religion in censuses and surveys and the keeping of individual records noting these characteristics on individuals. (Long, 1988; Rocard, 1991; Coleman, 1994, Schnapper, 1995). Germany, with its approach to citizenship based on *ius sanguinis* notions of German ancestry, also does not recognize concepts of 'ethnicity' in its state policy, in its census or in other forms of statistics collection (German Federal Ministry of the Interior, 1993), although paradoxically, the *ius sanguinis* is itself based on an ethnic or racial basis for German identity. However, these clear policies, which among other consequences prevent the collection of ethnic statistics, do not go unchallenged in either country (Barou, ; Heckmann, 1995).

West European countries regard themselves as nation-states. Even those with distinctive 'national' populations of non-immigrant origin ('autochthonous' in Euro-speak) have refrained from asking questions on ethnicity in their census. Spain, while united under a single crown, incorporates provinces which retain a lively sense of ancient ethnic identity and a widespread use of distinctive languages. Nonetheless no separate ethnic identities are recognized in the census. Each province, however, can choose to include non-compulsory questions on language, which serves an equivalent purpose in Catalonia and the Basque country. Belgium is divided into regions which are officially French or Dutch speaking (and Brussels) with parallel institutions and considerable autonomous powers. However the Belgian census makes no allusion to Walloon or Flemish identity or to French or Dutch language use. The UK responds to its ancient indigenous minorities by some regional subdivision in the census. The partly separate census organizations for England and Wales, Scotland and Northern Ireland, reflect the national privileges retained by Scotland since the Act of Union in 1707 and the variable level of autonomy enjoyed by (Northern) Ireland since the Act of Union of 1801 and the creation of the separate Province of Northern Ireland in 1922. Apart from the ethnic group question aimed at immigrant minorities, and the language questions noted below, the UK census otherwise resembles those in other Western European countries in avoiding questions which directly invite identification with ancient, indigenous ethnic minority populations of European origin, except through the traditional question on birthplace.

The Netherlands is the only other Western European country apart from Britain explicitly to recognize 'ethnic minorities' of immigrant (or any other) origin in law and in the publication of statistics, although the concept has also been used less formally in Sweden. In Britain and the Netherlands — more explicitly in the latter case — recognition of ethnic minorities has followed the adoption of 'multicultural' policies relating to law and administration, education, 'equal opportunities' and related measures, which accept or welcome new cultural diversity as a permanent part of the social structure, as a recognition of the rights of immigrant minorities, and as a means of recognizing disadvantaged populations (Rex, 1985; Hammar, 1990; Dieleman 1993). These provisions mostly refer to populations of recent immigrant origin, and are intended to advance their status, conditions of life and integration (NSCGP, 1990; Lithman, 1987). In theory, the Netherlands concept of 'ethnic minority', implies a temporarily disadvantaged status, recognised only for as long as the populations remain imperfectly integrated (Muus, 1991).

The Netherlands held its final census in 1971, before the ethnic minority concept was adopted. Ethnic data are derived indirectly through the statistics on birthplace, parents' birthplace and citizenship of the official registration system. Their compilation began after that country formally adopted a 'multicultural' policy following an official report in 1983 (Netherlands

Ministry of Home Affairs, 1983). As in the UK, ethnic statistics serve as the basis for monitoring in employment, the enforcement of which has led to considerable controversy. The British government has yet to issue a similar white paper, or debate the matter explicitly, but the general development of multicultural policy by UK central and especially local government policy in that direction has been apparent for some time (Cross, 1989) and the census ethnic group question marks its further establishment. In Sweden, there is no official question on ethnic origin or religion, although data on religious affiliation are published annually in the Statistical Yearbook of Sweden (1995: table 487), provided by the religious organizations them-selves.

The census in the United Kingdom asks questions on the use of the Scottish Gaelic, Welsh, and Irish Gaelic languages used by persons aged over 3 years, in Wales, Scotland and Northern Ireland respectively. In their modern form these questions date from 1881, 1891 and 1991 respectively, although a question on Irish Gaelic was asked from 1861 to 1911 (e.g. Census of Ireland 1901) when all Ireland was part of the United Kingdom. A similar question on the use of Irish Gaelic is still regularly asked in the census in the Irish Republic. In the UK, these questions relate to the use of these ancient languages only in their proper countries and provinces, the use of English being assumed (see Compton, Chapter 9). This practice dates from the 'ethnic revival' of such languages and more recently with a change of policy to support and subsidize them in order to respond to the needs of those who speak the languages or wish their children to do so. Proposals to supplement the 1991 British census ethnic question with a question on language, to be asked throughout Great Britain but aimed at ethnic minority groups of recent immigrant origin in order to refine ethnic categories (Sillitoe, 1987b), were not proceeded with.

A few other Western European countries ask questions on language in their censuses. All are either Scandinavian or German-speaking: Norway, Fin-land, Austria, Switzerland, (West) Germany. In Finland, the language ques-tion serves primarily to record the long-standing Swedish-speaking minor-ity dating from the former period of Swedish control. Austria likewise preserves a long tradition of such questions dating from the censuses of the multi-ethnic Austro-Hungarian Empire. Switzerland's unique structure as a voluntary association (confederation) of autonomous cantons with four indigenous official languages requires the census to ask questions on lan-guage. There are in fact two questions; one on preferred official language (four categories plus 'other' in 1990), the other on usual language (eight categories plus 'other' in 1990; mostly Swiss dialects). Recent immigrant languages are not included in the categories, although they can be written in. With these exceptions, questions on language are not asked in Western European censuses. In some cases such questions run counter to policy relating to national cohesion, for example in France, where 150 years of state effort has been devoted to turning provincial peasants and immigrants into Frenchmen (Weber, 1976; Watkins, 1990).

Religion can also be a component of ethnic identity, although religious differences need have no ethnic connotation. The religions traditionally identified in most of those Western European censuses which ask such a question do not have an obviously 'ethnic' base and the questions were not originally asked as surrogates for ethnicity. These census questions are of long standing and relate essentially to Catholic/Protestant differences, not to religions of recent immigrant origin, although the latter are now included in published tabulations. Outside Ireland, religion is asked in Western European censuses only in some Scandinavian and German-speaking countries where an established state church (Norway) or other recognized religious organisations (Germany, Switzerland) receive funding from registered adherents through the tax system. The census is not a direct instrument of taxation; neither is there official 'policy' towards religious groups, but the returns are useful to the religious organizations, which press for their continued retention in the census. Swiss census data are essential for the pro-rata distribution by the national government of church tax monies, collected at canton level, to the various officially recognized religious organizations. The question on religion in Norway, however, was dropped in the 1990 Census. The voluntary questions on religion in the Republic of Ireland and in Northern Ireland are closely connected with political divisions, as Compton describes in Chapter 9. A census question on religion throughout the UK, but directed at Asians only, was proposed in order to improve response both to the ethnic question intended for the 1981 Census and that asked in the 1991 census (Sillitoe, 1978; Sillitoe, 1987b). However, as with the similar language question, these proposals were dropped. In some countries it is explicitly illegal or unconstitutional to ask questions in public enquiries such as the census concerning religious affiliation, for example in France, Belgium, Denmark, Italy and Spain (see Courbage, 1995).

Finally it may be noted that the UK census is most unusual in not asking a question on the nationality (citizenship) of the population. Elsewhere in Europe, only Ireland, Norway, Spain, Sweden, Bulgaria, Hungary, Poland, and Slovenia do not ask questions on citizenship in their censuses. In Poland, Sweden and Norway this information is collected instead by the compulsory universal registration system. On the continent of Europe, statistics on immigrant or non-national populations are almost exclusively provided through the criteria of citizenship (legal nationality). As Salt shows in Chapter 5, Western European censuses, immigration data and vital statistics systems provide data on 'foreigners' defined by the citizenship which they possess, not by 'ethnic minority ' status or by immigrant status (although all these countries collect birthplace information in the census). But as Bulmer explains in Chapter 2 this question, asked in earlier British censuses, was abandoned after the 1961 Census. British citizenship then embraced that of the colonies from which many immigrants had recently arrived, and was further confused by the broader concept of 'British subject' or 'Commonwealth citizenship' status. Despite the reform and simplification of British citizenship through the British Nationality Act 1981, the question has never been re-introduced into the census, although it has been asked with apparent success in the Labour Force Survey since 1973 and in the International Passenger Survey. Because of their near-ubiquity, 'citizenship' and 'birthplace' questions are not included in Table 1.2.

Ethnicity and related topics in the censuses of Eastern and Central European countries

By contrast with Western Europe, in the Eastern and Central European countries and in the former Soviet Union ethnic or national origin questions in the census are widespread and have a long history. However these questions refer to indigenous, not to recent immigrant minorities. In the multi-ethnic Austro-Hungarian empire, which embraced Austria, Hungary, Czechoslovakia, Croatia, Bosnia, parts of Poland, Italy, Romania and other areas, everyday language (but not mother tongue) received explicit attention in the census from 1880 to 1910 (Kreager, 1992), although not without initial reluctance: the invitation in the census to identify with a national label may have accelerated that Empire's break-up (Hobsbawm, 1990). In the 19th century, the 'nationalities question'; the relationship between nation, population and in modern terms 'ethnicity' were much debated. In these areas, populations had not developed into ethnically or linguistically homogeneous nation-states, having been incorporated for centuries in Russian, Austro-Hungarian or Ottoman empires; (see Sellier and Sellier, 1992). Language data relating to ethnic origin was, and remains, a basis for identifying nations which might, given appropriate geographical concentration, claim to be nation-states (Kreager, 1992). From 1853, a series of International Statistical Congresses attempted to establish sound statistical and ethnographic criteria for the definition of 'populations' through such means as questions on language or national origin in censuses. The creation of new nation-states or federations at Versailles made extensive use of such census data. Interest in such statistics is now intense and is a commonplace of news reporting. The dissolution of the Soviet Union in 1991, of its hegemony over Eastern Europe from 1989 and the collapse of the two ethnic federations created at Versailles (Czechoslovakia and Yugoslavia) have gone hand in hand with revival of national aspirations and real or potential ethnic conflicts in many areas. The Council of Europe recently began an enquiry into the demographic situation of indigenous national minorities in Europe (see Courbage, 1995).

Questions on language and national origin were also posed in the first (and only) census of the multi-ethnic Russian Empire in 1897. Its Communist successor-state followed that example, although for different, somewhat convoluted and perhaps rather unexpected Marxist reasons developed by Stalin, an amateur of linguistics. The Soviet Union has routinely defined about 100 ' nationalities' since its first census in 1926. The Soviet census concept, usually translated as 'nationality', was close to that of 'ethnicity', not nationality in the sense of 'citizenship' and referred to populations of long standing in the Soviet territory, not to populations of recent immigrant origin (of which, in any case, there was none). The classification of 'nationalities' given for newly independent former Soviet Republics in Table 1.2 below is that used in the last Soviet census in 1989. No censuses have yet been held by those countries as independent states.

The boundaries of most of the new states created in Central and Eastern

Table 1.2 *Questions on race, colour, ethnicity, language and religion and number of categories used; censuses from 1970 in the industrial world*

Country	Race, colour, ethnicity, tribe	Language	Religion
Northern Europe			
Estonia 1989[1]	open	open	-
Finland 1970	-	10	5
Finland 1985	-	35	13
Channel Islands	3	-	-
Ireland 1981	-	2	open
Ireland 1991	-	2	open
Latvia 1989[1]	open	open	-
Lithuania 1989[1]	open	open	-
Norway 1980[2]	-	-	3
United Kingdom 1971	(parents' birthplace)	1 (Wales, Scotland)	open (N.Ireland)
United Kingdom 1981[3]	-	1(Wales, Scotland)	open (N.Ireland)
United Kingdom 1991[3]	8	1(Wales, Scotland, N. Ireland)	open (N.Ireland)
Western Europe			
Austria 1971	-	5	5
Austria 1981	-	5	6
Austria 1991	-	5	5
West Germany 1970[4]	-	-	4
West Germany 1987	-	-	6
Switzerland 1970[5]	-	14	6
Switzerland 1980	-	5	4
Switzerland 1990	-	4/8	3
Southern Europe			
Gibraltar 1970	-	3	5
Gibraltar 1981	-	?	5
Portugal 1981	-	-	8
Portugal 1991	-	-	8
Spain 1991[6]	-	open	-
Eastern Europe			
Bulgaria 1965	-	4	-
Bulgaria 1985	-	-	-
Bulgaria 1992	9	3	7
Czechoslovakia 1970	open	open	-
Czechoslovakia 1980	9	6	-
Czechoslovakia 1991	14	6	open
Hungary 1970[7]	-	9	-
Hungary 1980	9	9	-
Hungary 1990	yes	5	-
Macedonia 1991	-	3	3
Moldova 1989[1]	open	open	-
Poland[8]	-	open	-
Romania 1966	open	1 + open	-
Romania 1977	open	yes	-
Romania 1992	1 + open	1 + open	1 + open
Slovenia 1991	28		7
USSR 1970	open	open	-
USSR 1979	open	open	-
USSR 1989[1]	open	open	-
Yugoslavia 1971	open	open	-
Yugoslavia 1981	open	open	-
Yugoslavia 1991	open	open	open

Table 1.1 - *continued*

Country	Race, colour, ethnicity, tribe	Language	Religion
North America			
Canada 1971[9]	13	(3 questions)	13
Canada 1976	-	5	-
Canada 1981	15	(3 questions)	15
Canada 1986	15 + Indian	(3 questions)	-
Canada 1991	15 + Indian	(4 questions)	open
Canada 1996	(5 questions)	(4 questions)	-
United States 1970[10]	9/6	open	-
United States 1980[10]	14/5/open	open	-
United States 1990[10]	16/6/open	open	-
Oceania			
Australia 1976[11]	3	4	open
Australia 1981	3	(English ability)	open
Australia 1986[12]	3/open	(2 questions)	open
Australia 1991	3	(2 questions)	7
New Zealand 1976	2	-	open
New Zealand 1981[13]	9	-	8
New Zealand 1986[13]	8	-	15
New Zealand 1991[13]	8/open	-	8
New Zealand 1996[13,14]	14/open	4	10

Notes:
'open' indicates an open question with no pre-coded categories. '-' indicates that no question was asked. Questions with defined categories almost always include an open write-in category for 'other'. Consequently tabulations are available for more categories than are listed on the actual census schedule.

The number of categories used in 'tick-box' questions noted above excludes the categories 'other', 'unknown', 'not stated' but includes 'none' in the question on religion.

As far as possible these data are taken from the census schedules themselves. For Finland, Austria, Portugal, Slovenia the numbers of categories are those listed in the UNDY. Many derive from 'open' questions or have a 'write-in' 'other' category in addition to tick boxes.

States of the former Soviet Union, in all of whose territories the last 1989 Soviet Census was held, would have had the same 'open' questions. Questions on religion were not asked in the censuses of the Soviet Union (except in 1937) and in Eastern European countries under communist control, but were asked in some pre-war censuses (e.g. Poland 1920, 1930) and in some recent post-communist censuses (e.g. Bulgaria, Slovenia, Romania).

1. The Republics of the former Soviet Union all took part in the last Soviet Census of 1989 and the questions on 'nationalities' and 'language' were therefore identical. Differences may occur in published tabulations. Two open language questions were asked: 'native' and 'other'.
   The Baltic Republics, as independent states before Soviet invasion in 1940, asked questions on language, religion and ethnic origin in their censuses, following the recommendations of the International Conference of 1920 (Latvian census from 1920, Lithuanian from 1923, Estonian from 1922). Previous Baltic provincial census initiatives had asked questions on language and religion as early as 1881.
2. The question on religion was deleted from the 1990 Census of Norway.
3. United Kingdom. Only one category of language is noted as the question refers only to Welsh, Scottish or Irish Gaelic.
4. Religion has always been asked in the (West) German census.
5. Religion has been asked in the Swiss census since 1860. The question was modified in 1990 according to a new standard hierarchical format. (Bundesamt für Statistik 1991). There were two language questions in 1990 (best known official language, and usual language).
6. The question on language in Spain is asked only in certain Provinces: Pais Vasco (the Basque country) and Cataluña (Catalonia).
7. In Hungary, questions were asked on 'mother tongue' and 'everyday language'.

8. In Poland, questions on religion were asked in 1920 and 1930 but not after the Communist takeover in 1945. Language was asked after WW2, from which some estimate of 'nationalities' was made.
9. Questions on origin and religion has been asked in the Canadian census since its inception in 1871. The form of questions has changed over time and the questions are now too numerous to summarize in this table - see text and Statistics Canada 1994.
10. In US censuses, there are three separate 'origin' questions. The first number refers to the number of 'race' categories, the second to the number of 'Hispanic origin' categories (since 1970), The third 'ancestry' (ethnic) question (since 1980) is open-ended.
11. The optional question on religion in the Australian census has been asked since the first national census of 1911, its voluntary status clarified since 1933. Parent's birthplace is also asked.
12. The open-ended question on ancestry was asked for the first time in the 1986 Australian census.
13. The 'ethnic origin' question in the New Zealand census of 1976, which used the terms 'descent', and 'race' provided two categories plus write-in. That of 1981 lists 8 'full' categories plus write-in for other full and for mixed origin, that of 1986 8 categories plus write-in for 'other' (Review Committee on Ethnic Statistics, 1988).
14. The 8 and 14 categories in the 1991 and 1996 censuses respectively refer to 'ethnic group', the open write-in to Maori tribe or *iwi*. A question on usual language was introduced in 1996.

Sources: United Nations Demographic Yearbooks 1971, 1973, 1983, 1988, 1993 (Tables 27, 28, 29), National Census volumes, National Statistical Offices, Courbage (1995).

Europe at Versailles embraced substantial European ethnic minority populations, thanks to the long-term processes of migration and diffusion under the previous multi-ethnic empires and inept or punitive boundary-drawing. For example, areas with substantial Hungarian populations were allotted to Hungary's new neighbours (e.g. Slovakia, Romania), creating problems which remain lively today. The only major exception to this picture of diversity is Poland, whose previous diversity was tragically extinguished in the last war. It is one of the few to ask no question relating to ethnicity in its census. Most other states in Central and Eastern Europe ask census questions on the ethnicity or national origin, language or religion of their long-standing European ethnic minority populations (Table 1.2), some of which have constitutionally recognized positions (Kalibova, in press). These do not concern populations of recent immigrant origin. Until the 1990s these countries had experienced relatively little international migration.

Ethnicity and related topics in the censuses of the 'Neo-Europes'

The examples above show the originality of the British 1991 question on ethnic origin, directed at recent immigrant rather than ancient indigenous minorities, compared with all other European countries. With the exception of the Netherlands, it has little in common with the European approach to non-indigenous populations in censuses or with underlying policies towards them. Rather than placing itself at the heart of European census practice, Britain has instead followed in this respect the example of the English-speaking countries overseas: the United States, Canada, Australia and New Zealand. This is somewhat paradoxical, as the latter countries regard themselves as 'countries of immigration' with positive policies welcoming immigration (Papademetriou, 1994; Jupp and Kabala, 1993). The United Kingdom takes a diametrically opposite view. It does not officially regard itself as a 'country of immigration '; instead its immigration policy attempts to 'restrict severely the numbers coming to live permanently...in the UK' (Home Office, 1994, iii).

The United States, Canada, Australia and New Zealand have all been created by large-scale immigration, initially from European countries except for the black population of the US All also have indigenous non-European minorities, numerically relatively small except for the Maori in New Zealand (10 per cent of population in 1991). The ethnic and racial balance in these countries has been further diversified since the 1960s by a new immigration policy, which ended privileges once enjoyed by Britons and Europeans and which opened the door to new inflows from the third world. All have developed multicultural policies which institutionalize new ethnic differences (Castles, Cope, Kalantzis, and Morrissey, 1990; Chiswick, 1992). Their census practice reflects these diverse origins and pluralistic policies: all ask questions on race and/or ancestry in their censuses, directed to recent immigrants as well as to older minorities (these examples were considered during the debate on the British census ethnic question). In all these countries the census also asks questions on language, and (except the United States) on religion. In response to changing policies, fashions, and shifts in immigration the form of the census question asked has changed from one census to the next, notably in Canada, including at one stage questions on the origins of parents (Richmond, 1980). Great efforts have been devoted to producing definitive ethnic categorizations (e.g. Dept. of Statistics, 1993; Statistics Canada and US Bureau of the Census, 1993).

In Canada, successive censuses have asked increasingly detailed questions on ancestry and tribe: five in 1996 (Statistics Canada, 1994). A question on the two 'official' Canadian languages has a long history, recognizing the special position of the predominantly French-speaking population of Quebec and the substantial French-speaking minorities in other provinces. As in the other countries the numerous languages of indigenous peoples, and the growing number of those of recent immigrant origin, are also now recognized in the census.

In the United States, a question specifically on race dates back to the first census of 1790, recognizing the separate black population and later incorporating additional categories for American Indians, other indigenous minorities, Asian immigrant minorities (Chinese and Japanese) and — in 1930 only — Mexicans. US vital statistics from most States of the Union also record race and Hispanic origin as in the census but do not use the open-ended and very numerous 'ancestry' (ethnic) categories, which are confined to the census and to surveys. In the new ethnic awareness in the 1960s, a question on Hispanic origin was introduced into the US census in 1970. This was and remains quite separate from the race question; Hispanics can be of any race or colour. As part of the same political process a further, open-ended and separate third question on ancestry (ethnic origin) was made compulsory in the US census and official surveys in 1976. It first appeared in the census of 1980 (US Bureau of the Census, 1982; US Bureau of the Census, 1983).

Respondents can claim one or several origins. The Bureau of the Census coded over 1,000 in 1980. Partly as a result of representations from ethnic pressure groups, these three independent questions have been kept separate: on race (colour) with 15 fixed categories in 1990, Hispanic origin with 4 Hispanic categories in 1990 and ethnic origin, which is an open, write-in question. This does not work entirely as intended; in 1990, 9.8 million people, mostly Hispanic, did not respond to the race question (US Bureau of the Census, 1993). A question on language was first asked in 1890, one specifying foreign mother tongue from 1910. The results of these questions in the 1980 Census are analysed in a volume similar to this series (Lieberson and Waters, 1988).

In Australia, Aboriginals have been counted only since the 1971 Census. Apart from that, there is no question on 'race'. A question on ethnicity (actually 'ancestry', as in the US census) was adopted for the 1986 census, along with questions on country of birth of parents, language and religion (optional) (Population Census Ethnicity Committee, 1984). The ancestry question was open; multiple ancestries could be claimed (Castles, 1991b). The voluntary question on religion was also 'open' and yielded 1,500 different kinds of response, subsequently coded into 27 categories (Castles, 1991a). In New Zealand the major ethnic and racial divide is between Maori and other Pacific Islanders, and people of European origin. By 1986, the New Zealand census question had changed from one based on racial categories to one based on ethnic descent, with a separate question for Maori origin (Review Committee on Ethnic Statistics, 1988; Department of Statistics, 1993b). Categorization along these lines in census and vital registration statistics, is now routine. As elsewhere in the 'neo-Europes', the categories have become more diverse to include recent non-European immigrant groups (and in New Zealand, Maori tribal subdivisions and European ethnicities) following the growth of ethnic consciousness, and the change in immigration patterns.

1.9 The British ethnic group question compared with others

This brief survey reveals considerable international differences of practice in census questions on ethnicity, race and related topics. These reflects the historical origins of nations and perceptions as to their ancient unity or ethnic diversity, the volume and origins of their recent immigration streams, and the policy responses to ethnic diversity arising from different national constitutional traditions and political pressures. In choosing to ask a census question on ethnic origin directed to minorities of recent immigrant origin, Britain has made itself unique in Europe. In some respects it is following the census practices adopted in the United States and in the countries of the Old Commonwealth, developed in conjunction with a positive approach to immigration which Britain does not share. The British census ethnic group question differs from those used in the 'neo-Europes' in being a single question only and in being not open-ended but based on a short list of ostensibly 'ethnic' categories. Britain's approaches to the development of a multicultural society, which underlie the census question, however, do have something in common with policy in the US and the Old Commonwealth, through ethnic monitoring, targets and the legal recognition of group rights and privileges, much of which need ethnic statistics. This approach is well developed in only one other European country (Netherlands) and has been rejected by others. The ethnic or race census questions developed in the neo-Europes have often being revised from one census to the next. Stability of form is desirable for statistical continuity, but new opinions on ethnicity, and new immigration or political realities may be just as important. The process of debate on the form of the ethnic question in the British census of 2001, if there is to be one, has already begun. It will be interesting to see if the form of the question posed in 1991, on which so much effort has been bestowed, remains unchanged.

Acknowledgements

The editors wish to express their indebtedness to John Haskey of the OPCS for his encouragement, help and tireless attention to detail at all stages in the preparation of this volume. His comments on this chapter, together with those of Ceri Peach, Philip Kreager, Martin Bulmer and Mike Murphy, were most helpful. The Australian Bureau of Statistics, The Department of Statistics, New Zealand, Ms Manon Declos, Professor H-J Hoffmann-Nowotny, Ms Priska Gisler, Dr K Kalibova, Ms Julia Kirk, Dr Anton Kuijsten, Ms Camilla Palmer, Ms Ekaterina Shanova, Ms Marian Storkey and the London Research Centre, Dr A.G. Vishnevsky, Dr E. Voutiva, Dr P. Zvidrins and others provided useful material or corrections. All errors in this introductory chapter remain the responsibility of the authors.

Appendix 1.1

The full references to the legal cases cited in the text which define specific groups as falling under the protection of the race relations acts are:
Jews (Seide v Gillette Industries)
Gypsies (Commission for Racial Equality (CRE) v Dutton 1989 IRLR 8, CA)
Sikhs (Mandla v Dowell Lee 1983 2 AC 548, HL)
Irish (Bogdeniec v Sauer-Sundstrand Ltd 1988 COIT 1933/5)
Welsh (Cameron v Arfon BC 1987 COIT 1713/71)
Rastafarians (Crown Suppliers (PSA) v Dawkins 1991 IRLR 327, EAT) (failed)
Muslims (Tariq v Young and others 24773/88) (failed)
Note:
'COIT' is Central Office of Industrial Tribunals
'AC' is Appeal Case
'CA' is Court of Appeal
'HL' is House of Lords; the highest appeal court.
'EAT' is Employment Appeal Tribunal
'IRLR' is Industrial Relations Law Report'

This list of cases, which may not be complete, concerns only those groups whose protected status have been decided by the courts in cases of dispute. There is no comprehensive 'list' and no possibility of one.

References

Adelstein, A. M., MacDonald Davies, I. M., and Weatherall, J. A. C. (1980) *Perinatal and Infant Mortality: Social and Biological Factors 1975–1977. Studies on Medical and Population Subjects no 41.* London: HMSO.

Balarajan, R., and Bulusu, L. (1990) Mortality among Immigrants in England and Wales 1979-83. In M. Britton (Ed.), *Mortality and Geography. A review in the mid-1980s England and Wales. Series DS no. 9* (pp. 103–121). London: HMSO.

Balarajan, R., Bulusu, L., Adelstein, A. M., and Shukla, V. (1984) Patterns of Mortality among migrants to England and Wales from the Indian subcontinent. *British Medical Journal,* 289 (3 Nov 1984), 1185-1188.

Balarajan, R., and Raleigh, V. S. (1990) Variation in perinatal, neonatal, postneonatal and infant mortality by mothers' place of birth, 1982-85. In M. Britton (Ed.), *Mortality and Geography: a review in the mid-1980s. Series DS No. 9.* (pp. 123–137). London: HMSO.

Balarajan, R., Raleigh, V. S., and Botting, B. (1989) Sudden Infant Death Syndrome and postneonatal mortality among immigrants in England and Wales. *British Medical Journal,* 298, 716–720.

Ballard, R. and Khalra V.S.(1994) *The Ethnic Dimension of the 1991 Census: a preliminary report.* Census Microdata Unit, University of Manchester.

Banton, N. (1955) *The Coloured Quarter.* London, Jonathan Cape.

Barou, J. Le fait ethnique dans la France de demain. (pp. Chapter 10. 171–195 in typescript).

Benjamin, B. (1982) Variation of Mortality in the United Kingdom with special reference to immigrants and minority groups. In D. A. Coleman (Ed.), *The Demography of Immigrant and Minority Groups in the United Kingdom* (pp. 42–69). London: Academic Press.

Bertranpetit, J. *et al.* (1995) Human mitochondrial DNA variation and the origin of the Basques. *Annals of Human Genetics 59,* 63–81.

Brown, C. (1984) *Black and White Britain.* London: Policy Studies Institute/ Heinemann Educational.

Bundesamt für Statistik (1991) *Sprache und Religion.* Basel: Bundesamt für Statistik.

Castles, I. (1991a) *Census 86 - Religion in Australia. Census of Population and Housing, 30 June 1986.* Canberra: Australian Bureau of Statistics.

Castles, I. (1991b) *Multicultural Australia.* Canberra: Australian Bureau of Statistics.

Castles, S., Cope, B., Kalantzis, M., and Morrissey, M. (1990) *Mistaken Identity—Multiculturalism and the Demise of Nationalism in Australia (2nd edition).* Sydney: Pluto Press.

Cavalli-Sforza, L. L., Menozzi, P., and Piazza, A. (1988) *The History and Geography of the Human Genes.* Princeton: Princeton University Press.

Chiswick, B. R. (Ed.). (1992) *Immigration, language, and ethnicity : Canada and the United States.* Washington: AEI Press.

Coleman, D.A. (ed.) (1982) *The Demography of Immigrant and Ethnic Minority Groups in the UK,* London: Academic Press.

Coleman, D. A. (1994) Integration and Assimilation Policies in Europe. In M. Macura and D. A. Coleman (Eds.), *International Migration and Integration: Regional Pressures and processes. Economic Studies No 7.* New York and Geneva: United Nations Economic Commission for Europe.

Coleman, D. A. (1995) International Migration: demographic and socio-economic consequences in the UK and Europe. *International Migration Review,* 29(1), 155–206.

Coleman, D. A., and Salt, J. (1992) *The British Population: patterns, trends and processes*. Oxford: Oxford University Press.

Commission for Racial Equality (1989) *Positive Action and Racial Equality in Housing*. London: Commission for Racial Equality

Cross, M. (1989) Migrants and the New Minorities in Europe. In H. Enzinger and Carter (Eds.), *International Review of Comparative Public Policy vol - ume 1*. (pp. 153–178). Greenwich: JAI Press.

Cross, M., Johnson, M. R. D., and Cox, B. (1988) *Black Welfare and Local Government: Section 11 and Social Services Departments*. Warwick: Centre for Research in Ethnic Relations.

Courbage, Y. (1995) *Results of the survey on statistical information sources concerning national minorities in Europe. Paper prepared for the third meeting of the Group of Specialists on the Demographic Situation of National Minorities (POS-S-MIN)*. Strasburg: Council of Europe.

Department of Statistics (1993b) *1991 New Zealand Census of Population and Dwellings: New Zealand's Multicultural Society*. Wellington: Department of Statistics, New Zealand.

Department of Statistics (1993a) *New Zealand Standard Classification of Ethnicity*. Wellington: Department of Statistics, New Zealand.

Department of the Environment (1991) *Urban Programme Guidance Notes*. London: Department of the Environment.

Fryer, P. (1984). *Staying Power: the history of Black people in Britain*. London:

German Federal Ministry of the Interior (1993) Survey of the Policy and Law concerning foreigners in the Federal Republic of Germany. Bonn: German Federal Ministry of the Interior.

Gerzina, G. (1995) *Black England: life before emancipation*. London: John Murray.

Hammar, T. (1990) *Democracy and the Nation State: aliens, denizens and citizens in a world of international migration*. London: Avebury Gower.

Harris, H. (1980) *The Principles of Human Biochemical Genetics 3rd edition*. Amsterdam: Elsevier-North Holland.

Harrison, G. A. (1989) Human Geographical Variation. In M. Keynes and G. Ainsworth Harrison (Eds.), *Evolutionary Studies: a centenary celebration of the life of Julian Huxley*. (pp. 158–167). London: Macmillan.

Haskey, J. C. (1992) Demographic Characteristics of the Ethnic Minority Populations of Great Britain. In A. H. Bittles and. D. F. Roberts (Eds.), *Minority Populations: Genetics, Demography and Health*. (pp. 182–208.). London: Macmillan.

Heckmann, F. (1992) *Ethnische Minderheited, Volk und Nation*. Stuttgart: Enke.

HM Government (1978) *1981 Census of Population (Census White Paper) Cm 7146*. London: HMSO.

HM Government (1984) *The Government reply to the 2nd Report from the Home Affairs Committee Cmnd 9238*. London: HMSO.

HM Government (1988) *1991 Census of Population (Census White Paper) Cm 430*. London: HMSO.

Hobsbawm, E. (1990) *Nations and Nationalism since 1780*. Cambridge: Cambridge University Press.

Hollis, J. (1982) New Commonwealth Ethnic Groups: Populations in Greater London. In D. Coleman, (Ed.), *The Demography of Immigrants and Minority Groups in the United Kingdom*. London: Academic Press.

Home Affairs Committee (1983) *Ethnic and Racial Questions in the Census HC 33-1 Session 1982-83*. London: HMSO.

Home Office (1990) *Section 11 Guidance.* London: Home Office.

Home Office (I994) *Immigration and Nationality Department Annual Report 1994.* London: Home Office.

Immigrant Statistics Unit (1975) Country of Birth and Colour 1971-4. *Population Trends* 2, Winter 1975, 2-8.

Immigrant Statistics Unit (1977) New Commonwealth and Pakistani Population Estimates. *Population Trends* 9, 4-7.

Jenkinson, J. (1993) The 1919 Riots, In P. Panayi (Ed.), *Racial Violence in Britain 1840–950* (pp. 92–111.). Leicester: Leicester University Press.

Jones, D. (1979) The Chinese in Britain; origins and development of a community. *New Community,* 11.

Jupp, J., and Kabala, M. (1993) *The Politics of Australian Immigration.* Canberra: Australian Government Publishing Service.

Kalibova, K. (in press) Population Censuses and Ethnicity. *Acta Universitatis Carolinae. Geographica* no. 1-2.

Kreager, P. (1992) Quand une population est-elle une nation? Quand une nation est-elle un état? La démographie et l'émergence d'un dilemme moderne, 1770–1870. *Population,* 47(6), 1639–1656.

Langevin, B., Begeot, F., and Pearce, D. (1992) Censuses in the European Community. *Population Trends* 68, Summer 1992, 33–35.

LARRIE (1994).*The LARRIE Directory of Race Equality officers and Related Posts.* London: Local Authority Race Relations Information Exchange (LARRIE).

Lester, A., and Bindman, G. (1972) *Race and Law.* Harmondsworth: Penguin.

Lewontin, R. (1982) *Human Diversity.* New York: Scientific American.

Lieberson, S., and Waters, M. C. (1988) *From Many Strands: Ethnic and Racial Groups in Contemporary America.* New York: Russel Sage Foundation.

Lithman, E. L. (1987) *Immigration and Immigrant Policy in Sweden.* Stockholm: Swedish Institute.

Lomas, G. B. G. (1973) *Census 1971. The Coloured Population of Great Britain. Preliminary Report.* London: Runnymede Trust.

London Research Centre (1995) *Population projections of ethnic minority groups in London. Key findings for 2011.* London: London Research Centre.

Long, M. (1988) *Étre français aujourd'hui et demain. Rapport remis au Premier Ministre par Marceau Long.* Paris: La Documentation Française.

McKenzie, K.J. and N.S. Crowcroft (1994) Race, ethnicity, culture and science. *British Medical Journal* 309, 30 July 1994, 286–287.

Marmot, M., Adelstein, A., and Bulusu, L. (1983) *Immigrant Mortality in England and Wales 1970–1978: causes of death by country of birth. Studies in Medical and Population Subjects no 47.* London: HMSO.

Muus, P. J. (1991) *Migration, Minorities and Policy in the Netherlands: recent trends and developments. (Netherlands SOPEMI report 1991).* Amsterdam: Dept of Human Geography, University of Amsterdam.

Nanton, P. (1992) Official Statistics and Problems of Inappropriate Ethnic Categorisation. *Policy and Politics,* 20(4), 277–285.

Netherlands Ministry of Home Affairs (1983) *Minorities Policy Document.* The Hague: Staatsuitgeverij.

NSCGP (1990) *Immigrant Policy: summary of the 36th report.* The Hague: Netherlands Scientific Council for Government Policy.

OPCS (1979) *Projections of the New Commonwealth and Pakistani Population. OPCS Monitor PP2 79/1.* London: OPCS.

OPCS (1982) *Longitudinal Study: Socio-demographic Mortality Differentials 1971–5. Series LS no. 1.* London: HMSO.

OPCS (1983) *Mid-1981 Estimates of the Population of New Commonwealth and Pakistani Ethnic Origin. OPCS Monitor PP1 83/2.* London: OPCS.

OPCS (1985) *Labour Force Survey 1984. Country of Birth, Ethnic Group, Year of Entry and Nationality. OPCS Monitor LFS 85/1.* London: OPCS.

OPCS (1986) *Labour Force Survey 1985. Ethnic Group and Country of Birth. OPCS Monitor LFS 86/2.* London: OPCS.

OPCS (1994a).*Birth Statistics 1992, Review of the Registrar General on births and patterns of family building in England and Wales, 1992. Series FM1 No 21.* London: HMSO.

OPCS (1994b) *Mortality Statistics 1993 General England and Wales. Series DH1 No 27.* London: HMSO.

OPCS/GRO(S) (1993a) *1991 Census. Ethnic Group and Country of Birth Great Britain.* London: HMSO.

OPCS/GRO(S) (1993b) *1991 Census Supplement to Report on Ethnic Group and Country of Birth (Table A).* London: OPCS.

Owen, C. (1993) Using the Labour Force Survey to estimate Britain's ethnic minority populations. *Population Trends* 72 Summer 1993, 18–23.

Palmer, C. (1992) *Discrimination at Work (2nd edition).* London: Legal Action Group.

Papademetriou, D. G. (1994) International Migration in North America: Issues, Policies, Implications. In M. Macura and D. A. Coleman (Eds.), *International Migration: Regional Processes and Responses. Proceedings of a UN ECE/UN FPA informal Expert Group Meeting on International Migration.* (pp. 77–107). New York: United Nations.

Peach, G. C. K. (1966) Under-enumeration of West Indians in the 1961 Census. *Sociological Review,* 14, 73–80.

Peach, G. C. K., and Winchester, S.W.C., (1974) Birthplace, ethnicity and the under-enumeration of West Indians, Indians and Pakistanis in the Census of 1966 and 1971. *New Community,* 3, 386.

Peach, G.C.K., Robinson, V., Maxted, J. and J. Chance (1988) Immigration and Ethnicity. in Halsey, A.H. (ed.) *British Social Trends since 1900.* London: Macmillan. pp. 561–615.

Population Census Ethnicity Committee (1984) *The Measurement of Ethnicity in the Australian Census of Population and Housing. Report to the Australian Statistician by the 1986 Census Ethnicity Committee.* Canberra: Australian Bureau of Statistics.

Population Statistics Division (1986) Ethnic Minority Populations in Great Britain. *Population Trends,* 46, 18–21.

Registrar-General (1923) *Census of England and Wales 1921 General Tables* London: HMSO.

Registrar-General (1954) *Census of England and Wales 1951 General Report.* London: HMSO.

Registrar-General (1970) Estimate of population of New Commonwealth Ethnic Origin. *Registrar-General's Quarterly Return* (488).

Registrar-General for Scotland (1995) *Annual Report 1994 No 140.* Edinburgh: General Register Office for Scotland.

Review Committee on Ethnic Statistics (1988).*Report of the Review Committee on Ethnic Statistics (New Zealand).* Wellington: Department of Statistics.

Rex, J. (1985) *The concept of a multi-cultural society.* Warwick: Centre for Research in Ethnic Relations.

Richmond, A. H. (1980) Ethnic Questions in the Canadian Census. *New Community,* 8, 19.

Rocard, M. (1991) Le Devoir d'Intégration. Speech by the French Prime Minister at Villiers-le-Bel, 4 April 1991. London: French Embassy.

Scobie, E. (1972) *Black Britannia: A History of Blacks in Britain.* Chicago:

Sellier, A., and Sellier, J. (1992). *Atlas des Peuples d'Europe Centrale.* Paris: La Découverte.

Shaw, C. (1988) Latest estimates of ethnic minority populations. *Population Trends, 51,* 5–8.

Shyllon, F. O. (1974) *Black Slaves in Britain.* Oxford: Oxford University Press for the Institute of Race Relations.

Sillitoe, K. (1978) Ethnic Origins: the search for a question. *Population Trends, 13,* Autumn 1978, 25–29.

Sillitoe, K. (1987a) *Developing Questions on ethnicity and related topics for the Census. OPCS Occasional Paper 36.* London: OPCS.

Sillitoe, K. (1987b) Questions on race/ethnicity and related topics for the census. *Population Trends, 49,* 5–11.

Sokal, R. R., Jacquez, G. M., and Oden, N. I. (1993) Genetic Relationships of European Populations reflect their Ethnohistorical Affinities. *American Journal of Physical Anthropology, 91*(1), 55–76.

Statistics Canada (1994) Canadian Census Ethno-cultural questions 1871-1991. Ottawa: Centre for Ethnic Measurement, Statistics Canada.

Statistics Canada/US Bureau of the Census (1993). Challenges of Measuring an Ethnic World. Washington DC, US GPO.

Stewart, M., and Whitting, G. (1983) *Ethnic Minorities and the Urban Programme.* Bristol: School for Advanced Urban Studies, Bristol University.

Storkey, M. (1995) The size and projected numbers of London's Ethnic minority populations. Paper presented to the European Population Conference, Milan, Sepember 1995.

Tabili, L. (1994) *'We ask for British Justice' Workers and Racial Difference in Late Imperial Britain.* Ithaca and London: Cornell University Press.

Teague, A. (1993) Ethnic group: first results from the 1991 Census. *Population Trends 72,* Summer 1993, 12–17.

United Nations (1987) United Nations Statistical Commission and Economic Commission for Europe. Conference of European Statisticians. Statistical Standards and Studies - No. 40. *Recommendations for the 1990 Censuses of Population and Housing in the ECE Region.* New York: United Nations.

US Bureau of the Census (1982) *Ancestry and language in the United States: November 1979. Current Population Reports Special Studies Series P-23, No 116.* Washington DC: US Government Printing Office.

US Bureau of the Census (1983) *1980 Census of Population. Ancestry of the Population by State 1980. Supplementary Report. PC80-S1-10.* Washington DC: US Government Printing Office.

US Bureau of the Census (1993) *US Population Estimates by Age, Sex, Race and Hispanic Origin; 1980 to 1991. Current Population Reports P25-1095.* Washington DC: US Government Printing Office.

Visram, R. (1986) *Ayahs, Lascars and Princes: the story of Indians in Britain 1700–947.* London: Pluto Press.

Walvin, J. (1972) *The Black Presence: a documentary history of the Negro in England 1555–860.* New York:

Walvin, J. (1973) *Black and White: the Negro in English society 1555–945.* New York.

Watkins, S. C. (1990) From local to national communities: the transformation of demographic regimes in Western Europe 1870–1960. *Population and Development Review, 16,* 241–272.

Weber, E. (1976). *Peasants into Frenchmen.* Stanford: Stanford University Press.

Chapter 2
The ethnic group question in the 1991 Census of Population

Martin Bulmer

2.1 The question

The 1991 Census of Population included the questions on country of birth and ethnicity shown in Figure 2.1. (1)

Figure 2.1 *1991 Census of Population questions on country of birth and ethnic group*

10	**Country of birth**
Please tick the appropriate box.	England □ 1 Scotland □ 2 Wales □ 3 Northern Ireland □ 4 Irish Republic □ 5 Elsewhere □
If the 'Elsewhere' box is ticked, please write in the present name of the country in which the birthplace is now situated.	If elsewhere, please write in the present name of the country

11	**Ethnic group**
Please tick the appropriate box.	White □ 0 Black-Caribbean □ 1 Black-African □ 2 Black-Other □ *please describe*
	Indian □ 3 Pakistani □ 4 Bangladeshi □ 5 Chinese □ 6 Any other ethnic group □ *please describe*
If the person is descended from more than one ethnic or racial group, please tick the group to which the person considers he/she belongs, or tick the 'Any other ethnic group' box and describe the person's ancestry in the space provided.	

Source: 1991 Census of Population, H enumeration form for private households, reproduced in Dale and Marsh (1993), p.367.

The aim of this chapter is to trace the emergence of the question on ethnic group included for the first time in the 1991 Census and to discuss its effectiveness in identifying the main ethnic groups in Britain today. (This question is not a migration question and does not provide data on migration.) The emergence of new questions in the British Census of Population has typically in the past been the product of internal consultations and deliberations within the government, led by the Office of Population Censuses and Surveys and the General Register Office (Scotland), the government departments which conduct the census. (2) In recent censuses there has been an increasing amount of public consultation and debate, and this was particularly the case with the proposed ethnic group question, given its sensitivities and the problems encountered in 1981. Over the 15 years between 1975 and the finalisation of the census schedule in 1990 the process by which this question was developed, tested in various forms and introduced may be followed, with ministerial and parliamentary approval as the final stage of this process prior to the census itself.

Britain historically is a nation of ethnic and national mixture, despite being cut off by the sea from its nearest neighbours. Whether the migrants were Angles, Saxons, Normans, Huguenots, Irish or Jews, or members of other minority groups, the British population is by origin somewhat heterogeneous. However, until the nineteenth century, when large-scale Irish and Jewish immigration occurred from across the Irish sea and from Russia and eastern Europe, immigrant populations were small in relation to total population size and many, though not all, were assimilated into the indigenous population. Almost all of the migrants were White.

Census questions bear on important demographic and social variables about which the government of the day (including local and central government, quangos and statutory bodies) want information, where the information sought relates to the entire or a substantial part of the population and can therefore be sought through the census, and where it is judged technically feasible to ask the question successfully of the entire population.

2.2 Wider social trends

The phenomenon with which the 1991 Census ethnic group question is concerned is the substantial presence in Britain since the 1950s of members of ethnic minority groups originating from the West Indies and Guyana, the Indian subcontinent and Africa in particular, distinguishable in terms of darker skin colour. Members of earlier migrant ethnic minority groups, such as the Irish and the Jews, were not physically distinguishable from the majority White population, and their descendants living in Great Britain tended in subsequent generations to be less easily distinguishable to others as members of an ethnic minority group. From the late 1940s onwards, with increasing pace in the late 1950s and 1960s, substantial numbers of migrants from the New Commonwealth entered Britain and formed ethnic minority groups distinguishable in terms of colour from the White majority.

The New Commonwealth refers to Commonwealth countries in the Third World such as the Caribbean countries, African Commonwealth countries,

Mediterranean Commonwealth countries such as Cyprus and Malta, India and Bangladesh, Malaysia, Singapore and Hong Kong. Pakistan, which left the Commonwealth in 1972, is added to the New Commonwealth group since Pakistan is a major area of migration to Britain, and in any event rejoined the Commonwealth in 1989. This group of countries as a whole contrasts with the Old Commonwealth countries (Australia, Canada, New Zealand and South Africa, which left the Commonwealth in 1961 but re-joined in 1994) which, with the exception of South Africa, have predominantly White populations.

The immediate origin of the ethnic group question lay in the short term in political concerns voiced in the late 1960s and early 1970s about the numbers of people in Britain of West Indian, South Asian or Black African origin, and the politics involved in immigration control. For a period — relatively brief in retrospect — statistics of immigration and the population of 'New Commonwealth and Pakistan ethnic origin' became a hot political issue, with claim and counterclaim being made about the size of this group and its likely future population growth. One of the aims of the OPCS has been to provide reliable data which established the size and characteristics of these ethnic minority groups in as exact a form as possible (Moser, 1972). Subsequent demographic work on ethnic minority groups has enabled further estimates to be made of the size of the different groups by geographical area.

A subsequent and stronger rationale for including the question was the fact that ethnic minority groups were known to suffer discrimination and disadvantage, for example in relation to employment, housing and education. A census question would enable national and adequate local authority level data to be collected on these issues (Sillitoe and White, 1992) and used for planning services, monitoring the distribution of ethnic minority groups in relation to social provision, and in monitoring progress on combating inequality. During the 1980s, there was increasing government recognition of the need for these data.

2.3 Ethnicity and race

An ethnic group is a collectivity within a larger population having real or putative common ancestry, memories of a shared past, and a cultural focus upon one or more symbolic elements which define the group's identity, such as kinship, religion, language, shared territory, nationality or physical appearance. Members of an ethnic group are conscious of belonging to the group. There is no doubt that the inclusion of the question on ethnic minority group membership in the 1991 Census was aimed at identifying the size and distribution of the main *visible* ethnic minority groups in Britain, distinguishable in terms of skin colour from the majority population. To that extent the census question is concerned with 'race' rather than 'ethnicity'.

'Race' however is a controversial term, not least because of the political misuses that have been made of the concept, particularly in Nazi Germany. The idea that an objective classification of mankind's major biological categories into 'races' is either possible or useful, and that in turn individuals can be assigned to such categories, has been progressively discredited. Though there are discernible differences in skin colour, head form or type of hair among members of the human species, no satisfactory general classification of 'races' exists to which individuals may be assigned on the basis of these characteristics. This is evident, for example, in the wide variations in skin colour which exist within the population as a whole, or the variations within subgroups originating from particular geographical areas.(3) At the same time, it is the case that the visible difference in skin colour between most members of an ethnic minority group and the majority White population is an attribute to which social significance is attached.

Membership of an ethnic group is something which is subjectively meaningful to the person concerned, and this is the principal basis for ethnic categorisation. The census ethnic group question — which is essentially a self-assessed classificatory one — reflects the fact that members of both ethnic minority groups and the majority population perceive differences between groups in society and define the boundaries of such groups, taking into account a variety of charateristics including physical ones such as skin colour. What the census ethnic group question reflects is the inability to base ethnic identification upon objective, quantifiable information, as in the case of age or income, and the necessity to ask people which group they see themselves as belonging to.

2.4 Terminology

In order to ask a successful self-identification question about ethnicity or 'race', clear terminology must be used. One of the difficulties in this area is that the terminology in general use has changed markedly over time. The earliest studies of British race relations used the term 'Negroes', 'coloured' or 'coloured migrants' for persons of West Indian descent (Bulmer, 1986a). One study was entitled *Dark Strangers* (Patterson, 1963). As immigration from the Indian subcontinent increased in the 1960s, the term 'immigrants', 'coloured immigrants' or 'Commonwealth immigrants' became much more commonly used. The first national study of racial discrimination, published in 1968, referred to the 'Commonwealth coloured immigrant population' (Daniel, 1968). In the early 1970s, in official publications of statistics about ethnic minority groups, the term 'New Commonwealth and Pakistan ethnic origin' was intensively used for a period (see Moser, 1972).

In the few years immediately preceding the 1981 Census of Population there was a shift in empirical social research towards using terminology placing an emphasis upon area of origin. In the second Political and Economic Planning (PEP) national survey of race relations (Smith, 1976) the terms 'West Indian', 'African Asian' and 'Indians and Pakistanis' were used. West Indians were defined as people born in the West Indies or Guyana, or (if born in Britain) people whose families originally came from there. African Asians were defined as people who were racially Asian and who either were born in Africa or were living there immediately prior to coming to Britain, or belonged to families that were originally African Asian. Indians and

Pakistanis were defined as people who were not African Asians and were born in India or Pakistan or who belonged to families that originally came from India or Pakistan. 'Asian' was used to refer only to people coming from the Indian subcontinent. Other Asian groups such as Chinese or Japanese were not included in the sample. This classification had similarities with the OPCS estimates of the population of New Commonwealth and Pakistan ethnic origin, which was broken down by geographical area of origin.

Other studies of the time used this terminology in one form or another. In Ken Pryce's study of West Indian life-styles in Bristol (1979), those researched are referred to throughout as 'Jamaicans' or 'West Indians', whether born in the West Indies or Britain. Rex and Tomlinson (1979) and Ratcliffe (1981), in their studies of Handsworth in Birmingham use the terms 'West Indian' and 'Asian', with the term 'ethnic group' introduced as a more general term. The third national survey of race relations, carried out by Policy Studies Institute (PSI) in 1981 (Brown, 1984), used a broadly similar definition of 'West Indian', 'African Asian', 'Indian' and 'Pakistani' to that of the second PSI national survey in 1974.

2.5 Operationalisation

From the point of view of the census, the key issue is whether a workable question can be devised that would enable members of different ethnic groups to be identified. Various possible ways of operationalising the concept are available, and have been used over the years. These will now be reviewed. They are summarised for convenience in Table 2.1, which should be read in conjunction with the qualifications in the text that follows. The discussion relates to Great Britain, and this volume, except for Chapter 9, does not cover Northern Ireland. It is worth noting that Northern Ireland censuses have, exceptionally for the UK, included a question on religion.

Country of birth

The traditional question used in the census to identify people coming to Britain from outside the UK has been about where they were born, asked in censuses since 1841. In 1841 and 1851 birthplace was asked. From 1861 country of birth was asked, and data produced on this basis. This provides valuable information about the composition of the population, and some information about the composition of ethnic groups. Implicitly, a country of birth question is used in conjunction with a model of ethnic difference in which difference equates to recentness of arrival. It might be expected that someone born abroad will be more likely to differ in significant respects than someone born in this country. The converse of this is that as a person and their descendants born in this country live here, they become assimilated into the general population, and their children and grandchildren who are born in the UK (second- and third-generation 'immigrants') are no longer identifiable through a separate country of birth question. Indeed, beyond the first generation, the term 'immigrant' becomes a misnomer, and has been dropped from usage, to be replaced very widely by 'ethnic minority'.

Table 2.1 *Topics relating to country of origin and ethnicity in the Census of Population in Great Britain, 1801 to 1991*

Census question on	1801	'11	'21	'31	'41	'51	'61	'71	'81	'91	1901	'11	'21	'31	'51	'61	'66	'71	'81	'91
Birthplace/country of birth					GB	GB	GB	GB	GB	GB	GB	GB	GB	GB	GB	GB	GB	GB	GB	GB
Parents' country of birth																		GB		
Nationality					GB	GB	GB	GB	GB	GB	GB	GB	GB	GB	GB	GB	GB			
Language spoken																				
Gaelic									S	S	S	S	S	S	S	S		S	S	S
Welsh										W	W	W	W	W	W	W		W	W	W
Religion (separate voluntary inquiry)						GB														
Ethnic origin																				GB

GB = Great Britain;   S = Scotland;   W = Wales

Note: In the Census of Northern Ireland, a voluntary question on religion has been asked since. A question on language (Irish Gaelic) was asked for the first time in 1991.

This is true, for example, of both second- and third-generation 'immigrants' to the UK from Eire, and for the descendants of Jewish migrants who were part of the mass migration from Russia and Poland around the turn of the century. Thus statistically, it is very difficult to estimate the size of the Irish population in England, Scotland and Wales (assuming one includes people originating both from Eire and Northern Ireland) (OPCS/GRO(S), 1993). This group is likely to include those born in Eire and Northern Ireland enumerated in Great Britain, but the ethnic identity Irish also includes people of Irish descent who regard themselves as 'Irish'. A question on birthplace does not enable the identification of second-, third- and fourth-generation Irish people who may or may not still regard themselves as Irish and who are quite likely to have intermarried with people not of Irish descent. (See Chapter 9 by Paul Compton, and Chapter 10 in Volume 2 for further discussion of the Irish.) The question of whether the Irish in Great Britain should be treated as an ethnic group may be an issue in relation to the 2001 Census.

It is this limitation which led to the need to supplement a question on country of birth with other questions for migrants from the West Indies, Africa and South Asia coming to the UK in the last 40 years. The implicit model of assimilation applied to people of Jewish or Irish descent was clearly not applicable to the recent migrants, because as members of ethnic minority groups they retained physical differences — skin colour — which differentiated them from the majority White population, and was likely to mean that they would continue to receive different treatment and have different life chances from the majority population. There is continuing interest in identifying descendants of these ethnic minority group immigrants. Experience of 'melting pot' societies such as the United States and Australia, and a long tradition of studies in the sociology of race relations worldwide, suggested that members of such groups would be likely to have different life chances. So what additional questions could be used to identify second and subsequent generations of ethnic minority groups born in the UK?

Nationality

In theory a person's legal status as a citizen of a particular country would be a way of distinguishing members of minority groups originating outside the country. Within the EU as a whole it is the usual practice to distinguish people with citizenship rights from others, although the Netherlands identifies ethnic minority groups. In many continental countries with different legal systems, notably Germany, citizenship status is closely tied to legal position. Thus the law of *ius sanguinis* provides that those of German ancestry living outside Germany retain a right to citizenship and residence in the country. Other immigrants are defined *de jure* as foreigners unless naturalised. This is reflected in the national statistics produced, and these are the data used in studies of the position of ethnic minority groups in the society. The Labour Force Survey, referred to below, is the only survey held compulsorily in all EU countries (though individual response is voluntary). This survey includes a question on nationality, in terms of passport held. However, the UK is the only EU country to ask an additional question on ethnic origin, which is not one of the core questions for the Labour Force Survey in all countries.

In Britain the situation regarding the definition of citizenship or nationality is less clear cut than most other European countries. A question on nationality was asked in the British census from 1841 to 1961, and then dropped for good practical reasons. In 1841 it was asked only of those of Scottish and Irish birth, and from 1851 to 1891 respondents were only asked whether they were British or not. It appeared to work for migrants prior to mass immigration from the New Commonwealth, but then ran into difficulties over the complexities of legal status among persons of Commonwealth origin in the minefield of post-Imperial British nationality law. The basic limitation of a nationality question appeared to be that people in the UK tended to be confused about their nationality, in the sense that a census question asking people their nationality did not produce satisfactory results, and also generated the unfounded fear that people would be deported, or that new nationality laws would be formulated. In the 1979 Census test, it failed to meet a crucial requirement which census questions have to satisfy; too high a proportion of people refused to answer it. Such a question had been asked in the 1961 Census of Population, but the results were not usable.

A question on nationality has been asked in the Labour Force Survey, starting in 1973, but the first report covering 1973, 1975 and 1977, though reporting the inclusion of the question, did not present any data, and urged caution in the interpretation of any results (LFS, 1980). However, the question has continued to be asked, and it has yielded usable data for some purposes (see Salt, 1995).

Originally immigration by ethnic minority groups to the UK was by British subjects who were Commonwealth citizens and had a right to enter the UK by virtue of common membership of a political unit, the British Commonwealth. The narrower status of UK citizen was then open to those who established substantial connection to the UK by length of residence or marriage to a UK citizen. The automatic right of entry was restricted by legislation in 1962 and subsequently, but the distinction between the broader category of British subject and the narrower status of UK citizen remained. In addition, those from outside the British Commonwealth were legally aliens, and belonged to a different category. Immigrant aliens had enjoyed free entry to the UK prior to 1905, when legislation to limit entry was introduced at the peak of concern about Jewish immigration from eastern Europe.

The changes in citizenship status brought about by the British Nationality Act of 1981 may have clarified the position somewhat, but it was itself a politically controversial measure and indeed concern about its possible implications heightened resistance in the Census test of 1979 among members of ethnic minority groups (Sillitoe and White, 1992). In my view, a nationality question probably remains unfeasible in the foreseeable future in the census, given the anxieties it may raise among ethnic minorities about right of permanent abode in the UK, and the political exploitation of this issue by certain far right groups.

Language spoken at home

The British census has attempted language as a question only in respect of the minority of Gaelic-speakers in Scotland and Welsh-speakers in Wales. It has asked a question about the former since 1881 and the latter since 1891, but only in Scotland and Wales respectively. In 1991, a question was also asked regarding Irish Gaelic speakers in Northern Ireland. In 1901 and 1911 efforts were made to secure responses from east European Jewish immigrants by having the schedules printed in Yiddish and mobilising community support, though no question was asked about language spoken. For some ethnic minority groups, language spoken at home may be an effective way of distinguishing the members of these groups in a census. Such a question has commonly been asked in large national surveys of ethnic minority groups, not only to identify members of the minority but also to permit the matching of interviewer with respondent in cases where the interview is conducted in the indigenous language.

Thus in the 1981 national Policy Studies Institute (PSI) survey (Brown, 1984), respondents born in South Asia were asked what language they spoke most often at home, and which other languages they spoke fluently, with precodes for English/Urdu/Punjabi/Gujerati/Hindi/other. Such a question is asked in certain other countries' censuses, for example in the United States where estimating the proportion of the population which is Spanish-speaking is of major policy significance.

The report of the House of Commons Home Affairs Committee, *Ethnic and Racial Questions in the Census* (1983 a,b,c), recommended that a language question should be asked, both as to language spoken at home and English-speaking ability. Although such a question could be asked in Britain, and was tested thoroughly in the earlier field trials which formed part of the question development (Sillitoe, 1987), eliciting few objections, such a question would only apply to a small proportion of respondents in the census. It would thus not be a strong candidate for inclusion in the census, compared with other questions covering a much larger proportion of the population. There are also arguments that the census is not the best place to tackle the complexities of language use, which often requires more than one question.

Parents' country of birth in conjunction with country of birth

A more promising alternative was parents' country of birth, which taken together with country of birth, would enable data to be produced as a proxy variable for ethnic group about both first- and second-generation migrants to the UK. The 1971 Census collected data on this basis, though the inclusion of the question provoked criticism from the Liberal Party and a campaign for non-completion by the Young Liberals, which did not however materially affect the outcome of the census (Bulmer, 1979). The first analyses of these data, published in the mid-1970s, provided the first firm estimates of the size of the population of New Commonwealth ethnic origin, and showed that just over one third of this group was born in the UK (OPCS, 1975). The estimates were rather imprecise, in part because of non-response to the parents' country of birth question, and also because of a small but significant number of the White population who had been born in parts of the Empire/Commonwealth, and under this procedure were imputed as members of one or another ethnic minority group. Just as in 1901 and 1911 when attempts had been made to identify Jewish immigrants by means of analysis of surnames (Registrar General 1904: 139), after the 1971 Census limited efforts were made to estimate the size of this particular White population (cf OPCS 1975: 3).

Aside from the complexity of carrying out analyses using both variables together, which limited the usefulness of the two variables used in conjunction, and tended to confine the analyst to basic demographic counts, the increasing proportion of this group through the 1970s who were born in the UK meant that with time the two variables in combination were not an adequate measure of the ethnic minority population. In the event the question was not included in the 1981 Census on grounds of economy, so no time series of data was available between the two censuses. During the 1980s interest shifted to other possible questions.

Skin colour

Popular perceptions of ethnic difference — and to an extent for a period those of social science researchers — used terminology referring directly to skin colour. The term 'coloured' was widely used in the 1950s, but then fell out of use being regarded as pejorative and inaccurate. The metaphor of colour remained a powerful idea, however, and early discussions of a possible census question in the mid-1970s included references to measures of the appearance of different types of beer as an analogy to the measurement problems faced in the census in relation to ethnic minority groups.

In fact one attempt was made to gather data on skin colour by observation, in the General Household Survey (OPCS,1983). From its inception in 1971 until 1983, the interviewer in the General Household Survey was asked to record whether the respondent was White, Coloured or not known. No assessment was made by the interviewer of persons not seen, and most of these were children. From 1980 to 1983, if both parents were seen, the interviewer imputed their children's colour. This observational variable was then used to tabulate data. Its use was not particularly extensive, though some tables appeared in *Social Trends*. The question suffered both from the limitations of interviewer error in observation, and from the limited amount of information which it yielded. 'Coloured' was an ambiguous term, and it was not clear which ethnic groups it included. Did it, for example, include people of Maltese, Cypriot, or Arab origin; how were people of mixed racial origin classified, and so on? When both interviewer data on colour and the ethnic origin question (see below) were included in the GHS in 1983, and one was tabulated against the other, 99 per cent of those describing themselves as West Indian, 98 per cent of Indians, and 97 per cent of Pakistanis and Bangladeshis were classified by the interviewer as coloured, but of the remaining ethnic groups (including 'mixed ethnic origin'), one quarter were recorded by the interviewer as White (OPCS, 1983). The data did not provide a breakdown of the members of different ethnic minority groups, and this together with its imprecision accounted for its relative unpopularity.

A further development in the late 1970s and early 1980s was the use of the term Black to refer to members of certain ethnic minority groups. Although this might be used in a loose way to indicate members of ethnic minority groups, its use by members of ethnic minority groups themselves had more specific connotations in terms of promoting a positive self-identity among ethnic minority group members, and a sense of common political purpose. Not all people of South Asian descent, however, welcomed the term, and this led to the use by the Commission for Racial Equality (CRE) among others, of the phrase 'Black and Asian' to refer to the main ethnic minority groups.

The report of the House of Commons Home Affairs Committee, *Ethnic and Racial Questions in the Census* (1983 a,b,c), recommended that four questions be asked to identify a person's ethnic group in the census. These were:
  (a) Are you White?   Yes/no
  (b) Are you Black?   Yes/no
      If you are Black, are you: British/West Indian/African/Other?
      (tick as many boxes as apply)
  (c) Are you of Asian origin? Yes/no
      If *yes*, are you: British/Indian/Pakistani/Bangladeshi/West Indian/ Chinese/Vietnamese/Other?
      (tick as many boxes as apply)

(d) Other groups
   Are you: Mixed race/Arab/ Greek Cypriot/ Turkish Cypriot/None
   of these?
   (tick *one* box)

What remained ambiguous was whether Black referred primarily to persons of West Indian and African origin, or also included people of South Asian origin. Sometimes in political discourse it was more inclusive, but the tendency in research terms was to limit Black to the two former groups, and to talk about 'Black and Asian' when referring to the main ethnic minority groups in the UK. This indeed is the implication of the Select Committee question given above.

National/geographical origin

The Select Committee questions quoted above take the form of a direct question, relying on self-classification. This is the solution to the problem of trying to find a satisfactory ethnic origin question which has most commonly been adopted. It has been the practice, for example, in censuses in other multi-ethnic societies such as the United States and Canada. Instead of a proxy variable such as country of birth or nationality, a direct question is asked seeking the person's own categorisation of their ethnic group, or in the case of the census that of the member of the household completing the enumeration form.

When a question is framed in this way, the increasing tendency in the UK context in the last 15 years has been to rely on elements in the question which referred to national or geographical origin, with the accompanying assumption that these mapped on to ethnic groups. Thus the terms West Indian or Indian are taken as shorthand terms for members of ethnic groups originating in those parts of the world. White persons born in, for example, India, are taken not to belong to these groups, and would be expected to exclude themselves, choosing some other alternative such as White or English. In the case of migrant ethnic groups, combination of more than one identifier, as in East African Asian, can be used to differentiate between groups in a multi-ethnic society. In a sense one might argue that this is, if not a proxy variable, proxy terminology, since national or geographic origin is being used to identify people of a particular ethnic group.

The two previous in combination (e.g. Black–African)

A further development has been to combine national or geographical origin with a colour term such as Black, as in Black–African, to identify more precisely which group is being referred to for people originating from a part of the world which is itself multi-ethnic, such as the West Indies. The term Black–British has given rise to particular difficulties of meaning and use, and will be discussed more fully in the next section.

Racial group (for certain groups, e.g. Chinese)

Finally, there are a small number of cases where a classification is used which is more than an identification in terms of national origin or geography. Some of the OPCS tests of questions used categories such as Chinese or Arab, which are arguably in effect a racial classification of a kind, even if they also have to an extent certain geographical connotations.

2.6 Trials of the question in government continuous surveys

A question on ethnic minority group membership, in addition to being tested in the OPCS methodological research for the census, was introduced into a number of national surveys carried out by the OPCS for government departments. These provided a large-scale testing ground for the national feasibility of a question on ethnic origin, and the survey development is a very significant part of the story of the emergence of the census question. The first survey in which the question was used was the National Dwelling and Housing Survey, a very large-scale survey into the nation's housing carried out for the Department of the Environment in 1976 in the wake of the cancellation of the 1976 mid-term Census (DoE, 1980). This survey for the first time asked a question on ethnic origin. Respondents were handed a card and asked:

'To which of the groups listed on this card do you consider .... (person) belongs?'
01 White
02 West Indian
03 Indian
04 Pakistani
05 Bangladeshi
06 Chinese
07 Turkish
08 Other Asian
09 African
10 Arab
11 Other (give details)
12 Mixed origin
13 Refused

The first continuous survey to introduce the question was the Labour Force Survey (LFS) in 1979. (In its 1973, 1975 and 1977 rounds it had asked country of birth and nationality (LFS, 1980).) The question was not included in the 1981 Census, and the government stated that its policy would be to monitor the social and economic characteristics of the minority group population through voluntary sample surveys. The relatively large sample size of the LFS (one half of one percent of the adult population) made it very suitable for this purpose. In the 1979 LFS, this question, also with 13 somewhat different categories, had the following form (LFS, 1982a):

'From which of the groups listed on this card do you consider you are descended?' (Interviewers were instructed to enter the number, and specify further if the response was 03 or 11)
00 English, Welsh, Scottish or Irish
01 Polish
02 Italian

03 Other European
04 West Indian or Guyanese
05 African
06 Indian
07 Pakistani
08 Bangladeshi
09 Arab
10 Chinese
11 Any other racial or ethnic group or of mixed racial descent
12 No reply.

From 1981 onwards, the first four categories were merged into one, and termed White. There had been difficulties in respondents from continental Europe who had become integrated into British society responding to the 1979 question, and the LFS question thereafter has had the following format (LFS, 1982a; LFS, 1982b).
   'To which of the groups listed on this card do you consider you belong?'
   0 White
   1 West Indian or Guyanese
   2 Indian
   3 Pakistani
   4 Bangladeshi
   5 Chinese
   6 African
   7 Arab
   8 Mixed origin (SPECIFY)
   9 Other (SPECIFY)

If the respondents reply that they are Mixed or Other, the interviewer asks them to describe their ethnic origin in greater detail. If the description mentions only one of the named ethnic groups 1 to 7, they are reclassified to that group (Haskey, 1990). This question with the above modification of the White category proved workable and uncontroversial, though with some non-response (Owen, 1993).

From the 1983 round, the General Household Survey introduced a similar question on ethnic origin, directly asked of respondents, in addition to the interviewer's observation of the colour of the respondent. This had the form:
   'To which of the groups listed on this card do you consider ....
   belongs?'
   01 White
   05 West Indian or Guyanese
   02 Indian
   03 Pakistani
   04 Bangladeshi
   07 Chinese
   06 African
   08 Arab
   09 Mixed origin (SPECIFY)
   10 None of these

By 1992, the GHS question had been modified to the following:

'To which of the groups listed on this card do you consider ....
belongs?'

01 White
02 Black–Caribbean
03 Black–African
04 Black–Other (specify at (a))
05 Indian
06 Pakistani
07 Bangladeshi
08 Chinese
09 None of these (specify at (a))

If *Black Other* or *None of these*:

(a) How would you describe the racial or ethnic group to which ....
    does belong?

Although all the above questions had a general resemblance to each other, they differed in the particulars, partly in the terminology for certain ethnic minority groups and the majority White population, and partly in the number of categories used. Why was there no attempt at harmonisation? The answer probably lies in the decentralised system of statistics in British central government, and the fact that each survey had its own group of users in different departments, often with slightly different policy concerns in relation to ethnic minorities. This plurality of approaches underlined the importance of the work on a census question, which was continuing.

2.7 Development of the census question

Following the decision not to include a question on ethnicity in the 1981 Census, the Sub-committee on Race Relations and Immigration (SCORRI) of the House of Commons Home Affairs Committee considered the issue and recommended in its report, *Ethnic and Racial Questions in the Census* (1983 a,b,c), that a question on racial or ethnic origin should be included in future censuses, subject to confidentiality safeguards and a clear intention that the information gathered should be used to promote programmes against racial discrimination and disadvantage. The authority to ask such a question on race was contained in the Census Act of 1920, though it had never been previously invoked or contemplated. Their recommendations were accepted in principle by the government.

Development work on a possible census question on race and ethnicity had been underway within OPCS since 1975. Ken Sillitoe of OPCS Social Survey Division conducted this methodological research and development work trying out a large number of variant questions. Some of the earlier work is described in detail in Sillitoe (1987). Throughout, the aim was to frame a satisfactory direct question on race and ethnicity involving self-identification. A number of models for a direct question were available, for example from the United States and West Indian censuses. These, however, only showed the feasibility of such a question. The precise question to be asked in the census would need to be developed on the basis of careful testing to reflect the particular circumstances and ethnic composition of the population in Great Britain.

A full account of the later stages of the process is contained in Sillitoe and White (1992). Only the most salient points are presented here. The first relates to the political context in which census testing was undertaken. The Haringey Census Test of 1979 suggested to OPCS that an ethnicity question could not be asked successfully in the 1981 Census. This probably had less to do with the form of the question than the way in which the census was seen. Some local organisations campaigned for respondents in the voluntary test census (all residents of the London Borough of Haringey) not to complete questions on ethnicity, birthplace, parents' country of birth or nationality, on the grounds that collection of the information could be linked to the government's plans to change the nationality law, supposedly to the disadvantage of ethnic minority groups. Only just over half of households in the main census test returned the census form, and about one third of West Indian and Asian form-fillers in the test census who were asked the ethnicity question said they thought it wrong to include such a question in the census. Scepticism about the census question was not confined to the public or ethnic minority group organisations. Some academic researchers in the field of race relations also questioned the advisability of asking such a question in the census (for one example, see Booth, 1985).

When the Census Order was debated in the House of Commons on 29 April 1980, it was subject to a number of amendments (*Hansard*, Vol 983, No. 165, 1301, 1334). One, from Alex Lyon, MP for York, proposing the inclusion of ethnic origin as a question, was subject to heated exchanges and challenges to the arguments put forward by Patrick Jenkin, Secretary of State for Social Services, about the adverse experience of the test census, the worries of ethnic minorities, the risk of failure of the question and its effects on the census as a whole, and the aim of gathering such data by other means. However, the amendment was defeated by 116 votes to 14 (Coleman, 1980). It is notable that a census question was subject to debate in this way, and the debate indicated the groundswell of support which existed for such a question.

From the early 1980s onwards, political concern about the effects of a census question became much less intense, and there was no significant public opposition to the 1989 Census Test (as compared to that in 1979), nor significant public opposition at the time of the 1991 Census (as there had been in 1971). The question on ethnic minority group membership was broadly accepted by the public in the course of the 1991 Census of Population.

The use of the question in the NDHS, the LFS and the GHS had also demonstrated the question's feasibility, at least in a voluntary survey. Finding a satisfactory form for a census question became in the five years leading up to the 1991 Census therefore largely a technical matter. One of the most important issues to be resolved was whether the use of the terms Black–British or British–Asians produced meaningful results. The general finding was that the term British–Asian was not sufficiently discriminating, and that the term Black–British, although preferred by one in ten West

Indian respondents, also induced quite widespread confusion among those filling in the test forms. Sillitoe argued that the use of the term, because it blurred national or geographical origin in favour of skin colour and race, was in effect a classification based on race or skin colour rather than on ethnicity.

In July 1988 the White Paper, *1991 Census of Population* (Cmd 430), proposed that a question on ethnicity be included in the 1991 Census subject to a full dress rehearsal proving successful in the 1989 Census Test. An important innovation was the use of the term 'Black' which had previously been considered unacceptable. The question proposed had seven categories, White/Black/Indian/Pakistani/Bangladeshi/Chinese/any other ethnic group (please describe below), the first six being precoded tick boxes. This question was subsequently modified, following comments from the public and organisations representing ethnic minority groups, to a question almost identical to that used in the 1991 Census (see Figure 2.1), giving more detail on Black groups in terms of origin.

The 1989 Census Test, whose results are summarised by Dale and Marsh (1993), indicated much lower degrees of objection to an ethnic group question than in the 1979 Test Census. The Post-Enumeration Survey found that only 0.5 per cent of the total sample gave the ethnicity question as a reason for not completing the form (which was voluntary), and only 7 per cent of respondents objected to the ethnicity question — only 1 per cent higher than those objecting to the new question on long-standing illness. The Post-Enumeration Survey estimated the accuracy of the ethnic group data as between 85 and 90 per cent comparing interviewer's observations with the response on the form. On the basis of this test, the decision was taken by OPCS in 1990 to go ahead and include the question in the 1991 Census. The change from the 1981 situation was remarkable.

2.8 Quality of the 1991 Census data on ethnic group

No discussion of the 1991 Census question would be complete without some discussion of the quality of the data resulting from its introduction. This is touched on in a number of the subsequent chapters, but deserves some separate consideration at the outset. It may be considered under four headings: (a) coding procedure; (b) non-response to the question and imputation; (c) possible effects of census under-enumeration; and (d) adjustment factors to be applied to the published results.

Coding procedure

Both the country of birth question and the ethnic group question were coded for all census forms returned. For the question on ethnic group (Figure 2.1) nine tick boxes were provided, including seven pre-coded answers numbered 0 to 6, and two questions — Black–Other and Any other ethnic group — which asked for a description to be written in. The coding frame was based upon the seven pre-coded tick boxes plus a further 28 codes derived from written descriptions given in the Black–Other and Any other ethnic group boxes and from any multi-ticking of boxes. The full 35 categories are shown in Table 2.2. For most census output, these 35 codes were condensed into the 10 categories shown in Table 2.3 which form the ethnic group output classification.

Table 2.2   *The full coding frame of Ethnic Groups in 1991 Census data*

0	White		*Other ethnic group: non mixed origin*
1	Black–Caribbean	18	British - ethnic minority group indicated
2	Black–African	19	British - no ethnic minority group indicated
3	Indian	20	Caribbean Island, West Indies or Guyana
4	Pakistani	21	North African, Arab or Iranian
5	Bangladeshi	22	Other African countries
6	Chinese	23	East African Asian or Indo-Caribbean
		24	Indian subcontinent
	Black–Other: non-mixed origin	25	Other Asian
7	British	26	Irish
8	Caribbean Island, West Indies or Guyana	27	Greek (including Greek Cypriot)
9	North African, Arab or Iranian	28	Turkish (including Turkish Cypriot)
10	Other African countries	29	Other European
11	East African Asian or Indo-Caribbean	30	Other answers
12	Indian subcontinent		
13	Other–Asian		*Other ethnic group: mixed origin*
14	Other answers	31	Black/White
		32	Asian/White
	Black–Other: mixed origin	33	Mixed White
15	Black/White	34	Other mixed
16	Asian/White		
17	Other mixed		

Table 2.3   *The ten-category Ethnic Group classification used in 1991 Census output*

White
Black – Caribbean
Black – African
Black – Other
Indian
Pakistani
Bangladeshi
Chinese
Other groups – Asian
Other groups – Other

For five of the six Small Area Statistics tables, four collapsed categories are used:

White
Black
Indian, Pakistani and Bangladeshi
Chinese and other groups

The 1991 Census forms were manually coded and then keyed in at data

Figure 2.2 Flow chart showing coding steps for question 11, Ethnic Group, in the 1991 Census of Population

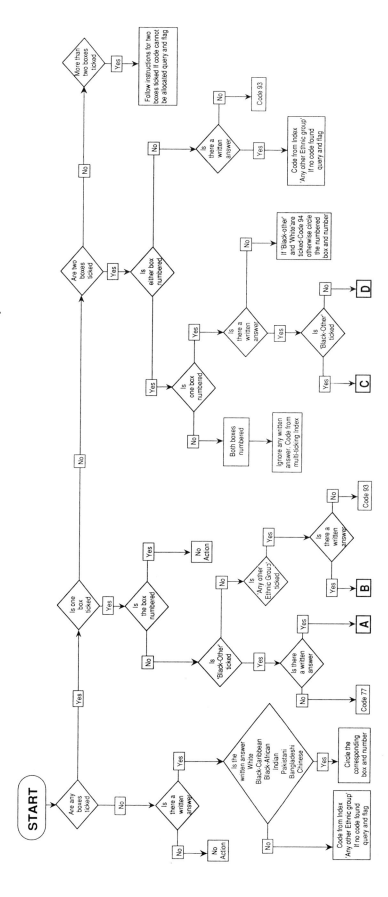

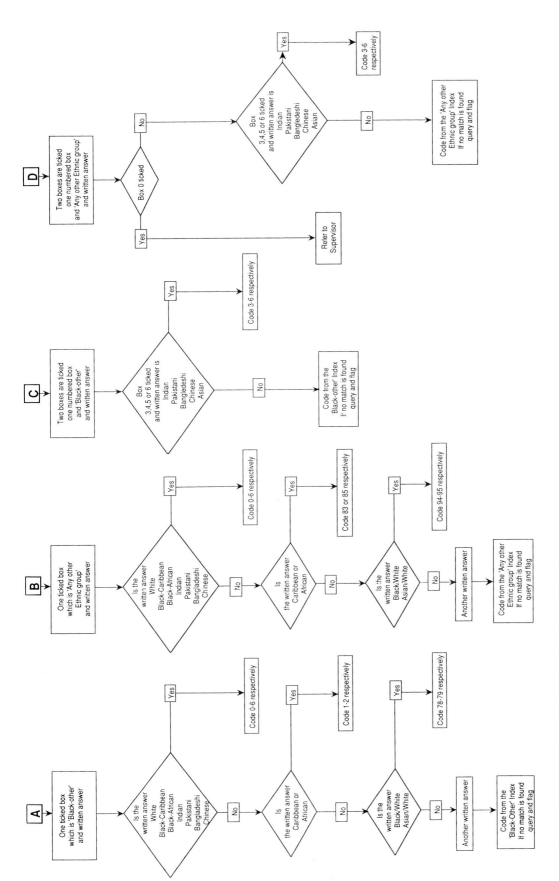

Source: OPCS, 1991 Census, Ethnic Group Flowchart and Index (internal document)

capture work stations. Instructions to census coders referred to the 35-category classification given above. These detailed instructions provided for the straightforward coding of unambiguous answers coded 0 to 6 in the question, and reference to a 235-item ethnic group index (or coding frame) giving various descriptive responses and the code appropriate to the response. (There was also a 42-item multiple ticking index for those forms where more than one box had been ticked.) Figure 2.2 shows how coders applied these rules in arriving at the ethnic group of census respondents.

Two categories, the Black–Other and Other–Other categories are particularly heterogeneous, containing a large number of different responses. This issue has considerable implications for how the data about these two groups are interpreted and is dealt with in more detail in Chapter 4. There will be some coder error due to data being entered incorrectly, but the scale of this given the procedures used is likely to have been very small.

Non-response to the question and imputation

Not all returned census forms are complete for all members of the household and for all items of information for a person, and the Census Offices have well-developed computerised procedures for the editing of data on forms for the 1991 Census, described by Mills and Teague (1991). After editing of data and consistency checks to correct a very small number of invalid or inconsistent responses (an example of the first would be a person age 140 years, of the second a person age 5 years and married), a process termed 'imputation' is applied to individual records which contain missing data for particular questions or invalid or inconsistent answers which cannot be corrected. The amount of imputation required for most items was 1 per cent or less in the 1981 Census. The imputation procedure fills in missing responses by predicting them from a series of tables reflecting the relationship between the item to be imputed and other census variables, and which are constantly updated during census processing using valid responses. For missing information on the ethnic origin of the first person in the household, this is inferred from their age, for the second and subsequent persons, from the ethnic group of the first member and the age of the person concerned (Mills and Teague, 1991). In all, invalid or missing items were imputed for 1.2 per cent of census forms in the 1991 Census.

In addition to missing items imputed, the 1991 Census was the first where whole households were imputed if there was evidence from a census enumerator that a household existed. Detailed imputed records for the missing household and the persons it contained were created by copying them from other forms which *had* been returned, using four key items: the type of area in which the household was located; the number of people noted or guessed by the enumerator while in the field; the number of rooms noted or guessed by the enumerator while in the field; and whether the accommodation was self-contained or not. In this way the characteristics of 869,098 persons (in 1.6 per cent of all households) were imputed, including 114,065 persons who were allocated to an ethnic minority group (13.12 per cent of those imputed). This represents 3.8 per cent of all persons from ethnic minority groups. Table 2.4 shows the national results.

Table 2.4 *Imputed residents of wholly absent households*

Age, marital status, long-term illness, economic position and ethnic group	Great Britain			England and Wales			England		
	Total	Males	Females	Total	Males	Females	Total	Males	Females
Total persons	**869,098**	**420,925**	**448,173**	**806,323**	**391,000**	**425,323**	**773,820**	**375,554**	**398,266**
0–5	138,340	70,286	68,054	129,161	65,574	63,587	124,521	63,216	61,305
16–17	13,990	6,895	7,094	13,013	6,400	6,613	12,491	6.156	6,335
18–29	210,953	103,002	107,951	196,424	95,763	100,661	189,964	92,477	97,487
30–44	184,795	99,328	85,467	171,748	92,150	79,598	165,582	88,737	76,845
45 up to pensionable age	146,508	85,297	61,211	135,731	79,188	56,543	129,862	75,724	54,138
Pensionable age and over	174,512	56,116	118,396	160,246	52,925	108,321	151,400	49,244	102,156
Single	401,458	211,135	190,323	374,317	196,914	177,403	361,866	190,211	171,655
Married	321,892	161,628	160,264	298,633	149,932	148,701	285,707	143,449	142,258
Widowed or divorced	145,748	48,162	97,586	133,373	44,154	89,219	126,247	41,894	84,353
With limiting long-term illness	118,283	53,033	65,250	108,239	46,681	59,558	101,746	45,830	55,916
In employment	384,056	217,245	166,811	357,610	202,177	155,433	345,188	194,903	150,285
Unemployed	63,110	41,838	21,272	58,482	38,706	19,776	56,525	37,362	19,163
Economically inactive	283,592	91,556	192,036	261,070	84,543	176,527	247,586	80,073	167,513
White	755,033	364,073	390,960	693,615	334,886	358,729	662,435	320,163	342,272
Other ethnic group	114,065	56,852	57,213	112,708	56,114	56,594	111,385	55,391	55,994

Source: 1991 Census, Report for Great Britain, Table 18, Part 1, p. 438

Some figures for areas with the highest incidence of imputation for ethnic minority groups are shown in Table 2.5.

Of the 17 districts listed in the table, 12 are in London, and all of those in which imputation accounted for more than 10 per cent of the ethnic minority group population were in London, mostly in central areas. This reflects in part the higher level of under-enumeration in these areas, which enumerators were able to limit partially by gathering some information about missing households. It reflects the high residential density with houses in multiple occupation, the higher proportion of single person households which are more difficult to enumerate in these areas, and the higher incidence of households which are not self-contained, but about which some information is available. In a majority of those districts with large imputation of ethnic minority group populations, Black–Caribbean people form the largest minority ethnic group. Some of the highest rates of under-enumeration are found among young men in this group and they are also undercounted in the Labour Force Survey. In addition to missing persons in enumerated households, and missing households about which the census enumerator gained some knowledge, both of which can be imputed, there are also those households not identified at all, and hence not enumerated. This gives rise to the problem of under-enumeration.

Table 2.5   *Districts with highest incidence of imputation for ethnic minority groups*

Local authority	Ethnic minority group	Per cent of population	No. imputed	Per cent of minorities imputed	Largest ethnic minority group in district
Lambeth	74,079	30.3	8,090	10.9	Black–Caribbean
Southwark	53,386	24.4	5,759	10.8	Black–Caribbean
Kensington & Chelsea	21,603	15.6	2,327	10.8	Other–Other
Westminster	37,439	21.4	3,753	10.0	Other–Other
Hackney	60,839	33.6	6,074	10.0	Black–Caribbean
Hammersmith & Fulham	25,989	17.5	2,031	7.8	Black–Caribbean
Haringey	58,667	29.0	4,551	7.8	Black–Caribbean
Islington	31,085	18.9	2,408	7.8	Black–Caribbean
Lewisham	50,749	22.0	3,839	7.6	Black–Caribbean
Camden	30,418	17.8	2,199	7.2	Bangladeshi
Manchester	51,183	12.6	2,987	5.8	Pakistani
Wandsworth	50,604	20.0	2,931	5.8	Black–Caribbean
Bristol	19,281	5.1	1,108	5.8	Black–Caribbean
Liverpool	17,046	3.8	928	5.4	Other–Other
Brighton	4,432	3.1	241	5.4	Other–Other
Brent	108,869	44.8	5,792	5.3	Indian
Leeds	39,725	5.8	2,005	5.1	Indian

Source: Compiled by David Owen, CRER, University of Warwick, from 1991 Census Local Base Statistics Crown Copyright, showing top 17 districts with number of cases imputed in 1991 Census exceeding 240.

Possible effects of census under-enumeration

There is clear evidence of a significant undercount of the 1991 population. Demographic estimates arrived at by taking the 1981 Census population, allowing for under-enumeration at that census, and surviving this population to 1991 by deducting deaths, adding births and making an allowance for net migration in the intervening 10 years, produced an estimated population of England and Wales in 1991 that was 1.21 million greater than the population enumerated in the 1991 Census, after allowing for the effects of imputing missing data (OPCS, 1993). The Census thus appears to have underestimated the actual population by 2.2 per cent.

A number of reasons have been suggested to account for the discrepancy, including the difficulties of enumeration in areas of high multi-occupancy of dwellings and with a high proportion of single-household residents, a traditional problem of census enumeration; mobile persons, particularly young people, ranging from the homeless to the floating population of students who may not be enumerated at their own residence and are treated statistically as visitors; the tendency of parents not to record newborn infants; the possibility that some of the institutional population were not recorded at their usual place of residence, leading to undercounting of the very elderly; and a factor particular to 1991, the avoidance of enumeration in the (incorrect) belief that census data would be linked to the poll tax register then maintained by local authorities for local taxation purposes.

The official Census Validation Survey (CVS), carried out immediately after the census, in which a sample of the population are interviewed and compared with their census returns, concluded that deliberate evasion remains a plausible hypothesis (Heady *et al.*, 1994).

What are the implications of this pattern of undercount for the data on ethnic minority groups? The grounds for preferring the demographic estimates are set out in the Registrar General's account (OPCS, 1993). Valuable information about the distribution of census coverage which is of use in estimating the effects of under-enumeration on results for ethnic minority groups is available from the CVS and the demographic estimates.

The demographic estimates of the undercount show differences by age, sex and area. The age-groups most likely to be under-represented were 0–4, 20–34 and 85 and over. Men were more likely to be under-represented in the 20–34 age-group and women in the 85+ age-group. There was no significant undercount for older children or for adults age 45–79. The undercount was estimated to be more concentrated in larger urban areas.

Given what is known of the sex and age breakdown of under-enumeration, it is likely that the impact of the undercount is greater for ethnic minority groups than for the White ethnic group. Their age structure is skewed to younger ages (see Chapter 4) and they are more concentrated in large urban areas. Assuming that the effects were the same for all ethnic minority groups together, it is possible to derive factors for an ethnic group such as those shown in Table 2.6. The adjustment factors shown in Table 2.6 reflect the differential effect of the undercount without having precise figures for each minority ethnic group.

The most marked effects of the undercount are for ethnic minority group men age 20–29. The table applies a standard factor to each group and makes no allowance for possible differences between ethnic minority groups. As suggested earlier, it is possible that the undercount for Black–Caribbean young men is higher than for all ethnic minority groups. Roger Ballard, in a preliminary demographic analysis of 1991 data looking at the numbers of men and women in the Black–Caribbean and Black–Other groups by age and sex, reports that there is likely to have been a higher undercount of this group (Ballard and Kalra, 1994). Marian Storkey of the London Research Centre is currently doing some work to investigate the matter looking at sex ratios in 1991 Census data among Black–Caribbeans in London. Initial analysis seems to support this view. Indirect evidence about under-enumeration of ethnic minority groups comes from the study of electoral registration carried out as part of the CVS, which showed that there was a substantially higher non-registration of these groups, and among them of the Black group in particular, though with much wider 95 per cent confidence intervals attached. Figure 2.3 shows the results.

'Black' includes Black–Caribbean, Black–African and Black–Other, while 'Other' includes Chinese and Any other ethnic group. The dot represents the proportion not registered and the line represents the upper and lower limits of the 95 per cent confidence interval.

Table 2.6 *Adjustment factors for estimated undercoverage by age, sex and ethnic group in the 1991 Census, Great Britain*

Age	Ethnic group										
	Total	White	Black Carib-bean	Black African	Black other	Indian	Pakist-ani	Bangla-deshi	Chinese	Other groups	
										Asian	Other
Persons, all ages	**1.02**	**1.02**	**1.03**	**1.05**	**1.04**	**1.03**	**1.03**	**1.03**	**1.03**	**1.03**	**1.03**
0- 4	1.03	1.03	1.04	1.04	1.04	10.3	10.3	10.4	1.03	1.04	1.04
5- 9	1.03	1.03	1.03	1.03	1.03	1.03	1.03	1.03	1.03	1.03	1.03
10-14	1.02	1.02	1.02	1.02	1.02	1.02	1.02	1.02	1.02	1.02	1.02
15-19	1.02	1.02	1.02	1.02	1.02	1.02	1.02	1.02	1.02	1.02	1.02
20-24	1.06	1.06	1.09	1.09	1.08	1.07	1.08	1.09	1.09	1.08	1.08
25-29	1.07	1.07	1.10	1.11	1.09	1.08	1.09	1.10	1.09	1.08	1.09
30-34	1.03	1.03	1.04	1.05	1.04	1.04	1.04	1.05	1.04	1.04	1.04
35-39	1.01	1.01	1.01	1.01	1.01	1.01	1.01	1.01	1.01	1.01	1.01
40-44	1.01	1.01	1.01	1.01	1.01	1.01	1.01	1.01	1.01	1.01	1.01
45-79	1.00	1.00	1.00	1.00	1.00	1.00	1.00	1.00	1.00	1.00	1.00
80-84	1.02	1.02	1.02	1.02	1.02	1.02	1.02	1.02	1.02	1.02	1.02
85+	1.04	1.04	1.04	1.04	1.04	1.04	1.04	1.04	1.04	1.04	1.04
Males, all ages	**1.03**	**1.03**	**1.05**	**1.07**	**1.06**	**1.04**	**1.04**	**1.04**	**1.05**	**1.05**	**1.05**
0- 4	1.04	1.04	1.04	1.04	1.04	1.04	1.04	1.04	1.04	1.04	1.04
5- 9	1.03	1.03	1.03	1.03	1.03	1.03	1.03	1.03	1.03	1.03	1.03
10-14	1.02	1.02	1.02	1.02	1.02	1.02	1.02	1.02	1.02	1.02	1.02
15-19	1.03	1.03	1.03	1.03	1.03	1.03	1.03	1.03	1.03	1.03	1.03
20-24	1.10	1.10	1.14	1.15	1.14	1.12	1.14	1.14	1.14	1.13	1.13
25-29	1.10	1.10	1.16	1.17	1.15	1.13	1.15	1.16	1.14	1.14	1.14
30-34	1.05	1.05	1.07	1.08	1.07	1.06	1.07	1.08	1.06	1.06	1.07
35-39	1.02	1.02	1.02	1.02	1.02	1.02	1.02	1.02	1.02	1.02	1.02
40-44	1.02	1.02	1.02	1.02	1.02	1.02	1.02	1.02	1.02	1.02	1.02
45-79	1.00	1.00	1.00	1.00	1.00	1.00	1.00	1.00	1.00	1.00	1.00
80-84	1.01	1.01	1.01	1.01	1.01	1.01	1.01	1.01	1.01	1.01	1.01
85+	1.01	1.01	1.01	1.01	1.01	1.01	1.01	1.01	1.01	1.01	1.01
Females, all ages	**1.01**	**1.01**	**1.02**	**1.02**	**1.03**	**1.02**	**1.02**	**1.02**	**1.02**	**1.02**	**1.02**
0- 4	1.03	1.03	1.03	1.04	1.03	1.03	1.03	1.03	1.03	1.03	1.03
5- 9	1.02	1.02	1.02	1.02	1.02	1.02	1.02	1.02	1.02	1.02	1.02
10-14	1.01	1.01	1.01	1.01	1.01	1.01	1.01	1.01	1.01	1.01	1.01
15-19	1.01	1.01	1.01	1.01	1.01	1.01	1.02	1.01	1.01	1.01	1.01
20-24	1.03	1.03	1.04	1.04	1.04	1.03	1.04	1.04	1.04	1.04	1.04
25-29	1.03	1.03	1.05	1.05	1.05	1.04	1.05	1.05	1.04	1.04	1.04
30-34	1.01	1.01	1.02	1.02	1.02	1.02	1.02	1.02	1.02	1.02	1.02
35-39	1.00	1.00	1.00	1.00	1.00	1.00	1.00	1.00	1.00	1.00	1.00
40-44	1.01	1.01	1.01	1.00	1.01	1.01	1.01	1.01	1.01	1.01	1.01
45-79	1.00	1.00	1.00	1.00	1.00	1.00	1.00	1.00	1.00	1.00	1.00
80-84	1.02	1.02	1.03	1.03	1.02	1.03	1.03	1.03	1.02	1.03	1.03
85+	1.06	1.06	1.06	1.06	1.06	1.06	1.06	1.06	1.05	10.6	1.06

Note: Derived entirely from factors by age, sex, and area of residence.

Source: OPCS/GRO(S) 1993, p.7.

Figure 2.3 *Non-registration in the electoral register by ethnic group in a national sample, 1991*

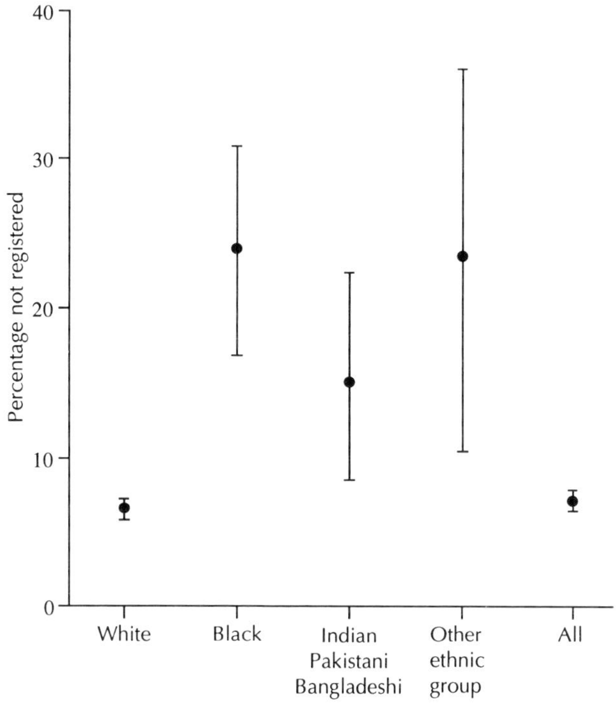

Source: Smith (1993) p11.

Adjustment factors to be applied to the published results

At the time of writing, the available adjustment factors to be applied to ethnic minority group data are those shown in Table 2.6, derived from official estimates of non-response in each of the 10 broad categories of ethnic minority group.

Work is currently underway on the incidence of under-enumeration at electoral ward level, involving the application of factors which reflect geographical differences in coverage between areas. This is important for purposes of local population estimates, and has considerable implications for resource distribution where ethnic minority group membership is a factor taken into account (Diamond, 1994; Simpson and Dorling, 1994; Simpson, 1994). Evidence from Bradford suggests that young children from ethnic minority groups were twice as likely to be missed in the census as young White children, using comparisons between the census population under 5 years and the local authority Child Health Register, but the generalisability of this finding is not yet known (Simpson, 1993). If the evidence in Table 2.5, relating to missing data and imputation in London local authorities in particular, is sound, it may be reasonable to infer that under-enumeration of Black–Caribbeans is higher in some areas than for other minority ethnic groups. Chapter 4 by Simpson considers these issues further.

At this point in time, caution is in order. The published OPCS adjustment factors should be used, but it is likely that further work will yield different weights to be used for different types of area, and possibly for different ethnic minority groups. The age effect, particularly for young males, is clearly established, and may be calculated where data broken down by age are being used. The Census Offices report that preliminary work suggests that undercoverage varies more among ethnic minority groups than is explained simply by their age, sex and geographical distribution, but it has not so far been possible to confirm or quantify such as effect (OPCS/GRO(S), 1993). More research is required into under-enumeration and its differential effects, particularly in preparation as the 2001 Census.

2.9 Conclusions

Implications for future censuses

A number of commentators have pointed out that the 1991 Census ethnic group classification does not permit respondents (or their parents in the case of children) to identify as being of mixed ethnic origin (e.g. Nanton, 1992). In the 1991 Census, this group is split between the Black–Other and Other–Other categories, with a small proportion in the Asian–Other group, a point developed by David Owen in Chapter 4. Ann Berrington in Chapter 7 points out that even by the late 1980s, about one in five of the 0–4 age-group of the total ethnic minority group population was of mixed ethnic origin, almost all UK-born. This mixed origin group is clearly growing, and its identification in future censuses is clearly a matter of importance, which will require careful consideration in the run-up to the 2001 Census. An earlier article by Chris Shaw using Labour Force Survey data suggested that one third of children of mixed parentage were described as White (Shaw, 1988). A recent report on the US census has commented upon the increase in inter-racial and inter-ethnic marriages and expanded numbers of peoples with multiple racial identities as changes which future censuses must take into account (National Academy of Sciences, 1994). The same report notes that problems of classification are likely to get much more complex as the ethnic and racial character of the American people changes, and calls for more research, particularly on public understanding on the concepts and acceptability of questions, comparability of census ethnic classifications with data from other survey and administrative sources, and the quality of data for small areas and specific groups, including attention to the problems of under-enumeration. They caution that the proliferation of ethnic categories in the census schedule may not be a practical solution.

The classification shown in Table 2.3 is a broad brush in other ways. It does not enable members of ethnic minority groups other than Black–Caribbean, Black–African, Indian, Pakistani, Bangladeshi and Chinese to be identified. For example, persons of Arab, Cypriot or Maltese origin cannot be identified. One advantage of the parents' country of birth question asked in 1971 was that it enabled the size of these groups to be estimated with some accuracy.

One of the most salient birthplace groups is that of those born in Ireland. The Census Offices issued a supplement (OPCS/GRO(S), 1994) to the main report on ethnic group and country of birth which covers those who recorded 'Irish' in response to the question on ethnic group, and relates this information to birthplace (whether in Eire or Northern Ireland). These however are not satisfactory, as they only relate to the 11,000 people (10,000 of whom were in Greater London) who chose to write in Irish instead of ticking White. As indicated earlier there are also limitations to taking birthplace data alone as an indication of Irish ethnic group membership. It is however for consideration whether a new category of Irish might be added to the ethnic group classification in 2001.

In addition to devising an ethnic group question which reflects the changing perceptions of ethnic minority identity in Britain by the year 2001, attention needs to be paid to the questions of census coverage and response, with particular efforts being made to improve census coverage in areas of significant ethnic minority group concentration.

Ineluctable fuzziness

The 1991 Census of Population has successfully introduced a question on ethnic group for the entire population of Great Britain, and has published the results. This volume and its three companions present the richness of data which this makes available and enhances our understanding of the multi-ethnic character of British society in 1991. Yet the successful inclusion of the question does not resolve all the issues which surround it. There remains an ineluctable fuzziness to the data which is probably inevitable, but which should be recognised by those who use it.

Conceptually, the census categories are a pragmatic compromise which identify some ethnic minority groups and do not identify others. It remains ambiguous whether the categories relate primarily to 'race' or to 'ethnicity'. The census ethnic group categories focus upon *visible* minorities, and quite significant groups, particularly those of mixed racial origin, and those of Irish origin, are not separately identifiable.

The wording of the census question combines more than one dimension, but this had been found to work in practice both in large OPCS surveys and in the census pretest. The precodes are based upon skin colour (White, Black), national origin (Caribbean, African, Indian, Pakistani, Bangladeshi) and race (Chinese). They include two open-ended categories allowing people to describe themselves if the seven precoded categories did not fit their self-identification. A list of 235 types of reply was used to reduce this complexity to 28 broad categories.

The quality of the census output has to be considered in relation to the issues of data imputation and under-enumeration discussed above. The existence of these adds a degree of uncertainty to the census information on ethnic minority groups, although the qualifications which may be required are relatively minor in relation to the value of the data on ethnic groups yielded by the census as a whole. The Census Offices have successfully introduced a new question which reflects a real differentiating factor within British society, so that ethnic group will come to take its place alongside variables such as age, sex, geographical origin and social class as key variables in analysis.

Notes

(1) The author is indebted to David Owen, author of Chapter 4, for comments on this chapter and for the use of some material by him, particularly Table 2.5, which has been incorporated into the section of this chapter on the quality of the 1991 Census data on ethnic group. For additional comments, he wishes to acknowledge the comments on an earlier draft of Roger Ballard, Ian Diamond, Steve Simpson, John Haskey of OPCS and the editors of this volume.

(2) OPCS is responsible for the conduct of the Census of Population in England and Wales, GRO(S) for its conduct in Scotland. They are separate departments with separate jurisdictions, each headed by the respective Registrar General, responsible to different ministers, but in practice they cooperate closely in many statistical matters including the conduct of the Census. OPCS was created in 1970 out of a merger between the General Register Office (GRO), established in 1837 and the Government Social Survey, established in 1941. The GRO was responsible for the Census and its history is outlined in Nissel (1987, Chapters 6 and 7). The Government Social Survey is discussed in Nissel (1987, Chapter 8), Moss (1991) and Barnes (1991).

(3) This is not to say that it is not possible to use race as a more fuzzy category in human biology to denote geographically discontinuous changes, or at least rates of change, in the frequency of phenotypic or genetic characteristics. Biologically defined human groups, however fuzzy and whether or not they are called 'races', have some empirical backing from multivariate clustering techniques applied to a wide variety of visible and invisible human and biological characteristics, in various attempts to trace the history of the evolutionary diversification of human populations (see Cavalli-Sforza and Bodmer, 1971). Polymorphisms of various kinds, both visible (such as skin colour) and invisible (such as blood group), do exist, although they tend to be clinal, that is to say that changes in gene frequency tend to occur gradually and evenly over distance. As American human biologist Frank Livingstone summed it up, 'There are no races, only clines' (quoted in Harrison, 1989, p. 160). This renders classification into discrete groups almost impossible. I am indebted to David Coleman for some of these points.

References

Ballard, R. and Kalra, V.S. (1994) *The ethnic dimension of the 1991 Census: a preliminary report*. Manchester: Census Research Group, University of Manchester.

Barnes, B. (1991) Social Survey Division in the 1990s. *Population Trends*, 64, 9–18.

Booth, H. (1985) Which 'ethnic question'? the development of questions identifying ethnic origin in official statistics. *The Sociological Review*, 33 (2), 254–74.

Brown, C. (1984) *Black and White Britain*. London: Heinemann.

Bulmer, M. (ed.) (1979) *Censuses, Surveys and Privacy*. London: Macmillan.

Bulmer, M. (1986a) Race and Ethnicity. In: R.G. Burgess (ed.), *Key Variables in Social Investigation*. London: Routledge, pp. 54–75.

Bulmer, M. (1986b) A controversial census topic: race and ethnicity in the British Census. *Journal of Official Statistics*, 2(4): 471–80.

Cavalli-Sforza L. L. and Bodmer, W. (1971) *The Genetics of Human Populations*. San Francisco: WH Freeman.

Coleman, D. (1980) The 1981 Census: a missed opportunity. *Bulletin of the Eugenics Society*, vol 12, no 3, pp. 73–9.

Dale, A. and Marsh, C. (eds) (1993) *The 1991 Census Users' Guide*. London: HMSO.

Daniel, W.W. (1968) *Racial Discrimination in England*. Harmondsworth: Penguin.

Diamond, I. (1994) Where and who are the missing million? measures of Census of Population undercount. In: *Statistics Users Council, Regional and Local Statistics*. Esher, Surrey: IMAC Ltd.

DoE (1980) *National Dwelling and Housing Survey 1976*. London: HMSO.

Harrison, G.A. (1989) Human Geographical Variation. In M. Keynes and G. A. Harrison (eds), *Evolutionary Studies: a centenary celebration of the life of Julian Huxley*. London: Macmillan, pp.158–67.

Haskey, J. (1990) The ethnic minority group populations of Great Britain: estimates by ethnic group and country of birth. *Population Trends*, 60, 35–8.

Heady, P., Smith, S. and Avery, V. (1994) *1991 Census Validation Survey: Coverage Report*. London: HMSO.

House of Commons Home Affairs Committee (1983 a,b,c) *Ethnic and Racial Questions in the Census*. London: HMSO, House of Commons Paper HC 33- I, II and III, Session 1982–83, Volume 1, Report; Volume 2, Minutes of Evidence; Volume 3, Appendices.

LFS (1980) *Labour Force Survey 1973, 1975 and 1977* London: HMSO

LFS (1982a) *Labour Force Survey 1979* London: HMSO

LFS (1982b) *Labour Force Survey 1981* London:HMSO

Mills, I. and Teague, A. (1991) Samples of anonymised records from the 1991 Census *Population Trends*, 69: 17-26.

Moser, C. (1972) Statistics about immigrants: objectives, sources, methods and problems. *Social Trends*, 3, 20–30.

Moss, L. (1991) *The Government Social Survey: a history*. London: HMSO.

National Academy of Sciences (1994) *Modernizing the U.S. Census*. Washington DC: National Academy Press, National Research Council.

Nissel, M. (1987) *People Count: a history of the General Register Office*. London: HMSO.

OPCS (1975) Country of birth and colour. *Population Trends*, 2, 2–8.

OPCS (1985) *General Household Survey 1983*. London: HMSO.

OPCS (1993) How complete was the 1991 Census? *Population Trends*, 71, 22–5.

OPCS/GRO(S) (1993) *Ethnic Group and Country of Birth, Great Britain*. Two volumes, Ref CEN91 ECGB. London: HMSO.

OPCS/GRO(S) (1994) *Supplement to Report on Ethnic Group and Country of Birth: 1991 Census*. London: OPCS.

Owen, C. (1993) Using the Labour Force Survey to estimate Britain's ethnic minority populations. *Population Trends*, 72, Summer, 18–23.

Patterson, S. (1963) *Dark Strangers: a study of West Indians in London*. Harmondsworth: Penguin.

Pryce, K. (1979) *Endless Pressure: a study of West Indian life-styles in Bristol*. Harmondsworth: Penguin.

Ratcliffe, P. (1981) *Racism and Reaction: a profile of Handsworth*. London: Routledge and Kegan Paul.

Registrar-General (1904) Census of Great Britain, 1901, *General Report*. London: HMSO.

Rex, J. and Tomlinson, S. (1979) *Colonial Immigrants in a British City: a class analysis*. London: Routledge and Kegan Paul.

Salt, J. (1995) Foreign workers and the UK labour market. Department of *Employment Gazette*, 11–19

Shaw, C. (1988) Latest estimates of ethnic minority populations. *Population Trends*, 51, 5–9

Sillitoe, K. (1987) *Developing Questions on Ethnicity and related topics for the Census*. OPCS Occasional Paper 36, SS 1246/1261. London: OPCS.

Sillitoe, K. and White, P.H. (1992) Ethnic group and the British Census: the search for a question. *Journal of the Royal Statistical Society, Series A*, 55 (1), 141–63.

Simpson, S.N. (1993) Measuring and coping with local underenumeration in the 1991 Census. Paper given at the conference on Research on the 1991 Census, Newcastle, September 1993.

Simpson, S.N. (1994) Editorial: Coverage of the Great Britain Census of Population and Housing. *Journal of the Royal Statistical Society, Series A*, 157 (3): 313–16.

Simpson, S.N. and Dorling, D. (1994) Those missing millions: implications for social statistics of non-response to the 1991 Census. *Journal of Social Policy*, 23 (4), 543–67.

Smith, D.J. (1976) *The Facts of Racial Disadvantage: a national survey*. London: Political and Economic Planning, PEP Broadsheet no 560.

Smith, S. (1993) *Electoral Registration in 1991*. OPCS Series SS1301 London: HMSO.

Chapter 3

Non-response to the 1991 Census: the effect on ethnic group enumeration

Stephen Simpson

3.1 Introduction

Chapter 2 of this volume reviews the following findings concerning the response of residents in the 1991 Census. While the overall level of response was reassuringly high at 97.8 per cent, it was significantly lower among young children, young adults and very elderly people, in particular among men aged 20–34 in city districts. This pattern implies greater national undercount for subpopulations concentrated in these age groups and areas, including all the Black and Asian ethnic groups classified by the 1991 Census (Chapter 2, Table 2.6). It also highlights the fact that there may be other characteristics of each ethnic group which cause it to be more or less covered by the census than others. It urges caution and identifies a need for more research into under-enumeration and its differential effects, particularly so far as the 2001 Census is concerned.

This chapter summarises further research undertaken in 1995 which provides evidence of differential undercount between census ethnic groups. Two approaches are taken. First, given the known characteristics of those who were missed by the census, the association of these with each ethnic group implies a probable differential under-enumeration. This evidence relies on a detailed geography and demography of the census under-enumeration estimated for electoral wards in England and Wales, and concludes that a larger proportion of each of the ethnic minority groups than the White group were probably missed by the census because of their location in areas and age-groups that are difficult to enumerate. A brief consideration of other attributes associated with non-response in the 1991 Census is inconclusive.

Second, the 1991 Census results can be assessed directly by comparison with other data sources. Lack of sufficiently comprehensive data with an ethnic group marker other than the census, means these comparisons are mainly based on a classification of country of birth. The evidence presented below relates to children's mothers' country of birth, and to sex ratio changes between the 1981 and 1991 Censuses. Comparison between the 1991 Census and other data sources is always approximate. The nature of these approximations are discussed but do not appear to detract from the main conclusion: that Black populations and South Asian populations were missed considerably more often than their White neighbours.

3.2 Characteristics of those missed by the census

Geography and demography of missing residents

UK government offices have provided an estimate of the number of residents not included in the census count, disaggregated by age and sex, separately for each of eleven types of local authority district (Heady *et al.*, 1994; Simpson and Dorling, 1994). These have been further disaggregated to local authority wards by the 'Estimating with Confidence' project, following consultation regarding a plausible and acceptable local pattern of census non-response in 1991 (Tye, 1995; Simpson *et al.*, 1995). These are estimates of census non-response and as such can be seen as means for improving the accuracy of the census; however, conclusions based on them carry an unknown degree of uncertainty.

For 1991 there is no hard evidence from which to estimate local under-enumeration directly, or even to estimate *correlates* of undercount that could be applied to local area characteristics. Instead the 'Estimating with Confidence' project divides the level of undercount in each district as estimated by OPCS, to smaller areas according to local indicators which are:

- *plausible* in their construction
- *acceptable*, in the sense of providing results which are no less plausible than any other practical proxy
- *consistent* with the (little) relevant evidence of the size of adjustment required.

Plausibility and acceptability were assessed for eight candidate indicators of non-response, first through several academic presentations and second, and very importantly, through focus groups and correspondence with local authority staff from 13 counties who had knowledge of the local areas within their authorities. As a result, the following indicators were used:

- unemployment of males aged 20–34, indicating areas with poor social conditions, which are found in social surveys to have poorer response rates.
- residents imputed in the census, indicating areas with concentrations of non-cooperative households, mobile populations, homeless people, or less successful enumerators.

These two indicators were used with equal weight; thus a local ward with 10 per cent of its district's unemployed males aged 20–24 and 6 per cent of the district's imputed residents received 8 per cent of the district's non-response. The undercount for each five-year age-group under age 45 was distributed in this way. The smaller undercount at older ages was distributed 'evenly', proportionately to the census count of residents in each local area.

Under-enumeration of the armed forces (common in British and other censuses) was handled differently, by distributing the OPCS estimates of non-response among members of the armed forces in a district to those local areas with some members of the armed services enumerated on or off bases.

The resulting estimates show that census undercount was higher within inner city areas of urban districts, and to some extent in the poorest housing estate areas. No electoral ward in England and Wales is estimated to have as high as 10 per cent of its total population under-enumerated, but a few wards are estimated to have as much as 50 per cent of the male population in their twenties missing from census counts. Further detail is given in Simpson *et al.* (1995).

It is not certain that the pattern of local under-enumeration estimated in this way is correct. Even if broadly correct, as indicated by its wide acceptance and use, it represents an approximation to an unknown degree in each local area. In this chapter the undercount estimated as above is applied equally to each ethnic group in a ward. The concentration of some ethnic groups in areas and age–sex groups that were difficult to enumerate implies greater undercount of those ethnic groups at the national level.

None the less, from these estimates of those not included (u) in the census count of residents (c), census users are advised to use adjustment factors (equal to (u+c)/c) to gross up census counts to the full resident count, wherever under-enumeration may affect the analyses that the user has undertaken. The adjustment factors differ for each age, sex and geographical location, and are highest where there was greatest estimated under-enumeration in the 1991 Census. For example, the adjustment factor for females aged under five in most areas is 1.03, whereas for males aged 20–24 in the wards estimated to be worst enumerated, the factor rises to 2.0, implying that half that population was missed. The two sets of estimates for under-enumeration provided two consistent sets of age–sex adjustment factors; the first is for local authority districts, as used for Table 2.6 in Chapter 2 of this volume. The second and more recent is for local authority wards and thus allows adjustments more sensitive to local geographical variations to be made.

Table 3.1 and Figure 3.1 show the results of applying the ward adjustment factors to the ward census data for ethnic groups. This was a straightforward but large task, multiplying the published census count for every ethnic group in an age–sex category for a local area, by the relevant adjustment factor, and summing the results for every local area in England and Wales to give an adjusted count for the total population of that ethnic group.

These adjusted national populations relate to the census counts as shown in the final column of Table 3.1. The results reflect each ethnic group's concentration within age–sex groups and areas that were relatively poorly enumerated, such as inner city wards. Table 3.1 assumes no ethnic group differential under-enumeration within an age–sex group of a local area.

However, each ethnic minority group (excepting those born in Ireland) is shown to be affected by the geography and demography of undercount more than the White group. The Black–Caribbean, Pakistani, Bangladeshi,

Table 3 .1   Implications of the local ward census undercount, 1991 England and Wales

Ethnic group	Published census count of residents	Total population including estimated undercount	Overall adjustment factor
White	46,938,466	47,935,395	1.021
Black - Caribbean	499,325	518,465	1.038
Black - African	209,665	220,603	1.052
Black - Other	175,493	184,062	1.049
Indian	829,966	856,474	1.032
Pakistan	455,443	474,364	1.042
Bangladeshi	161,626	167,618	1.037
Chinese	146,156	152,365	1.042
Other groups - Asian	192,857	200,043	1.037
Other groups - Other	281,496	293,077	1.041
Ireland-born	788,597	802,611	1.018
All groups	**49,890,493**	**51,002,465**	**1.022**

Sources: 1991 Census LBS Table L06 (ESRC/JISC purchase). Crown Copyright. Ward non-response estimates from the 'Estimating with Confidence' project.

Figure 3.1 *National adjustment for non-response, resulting from geographical and demographic location of each ethnic group*

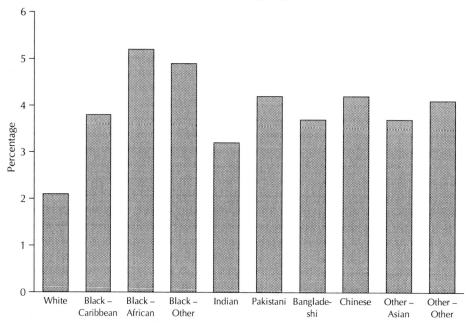

Chinese, Other – Asian and Other – Other groups are all adjusted, nation-ally, by 4 per cent, while the Black–African and Black–Other groups are adjusted by 5 per cent, more than twice the the adjustment to the White group.

For most ethnic groups, the estimates of non-response in Table 3.1 are slightly higher than those of Table 2.6 in Chapter 2 (its first row is equivalent to the final column of Table 3.1). This shows that within the districts in which they are found, these ethnic groups are concentrated in the wards with lower census coverage, a result generally consistent with the location of ethnic minority groups in city areas of high unemployment, as described in other volumes in this series.

Table 3.1a shows the detailed distribution by age and sex of the adjusted populations, and Table 3.1b shows the national adjustment factors for each age and sex derived from the process of adjusting populations in each locality. The populations in Table 3.1 and Table 3.1a can be seen to be better estimates of the number of residents in each ethnic group than are the published census counts because they include an estimate of residents not counted in the census. However, there is considerable uncertainty attached to each figure.

Other characteristics

In Chapter 2 it was observed that it is generally more difficult for a census to enumerate those residents who live in multi-household dwellings, single person households, and residents recently migrated. The 1991 Census Validation Survey does not throw much light on these issues. Although it does show a relatively high number of missed residents among private rented households (Heady *et al.*, 1994, Chapter 4), one-person households particularly in shared and converted accommodation, single or divorced residents, students and Black ethnic groups, none of these results were statistically significant. The validation survey itself suffered from non-response. In short, the other characteristics of those missed from the census are not sufficiently quantified to associate them properly with one or other ethnic group.

3.3   Comparison with other data sources

Children and country of birth of mother

A comparison of census counts of children with the number of births registered through the civil registration system has established, for all births, that 3 per cent of infants under the age of one were missed from census forms, and were more likely to be missed in some areas than others (OPCS, 1993). Undercoverage of infants is a common feature of population censuses (Werner, 1984). A suitable adjustment was applied to the local census results when the UK government published population estimates. Children of other ages are also missed, and their geographical pattern closely matches that for under-enumeration of adults, i.e. it is concentrated in city districts and in particular in inner London (Simpson, 1993).

Table 3.2 shows the same comparison between children in the census and

Table 3.1(a) *1991 Census populations by ethnic group, adjusted for estimated undercoverage, England and Wales, thousands*

Derived entirely by applying adjustment factors by age, sex, and electoral ward of residence.

	Total	White	Black–Caribbean	Black–African	Black–Other	Indian
Persons, all ages	**51002.5**	**47935.4**	**518.5**	**220.6**	**184.1**	**856.5**
0- 4	3421.6	3080.1	39.4	26.0	37.2	76.0
5- 9	3212.8	2885.1	36.9	19.6	29.2	83.5
10-14	3040.6	2753.8	30.8	15.3	21.8	79.0
15-19	3281.1	3028.7	31.8	14.7	18.1	70.4
20-24	3958.7	3655.4	53.7	25.8	21.5	77.0
25-29	4238.6	3914.6	70.9	36.5	23.0	78.5
30-34	3744.3	3457.4	51.1	28.6	12.4	82.8
35-39	3354.9	3125.4	31.0	17.2	6.0	77.8
40-44	3710.6	3542.1	20.9	11.9	4.0	59.8
45-49	3079.4	2951.6	25.9	8.3	3.1	42.1
50-54	2722.9	2587.1	37.3	7.0	2.3	40.8
55-59	2570.5	2460.7	34.9	4.0	1.9	31.9
60-64	2558.0	2480.9	25.9	2.5	1.4	22.9
65-69	2487.6	2442.0	14.9	1.5	1.0	14.9
70-74	2014.4	1989.0	7.4	.8	.6	9.3
75-79	1667.0	1653.4	3.6	.4	.3	5.2
80-84	1137.7	1131.0	1.4	.2	.2	2.7
85+	801.7	797.1	.8	.2	.1	1.9
Males, all ages	**24945.9**	**23389.1**	**252.5**	**113.1**	**91.7**	**436.5**
0- 4	1756.2	1582.2	19.8	13.2	18.8	39.0
5- 9	1651.9	1484.4	18.9	10.0	14.8	42.5
10-14	1564.3	1416.9	15.6	7.8	11.1	40.4
15-19	1688.6	1558.5	15.8	7.3	9.0	36.2
20-24	2020.5	1867.8	26.1	12.9	10.4	39.0
25-29	2160.1	2000.9	33.5	18.2	10.9	38.3
30-34	1894.7	1752.1	23.0	15.0	6.0	41.3
35-39	1684.4	1570.0	13.4	9.1	3.0	40.2
40-44	1860.5	1781.2	8.3	5.8	2.1	30.2
45-49	1541.6	1480.4	10.9	4.0	1.5	20.9
50-54	1362.3	1289.2	18.6	4.0	1.2	21.7
55-59	1278.5	1216.9	18.6	2.5	1.0	17.4
60-64	1235.5	1191.7	14.5	1.5	.7	12.3
65-69	1153.1	1127.5	8.6	1.0	.5	7.8
70-74	870.4	857.0	4.2	.5	.3	4.7
75-79	651.9	645.6	1.7	.2	.2	2.4
80-84	379.6	376.8	.6	.1	.1	1.2
85+	191.7	189.9	.2	.1	.1	.9
Females, all ages	**26056.5**	**24546.3**	**265.9**	**107.5**	**92.4**	**419.9**
0- 4	1665.3	1497.9	19.6	12.9	18.4	37.0
5- 9	1560.9	1400.6	18.0	9.7	14.4	41.0
10-14	1476.3	1336.9	15.2	7.6	10.7	38.5
15-19	1592.5	1470.2	15.9	7.4	9.1	34.2
20-24	1938.2	1787.5	27.6	12.9	11.1	37.9
25-29	2078.4	1913.6	37.4	18.3	12.1	40.1
30-34	1849.6	1705.4	28.0	13.6	6.4	41.5
35-39	1670.5	1555.4	17.6	8.2	3.0	37.6
40-44	1850.2	1760.9	12.6	6.1	2.0	29.7
45-49	1537.8	1471.2	15.1	4.3	1.6	21.2
50-54	1360.5	1297.9	18.7	3.0	1.1	19.1
55-59	1292.0	1243.8	16.3	1.5	.9	14.6
60-64	1322.5	1289.2	11.4	1.0	.7	10.6
65-69	1334.5	1314.5	6.3	.5	.4	7.1
70-74	1144.0	1132.0	3.2	.3	.3	4.6
75-79	1015.1	1007.8	1.8	.2	.2	2.8
80-84	758.1	754.2	.8	.1	.1	1.5
85+	610.0	607.2	.5	.1	.1	.9

Note: Figures will not always add to totals due to the effect of rounding.

Pakistani	Bangladishi	Chinese	Other Asian	Other–Other	Irish–born	
474.4	**167.6**	**152.4**	**200.0**	**293.1**	**802.6**	**Persons, all ages**
62.5	25.4	10.7	16.1	48.2	5.6	0- 4
66.8	25.5	11.0	16.0	39.0	11.5	5- 9
62.4	23.5	10.8	14.0	29.3	11.5	10-14
47.7	20.2	12.7	13.3	23.6	14.8	15-19
47.0	14.2	17.8	19.7	26.8	47.4	20-24
33.3	10.4	19.1	21.9	30.3	61.0	25-29
36.7	10.5	17.5	23.0	24.3	50.6	30-34
33.3	9.0	14.8	21.9	18.5	57.6	35-39
20.3	5.1	11.9	20.2	14.4	72.1	40-44
14.6	4.8	6.5	12.1	10.2	78.8	45-49
17.9	8.0	6.2	8.5	7.8	76.4	50-54
14.8	5.7	4.9	5.3	6.3	75.1	55-59
9.0	3.3	3.4	3.4	5.2	69.8	60-64
4.3	1.1	2.1	2.1	3.7	62.8	65-69
1.9	.5	1.4	1.2	2.3	49.2	70-74
.9	.2	.8	.8	1.5	33.4	75-79
.5	.1	.5	.3	.8	16.1	80-84
.4	.1	.3	.2	.6	8.9	85+
247.9	**88.5**	**76.5**	**96.5**	**153.5**	**381.4**	**Males, all ages**
32.0	12.9	5.5	8.1	24.7	2.9	0- 4
34.3	13.2	5.7	8.2	20.0	5.9	5- 9
32.6	12.4	5.6	7.1	14.9	5.8	10-14
25.5	10.9	6.6	6.9	11.9	7.3	15-19
23.7	6.9	9.7	10.4	13.6	22.2	20-24
16.3	5.3	10.2	10.4	16.2	31.8	25-29
18.4	5.9	8.7	10.6	13.6	25.4	30-34
17.9	4.0	6.6	9.8	10.4	27.5	35-39
9.8	1.4	5.2	8.7	7.8	34.7	40-44
7.3	2.3	3.2	5.7	5.5	38.3	45-49
10.6	5.2	3.2	4.3	4.3	37.6	50-54
9.0	4.1	2.6	2.8	3.6	37.2	55-59
5.7	2.7	1.8	1.6	2.9	33.3	60-64
2.9	.8	1.0	.9	1.9	28.9	65-69
1.2	.3	.6	.5	1.1	21.4	70-74
.4	.1	.3	.3	.6	13.4	75-79
.2	.1	.1	.1	.3	5.5	80-84
.2	.0	.1	.1	.2	2.2	85+
226.5	**79.1**	**75.8**	**103.5**	**139.5**	**421.2**	**Females, all ages**
30.5	12.5	5.2	8.0	23.4	2.8	0- 4
32.5	12.3	5.3	7.9	19.1	5.6	5- 9
29.8	11.1	5.2	6.9	14.5	5.7	10-14
22.2	9.3	6.1	6.4	11.7	7.5	15-19
23.3	7.3	8.1	9.4	13.1	25.2	20-24
17.1	5.1	9.0	11.5	14.2	29.2	25-29
18.3	4.5	8.8	12.4	10.7	25.1	30-34
15.3	5.0	8.2	12.1	8.1	30.1	35-39
10.5	3.7	6.7	11.4	6.6	37.4	40-44
7.3	2.6	3.4	6.4	4.7	40.5	45-49
7.3	2.8	3.0	4.2	3.5	38.8	50-54
5.8	1.6	2.3	2.5	2.7	38.0	55-59
3.3	.6	1.7	1.7	2.3	36.6	60-64
1.3	.2	1.1	1.1	1.9	33.8	65-69
.8	.2	.8	.7	1.2	27.7	70-74
.4	.1	.5	.5	.9	20.0	75-79
.3	.1	.3	.2	.5	10.6	80-84
.2	.0	.2	.2	.4	6.7	85+

Table 3.1(b) *Adjustment factors for estimated undercoverage by age, sex and ethnic group in the 1991 Census England and Wales*

Derived entirely by applying adjustment factors by age, sex, and electoral ward of residence.

	Total	White	Black–Caribbean	Black–African	Black–Other	Indian
Persons, all ages	**1.022**	**1.021**	**1.038**	**1.052**	**1.049**	**1.032**
0- 4	1.032	1.031	1.043	1.045	1.042	1.039
5- 9	1.029	1.028	1.032	1.033	1.035	1.031
10-14	1.018	1.018	1.019	1.021	1.022	1.020
15-19	1.023	1.023	1.027	1.028	1.029	1.027
20-24	1.061	1.058	1.095	1.101	1.095	1.080
25-29	1.067	1.064	1.113	1.121	1.109	1.092
30-34	1.034	1.032	1.051	1.063	1.059	1.041
35-39	1.014	1.014	1.013	1.016	1.030	1.015
40-44	1.013	1.013	1.014	1.015	1.020	1.016
45-49	1.002	1.002	1.000	1.000	1.002	1.001
50-54	1.001	1.001	1.001	1.000	1.001	1.001
55-59	1.002	1.002	1.001	1.002	1.001	1.001
60-64	1.000	1.000	.997	.997	.998	.999
65-69	.999	.999	.996	.996	.997	.997
70-74	1.000	1.000	.998	.999	.999	.999
75-79	1.002	1.002	1.001	1.002	1.002	1.001
80-84	1.022	1.022	1.020	1.021	1.022	1.021
85+	1.051	1.051	1.044	1.041	1.039	1.037
Males, all ages	**1.032**	**1.030**	**1.057**	**1.076**	**1.066**	**1.045**
0- 4	1.035	1.034	1.047	1.050	1.047	1.043
5- 9	1.033	1.032	1.036	1.037	1.039	1.036
10-14	1.021	1.021	1.023	1.024	1.026	1.023
15-19	1.032	1.031	1.039	1.040	1.040	1.038
20-24	1.095	1.091	1.157	1.166	1.154	1.128
25-29	1.103	1.098	1.183	1.193	1.171	1.147
30-34	1.052	1.050	1.085	1.098	1.089	1.065
35-39	1.024	1.023	1.026	1.027	1.043	1.025
40-44	1.020	1.020	1.024	1.025	1.029	1.024
45-49	1.003	1.003	1.002	1.003	1.004	1.002
50-54	1.001	1.001	1.000	1.000	1.001	1.001
55-59	1.003	1.003	1.003	1.004	1.004	1.003
60-64	1.000	1.000	.997	.997	.997	.998
65-69	1.000	1.000	.998	.998	.998	.999
70-74	1.000	1.000	.999	1.000	.999	.999
75-79	1.001	1.001	1.000	1.001	1.001	1.001
80-84	1.014	1.014	1.014	1.015	1.015	1.014
85+	1.016	1.016	1.008	1.010	1.007	1.013
Females, all ages	**1.014**	**1.013**	**1.021**	**1.028**	**1.032**	**1.018**
0- 4	1.028	1.027	1.039	1.041	1.038	1.035
5- 9	1.025	1.024	1.027	1.028	1.031	1.027
10-14	1.014	1.014	1.015	1.017	1.019	1.016
15-19	1.014	1.014	1.016	1.016	1.018	1.016
20-24	1.027	1.026	1.042	1.043	1.045	1.034
25-29	1.033	1.031	1.057	1.059	1.059	1.044
30-34	1.015	1.015	1.025	1.028	1.032	1.018
35-39	1.005	1.005	1.004	1.003	1.016	1.004
40-44	1.007	1.007	1.007	1.006	1.010	1.008
45-49	1.001	1.001	.999	.998	1.000	1.000
50-54	1.001	1.001	1.001	1.001	1.002	1.001
55-59	1.000	1.000	.998	.998	.999	1.000
60-64	1.000	1.000	.997	.996	.998	.999
65-69	.998	.998	.993	.993	.995	.996
70-74	1.000	1.000	.998	.998	.999	.999
75-79	1.003	1.003	1.002	1.004	1.003	1.002
80-84	1.026	1.026	1.026	1.025	1.026	1.026
85+	1.063	1.063	1.061	1.061	1.061	1.061

Note: Each adjustment factor is derived as (census + estimated non-response)/census. An adjustment factor under 1.0 implies over-estimation of resident population by the census published counts, due to over-imputation.

Pakistani	Bangladeshi	Chinese	Other Asian	Other–Other	Irish–born	
1.042	**1.037**	**1.042**	**1.037**	**1.041**	**1.018**	**Persons, all ages**
1.043	1.043	1.038	1.043	1.041	1.036	0- 4
1.036	1.033	1.032	1.033	1.034	1.031	5- 9
1.023	1.020	1.020	1.020	1.021	1.019	10-14
1.032	1.028	1.028	1.028	1.028	1.027	15-19
1.099	1.092	1.107	1.099	1.093	1.074	20-24
1.127	1.120	1.116	1.098	1.108	1.086	25-29
1.061	1.064	1.048	1.046	1.054	1.040	30-34
1.019	1.014	1.015	1.015	1.020	1.014	35-39
1.020	1.013	1.014	1.014	1.016	1.014	40-44
1.002	1.000	1.002	1.001	1.002	1.002	45-49
1.001	1.000	1.001	1.001	1.001	1.001	50-54
1.002	1.000	1.002	1.002	1.002	1.002	55-59
.999	.996	.999	.998	.998	.999	60-64
.999	.997	.997	.996	.997	.998	65-69
1.000	.998	1.000	.999	.999	1.000	70-74
1.002	.999	1.002	1.002	1.002	1.003	75-79
1.022	1.018	1.023	1.021	1.021	1.022	80-84
1.040	1.042	1.050	1.046	1.046	1.050	85+
1.056	**1.049**	**1.065**	**1.056**	**1.056**	**1.027**	**Males, all ages**
1.048	1.048	1.042	1.047	1.046	1.041	0- 4
1.041	1.037	1.036	1.037	1.038	1.035	5- 9
1.027	1.024	1.023	1.024	1.025	1.022	10-14
1.043	1.039	1.038	1.038	1.039	1.038	15-19
1.161	1.152	1.168	1.157	1.148	1.124	20-24
1.202	1.186	1.180	1.158	1.164	1.132	25-29
1.096	1.095	1.077	1.075	1.079	1.064	30-34
1.031	1.027	1.027	1.026	1.030	1.025	35-39
1.031	1.027	1.023	1.023	1.024	1.022	40-44
1.003	1.002	1.004	1.003	1.004	1.003	45-49
1.001	1.000	1.001	1.001	1.001	1.001	50-54
1.003	1.001	1.004	1.004	1.004	1.003	55-59
.999	.996	.999	.998	.998	.999	60-64
.999	.997	.999	.998	1.000	1.000	65-69
1.000	.998	1.000	.999	1.000	1.000	70-74
1.001	.999	1.001	1.000	1.000	1.001	75-79
1.015	1.013	1.014	1.013	1.014	1.014	80-84
1.013	1.015	1.017	1.009	1.012	1.015	85+
1.026	**1.024**	**1.021**	**1.020**	**1.025**	**1.009**	**Females, all ages**
1.038	1.038	1.034	1.039	1.037	1.032	0- 4
1.031	1.028	1.027	1.028	1.029	1.026	5- 9
1.018	1.016	1.016	1.017	1.018	1.015	10-14
1.019	1.016	1.017	1.017	1.017	1.016	15-19
1.043	1.042	1.043	1.042	1.041	1.033	20-24
1.063	1.059	1.051	1.049	1.051	1.040	25-29
1.028	1.026	1.020	1.021	1.024	1.017	30-34
1.006	1.004	1.005	1.006	1.006	1.005	35-39
1.011	1.008	1.007	1.007	1.007	1.007	40-44
1.000	.999	1.000	1.000	1.000	1.001	45-49
1.002	1.001	1.002	1.001	1.002	1.001	50-54
1.000	.998	1.000	.999	1.000	1.000	55-59
.999	.995	.999	.998	.998	.999	60-64
.997	.994	.996	.994	.995	.996	65-69
1.000	.997	.999	.998	.999	1.000	70-74
1.003	1.000	1.003	1.003	1.004	1.004	75-79
1.027	1.024	1.026	1.027	1.026	1.026	80-84
1.062	1.060	1.062	1.062	1.062	1.063	85+

Table 3.2 *Children under 5, Bradford. Deficit of the 1991 Census residents aged under 5, when compared with registered births in the previous five years Bradford Metropolitan District, by ethnic group*

Ethnic group	Registered births	1991 Census	Census deficit (%)
All	**37,256**	**35,287**	**6%**
White	26,495	25,825	3%
All other groups	10,648	9,462	13%
Pakistani	7,675	6,299	22%
Indian	1,081	1,032	5%
Bangladeshi	465	543	-14%
African - Caribbean	569	652	-13%
Other	858	936	-8%
Unknown	113	-	

Sources: 1991 Census LBS Table L06 and unpublished National Health Service maternity records held by Bradford Health Authority.

Notes: the ethnic group classification is the closest fit between the categories of the 1991 census and the Bradford maternity service. 'Census deficit' is shown less than zero when the census enumeration exceeds the registered births.

births before the census for Bradford, one of the few areas where ethnic group was recorded on maternity records and collated on the Child Health Register in the years prior to 1991. The numbers are small, the comparison is inexact due in particular to migration between birth and census day, and the results for some groups suggest, oddly, over-enumeration, perhaps due to a mismatch in the classifications and the quality of data collection. However it does seem clear that children of the largest ethnic minority group – Pakistanis – were counted in the census with considerably lower coverage than the average.

While ethnic group is not generally recorded on birth monitoring systems, the mother's country of birth is included on all birth registrations. Mother's country of birth is available for children enumerated in the census on the 1% household Sample of Anonymised Records, using the family membership variable developed by the Census Microdata Unit (Holdsworth, 1995).

Table 3.3 and Figure 3.2 show the number of children in England and Wales counted in the census by comparison with the number of births registered 1, 5 and 10 years prior to the census, using published data from OPCS, by mother's country of birth. Due to census under-enumeration, the percentage of registered births that are represented in the census counts is usually less than 100. For some countries of birth, this percentage is much lower than for all countries of birth combined, and where this difference is statistically significant at the 95 per cent level, the figure has been underlined. Details of the method of comparison and the approximations involved, are outlined in Appendix 3.1.

The only approximation likely to bias the comparison shown in Table 3.3 is the assumption that there has been zero net migration between the time of birth and 1991 when children should have been enumerated in the census. The continued net inflow of children from the New Commonwealth recorded in official statistics of international migration suggests that the deficit in the census may, if anything, be larger than that estimated in Table 3.3 for New Commonwealth origins. In spite of small samples and wide confidence intervals for some groups, the patterns in Table 3.3 seem to be clear.

Almost every non-UK origin category has more children missed in the census than the UK origin category, whether comparing children under 1, under 5 or under 10 with the relevant births. The low coverage of children of USA mothers stands out. It is probably related to the traditional census undercount of armed services personnel and their dependants. It is probably also related to family migration back to the USA before the 1991 Census.

Table 3.3 *Children, by mother's country of birth. Children counted in the census, compared with children born before the census, by origin of mother, England and Wales*

Country of Birth of Mother	Children in census 1% household SAR (A)			Registered births 00s (B)			Children in census as % of relevant births (100* A/B)			SAR Design Factor
	[0]	[0-4]	[0-9]	1 year before census	5 years before census	10 years before census	[0]	[0-4]	[0-9]	
UK	5,951	28,868	55,733	6,221	30,357	58,213	95.7	95.1	95.7	1.410
Eire	49	265	649	63	316	660	77.7	83.8	98.4	1.230
Australia,Canada,New Zealand	22	113	208	30	136	251	72.6	83.2	83.0	1.230
India	86	391	899	84	468	1,045	102.2	83.6	*86.0*	1.377
Pakistan	104	523	1,108	124	633	1,306	83.6	82.6	*84.8*	1.655
Bangladesh	32	192	419	56	253	445	*57.2*	75.8	94.1	1.969
African Commonwealth	94	426	848	116	565	1082	80.9	*75.4*	*78.4*	1.457
Caribbean Commonwealth	19	180	396	37	209	480	51.3	86.0	82.5	1.286
Far East Commonwealth	35	129	257	39	197	377	89.2	*65.6*	*68.2*	1.343
Mediterranean Commonwealth	18	121	250	23	128	272	77.2	94.3	92.0	1.280
Rest of Commonwealth	14	64	126	16	78	158	87.5	81.7	79.6	1.306
Other EC (1986)	63	350	700	76	363	694	83.2	96.5	100.8	1.204
Other Europe and USSR	18	92	187	25	105	198	73.0	87.9	94.4	1.215
USA	23	116	224	33	163	302	69.6	*71.2*	*74.1*	1.366
Other	75	419	819	96	444	832	78.2	94.4	98.4	1.061
Not known	53	165	301	0	3	12				
All origins	**6,656**	**32,414**	**63,124**	**7,040**	**34,418**	**66,327**	**94.5**	**94.2**	**95.2**	
South Asia	222	1,106	2,426	265	1,354	2,797	83.9	*81.7*	*86.7*	1.621
All except UK	705	3,546	7,391	819	4,061	8,114	*86.0*	*87.3*	*91.1*	1.410
New Commonwealth	402	2,026	4,303	496	2,531	5,165	*81.0*	*80.0*	*83.3*	1.517
All except New Commonwealth	6,254	30,388	58,821	6,544	31,886	61,162	95.6	95.3	96.2	1.517

Sources: 1991 Census SARs (ESRC/JISC purchase) 1% household sample. OPCS series FM1 *Birth Statistics*, annual. London: HMSO.
Notes: Registered births are shown summarised in hundreds but calculations used unit figures as published.
Underlined percentages are significantly different from the 'All origins' value (see Appendix 3.1).

Figure 3.2 *Deficit of children under 10 by mother's country of birth*

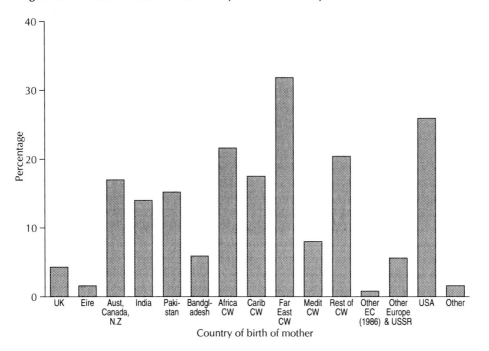

The generally high deficit of other origins, including 17 per cent of all children under 10 whose mothers were born in the New Commonwealth, is not so easily explained. To some extent, non-UK-born mothers tend to live in inner city areas that are difficult to enumerate. But the differences are larger than can be explained by this geographical element (summarised earlier in this chapter) alone. Perhaps the estimated geographical adjustment factors are too homogeneous for children, but it does also seem that children of New Commonwealth mothers (and therefore generally Black and Asian families) were considerably more difficult to enumerate in the 1991 Census than their neighbours in the same areas.

Sex ratios

Nationally in 1991, the non-response for adults aged 20–34 was predominantly among men. The evidence for differential non-response between local authority districts in England and Wales was based on a study of sex ratios in 1991, comparing them with previous census years (Heady *et al.*, 1994, Chapter 5). Greater levels of under-enumeration were inferred for areas where there was a lower proportion of men enumerated in the census than expected from previous decades' sex ratios.

A similar analysis provides some further evidence for differential under-enumeration for some origins. This analysis again focuses on country of birth categories which are available in the output of both the 1981 and the 1991 Censuses. Table 3.4 shows the sex ratios for selected countries of birth and various age groups as published in 1981, and the nearest equivalent cohort published for the same countries of birth in 1991. For example the sex ratio of those aged 20–24 in 1981 is set against that of those aged 30–34 in

1991. The figures are unadjusted census counts of residents. These will be the same residents in 1981 and 1991, except for the effects of migration, mortality and changes in census coverage between 1981 and 1991.

Concentrating on the largest changes in sex ratio between 1981 and 1991, a deficit of males born in the UK is indicated for those aged 25–29 in 1991 compared to that expected from the sex ratio in 1981, and to a lesser extent for those aged 15–24 and 30–34 in 1991. This reflects what is known of the under-enumeration in the whole population, most of whom are born in the UK. The reduction in sex ratio, indicating fewer males than expected from

Table 3.4 *Sex ratios 1981-1991, Selected countries of birth, Great Britain*

Age in 1981	1981		M/F Ratio	Age in 1991	1991		M/F Ratio	% change in ratio 1981-91
	Males	Females			Males	Females		
Born in the UK								
5-15	4,324,151	4,112,270	1.052	15-24!	3,624,702	3,578,807	1.013	-3.68
16-19	1,733,877	1,663,003	1.043	25!-29	1,971,695	2,021,010	0.976	-6.43
20-24	1,842,077	1,788,511	1.030	30-34	1,787,101	1,805,674	0.990	-3.91
25-29	1,642,803	1,616,237	1.016	35-39	1,628,850	1,637,541	0.995	-2.14
Born in Commonwealth Africa								
5-15	18,681	18,494	1.010	15-24!	23,155	24,899	0.930	-7.94
16-19	15,823	15,285	1.035	25!-29	24,789	27,218	0.911	-12.02
20-24	26,954	25,809	1.044	30-34	32,536	31,678	1.027	-1.65
25-29	25,856	22,647	1.142	35-39	27,151	24,434	1.111	-2.67
Born in Commonwealth Caribbean								
5-15	2,974	3,041	0.978	15-24!	3,560	4,539	0.784	-19.80
16-19	3,808	4,087	0.932	25!-29	4,393	5,867	0.749	-19.64
20-24	14,059	17,170	0.819	30-34	12,349	16,842	0.733	-10.45
25-29	13,945	18,515	0.753	35-39	12,868	17,752	0.725	-3.76
Born in India								
5-15	8,556	7,582	1.128	15-24!	10,580	13,469	0.786	-30.39
16-19	8,588	9,082	0.946	25!-29	14,661	19,581	0.749	-20.82
20-24	15,876	18,981	0.836	30-34	20,905	24,054	0.869	3.91
25-29	22,861	22,719	1.006	35-39	24,820	24,817	1.000	-0.61
Born in Bangladesh								
5-15	5,783	3,400	1.701	15-24!	12,958	12,825	1.010	-40.60
16-19	2,351	1,133	2.075	25!-29	4,142	4,569	0.907	-56.31
20-24	3,660	2,217	1.651	30-34	5,356	4,398	1.218	-26.23
25-29	2,951	2,183	1.352	35-39	3,945	4,969	0.794	-41.27
Born in Pakistan								
5-15	15,040	10,469	1.437	15-24!	18,011	19,283	0.934	-34.98
16-19	6,938	5,514	1.258	25!-29	11,266	13,885	0.811	-35.52
20-24	13,866	14,185	0.978	30-34	16,656	17,688	0.942	-3.67
25-29	16,607	13,215	1.257	35-39	17,676	15,088	1.172	-6.78

Sources: 1991 Census Ethnic Group and Country of Birth Topic Report (vol. 1). 1981 Census Country of Birth Topic Report. Crown Copyright.

Note: Age groups marked ! are not exact matches to the cohort shown in 1981, but are the closest available from 1991 Census publications.

the 1981 enumeration, is stronger in these same age groups for the five other birth origins shown, particularly for those aged 15–24 and 25–29 in 1991, and those born in the Caribbean Commonwealth countries and in each of the three South Asia countries.

There is however a severe caution to apply before taking these changes as evidence of decreased coverage in 1991 compared to 1981. Over the decade, migration between Britain and the countries shown in Table 3.4 has affected the sex ratios shown. Official statistics show that half the net inflow of migration to the United Kingdom by New Commonwealth citizens is of those aged 15–24, and within this age-group females generally exceed males by several hundred each year (OPCS, 1992 (and previous years), Table 3.5). The increase in each of these populations between 1981 and 1991 (shown in Table 3.4) testifies to the continued importance of net immigration. Thus the lower sex ratios in 1991 are partly, and perhaps wholly, due to migration in the intervening period.

These sex ratios show some consistency with the notion of differential non-response, but cannot be used to quantify that differential because of the lack of detailed international migration data.

3.4   Conclusions

This chapter began with an analysis which assumed that within any local area (or electoral ward) each ethnic group was enumerated with the same success by the 1991 Census. However, the Black and Asian ethnic groups are relatively poorly enumerated in the country as whole, purely due to their demographic concentration within low-coverage areas of Britain. This effect is greatest for the Black–African and Black–Other groups for whom, on this basis, 5 per cent of their population overall are estimated to have been missed, compared to 4 per cent for most other ethnic minority groups and 2 per cent for the White group.

This analysis provides adjustment factors that should be applied to census data wherever it may be misleading not to do so. The 2% individual Sample of Anonymised Records includes a weighting variable to reflect the census coverage estimates at its relatively coarse geographical level, which does make adjustments to census analyses routinely feasible with this dataset.

However, other evidence presented in this chapter suggests that the assumption of local homogeneity of coverage is unlikely to have been true in reality. It provides an estimate of 17 per cent of children under the age of 10 born to New Commonwealth-born mothers missed from the census. Since it is still the case that four in five South Asian parents and one third of the parents in Black groups were born in the New Commonwealth, the proportion of ethnic minority children missed may also be higher than 10 per cent. Caution should be used with this figure, as there is some uncertainty in the estimating procedure. It does however suggest that census figures provide a serious underestimate of the numbers of ethnic minority group children. This topic is discussed further in Chapter 4 by David Owen.

It is possible that children were missed from census forms through a misunderstanding that the census applied only to adults. But it seems likely that adults within their household were missed too. The study of sex ratios supports the notion that adults aged 15–34 of ethnic minority groups were also disproportionately missed by the census, but does not allow estimation of the size of this effect. These results are supported by the other evidence in Chapter 2 from imputation and a study of electoral registration, that Black and Asian groups were more susceptible to omission from official enquiries in 1991 than the White group.

If quantification of residents missed by the census remains hazy, under-standing of why people are missed from the census is still more unfathomed. Ethnographic study of how people fill in the census forms, and individual census validation data including local place of residence, could give a better understanding of non-response to a census. Language difficulties in making sense of the census schedule, and attitudes to official enquiries could be usefully explored for their effects on response rates. Although too late for the 1991 Census, these may be useful avenues for validation of the 2001 Census.

References

Heady, P., Smith, S. and Avery, V. (1994) *1991 Census Validation Survey: coverage report,* OPCS Social Survey report SS1334. London: HMSO.

Holdsworth, C. (1995) Minimal Household Units. *SARs newsletter,* 5 (May 1995), University of Manchester Census Microdata Unit.

OPCS (1991) *Birth Statistics.* OPCS series FM1. London: HMSO.

OPCS (1992) *International migration 1990.* Series MN no.17. London: HMSO.

OPCS (1993) Rebasing the annual population estimates. *Population Trends,* 73, 27–31.

Simpson, S. (1993) Measuring and coping with local under-enumeration in the 1991 Census. Paper to the conference on 'Research in the 1991 Census', Newcastle. Available from the author at Bradford Metropoli-tan Council, City Hall, Bradford BD1 1HY.

Simpson, S. and Dorling, D. (1994) Those missing millions: implications for social statistics of non-response to the 1991 Census. *Journal of Social Policy*, 23(4), 543–67.

Simpson, S., Tye, R. and Diamond, I. (1995) *What was the true population of local areas in mid-1991?* Working Paper 10, Estimating with Confidence Project. Southampton: Department of Social Statistics of the University of Southampton.

Tye, R. (1995) The missing millions! *Manchester Computing Centre MIDAS newsletter*, March, 2–4.

Werner, B. (1984) Infants aged under 1 in the census, 1861–1981. *Population Trends*, 38, 18–24.

Acknowledgements

Thanks to Tracey Schofield and Andy Peloe, who helped with some of the figurework in this chapter; to Marian Storkey of London Research Centre for suggesting the analysis shown in Table 3.4, and to her, Martin Bulmer, Ian Diamond, Rachel Leeser, David Owen and Andy Teague for very useful comments on interpretation of the figurework.

Appendix 3.1   Country of birth of mother: comparing the census and civil registration of births

Deriving the census count of children by country of birth of mother

To each person on the 1% household Sample of Anonymised Records (SAR) is attached their family membership (variable FAMMEMB), to identify mothers. The number of children of each single age in a family is derived by aggregation within families (variable FAMID). For the small number of census children in male lone parent families, the father's country of birth has been taken in place of mother's country of birth, which is unknown.

301 (0.5 per cent) children are not in a family in the SAR and so have unknown country of birth of mother. This is usually because they are fostered or in some other way unrelated to others in the household, or because they are living with aunts, siblings or other non-parents.

The household SAR excluded 0.3 per cent of children who did not live in census households but in communal establishments, rising to 1.0 per cent of children in Black ethnic groups; 1.3 per cent of children who in other census output are imputed as residents in absent households not returning a census form. In all, this accounts for a census deficit of up to 2–3 per cent in the comparisons of Table 3.3.

Deriving the count of births in years before the census, by country of birth of mother

These are published for calendar years (eg. OPCS, 1991), which have been combined to reflect the 21 April date. This is an approximation but should not bias the comparisons of Table 3.3.

Migration between births and census

Some children in the census will have been born abroad, and some registered births will have left the country before the census. This mostly affects the comparisons with children enumerated in the census when aged under 5 and under 10. If anything, this would increase the numbers of children expected in the census from New Commonwealth origins, whose numbers have grown through net immigration during the 1980s (OPCS, 1992 and earlier), and thus increase the deficits estimated in Table 3.3.

Sampling error

Where the percentage of children enumerated for a country origin is significantly further from the national percentage than one would expect from the household SAR sampling error at the 95 per cent level, that ratio is underlined. The Census Microdata Unit has provided Design Factors, showing the extra imprecision of the household SAR over a simple random sample for country of birth categories. They are shown in the final column of Table 3.3. These tend to be higher than one because country of birth is highly clustered within households. The design factors have been used in calculating the confidence intervals for the estimated ratio of census to registered births for children under the age of 5 and under 10. They have not been used for children under 1 year old, as the likelihood of having two 0-year-olds sampled from the same household is slight.

Among the many ratios displayed in Table 3.3, one would expect about 1 in 20 to be as 'significant' purely by chance. The interpretation of the results takes into account the size of the ratios as well as their statistical significance.

Chapter 4
Size, structure and growth of the ethnic minority populations

David Owen

4.1 Introduction

This chapter is concerned with the size, structure, growth and geographical distribution of ethnic minority populations resident in Great Britain in 1991, and compares individual minority groups with the White population. It provides the context for the more detailed analysis of ethnic minority groups presented elsewhere in this and the other three companion volumes. The prime source of data upon which it is based is the 1991 Census, but it also draws upon information from previous censuses and other large socio-economic data sets.

The preceding chapters in this volume have already emphasised that the 1991 Census provided the first comprehensive information on the ethnic composition of Great Britain, and discussed how a question on ethnic group came to be incorporated into the British census. Until the results were published, those interested in the situation of ethnic minority groups in Great Britain were limited to using estimates, based on the results of large-scale surveys (such as the National Dwelling and Household Survey in the 1970s and the Labour Force and General Household Surveys in the 1980s, discussed in Chapter 2) or derived from census information on the country of birth of individuals or their parents. These sources still provide the only information on trends over time in the populations of ethnic minority groups, which are reviewed in the first part of this chapter.

The chapter then moves on to analyse the demographic structure and geographical distribution of each ethnic group in 1991, discussing the age structure of individual ethnic groups in some detail. This section also illustrates the probable influence of under-enumeration in the census upon the age and sex structure of individual ethnic groups, while providing a broad overview of the contrasting structures of the various ethnic groups resident in Great Britain in 1991.

4.2 Trends over time in the ethnic minority population

Though members of ethnic minority groups were present in Britain through-out the period of empire, their numbers have increased dramatically since the Second World War. This growth was initiated by the mass immigration from the countries of the 'New Commonwealth' which followed the passing of the 1948 British Nationality Act, and was substantially curtailed by the

Commonwealth Immigrants Acts of 1962 and 1968, and the Immigration Act of 1971. However, the migration of dependants and new spouses, and some workers continued, as described in Chapter 5 (see also page 5), while immigration from non-Commonwealth countries (e.g. the rest of the European Union, South-East Asia and Africa) has increased in recent years (OPCS, 1994a). The peak of immigration from the Caribbean occurred in the early 1960s, while immigration from India and Pakistan was at its peak in the late 1960s and early 1970s. Total immigration from the New Commonwealth declined through the 1970s and 1980s until 1983, afterwards increasing due to growing numbers of migrants from Bangladesh, Hong Kong and Africa.

From the mid-1980s onwards there was a dramatic increase in the number of asylum seekers, many of whom also came from New Commonwealth countries. For example, there were 32,800 applications for asylum in 1994, not including dependants. Of the 20,990 cases on which a decision was made in that year (many applicants would have arrived in the previous year or earlier) only 825 people (3.9 per cent) were accepted as refugees under the Geneva Convention. A further 2,660 (17.4 per cent) were granted exceptional leave to remain, and the remaining 16,500 (78.6 per cent) were refused asylum. However, few of those refused leave to remain are definitely known to have left the UK. Immigration patterns are discussed further in Chapter 5.

The number of people living in Great Britain who had been born in the New Commonwealth and Pakistan stood at 256,000 in 1951, and increased to 523,000 in 1961, but the share of White people among those born in the New Commonwealth was still substantial at that time. Thus, the ethnic minority group population of England and Wales was estimated to be 103,000 in 1951 – less than half the total born in the New Commonwealth – rising to 415,000 in 1961 (Eversley and Sukdeo, 1969).

On the other hand, it has been argued (by Peach, 1968; Peach and Winchester, 1974 and Rose et al., 1969) that the 1961 and 1966 (sample) Censuses substantially underestimated the New Commonwealth-born population, and hence that the growth in the ethnic minority population during the 1950s may have been even faster. It is possible that later censuses have also underestimated the size of the ethnic minority population (but to a lesser degree). For example, the parents' country of birth question in 1971 (which was used in estimating the number of people from ethnic minority groups) suffered from a relatively high degree of non-response, while the degree of under-enumeration is thought to have been greater for ethnic minority groups than for the White ethnic group in 1991 (see Chapters 2 and 3).

The lack of data on persons defined by ethnic group greatly hampers the assessment of trends over time in the ethnic minority population of Great Britain. As there is no consistently defined time-series of such information, the analysis of population change must proceed by bringing together information from a range of different data sources, including the Census of Population, the Labour Force Survey and OPCS estimates of the numbers of persons of 'New Commonwealth and Pakistan (NCWP) ethnic origin' (OPCS

Immigrant Statistics Unit, 1976 and 1977). The OPCS estimates of the New Commonwealth and Pakistan population were based on 1971 Census data on the country of birth of individuals and that of their parents. The population in 1971 was estimated by including all those born in the New Commonwealth and Pakistan or with parents born in these countries, and used an analysis of surnames (of Asian countries of birth) to determine whether or not persons with one parent born in the New Commonwealth and Pakistan were of 'NCWP' ethnic origin. The 1971 estimate was then updated by adjusting annual data on births, deaths and international migration by country of birth through an analysis of surnames, to yield estimates of these three quantities for the NCWP population.

Figure 4.1 illustrates the trend in the total ethnic minority population from 1966–7 to 1989–91. The figures for 1967–8 to 1980–81 are annual OPCS estimates of the NCWP population, derived from country of birth information, while those from 1981–3 onwards are the total of all ethnic minority groups, averaged across three successive Labour Force Surveys. It reveals almost continuous growth in both total numbers and the percentage of the total population from ethnic minority groups. Over the 14 years from 1966 to 1980, the number of people from ethnic minority groups more than doubled, from 886,000 to 2.1 million. The LFS reveals a further growth of over half a million during the 1980s, with ethnic minority groups forming nearly 5 per cent of the population by 1989–91. However, there are considerable annual fluctuations in the annual estimates from the LFS, even after averaging. Indeed, the LFS estimate of the ethnic minority group population fell in 1984; this was attributed to the increased level of non-response in that year's survey (OPCS Population Statistics Division, 1986).

This source also appears to underestimate the ethnic minority group population in comparison with the 1991 Census, which (before adjustment for under-enumeration) found that 3.015 million people, or 5.5 per cent of the population, were from ethnic minority groups. Owen (1993) notes that response rates to the LFS are lowest in Inner London and the other metropolitan areas that contain the largest ethnic minority populations. He argues that evidence from the experience of a range of census tests and surveys such as the British Social Attitudes Survey has demonstrated that ethnic minority groups are less likely then White people to be contacted, or to respond, while the General Household Survey has shown that ethnic minority groups are less likely than White ethnic groups to answer a question on ethnic group. He suggested that if the LFS estimate of ethnic minority populations in 1991 was adjusted on the basis that people from ethnic minorities were twice as likely as White people not to respond, then this would raise their share of the British population to '5.9 per cent rather than 4.9 per cent, an increase of 21 per cent' (Owen, 1993, 21). The Quarterly Labour Force Survey, which began in April 1992 using an improved methodology, yielded an estimate of the ethnic minority share of the population of 5.8 per cent for 1992-3 (Sly, 1993).

The 1991 Census figure is broadly consistent with OPCS projections of the growth of the NCWP population from 1976 to 1991, made in 1979 (OPCS Immigrant Statistics Unit, 1979). Their projection was that the number of people of 'wholly' NCWP origin would lie between 2.47 and 2.94 million

Figure 4.1 *Trend in total ethnic minority population, 1966-7 to 1989-91*

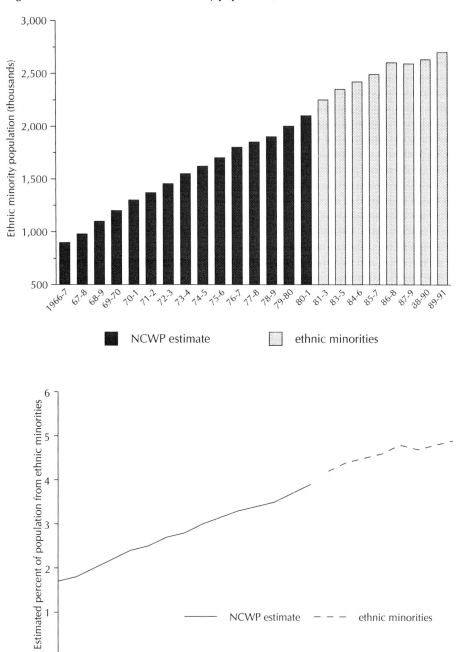

people in 1991, and that the number of 'NCWP ethnic origin' (those born in the New Commonwealth and Pakistan, their children and children of mixed parentage) would be between 2.75 and 3.25 million people in 1991.

The lack of an ethnic question in the census before 1991 and inconsistencies in the definitions used for ethnic groups between data sources makes the estimation of change in the ethnic composition of Great Britain over time problematic. As described earlier, estimates of the size of the ethnic minority population in 1971 were based on the number of people with parents born in the New Commonwealth and Pakistan. In 1981, estimates of the ethnic group composition of the population (made by OPCS or local government) took as their starting point the number of people living in a household headed by a person born in the New Commonwealth or Pakistan (OPCS Population Statistics Division, 1986; Howes, 1986). Persons were therefore classified into broadly 'national' ethnic groups, such as Indians, West Indians and Pakistanis. These same categories were used in the ethnic group questions adopted by the Labour Force and General Household Surveys and by the 1991 Census.

Figure 4.2 depicts the changing estimated size of the largest ethnic minority groups during the 1970s, based on the estimates made by OPCS. In 1971, the bulk of the ethnic minority group population was accounted for by those of West Indian ethnic origin. The estimate series shows their numbers reaching a peak in 1976 and thereafter declining in the years up to 1981, at which time their population was 3 per cent smaller than in 1971. Peach (1991) notes that the decline in the Caribbean born population had started by 1966. The growth of the ethnic minority population of Britain during the 1970s was therefore due to the faster growth of those of Indian (including East African Asian), Pakistani and Bangladeshi and Other (including those of Mediterranean, Chinese and mixed ethnic origins) ethnic origins. By 1981, Indians had

Figure 4.2 *Ethnic minority group population change, 1971 to 81*

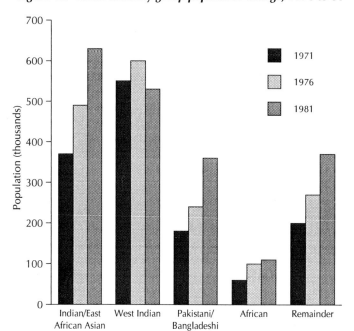

overtaken West Indians as the largest ethnic minority group, having increased by two thirds during the decade 1971–81. The number of Pakistanis and Bangladeshis more than doubled over the decade, but their growth was nearly matched by those from the remainder of the New Commonwealth.

The Labour Force Survey has provided annual estimates of the population disaggregated by ethnic group since 1981. Substantial variations exist between the 10 ethnic groups identified by the LFS in rates of population change during the 1980s (Table 4.1). The White population grew by only 1 per cent over the decade (compared to 2 per cent for the population as a whole), while the ethnic minority population increased by 28 per cent. The broad trends of population change by ethnic group established in the 1970s continued into the 1980s. The number of people in the West Indian and Guyanese ethnic group continued to decline (by 14 per cent), and by the end of the decade, the Pakistani ethnic group had overtaken it in size to become the second largest ethnic group.

The Indian ethnic group was the largest of the ethnic minority groups, numbering nearly 800,000 by 1989–91. However, the rate of growth of the Indian population, as estimated by the LFS, was only 8 per cent between 1981 and 1991, a considerable apparent slowing in the growth rate relative to the 1970s. The growth of the Indian ethnic group in the 1970s may have been even faster, as there is a discrepancy of 100,000 in the estimated size of the Indian ethnic group between the OPCS estimates and those of the Labour Force Survey in 1981. This appears to have been largely due to underestimation of the number of people of Indian ethnic origin born outside the UK, many of whom were allocated to the Other category in the OPCS estimates series (OPCS Population Statistics Division, 1986). However, as already mentioned, the LFS estimates of the ethnic composition of the population are subject to uncertainty, due to both sampling variability relative to small populations and the possibility of under-enumeration.

Table 4.1 *Estimated population of Great Britain by ethnic group, 1981 and 1989-91*

Ethnic group	Estimated Population			
	1981 (000s)	1989-91 (000s)	Change (000s)	Change (%)
White	51,000	51,808	808	1
All ethnic minority groups	2,092	2,677	585	28
West Indian	528	455	-73	-14
African	80	150	70	88
Indian	727	792	65	9
Pakistani	284	485	201	71
Bangladeshi	52	127	75	144
Chinese	92	137	45	49
Arab	53	67	14	26
Mixed	217	309	92	42
Other	60	154	94	157
Not stated	608	495	-113	-19
All ethnic groups	53,700	54,979	1,279	2

Source: Population Trends, 67, and OPCS (1992), Table 6.29.

The ethnic groups which displayed the fastest population growth during the 1980s were the Others and Bangladeshis, whose numbers more than doubled. Smaller ethnic minority groups, such as African and Chinese people, also experienced high rates of population growth. The numerical increase of the Pakistani ethnic group over this period (201,000) was the greatest of all the ethnic minorities. International migration was still a strong influence on the growth of the number of people of South Asian ethnic origin in Great Britain, despite the growing numbers of British-born, most immigration being accounted for by the entry of dependants. Over the period 1981–90, net immigration to the UK from India, Bangladeshi and Sri Lanka totalled 105,500 people, with net immigration of a further 77,900 people from Pakistan (compared with net immigration to the UK of only 3,100 from the Caribbean). Net immigration from Africa totalled 54,300 people over the same period, strongly influencing the 88 per cent growth of the African ethnic group between 1981 and 1991. The Mixed and Other ethnic groups also displayed rapid growth between 1981 and 1989–91, indicative of the growing numbers of people with more complex ethnic identification and of children with parents from different ethnic groups. However, the number of 'not stated' answers declined during the 1980s, as the quality of response to the ethnic group question improved.

Though the 1991 Census provides the best indication so far of the ethnic composition of the British population, temporal comparison is complicated by the adoption of a different classification of ethnic group to that used by the Labour Force Survey (the Labour Force Survey adopted the census ethnic group classification from April 1992), and the lack of an ethnic group question in 1981.

Another perspective on the changing ethnic composition of Great Britain can therefore be gained by comparing 1981 and 1991 Census data, using the 1981 census definition of ethnic minority groups: persons resident in a household headed by a person born in the New Commonwealth. The pattern of change revealed was similar to that shown by the Labour Force Survey, but there are significant differences (Table 4.2). The overall rate of increase was slightly slower than that of the ethnic minority population, but the pattern of decline in persons in Caribbean-headed households, slow growth of the population of Indian-headed households and rapid growth in the number living in Bangladeshi-headed households mirrored the pattern of change in the corresponding ethnic groups. However, rates of change tended to be underestimated relative to the LFS, notably for persons in Pakistani-headed households, while the census figures yielded a much larger estimate of the number of Bangladeshis than does the LFS.

The growth in the number of households headed by an ethnic minority person born in the UK results in the estimates of ethnic group populations becoming increasingly inaccurate over time. The effect was greatest for the Black–Caribbean and Indian ethnic groups, because the ethnic group question indicates that these two ethnic groups are much larger than country-of-birth data suggests, and hence their rate of growth in the 1980s was understated. On the other hand, the estimated rates of growth in the number of Bangladeshis and Pakistanis are more likely to be accurate, since the migration of these ethnic groups was more recent.

Table 4.2 *Change in the number of persons resident in households headed by persons born in New Commonwealth countries, 1981-91*

Country of birth of household head	1981 (000s)	1991 (000s)	Change 1981-91 (000s)	Percentage change
East Africa	181	312	131	72.2
Other Africa	n/a	150	-	-
Caribbean	546	434	-112	-20.5
Bangladesh	65	161	97	149.7
India	674	693	19	2.8
Pakistan	295	442	164	49.6
South East Asia	120	175	55	46.1
Cyprus	170	118	-52	-30.4
Other New Commonwealth	156	150	-6	-3.9
New Commonwealth	2,207	2,635	428	19.4

Source: 1981 Census Country of Birth report for Great Britain and 1991 Census Local Base Statistics.

4.3 The ethnic composition of Great Britain in 1991

Table 4.3 presents the ethnic composition of Great Britain in 1991, drawn from the responses to the ethnic group question in the 1991 Census. It also shows how the 10 published ethnic groups were built up from the answers to the question. People who ticked one of the Other boxes and wrote in a description of their ethnic origin were reallocated to one of the major ethnic groups or one of the three Other ethnic groups, using the 35-fold classification of written answers derived from the results of the 1989 Census Test. The flowchart which was devised to guide the processing of responses to the ethnic group question is given in Chapter 2 (see Figure 2.2, pp50-51).

The ethnic group question from the 1991 Census was broadly successful. It yielded a higher figure for the ethnic minority population than either the Labour Force Survey or country of birth-based estimates discussed in the previous section, at just over 3 million, or 5.5 per cent of the population of Great Britain. The magnitude of individual ethnic groups was broadly consistent with estimates made from other sources. The census revealed that South Asians represented half of the ethnic minority population of Britain. Indians were the largest single ethnic minority group, with 840,000 people (2.7 per cent of the population), while Black ethnic groups formed a further 1.5 per cent of the population. In contrast with the LFS, Black–Caribbeans (with just under half a million people) were the second largest ethnic minority group, just outnumbering the Pakistani ethnic group. Though the Pakistani ethnic group is smaller in the census data, both the Bangladeshi and Chinese ethnic groups were estimated to be larger by the Census than by the LFS. The Black–African population was two fifths the size of the Black–Caribbean ethnic group, while the Black–Other ethnic group accounted for a fifth of all people from Black ethnic groups. The Chinese ethnic group was the smallest of the seven 'pre-coded' ethnic groups, and may be submerged in much census data (such as the Small Area Statistics and Special Migration Statistics) which use a four-fold ethnic group classification, since both the Other – Other and Other–Asian ethnic groups contained more people.

Table 4.3 *Ethnic composition of Great Britain in 1991, and the relationship of answers to the ethnic group question with published totals for ethnic group data*

Ethnic group	Population of GB		Main ethnic group ticked	Number	Black - Other (write in*)	Number	Any other ethnic group (write in*)	Numbe
	Number	%						
White	51,873,794	94.5	White	51,810,555			Irish	45
							Greek (inc. Cypriot)	17,98
							Turkish (inc. Cypriot)	18,87
							Other European	22,14
							Mixed White	3,77
Ethnic minority groups	3,015,051	5.5						
Black ethnic groups	890,727	1.6						
Black-Caribbean	499,964	0.9	Black-	493,339	Caribbean	3,093	Caribbean Island	3,53
Black-African	212,362	0.4	Black-African	208,110	Other African countries	927	Other African countries	3,32
Black-Other	178,401	0.3			British	58,106		
					Other answers	44,940		
					Mixed Black/ White	24,687		
					Other Mixed	50,668		
South Asian	1,479,645	2.7						
Indian	840,255	1.5	Indian	840,255				
Pakistani	476,555	0.9	Pakistani	476,555				
Bangladeshi	162,835	0.3	Bangladeshi	162,835				
Chinese and Other	644,678	1.2						
Chinese	156,938	0.3	Chinese	156,938				
Other-Asian	197,534	0.4			East African/ Indo-Caribbean	1271	East African/Indo-Caribbean	6,11
					Indian sub-continent(nes)	4005	Indian sub-continent(nes)	41,33
					Other Asian	24854	Other Asian	119,96
Other-Other	290,206	0.5			North African/ Arab/Iranian	6471	British ethnic minority	16,17
					Mixed Asian/ White	69	British no ethnic minority indicated	13,97
							North African/ Arab/Iranian	58,72
							Other answers	41,72
							Mixed Black/White	29,88
							Mixed Asian/White	61,80
							Other mixed	61,39
Entire population	54,888,844	100.0						

*Answers written on census form.

Source: 1991 Census Country of Birth and Ethnic Group report (Table A).

Growth in the number of people in Other and mixed ethnic categories has been a consistent feature of the last two decades. The 1991 Census does not include a category for people of mixed ethnic origins, who are instead included in one of the three Other categories (though 3,800 people of mixed White ethnic origin are included in the White ethnic group). This is problematical, because it confounds the characteristics of people of mixed parentage with those of people from less numerous ethnic groups and those of people who had a perception of their ethnic identity which did not match the seven major categories used in the ethnic group question. The 35-fold coding scheme was intended to allocate persons who wrote in a description of their ethnic identity as accurately as possible (in the perception of the Census Offices) into the Black, Asian and Other ethnic groups, and prevent persons of Asian or part Asian ethnic origin from being identified as Black (even if their response to the question indicated that they might like to be identified as such). Thus, the coding scheme yielded a more precise measure of the broad ethnic categories, but at the considerable cost of yielding only vague information on the characteristics of people with parents from different ethnic groups. It is notable that the mixed ethnic groups together contain rather fewer people than the corresponding category in the LFS estimates.

The way in which the Other categories were constructed is detailed in Table 4.3. The largest component of the Black–Other category in 1991 was people who identified themselves as British (32.5 per cent). Half of the category were persons of mixed parentage, but the number providing other answers was also substantial, and would include groups such as Black US servicemen. This accounts for the large presence of Black–Other people in Suffolk and Argyll, which are otherwise remote from concentrations of people from ethnic minorities (see below and Owen, 1995).

The Other–Asian category largely comprised Asian people (144,800, or 73.3 per cent of the entire category) who could not adequately describe their ethnic origin in the standard categories (e.g. Vietnamese or Filipino people), followed by 45,300 people (23 per cent) with ethnic origins in the Indian subcontinent other than the three main groups (an example would be Sri Lankans). A small part of this ethnic category was accounted for by Indo-Caribbean or East African Asian people. This is probably an underestimate, because the form of the question invites Indo-Caribbean people to identify themselves as either Black–Caribbean or Indian, and most East African Asians appear to have identified themselves as Indian.

The Other – Other category contained 290,000 people (0.5 per cent of the population), outnumbering the Black–African, Bangladeshi and Chinese ethnic groups. It was the most heterogeneous of the three Other categories, and submerged a number of ethnic groups, some of whom could be identified from LFS data. For example, North Africans, Arabs and Iranians cannot be separately distinguished even in the 35-fold census classification, but formed 22.5 per cent of the Other–Other category, and will be more significant in localities containing higher education establishments (as many members of these ethnic groups will be overseas students and refugees working in higher education). This category also obscures relatively large groups of people of mixed Black and White, Asian and White, and other mixed parentage (together 153,000 or 52.8 per cent of the category), which also vary in their relative magnitude between localities.

In amalgamating a diverse range of ethnic groups together with persons of mixed parentage and those who have given answers which may be inaccurate or deliberately misleading, census data has severe limitations for the detailed study of the ethnic mix of cities such as Cardiff and Liverpool, in which ethnic minority communities are long-established and where the mixed ethnic groups will thus be relatively substantial. Moreover, an estimate of all people of mixed ethnic origin broadly consistent with the LFS definition (up to 1992) should combine these components with the mixed components of the Black–Other ethnic group, but it is not possible to disaggregate these ethnic groupings in the Local Base Statistics produced by the census.

A further problem with the ethnic group classification is that other ethnic groups that are locally significant, such as Greeks, Cypriots and Turks, are allocated to the White ethnic group. Table A in the 1991 Census *Ethnic Group and Country of Birth* report partly makes up for this in presenting an analysis of the number of people who wrote in a number of common ethnic origins in the 'any other ethnic group' box. Unfortunately, the census data is structured so as to make it impossible to distinguish Cypriots from Greeks and Turks. As the number of people born in Greece, Turkey and Cyprus outnumber those identifying their ethnic origin in these countries, it is possible that most ticked the White box, rather than writing in the ethnic group with which they identified. Indeed, Storkey and Lewis (1995) estimate that the Cypriot population of greater London is about twice that revealed by the country-of-birth data.

Another ethnic group of growing political significance that is not adequately identified by the census is the Irish. An attempt by Irish community groups to have the Irish recognised by the Census Offices as an ethnic group in the 1991 Census was unsuccessful, and they responded by organising a campaign to persuade Irish people to write in 'Irish' on the census form. About 11,000 people wrote Irish in the 'any other ethnic group' box, and a further 20,000 both ticked the White box and wrote Irish in the 'any other ethnic group' box. (Table A of the 1991 Census *Ethnic Group and Country of Birth* report reported only 457 Irish people, because much of this information was initially lost due to a processing error by the Census Offices. Estimates were later made to compensate for the initial error (OPCS/GRO(S) (1994b)) However, there were 837,400 people living in Great Britain who had been born in either Northern Ireland or the Irish Republic at the time of the Census. Thus, the vast majority of Irish people did not identify themselves as such on the census form. The Census Offices decided to include a column for people born in Ireland in the tables disaggregated by ethnic group, but this provides no information on people who regard themselves as being ethnically Irish, but who were born in Great Britain.

4.4 The geography of ethnic minorities in Great Britain

Regional-level variations in ethnic mix within Britain

The ethnic composition of the population varies greatly within Great Britain. The bulk of people from ethnic minority groups live in the most populous areas of England, and these ethnic groups are also more geographically concentrated than people from the White ethnic group within these regions. This is illustrated in Table 4.4, in which the 1991 population of each ethnic group is expressed as a percentage of the Great Britain total for each region and metropolitan county. The regional population share for each ethnic group is compared with that region's share of the total national population.

More than half of all people from ethnic minority groups lived in the South East standard region, compared to less than a third of people from the White ethnic group. Greater London alone contained 44.8 per cent of all people from ethnic minority groups in Britain, though it only contained 10.3 per cent of the White population. The other main concentration of people from ethnic minority groups occurred in the West Midlands; in particular the former metropolitan county centred upon Birmingham. This region accounted for more than 14 per cent of all people from ethnic minority groups, but only 9 per cent of the White population. Further north, West Yorkshire and Greater Manchester had the next highest relative concentrations of

Table 4.4 *Regional ethnic group distribution of total population of Great Britain, 1991*

Region or metropolitan county	Percentage of resident population											
	Entire popul-ation	White	Min-ority ethnic groups	Black			Ind-ian	Paki-stani	Bang-lade-shi	Chin-ese	Other Asian	Other Other
				Carib-bean	Afri-can	Other						
South East	31.4	29.9	**56.2**	**66.3**	**83.5**	**56.6**	**52.9**	29.9	**63.6**	**53.3**	**72.4**	**57.9**
Greater London	*12.2*	*10.3*	*44.6*	*58.2*	*77.1*	*45.2*	*41.3*	*18.4*	*52.7*	*36.1*	*57.1*	*41.7*
East Anglia	3.7	**3.8**	1.4	1.0	1.1	**4.0**	0.8	1.2	1.0	2.4	1.9	2.6
South West	8.4	**8.8**	2.1	2.5	1.3	3.7	1.3	0.8	1.4	4.3	2.3	4.3
West Midlands	9.4	9.1	**14.1**	**15.6**	2.5	**10.5**	**18.9**	**20.7**	**11.9**	6.1	5.8	8.4
West Midlands MC	*4.6*	*4.2*	*12.4*	*14.4*	*1.9*	*8.8*	*16.8*	*18.5*	*11.1*	*3.9*	*4.5*	*6.5*
East Midlands	7.2	**7.3**	6.2	4.9	1.6	6.0	**11.8**	3.7	2.6	4.8	3.7	4.9
Yorks & Humberside	8.8	**8.9**	7.1	4.3	2.3	5.7	4.8	**19.9**	5.1	5.2	3.7	6.2
South Yorkshire	*2.3*	*2.4*	*1.2*	*1.2*	*0.6*	*1.4*	*0.4*	*2.8*	*0.7*	*1.4*	*0.7*	*1.6*
West Yorkshire	*3.7*	*3.6*	*5.4*	*3.0*	*1.2*	*3.7*	*4.1*	*16.9*	*3.7*	*2.5*	*2.3*	*3.6*
North West	11.4	**11.6**	8.1	4.3	4.4	9.0	6.6	**16.2**	9.1	11.1	4.5	8.2
Greater Manchester	*4.6*	*4.5*	*4.9*	*3.4*	*2.5*	*5.2*	*3.5*	*10.4*	*7.0*	*5.3*	*2.5*	*4.4*
Merseyside	*2.6*	*2.7*	*0.9*	*0.4*	*1.4*	*2.4*	*0.3*	*0.2*	*0.4*	*3.6*	*0.6*	*1.9*
North	5.5	**5.8**	1.3	0.2	0.7	1.1	0.9	2.0	2.2	3.2	1.6	1.8
Tyne & Wear	*2.0*	*2.1*	*0.7*	*0.1*	*0.4*	*0.5*	*0.5*	*0.8*	*1.7*	*1.8*	*0.8*	*0.9*
Wales	5.2	**5.4**	1.4	0.7	1.3	1.9	0.8	1.2	2.3	3.1	1.9	2.6
Scotland	9.1	**9.5**	2.1	0.2	1.3	1.5	1.2	4.4	0.7	6.7	2.3	3.0

Source: 1991 Census Local Base Statistics within Great Britain (ESRC purchase); Crown copyright.

people from ethnic minority groups. People from ethnic minority groups were much less likely than White people to live in Wales, Scotland and the more peripheral regions of England.

The three *Black* groups were clearly heavily concentrated in the South-East and West Midlands; nearly 80 per cent of Black–Africans and nearly 60 per cent of Black–Caribbeans lived in Greater London in 1991. However, Black–Others were more widely distributed in Britain, with a substantial representation in North West England and a more substantial presence in the less populous parts of Britain than the other two Black ethnic groups.

There were marked differences in settlement patterns between the *South Asian* ethnic groups: Indians, Pakistanis and Bangladeshis. More than half of all Bangladeshis and two fifths of Indians lived in Greater London in 1991, compared to only a fifth of Pakistanis. The major concentrations of the latter ethnic group were in the West Midlands, the North West and West Yorkshire, with a substantial presence in Scotland. Table 4.4 also picks out the relative concentrations of Bangladeshis in West Yorkshire, Greater Manchester and Tyne & Wear.

In the *Other* category, Other–Asians were more strongly concentrated in London and the South East than most other ethnic minority groups. This contrasts with the relatively even spatial distribution of the Chinese ethnic group, for which the main regional concentrations outside London were in North West England. Other– Others had a broadly similar distribution, but displayed a stronger presence in the West Midlands.

The geographical distribution of ethnic minority groups can also be considered in terms of variations in the share of the resident population accounted for by each ethnic minority group. This is presented for standard regions, countries and former metropolitan counties in Table 4.5. Greater London stands out as having a very different ethnic mix to the rest of Britain; more than a fifth of its population (and more than a quarter of the population of Inner London) was from ethnic minority groups in 1991. The Black ethnic groups formed the largest component of the ethnic minority groups, accounting for 8 per cent of the population. Only the West Midlands (former) metropolitan county came close in terms of the ethnic minority group share of its population (14.6 per cent). But while this conurbation contains the second largest concentration of people from Black ethnic groups, South Asians outnumbered them, forming 9.7 per cent of the population.

Of the other metropolitan counties, the percentage of the population from ethnic minority groups was greatest in West Yorkshire (8.2 per cent), where Pakistanis were the largest ethnic minority group, and Greater Manchester (5.9 per cent), where Pakistanis and Indians were the largest minority groups. The share of ethnic minority groups in the population of the East Midlands was also relatively high (largely because of large minority populations in the major cities of the region; in 1991, 28.5 per cent of the population of Leicester were from ethnic minority groups), where Indians were the largest minority group. The share of ethnic minority groups in the population of more remote regions of England, Wales and Scotland, was

Table 4.5 *Regional variations in ethnic composition, within Great Britain 1991*

Region or metropolitan county	Percentage of resident population									
	All ethnic minorities	Black			Indian	Paki-stani	Bangla-deshi	Chin-ese	Oth. Asian	Other Other
		Carib-bean	Afri-can	Other						
South East	9.9	1.9	1.0	0.6	2.6	0.8	0.6	0.5	0.8	1.0
Greater London	*20.2*	*4.4*	*2.4*	*1.2*	*5.2*	*1.3*	*1.3*	*0.8*	*1.7*	*1.8*
East Anglia	2.1	0.2	0.1	0.4	0.3	0.3	0.1	0.2	0.2	0.4
South West	1.4	0.3	0.1	0.1	0.2	0.1	0.1	0.1	0.1	0.3
West Midlands	8.2	1.5	0.1	0.4	3.1	1.9	0.4	0.2	0.2	0.5
West Midlands MC	*14.6*	*2.8*	*0.2*	*0.6*	*5.5*	*3.5*	*0.7*	*0.2*	*0.3*	*0.7*
East Midlands	4.8	0.6	0.1	0.3	2.5	0.4	0.1	0.2	0.2	0.4
Yorks & Humberside	4.4	0.4	0.1	0.2	0.8	2.0	0.2	0.2	0.2	0.4
South Yorkshire	*2.9*	*0.5*	*0.1*	*0.2*	*0.3*	*1.0*	*0.1*	*0.2*	*0.1*	*0.4*
West Yorkshire	*8.2*	*0.7*	*0.1*	*0.3*	*1.7*	*4.0*	*0.3*	*0.2*	*0.2*	*0.5*
North West	3.9	0.3	0.1	0.3	0.9	1.2	0.2	0.3	0.1	0.4
Greater Manchester	*5.9*	*0.7*	*0.2*	*0.4*	*1.2*	*2.0*	*0.5*	*0.3*	*0.2*	*0.5*
Merseyside	*1.8*	*0.2*	*0.2*	*0.3*	*0.2*	*0.1*	*0.1*	*0.4*	*0.1*	*0.4*
North	1.3	0.0	0.0	0.1	0.3	0.3	0.1	0.2	0.1	0.2
Tyne & Wear	*1.8*	*0.0*	*0.1*	*0.1*	*0.4*	*0.3*	*0.3*	*0.3*	*0.1*	*0.2*
Wales	1.5	0.1	0.1	0.1	0.2	0.2	0.1	0.2	0.1	0.3
Scotland	1.3	0.0	0.1	0.1	0.2	0.4	0.0	0.2	0.1	0.2
Great Britain	5.5	0.9	0.4	0.3	1.5	0.9	0.3	0.3	0.4	0.5

Source: 1991 Census Local Base Statistics (ESRC purchase); Crown copyright.

much lower, and people from Black ethnic groups were much less common. The largest ethnic minority group in Scotland was Pakistanis and in Wales the Other–Other ethnic group was largest, followed by Indians and Pakistanis.

Local concentrations of ethnic minority groups

The regional-level pattern conceals an even stronger tendency for ethnic minority groups to concentrate in particular localities. This is clearly illustrated in Figure 4.3, which maps the percentage of the population of each local authority district from ethnic minority groups in 1991 (note that Rees and Phillips (1995) present maps of the number of people from each ethnic minority group, and lists of the local authority districts in which the share of the population from each ethnic group was greatest). The pattern revealed was of greatest concentration in inner London boroughs, with two subsidiary areas of concentration. The first was a broadly triangular area stretching north from London to the southern Midlands, with concentrations of ethnic minority groups west of London, in the West Midlands metropolitan county, the cities of the East Midlands (notably Leicester), in the New and Expanded Towns of the southern East Midlands and northern South East (Northampton and Peterborough), Luton and the university towns of Oxford and Cambridge. The second major area of concentration covered the 'mill towns' of Lancashire, Greater Manchester and Yorkshire. Other scattered concentrations occurred in places such as Cardiff and

Gloucester. However, this is very much an average picture and conceals marked differences in the location of individual ethnic groups, which will now be described in greater detail.

Location patterns for Black ethnic groups

Though the Black ethnic groups are often treated as being homogeneous, there were considerable differences in the characteristics of the three component ethnic groups (some of which are illustrated in later sections of this chapter), and the geographical distribution of each displayed distinctive features. Nevertheless, members of these ethnic groups often regard themselves as having more in common with each other than with other ethnic groups, and indeed, members of the Black–Other ethnic group may be the children of people from the Black–Caribbean ethnic group. Hence local concentrations of the *Black* ethnic groups as a whole in 1991 are mapped in Figure 4.4 (a).

This map has some similarities with the distribution of ethnic minority groups as a whole, but there are also substantial differences. The degree of concentration of Black people in Inner London was greater than for all minority groups, but elsewhere Black ethnic groups were more sparsely distributed. The area of highest concentration described a broad axis north-westward from London through the south-east Midlands and into the West Midlands metropolitan county. In northern England, the percentage of the population from Black ethnic groups was highest in Manchester and Leeds. Elsewhere, the port cities of Cardiff and Bristol had substantial representations of Black people. However, the distribution of each of the component ethnic groups diverged considerably around this average pattern, and these distributions will now be considered in turn.

People of *Black–Caribbean* ethnic origin had a geographical distribution much more narrowly restricted to the largest urban areas (Figure 4.4 (b)) and were much more strongly concentrated in inner and south London and Birmingham than Black ethnic groups as a whole. The pattern for *Black–Africans* was radically different (Figure 4.4 (c)). Concentrations of this group occurred in inner and north-west London, the port cities of Cardiff and Liverpool, Manchester, and in Oxford and Cambridge. The spatial distribution of the Black–Other ethnic group was again markedly different from the group average (Figure 4.4 (d)), but in the direction of greater dispersal. Local concentrations of people from this ethnic group occurred in most areas of ethnic minority group settlement, with relatively high percentages of the population also occurring in Suffolk and in Argyll and Bute district in Strathclyde Region (these reflect the location of US military bases, due to the presence of Black Americans (Owen, 1995)).

Location patterns for South Asian ethnic groups

The geographical distribution of people of *South Asian* ethnic origin as a whole in 1991 is mapped in Figure 4.5 (a). This pattern is different both from those of ethnic minority groups as a whole and of Black ethnic groups. Once again, there was a concentration of population in Greater London, but this time in boroughs in the west and north-east. The high percentages of the population from South Asian ethnic groups in Slough and districts west of the capital was mirrored south of the Thames estuary, in Kent. Local concentrations of South Asian people stretched through Hertfordshire and Bedfordshire into the East and West Midlands. These ethnic groups were distributed more widely than the Black ethnic groups in these regions, while the concentration of South Asians in Birmingham was matched by that in Leicester (the local authority district with the largest percentage of its population from ethnic minority groups outside Greater London).

In northern England, concentrations of South Asian ethnic groups occurred in much of Greater Manchester, West Yorkshire and south Lancashire (notably in Blackburn), while an isolated local concentration in Middlesborough is also highlighted by the map. On a more detailed spatial scale, Peach and Rossiter (1995) showed that South Asian ethnic groups had a greater tendency to cluster together than other ethnic groups in 1991, and Owen (1994) demonstrated that some of the highest degrees of segregation experienced by these ethnic groups occurred in the Pennine towns.

However, this average pattern once again disguises marked differences in geographical distribution between the three component ethnic groups. The spatial distribution of people of *Indian* ethnic origin strongly resembles that for South Asian people as a whole (Figure 4.5 (b)). However, there are notable differences in the Midlands and northern England. Indians were less widely distributed than all South Asians in Lancashire, West Yorkshire and Greater Manchester, and were concentrated in Wolverhampton and Sandwell rather than Birmingham in the West Midlands. In the East Midlands, the Indian ethnic group made up more than a fifth of the population of Leicester, and was also strongly represented in the commuting hinterland of the city.

Pakistanis displayed a strongly contrasting spatial distribution (Figure 4.5 (c)). Their main concentrations within the South East standard region were in north east London, west London, Slough, Buckinghamshire and Luton. In the Midlands, their shares of the resident population were highest in Birmingham, Stafford and Peterborough. However, the most notable feature of the map is the ring of 'textile towns' stretching through south Lancashire into Greater Manchester and West Yorkshire, in which their representation was more than five times the British average. Local concentrations of Pakistanis also occurred in Middlesbrough, Newcastle, Lanarkshire, Newport and Cardiff.

The greatest local concentrations of *Bangladeshis* (Figure 4.5 (d)) were found in north central London (notably Tower Hamlets), Luton and Oldham. They were also strongly represented in the West Midlands metropolitan county, areas to the north and west of London, Newcastle, Scunthorpe, some Pennine mill towns and in the major cities of South Wales.

Location patterns for Chinese and Other ethnic groups

The *Chinese and Other* grouping is the most heterogeneous of the three, combining people of South East Asian ethnic origin with people of North African, Near and Middle Eastern ethnic origins and mixed parentage. The purpose of presenting an overall distribution pattern for the three ethnic groups combined is thus purely to provide a comparison with the other two broad groupings and a context for the use of data sets (such as the Special Migration Statistics) in which this ethnic group is not disaggregated. People from these three ethnic groups display less marked local clustering than either the Black or the South Asian groupings (Figure 4.6 (a)). The degree of geographical segregation of these ethnic groups was also much less than for the South Asian ethnic groups (Peach and Rossiter, 1995).

The share of Chinese and Other ethnic groups in the resident population in 1991 was greatest in north west London boroughs, where it was five times higher than the British average. Concentrations of these ethnic groups were also found in the Home Counties on the north, west and south sides of London. Elsewhere, in the cities of the south and east of England, including Brighton, Cambridge, Ipswich and Peterborough, a relatively high percentage of their population was from the Chinese and Other ethnic groups. In the Midlands, local concentrations occurred in Northampton, Birmingham and Leicester. Chinese and Other ethnic groups were also strongly represented in Liverpool, Manchester, Sheffield, Blackburn, Newcastle and Cardiff. Once again, this overall pattern disguises significant differences between ethnic groups.

The geographical distribution of *Chinese* people was similar to that of the Chinese and Other group as a whole, except that the concentration in London was much less marked, while stronger local concentrations occurred in Merseyside and Greater Manchester (Figure 4.6 (b)). Further local concentrations were found in Bristol, Cardiff, Edinburgh, Aberdeen and Lanarkshire.

In contrast, the spatial distribution of the *Other–Asian* ethnic groups (Figure 4.6 (c)) were much more strongly orientated towards southern England and the south Midlands. The main concentrations were in west London, districts to the west of London, Brighton, Ipswich, Forest Heath, Cambridge, Peterborough, Leicester and Birmingham. Elsewhere, their representation in the local population exceeded the national average in Manchester, Blackburn, Newcastle and Cardiff.

The geographical distribution of the *Other–Other* ethnic group largely followed the band of greatest urban development stretching from London to Leeds (Figure 4.6 (d)). These ethnic groups again displayed concentrations in the western part of London, and in districts on the western side of London. However, there were also larger than average percentages of the population from these ethnic groups in the West Midlands and the conurbations of northern England. These ethnic groups were also strongly represented in the port cities of Liverpool, Bristol, Cardiff and Newport. This is because ethnic minority groups were longer established here than elsewhere, and hence the degree of ethnic intermarriage was greater. Moreover, their status as ports had led a diverse range of nationalities and ethnic groups to settle within them, this diversity being reinforced by the presence of higher education establishments (which recruit overseas students).

Figure 4.3 *Percentage of district population from minority ethnic groups, 1991*

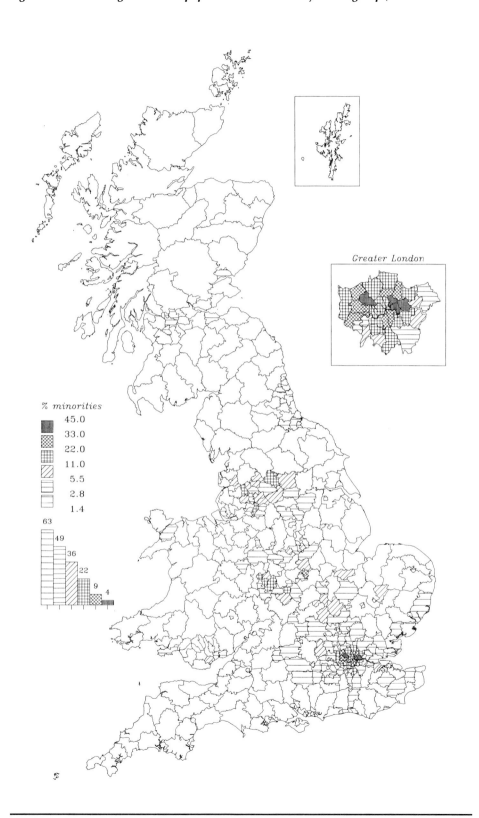

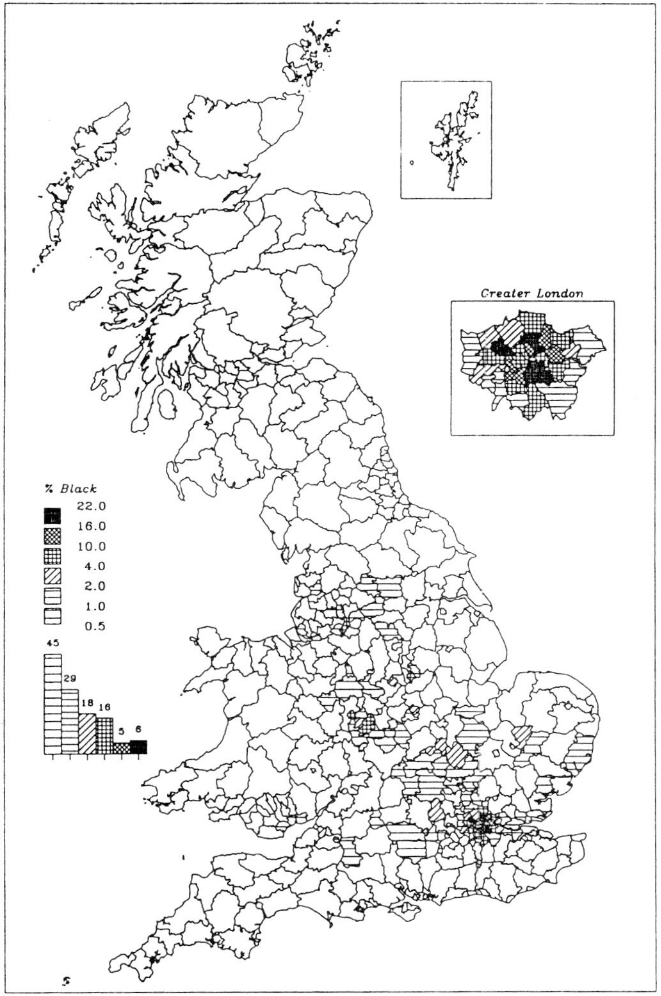

Figure 4.4b: *Black-Caribbeans*

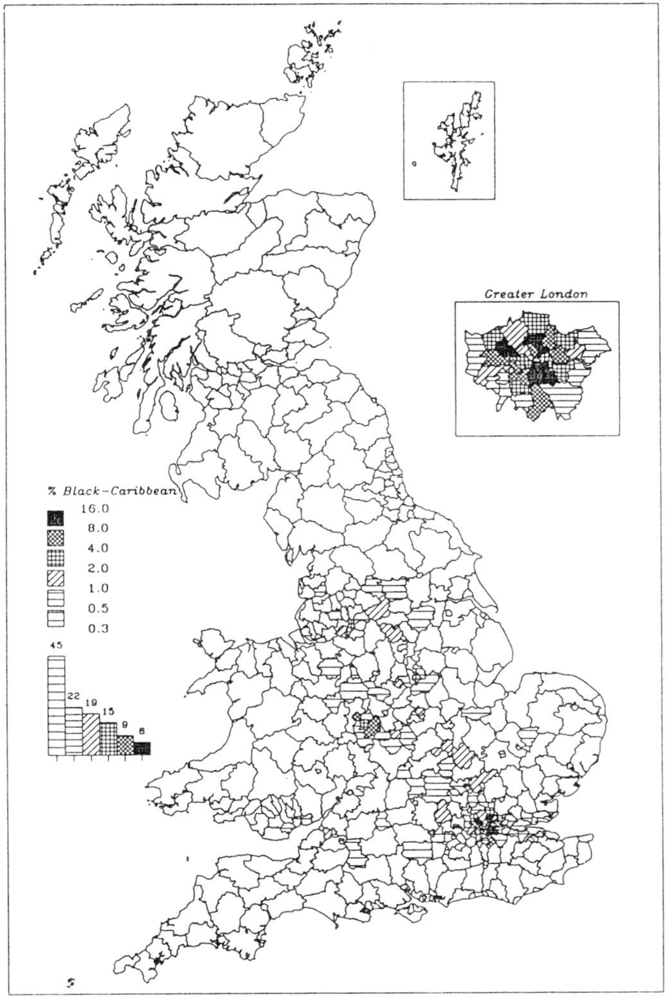

Figure 4.4a *Black ethnic groups*

Demographic characteristics of the ethnic minority populations

Figure 4.4d: *Black-Others*

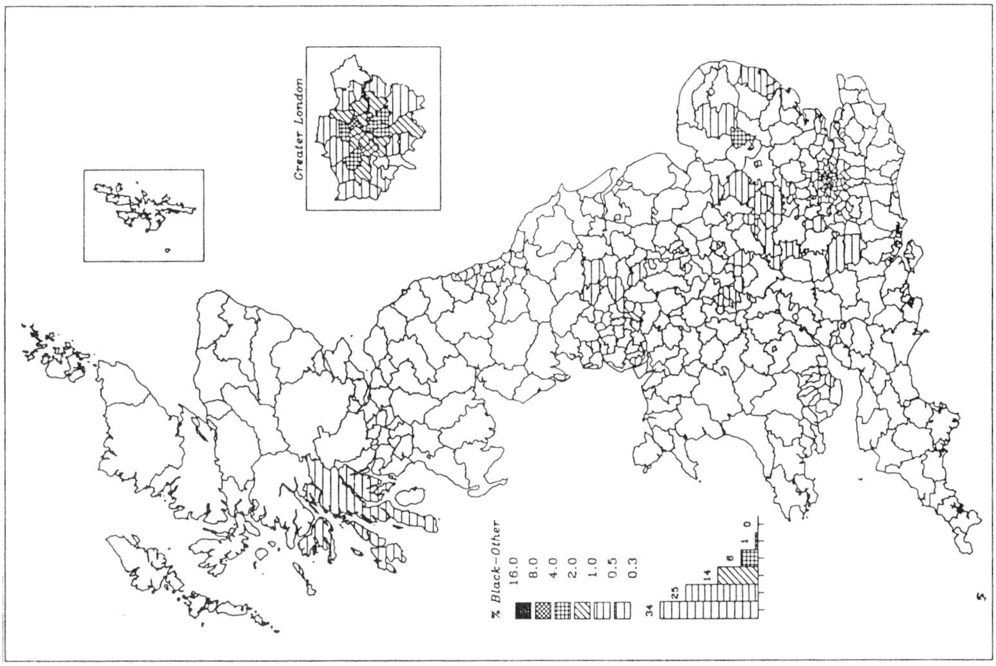

Figure 4.4:c: *Black Africans*

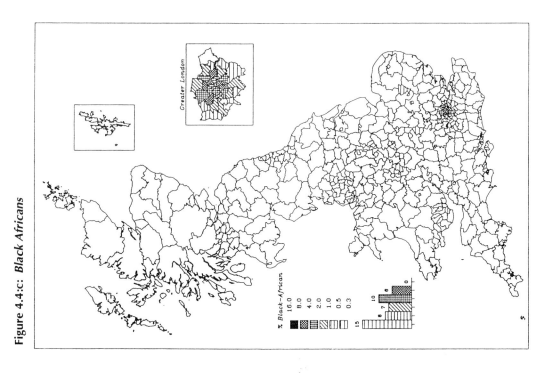

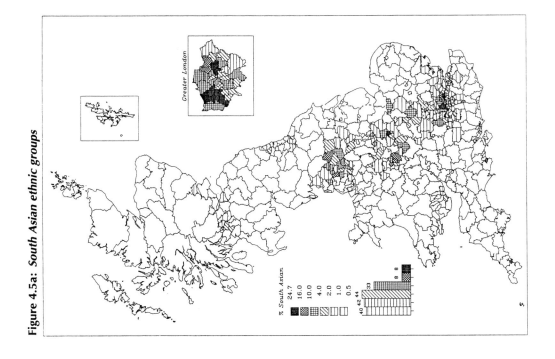

Figure 4.5b: *Indian*

Figure 4.5a: *South Asian ethnic groups*

Demographic characteristics of the ethnic minority populations

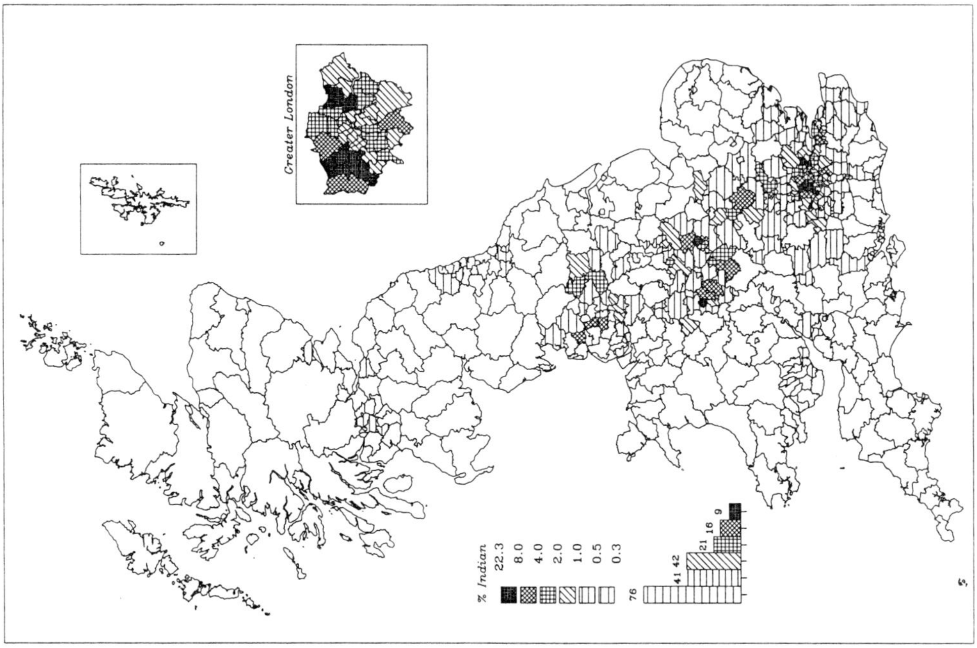

Figure 4.5d: Bangladeshis

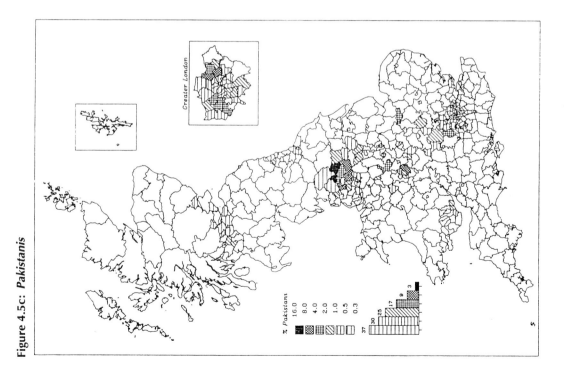

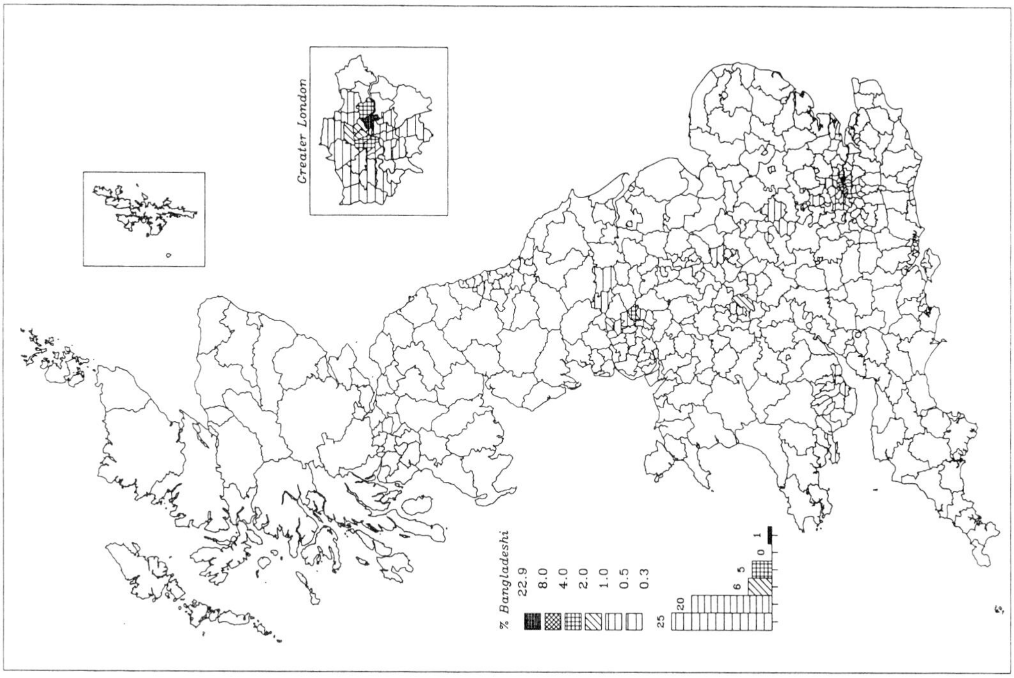

Figure 4.5c: Pakistanis

Figure 4.6b: *Chinese*

Figure 4.6a: *Chinese and Other ethnic groups*

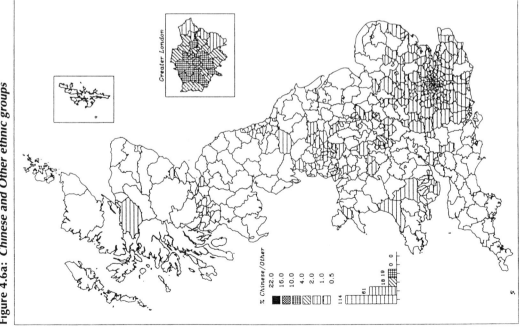

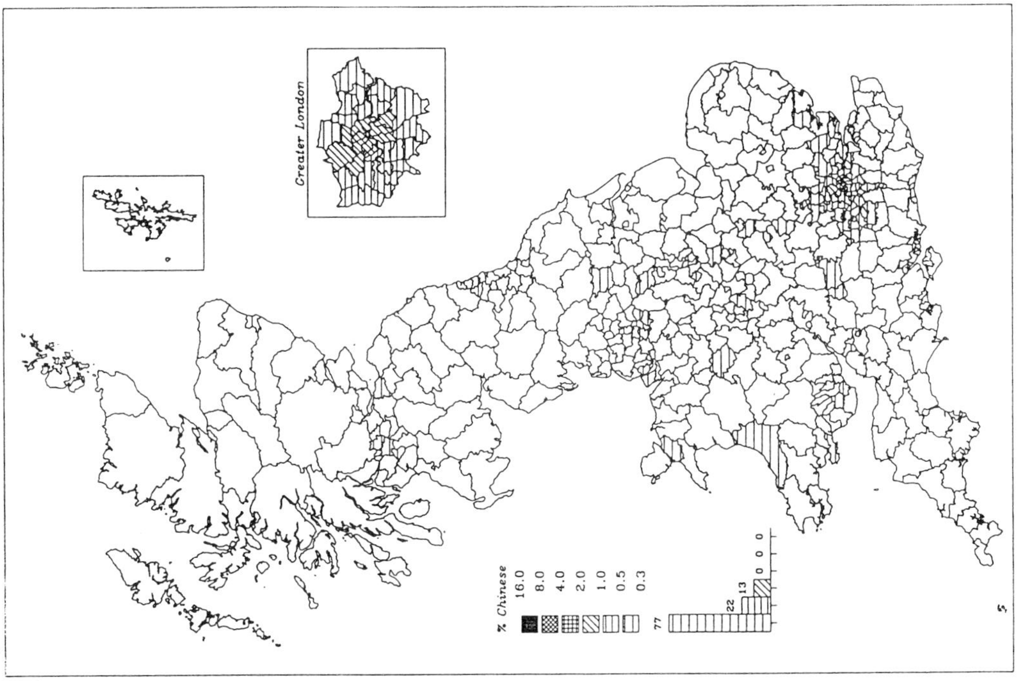

Demographic characteristics of the ethnic minority populations

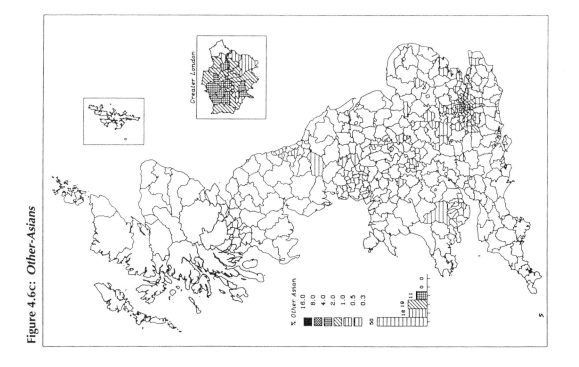

Figure 4.6d: *Other-Others*

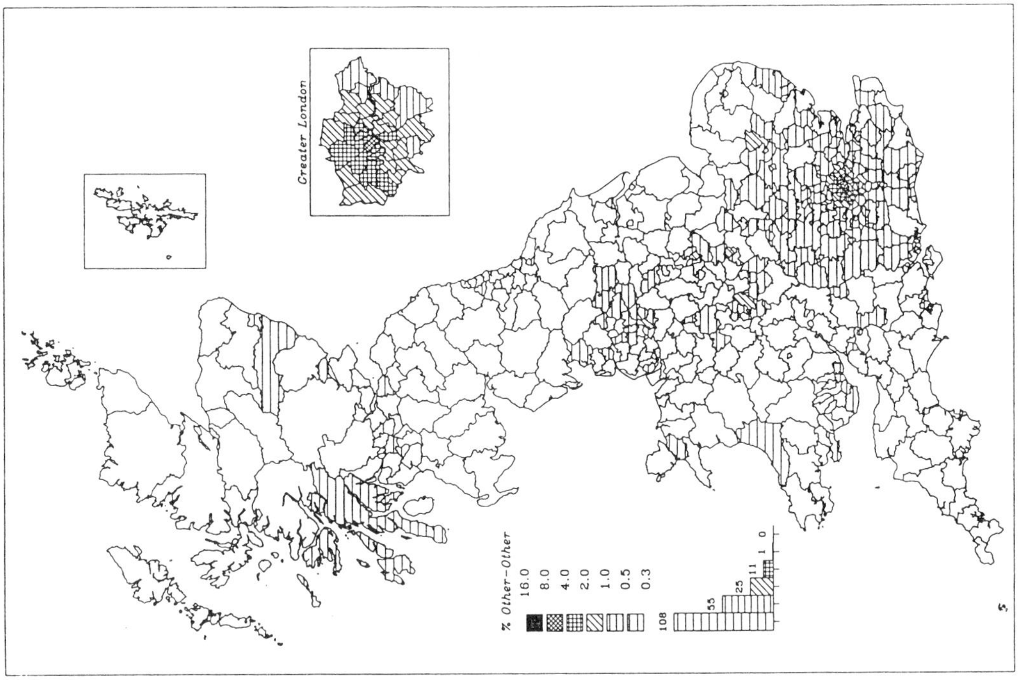

Figure 4.6c: *Other-Asians*

4.5 Age and sex structure of ethnic minority groups in Great Britain

In this section, the broad demographic features of ethnic minority groups at the time of the 1991 Census are discussed, and compared with those of the White ethnic group. The age and sex structure of each ethnic group is presented in the population pyramids in Figures 4.7 to 4.10. The male and female population in each five-year age-group is represented in graphical form, with the youngest age-groups at the base and the oldest at the apex. The figures also depict the probable impact of the problem of under-enumeration in the 1991 Census (discussed in Chapter 2) upon the age and sex structure information (the dark shading at the end of each bar).

Figure 4.7 contrasts the population structure of the White ethnic group (which is very similar to that for the entire British population) with that of the ethnic minority groups as a whole. The shape of Figure 4.7 (a) is typical of a population experiencing slow population growth, with age cohorts of broadly equal size up to retirement age, after which the population diminishes, more rapidly for males than females (as a result of the longer life expectancy of women relative to men). The two post-Second World War 'baby booms' are reflected in the broadening of the 1991 pyramid for people aged 25–29 and 40–44. For ethnic minority groups as a whole, the figure has a more triangular shape, with a broad base (representing large numbers of children and young people) narrowing with successively older age-groups, and reaching a very narrow apex (representing the relatively small number of old people in ethnic minority groups) (Figure 4.7 (b)). However, there are also some 'bulges' in this pyramid, notably for people in their twenties and early thirties, and for men in their fifties.

The pyramids for *Black* groups (Figures 4.8 (a) to (d)) contrast strongly with those for South Asians (Figures 4.9 (a) to (d)), and each other. The overall

Figure 4.7 *Population structure of the White ethnic group and the eithnic minority groups*

(a) White ethnic group

(b) Ethnic minority groups

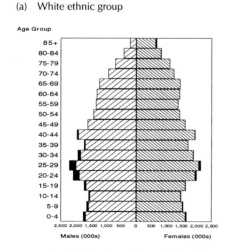
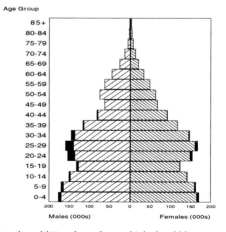

Note: the dark shading at the end of each bar represents the additional numbers which should be added to compensate for under-enumeration

shape of the Black pyramid (Figure 4.8 (a)) was broadly pyramidical, but with a substantial bulge in the 20–35 age range, centred on 25–29-year-olds, and a further bulge corresponding with 50–65-year-olds. Women form the majority of 20–35-year-olds, with a majority of men in the middle-aged bulge. The latter represents the early migrants from the Caribbean, and the former the generation of children born in Britain to migrant parents (which will be illustrated later in this chapter).

Figure 4.8 *Population structure of Black ethnic group*

(a) Black ethnic groups

(b) Black–Caribbeans

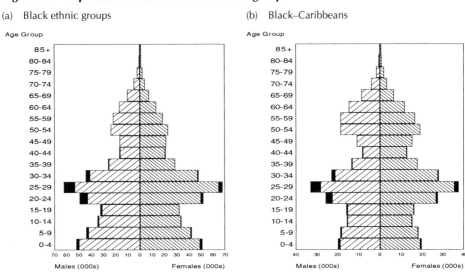

(c) Black–African

(d) Black–Others

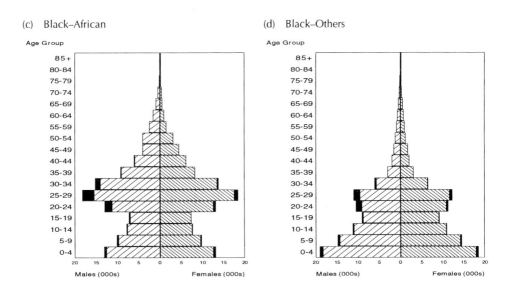

Note: the dark shading at the end of each bar represents the additional numbers which should be added to compensate for under-enumeration

The number of teenagers was much smaller than that of young adults and the wide base of the pyramid represents the emerging 'third generation' of people from Black ethnic groups. These population pyramids illustrate the diversity of the Black ethnic groups. The young adult and middle age bulges are much more pronounced for the Black–Caribbean ethnic group (Figure 4.8 (b)), among whom the bulge corresponding to young children is far less prominent. Females were in the majority in all but the oldest age groups. The pyramid for Black–African people (Figure 4.8 (c)) displays only two bulges – for young adults and for children – with the former more numerous. The two sexes were broadly in balance throughout the age range. Black–Other people (Figure 4.8 (d)) were predominantly British-born, and young adults formed only a minor bulge in the sharply tapering pyramid. Males were in the majority among children, but females outnumbered males in the young adult age range.

The pyramids for *South Asian* ethnic groups had a pyramidical age and sex structure, with a wide base, narrowing in the youngest age-groups (Figure 4.9 (a)), indicative of a youthful population whose rate of growth was beginning to decline. There is a marked contrast between the pyramids for the Indian ethnic group (Figure 4.9 (b)) in which this process is more advanced, since age-groups were of similar size up to the age of 40, afterwards declining in numbers, and the Pakistani and Bangladeshi ethnic groups.

The Pakistani ethnic group had a very youthful population pyramid (Figure 4.9 (c)), notable for the large numbers of children of school age, most of whom were boys. There was a deficit of people in their twenties, which was most marked for young men. Males were in the majority in most age-groups, notably for those aged from 50 to retirement age, though there were more women than men among people in their forties.

The population pyramid for Bangladeshis (Figure 4.9 (d)) was a more exaggerated version of that for Pakistanis. The population was dominated by persons aged under 20, among whom males were in the majority. The size of each age cohort for those over 20 was much smaller, declining gradually with increasing age. Women formed the majority of the population aged over 30, with the exception of a bulge of men aged 50 and over, representing the early migrants, who waited an unusually long time before bringing their families to join them in the 1970s and (especially) the 1980s.

The population pyramid for *Chinese and Other* people differs greatly from those for Black and South Asian people, being dominated by people in the 20–45 age range, and having a relatively broad apex and narrow base (Figure 4.10 (a)). The population pyramids for the three component ethnic groups demonstrate clearly the artificiality of this grouping, with the characteristics of the Other–Other ethnic groups being much more similar to those of the Black–Other ethnic groups than for the Other–Asian and Other – Other groups. The *Chinese* pyramid is similar to the overall average of the three ethnic groups, with more people in the cohorts aged between 20 and 45 than in older or younger age-groups (Figure 4.10 (b)). Women were in the majority in these age-groups, with a majority of males in younger age-

Figure 4.9 *Population structure of South Asian ethnic group*

(a) South Asian ethnic groups

(b) Indians

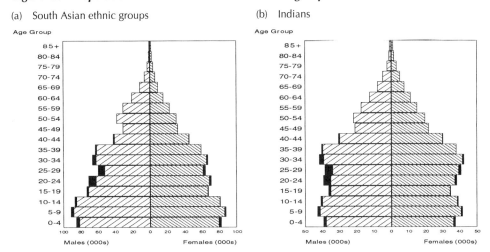

(c) Pakistanis

(d) Bangladeshis

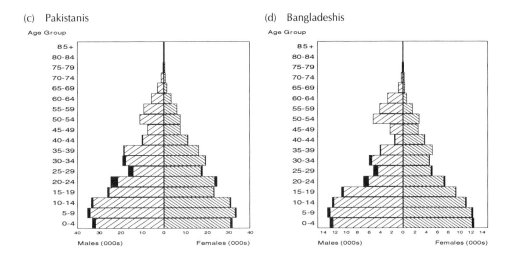

Note: the dark shading at the end of each bar represents the additional numbers which should be added to compensate for under-enumeration

groups. The narrowing base of the pyramid suggests a decline in family size in the second generation. This pattern is even more marked for Other–Asians (Figure 4.10 (c)). The age and sex structure of the Other – Other group (Figure 4.10 (d)) was very different from the other two ethnic groups, being much more youthful and having a preponderance of males in most age-groups.

Indeed, the ethnic groups with the most youthful population structures of all were the Black–Other (Figure 4.8 (d)) and Other – Other (Figure 4.10 (d)) ethnic groups. For each, the population pyramid broadened with declining age, indicative of rapid recent population growth. This is a reflection of the growing number of children with parents from different ethnic groups, but it may also indicate a greater tendency for parents of Black children to identify them as British, rather than by reference to the ultimate geographical region of their ethnic origin (the Caribbean or Africa). Their population pyramids contrast with those of the Pakistanis and Bangladeshis, for whom the similar size of the three youngest age-groups implies a slowing in birth rate during the 1980s.

Figure 4.10 *Population structure of Chinese and Other ethnic groups*

(a) Chinese and Other ethnic groups

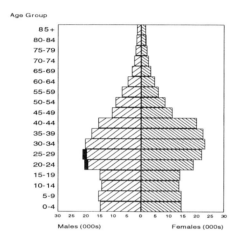

(b) Chinese

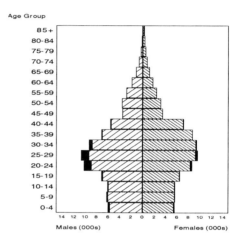

(c) Other-Asians

(d) Other-Others

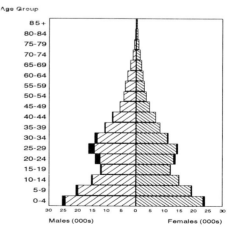

Note: the dark shading at the end of each bar represents the additional numbers which should be added to compensate for under-enumeration

The impact of census under-enumeration, discussed in Chapter 3, is illustrated here by applying the adjustment factors calculated by the Census Offices (these factors are shown in Table 2.6 in Chapter 2) to each age and sex group. As already mentioned, under-enumeration was greatest for 0–4-year-olds, for men aged 20–34 and for women aged over 85, and the census coverage of males was lower than that of females. These features are common across ethnic groups, but vary in intensity between ethnic groups, because of their different age and sex structures. The overall effect is that the census coverage was lower for ethnic minority groups, particularly the Black ethnic groups, than for the White ethnic group (Table 4.6). The population pyramids clearly show that the under-enumeration of young men and young children has a greater impact upon data for ethnic minority groups than for the White ethnic group. The impact of under-enumeration is much more severe for men from ethnic minority groups than for White men in the 20–34 age range, and is most severe for Black–African, Black–Caribbean and Bangladeshi men aged 25–29. The effect of adjusting for under-enumeration for the Black ethnic groups is to increase further the bulge in the number of young adults. In the South Asian ethnic groups, it does not quite compensate for the deficit of young Pakistani and Bangladeshi men relative to women in the same age-groups, indicating that the undercount of young men in these ethnic groups was even more severe.

The previous section demonstrated that ethnic minority groups are relatively concentrated in the most urbanised areas of Great Britain, particularly in the inner cities. OPCS/GRO(S) (1994a) found that the degree of under-enumeration was also highest in inner urban areas, thus adding a further factor that acts to magnify the potential under-enumeration of ethnic minorities. Additionally, the difficulty of contacting households in such areas meant that a relatively high percentage of the data for ethnic minority groups was imputed in these types of area. It is thus likely that the estimates of the undercount already made do not fully account for the under-enumeration of ethnic minority groups.

Table 4.6 *Estimated coverage of ethnic groups in Great Britain, 1991*

Ethnic group	Persons (%)	Males (%)	Females (%)
White	98	97	99
Black - Caribbean	97	95	98
Black - African	95	93	98
Black - Other	96	94	97
Indian	97	96	98
Pakistani	97	96	98
Bangladeshi	97	96	98
Chinese	97	95	98
Other - Asians	97	95	98
Other - Other	97	95	98
Entire population	98	97	99

Source: 1991 Census User Guide 58

The geographical factors underlying the undercount can be more accurately approximated by comparing census data with demographically-based estimates of the populations of small areas (as in the ESRC-sponsored 'Estimating with Confidence' project). However, there are additional factors specific to ethnic minority groups which have an unknown effect upon their enumeration. For example, Asian households tend to be larger than average, and hence any tendency for the number of people in a household to be understated resulting from an attempt to avoid registration for the poll tax or council tax might be expected to be strongest for these ethnic groups. Additionally, Simpson (1993) found that failure to include new-born babies in census returns in Bradford was particularly marked in the city centre wards where the percentage of South Asians in the population was greatest. The ethnic minority population also includes a number of refugees and asylum seekers, many of whom avoid responding to surveys for fear of contact with state officials. Clearly, even adjusted census data is still subject to an unknown degree of uncertainty.

The remainder of this section discusses the demographic structure of each ethnic group in greater detail, using data adjusted for under-enumeration.

Sex distribution

Table 4.7 presents the sex ratio (the number of males per 1,000 females) for each ethnic group in Great Britain for 1991. Overall, females formed the majority of the British population, but there was near equality in the number of males and females in the ethnic minority population as a whole. Within this overall average, considerable variations existed between ethnic groups. The lowest ratios of males to females occurred in the Other–Asian, Black–Caribbean, and White ethnic groups. In contrast, there was a marked excess of males over females in all three South Asian ethnic groups. The greatest excess was experienced by the Bangladeshi ethnic group, for which the number of males was over 9 per cent greater than the number of females. This pattern reflects the more youthful age structure of ethnic minority groups compared to the White ethnic group, because women are in the majority in the oldest age-groups. However, the youthful Black–Other category also has an excess of females over males.

A more powerful influence upon this pattern is the different migration histories of each ethnic group. The Black–Caribbean ethnic group was the earliest to migrate to Great Britain, and its period of mass immigration ended earliest (Booth, 1993). Moreover, Black–Caribbean women were relatively early migrants, and often migrated independently from men (Peach, 1991). In contrast, the pattern of South Asian migration was typically one of men migrating first and being joined later by their wives and children. People from the Indian ethnic group completed migration of families earlier than Pakistanis, while the Bangladeshi ethnic group was the slowest of the South Asian ethnic groups to reunite male migrants with their families.

The Black–African ethnic group also had an excess of males over females in 1991. Migration from Africa was relatively rapid in the 1980s, strongly

Table 4.7 *Population size of ethnic groups in Great Britain, 1991; males, females and sex ratio*

Ethnic group	Persons (000s)	Males (000s)	Females (000s)	Males per 1000 females
White	52,893.9	25,818.4	27,075.5	954
Ethnic minorities	3,117.0	1,579.5	1,537.5	1,027
Black	*925.5*	*458.5*	*467.0*	*982*
Black-Caribbean	517.1	251.5	265.7	946
Black-African	221.9	114.3	107.7	1,061
Black-Other	186.4	92.8	93.6	991
South Asian	*1,524.3*	*783.5*	*740.8*	*1,058*
Indian	865.5	439.8	425.7	1,033
Pakistani	491.0	255.4	235.6	1,084
Bangladeshi	167.8	88.3	79.4	1,112
Chinese and others	*667.2*	*337.4*	*329.8*	*1,023*
Chinese	162.4	81.6	80.9	1,009
Other Asians	204.3	98.3	106.0	927
Other - Other	300.5	157.6	142.9	1,103
Entire population	**55,969.2**	**27,372.2**	**28,597.0**	**957**

Source: 1991 Census Local Base Statistics (ESRC purchase); Crown Copyright.
Note: These figures have been adjusted for Census under-enumeration.

influenced by the migration of men coming to the UK for higher education. In contrast, many migrants to Britain in the Other–Asian ethnic group are women who have migrated to fill service sector jobs, and the bulk of their migration has been quite recent. The summary comparison with the sex ratio of the population living in households headed by persons born in the New Commonwealth in 1981 shows how the population of ethnic minorities became more balanced in its sex composition over the decade 1981–91 as the process of family reunification proceeded.

Median ages, country of birth and migration

Women have a greater life expectancy than men, and consequently the median age of females was three years higher than that of males for the population as a whole in 1991, at nearly 38 years (Table 4.8). The median age of both males and females in the White ethnic group was nearly a year greater than this aggregate figure. In contrast, the median age of people from ethnic minority groups was just over 25, with very little difference between the sexes. Black people as a whole were slightly older and South Asians slightly younger than the ethnic minority population average. In the Chinese and Other group, males were considerably older and females considerably younger than the overall ethnic minority population figure. There were striking differences within the three broad ethnic minority categories. The median age of Black–Caribbean people was nearly twice that of Black–Other people, with a similar difference between the median ages of people from the Indian and Bangladeshi ethnic groups.

Table 4.8 *Median age of males and females by ethnic group in Great Britain, 1991*

Ethnic group	Persons	Males	Females	Percent born in UK	% living outside UK in 1990
White	36.7	34.9	38.6	95.8	0.5
Ethnic minority groups	25.4	25.2	25.5	46.8	2.7
Black	*26.6*	*26.4*	*26.7*	*55.7*	*2.4*
Black - Caribbean	29.8	29.6	30.0	53.7	0.6
Black - African	26.3	26.7	25.9	36.4	7.3
Black - Other	16.2	15.6	16.8	84.4	1.7
South Asian	*23.9*	*23.9*	*23.9*	*44.1*	*1.4*
Indian	27.8	27.8	27.8	42.0	1.2
Pakistani	19.8	19.9	19.7	50.5	1.6
Bangladeshi	17.1	17.3	16.9	36.7	2.1
Chinese and Other	*26.0*	*25.7*	*26.4*	*40.6*	*5.8*
Chinese	28.4	27.5	29.4	28.4	5.1
Other - Asian	29.9	28.8	30.7	21.9	9.2
Other - Other	21.2	22.0	20.5	59.8	3.9
Entire population	**35.8**	**34.2**	**37.5**	**93.1**	**0.6**

Source: 1991 Census Local Base Statistics (ESRC purchase); Crown Copyright.
Note: Medians based on data adjusted for Census under-enumeration.

The ethnic minority groups with the oldest average ages were the Black–Caribbean, Other–Asian, Chinese and Indian ethnic groups, for all of whom the median age was around 30 years. The very young median ages of Black–Others, Bangladeshis, Pakistanis, and Other – Others is striking; for the former pair, about half their populations were of school age or below in 1991. Overall, the 'older' ethnic groups are those containing earlier migrants to the UK, and hence the percentage born in the UK in these ethnic groups tends to be below the average figure of 46.8 per cent for all ethnic minority groups (with the exception of Black–Caribbeans). However, the opposite pattern did not hold among the younger ethnic groups. There was a marked contrast between the Black–Other and Other – Other ethnic groups, which were predominantly made up of people born in the UK, and the Bangladeshis, only 36.7 per cent of whom were born in the UK.

The pattern of international migration by age across ethnic groups is illustrated in Figure 4.11, in which the black shading in each population pyramid represents the percentage of each ethnic group population born outside the UK in each age and sex group (these figures were derived using the 2 per cent individual SAR). For ethnic minority groups as a whole (Figure 4.11 (c)), the UK-born population had a very marked triangular pattern, with the oldest being aged 45–49. Nearly all older people had been born outside the UK, but there were migrants in all age-groups, with the percentage born in the UK steadily increasing with decreasing age. In contrast, there was a sharp divide in the Black–Caribbean ethnic group, in which nearly all those aged over 35 had been born outside the UK, and nearly all younger people in the UK (Figure 4.11 (g)). The pattern for the Black–African ethnic group was highly distinctive (Figure 4.11 (h)). The population pyramid was widest in the 25–34 age range, which is dominated by people born outside the UK. Most UK-born people were aged under 40, with an the percentage born in the UK increasing as age decreases. Nearly all Black–Other people had been born in the UK, over the entire age range.

Figure 4.11 *Age and sex distribution of persons born within and outside the UK by ethnic group 1991*

(a) All   (b) White   (c) Ethnic minorities

(d) Black   (e) South Asian   (f) Chinese & Other

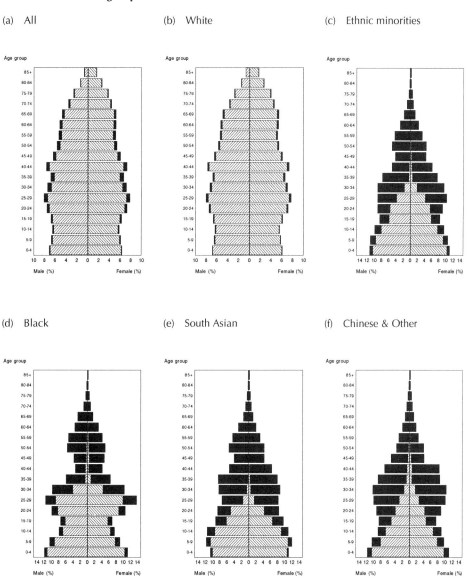

Note: black shading represents persons born outside the UK.

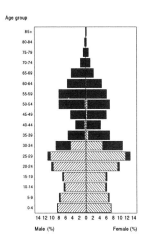

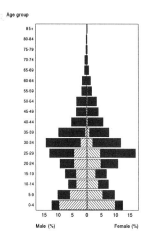

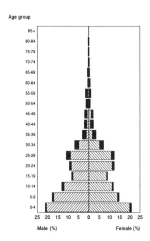

(j) Indian   (k) Pakistani   (l) Bangladeshi

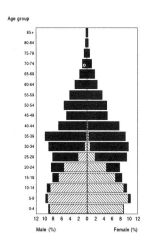

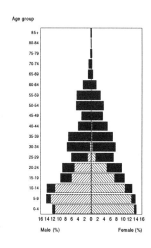

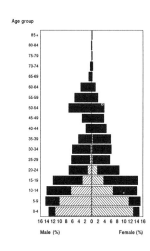

(m) Chinese   (n) Other - Asian   (o) Other - Other

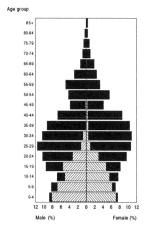

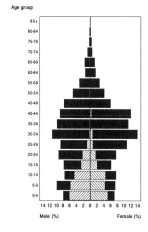

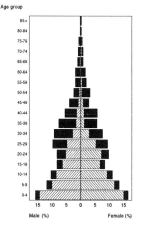

The patterns for the three South Asian ethnic groups were very similar (Figures 4.11 (j) to (l)). In the Indian ethnic group, nearly all those aged over 35 had been born outside the UK, with the percentage born outside the UK diminishing to a very small level for people below the age of 15. The UK-born were predominantly of school age or young adults. The Pakistani ethnic group displays a similar pattern, but at younger ages; most people aged over 30 were born outside the UK. The pattern for Bangladeshis (Figure 4.11 (l)) is similar, but people born outside the UK formed a larger percentage of the population throughout the age range; at least half of those aged 10 and over were born outside the UK.

The Chinese and Other–Asian ethnic groups (Figures 4.11 (m) and (n)) displayed similar patterns, with the largest part of the population being of working age, and overwhelmingly born outside the UK. The UK-born population in both ethnic groups was predominantly aged under 35, and increasing in size. In the Other–Asian ethnic groups, nearly all people aged over 25 were born outside the UK. In the Other – Other ethnic groups, those born outside the UK were in the minority, and mostly aged over 25. The UK-born population was not quite as youthful as the Black–Other ethnic group, but also demonstrated rapid growth.

Age structure

Table 4.9 presents the breakdown of the 10 census ethnic groups into broad age categories for Great Britain as a whole, corresponding to pre-school age children (0–4), school children (5–15), young adults (16–24), the main working age-groups and the elderly population (65 and over). The relative youth of the ethnic minority groups is immediately apparent. Children formed a third of the ethnic minority population in 1991, compared to under a fifth of the White population. In contrast, the proportion of the ethnic minority population aged over 45 was far smaller than that for the White population. While 16 per cent of the population as a whole was aged over 65, only just over 3 per cent of the ethnic minority population fell within this age-group.

There were substantial variations in age structure between ethnic minority groups. Turning first to the Black ethnic groups, it was shown above that Black–Caribbeans were older on average than those from the Black–African and Black–Other ethnic groups, and hence a higher percentage of people (higher than in any other ethnic minority) from the former ethnic group were aged 65 and above. In contrast, 90 per cent of the Black–Other ethnic groups were aged under 45, and half aged 0–15 in 1991. People from the Other – Other ethnic groups had a similar but less extreme age structure.

Indian people displayed the most elderly age structure of all the South Asian ethnic groups, but even so, children still accounted for a much higher proportion of their population than the average for all ethnic groups. Moreover, the great majority of Indians were aged under 45 in 1991. The Pakistanis and Bangladeshis were much younger on average, with nearly a third of the population of each being of school age in 1991. The Chinese and Other–Asian ethnic groups displayed another type of age structure, with the majority of each ethnic group being of working age, primarily in the 25–44 age-group.

Table 4.9 *Age breakdown of ethnic groups in Great Britain, 1991*

Ethnic group	Total Population	Percentage of total population					
		Aged 0-4	Aged 5-15	Aged 16-24	Aged 25-44	Aged 45-64	Aged 65+
White	52,893.9	6.5	13.0	12.9	29.3	19.2	19.3
Ethnic minority groups	3,117.0	11.1	21.7	16.4	32.9	13.6	4.2
Black	*925.5*	*11.1*	*18.0*	*16.5*	*33.8*	*15.4*	*5.1*
Black - Caribbean	517.1	7.6	14.1	15.3	33.4	21.8	7.7
Black - African	221.9	11.8	17.1	17.0	42.7	9.5	1.8
Black - Other	186.4	20.1	29.6	19.3	24.6	4.4	1.6
South Asian	*1,524.3*	*10.9*	*24.6*	*16.5*	*30.5*	*13.5*	*3.9*
Indian	865.5	8.9	20.5	15.5	34.9	14.9	5.2
Pakistani	491.0	13.2	29.2	17.9	26.1	11.3	2.4
Bangladeshi	167.8	15.1	31.9	17.9	20.8	12.7	1.5
Chinese and Other	*667.2*	*11.6*	*20.1*	*16.1*	*36.9*	*11.4*	*3.8*
Chinese	162.4	7.1	16.0	18.4	41.4	12.7	4.4
Other - Asians	204.3	8.0	16.2	15.1	43.6	13.7	3.1
Other - Other	300.5	16.4	25.0	15.5	29.9	9.2	3.9
Entire population	**55,969.2**	**6.7**	**13.5**	**13.1**	**29.5**	**18.9**	**18.5**

Source: 1991 Census Local Base Statistics (ESRC purchase); Crown Copyright.
Note: Based on data adjusted for Census underenumeration.

An alternative perspective on contrasts in age structure is presented in Table 4.10. Here, the share of the total British population in each age-group which is accounted for by each ethnic group is presented, illustrating how particular ethnic minority groups were relatively more prominent in different sections of the British population. White people dominated all age-groups, but their share of the youngest age-groups was smallest, increasing to a maximum in the oldest age-groups. Conversely, the percentage of the population accounted for by each ethnic minority group declined with increasing age. The main exception to this was the Black–Caribbean ethnic group, whose share of the total population was fairly constant in all age-groups up to retirement age. The share of South Asians in the population was greatest for 0–15-year-olds, with the fall in percentage share with age being more rapid for Pakistanis and Bangladeshis than for Indians. The Chinese and Other–Asian shares of the population were greatest in the 16–24 and 25–44 year age-groups.

For pre-school age children, the share of each of the main ethnic groups was smaller than their share of children of school age, while the percentage accounted for by Black–Others and Other – Others was larger. This implies that children from these two ethnic groups will form a growing percentage of the population of school age during the 1990s. They are also likely, together with the three South Asian ethnic groups, to form a growing percentage of young people entering further/higher education and the labour market during the course of this decade. At the other end of the age

Table 4.10 *Ethnic group share of each age group in Great Britain, 1991*

Ethnic group	Overall share of population (%)	Percentage of total population					
		Aged 0-4	Aged 5-15	Aged 16-24	Aged 25-44	Aged 45-64	Aged 65+
White	94.5	90.8	91.0	93.1	93.9	96.0	98.7
Ethnic minority groups	5.5	9.2	9.0	7.0	6.2	4.0	1.3
Black	*1.7*	*2.7*	*2.2*	*2.1*	*1.9*	*1.3*	*0.5*
Black - Caribbean	0.9	1.0	1.0	1.1	1.0	1.1	0.4
Black - African	0.4	0.7	0.5	0.5	0.6	0.2	0.0
Black - Other	0.3	1.0	0.7	0.5	0.3	0.1	0.0
South Asian	*2.7*	*4.4*	*5.0*	*3.4*	*2.8*	*1.9*	*0.6*
Indian	1.5	2.0	2.4	1.8	1.8	1.2	0.4
Pakistani	0.9	1.7	1.9	1.2	0.8	0.5	0.1
Bangladeshi	0.3	0.7	0.7	0.4	0.2	0.2	0.0
Chinese and Other	*1.2*	*2.1*	*1.8*	*1.5*	*1.5*	*0.7*	*0.2*
Chinese	0.3	0.3	0.3	0.4	0.4	0.2	0.1
Other - Asians	0.4	0.4	0.4	0.4	0.5	0.3	0.1
Other - Other	0.5	1.3	1.0	0.6	0.5	0.3	0.1
Entire population	**100.0**	**100.0**	**100.0**	**100.0**	**100.0**	**100.0**	**100.0**

Source: 1991 Census Local Base Statistics (ESRC purchase); Crown Copyright.
Note: Based on data adjusted for Census underenumeration.

range, Black–Caribbeans, Indians and (to a lesser extent) Pakistanis will account for an increasing percentage of people reaching retirement age during the decade (though pensioners will still be overwhelmingly from the White ethnic group).

Dependency ratios

The age structure data can also be expressed in the form of a *dependency ratio*. This is defined here as the ratio of the dependent sectors of the population – children (under the school leaving age of 16) and old people (above pensionable age) – to the population of working age (aged from 16 to 59 for women or 64 for men – see Box 4.1). It may be regarded as measuring the 'burden' of the old and young upon the age-group which contains those people of working age and the primary bearers of family responsibilities. Overall, the population in the non-productive age-groups was nearly two thirds the size of the population of working age. This varied considerably between ethnic groups, as did the contribution of children and old people to the overall dependency ratio (Table 4.11).

Among the White ethnic group, the contribution of children and the elderly to the dependency ratio was about equal. In contrast, the dependency ratios for ethnic minority groups were largely determined by the size of the child population, with the exception of Black–Caribbeans. Dependency ratios

Box 4.1 Dependency ratios

The *child dependency ratio is defined here as:*

$$100 \times \frac{\text{number of persons aged 0--15}}{\text{men aged 16--64 plus women aged 16--59}}$$

and the 'elderly dependency ratio' is defined here as:

$$100 \times \frac{\text{men aged 65 and over plus women aged 60 and over}}{\text{men aged 16-64 plus women aged 16--69}}$$

The *total dependency ratio* is the sum of these two ratios

Note: These age-groups are chosen to suit UK conditions. Conventional demographic age-groups are 0-14, 15-64, 65 and over.

Table 4.11 *Dependency ratios for ethnic groups in Great Britain, 1991*

Ethnic group	Child dependency ratio	Elderly dependency ratio	Total dependency ratio
White	31.7	31.4	63.1
Ethnic minority groups	52.1	6.7	58.8
Black	*44.2*	*7.7*	*51.9*
Black - Caribbean	30.8	10.9	41.7
Black - African	41.7	2.7	44.4
Black - Other	103.0	3.3	106.3
South Asian	*58.7*	*6.4*	*65.1*
Indian	45.1	8.0	53.0
Pakistani	76.7	4.3	81.0
Bangladeshi	91.2	3.0	94.2
Chinese and Other	*49.2*	*5.9*	*55.1*
Chinese	31.9	6.0	37.9
Other - Asians	33.5	4.4	37.8
Other - Other	75.8	7.1	82.9
Entire population	**32.8**	**30.0**	**62.9**

Source: 1991 Census Local Base Statistics (ESRC purchase); Crown Copyright.
Note: Based on data adjusted for Census underenumeration.

were lowest for the Other–Asian, Chinese, Black–Caribbean and Black–African ethnic groups, at about two fifths of the population of working age. The ratio reached over 50 per cent for the Indian ethnic group, and over 80 per cent for the Pakistani and Other – Other ethnic groups. The highest ratios were displayed by the Bangladeshi and Black–Other ethnic groups, for whom there were as many or more dependants as persons of working age. This pattern is strongly influenced by the larger family sizes of South Asian ethnic groups, but the dependency rates for Black–Others may be inflated by a greater tendency for children than adults to fall into the Other category, either through mixed parentage or a preference for identification as Black–British.

Marital status

Here, the substantial differences which existed between ethnic groups in marital status are briefly discussed, focusing upon the aggregate pattern for all persons aged over 16 (Table 4.12). Chapter 7 of this volume analyses patterns of marriage and partnership in much greater detail, examining the detailed variations across the age range.

Perhaps surprisingly, a smaller percentage of women than men were married in most ethnic groups. This largely reflects their greater life expectancy, since the percentage of women who were widowed or divorced was twice as high as the percentage of men, and the percentage single was much smaller for women than for men. The percentage of single people was higher and the incidence of marriage and widowhood/divorce was lower for ethnic minority groups as a whole than for the White ethnic group, for both men and women. There were marked contrasts between ethnic minority groups. While about half of all people from Black ethnic groups were single, only

Table 4.12 *Marital status distributions of the different ethnic groups in Great Britain, 1991*

Ethnic group	Males aged 16 and over			Females aged 16 and over		
	Single	Married	Widowed /divorced	Single	Married	Widowed /divorced
	(%)	(%)	(%)	(%)	(%)	(%)
White	29.5	61.0	9.4	22.6	56.1	21.3
Ethnic minority groups	37.1	58.0	4.9	33.4	56.2	10.5
Black	*49.4*	*42.1*	*8.4*	*50.5*	*36.7*	*12.9*
Black - Caribbean	47.2	42.2	10.6	50.0	35.2	14.9
Black - African	46.9	48.2	4.9	43.3	46.5	10.2
Black - Other	63.6	31.0	5.5	64.2	27.5	8.4
South Asian	*28.1*	*69.0*	*2.9*	*21.5*	*69.4*	*9.1*
Indian	27.0	69.6	3.5	21.2	68.3	10.5
Pakistani	29.2	68.7	2.2	21.9	71.3	6.8
Bangladeshi	32.7	66.2	1.1	21.5	71.4	7.1
Chinese and Other	*39.8*	*55.7*	*4.5*	*33.3*	*57.0*	*9.7*
Chinese	40.5	56.5	2.9	31.4	60.5	8.1
Other - Asians	34.7	62.0	3.4	27.0	64.4	8.6
Other - Other	43.3	50.2	6.4	40.9	47.1	12.0
Entire population	29.9	60.9	9.2	23.1	56.1	20.8

Source: 1991 Census Local Base Statistics (ESRC purchase); Crown Copyright.

28.1 per cent of South Asian men and 21.5 per cent of South Asian women were in this marital status, and the corresponding figures for Chinese and Other ethnic groups were 39.8 and 33.3 per cent respectively. Marriage was twice as common for South Asian women than for Black women, while the differential was almost as great for men.

Within the Black ethnic groups, nearly two thirds of the Black–Other group and about half of the Black–Caribbean group were single in 1991. The incidence of marriage was much lower than for South Asians in all Black ethnic groups, being highest for Black–Africans and lowest for Black–Others. The incidence of widowhood and divorce was also much higher for women from Black ethnic groups (especially Black–Caribbean women) than for women from other ethnic minority groups.

Among South Asians, the percentage single was highest for Bangladeshi men, as a consequence of their relative youth. The sexual differentials in the percentages married and single were quite narrow for South Asians, with two thirds or more of both men and women married. Widowhood and divorce were more common for women than men, with the incidence highest for Indian women.

The Chinese and Other ethnic groups experienced a pattern intermediate between the Black and South Asian ethnic groups. The percentage single was highest and percentage married lowest in the Other – Other ethnic group, once again largely a consequence of the low median age of this group. The percentage single was above the average of all ethnic minority groups for Chinese men and slightly below the ethnic minority group average for Chinese women. Both sexes were less likely to be widowed or divorced than the average for ethnic minority groups, while men were slightly less likely, and women slightly more likely than average to be married. Other–Asian men and women were more likely than Chinese people to be married.

4.6 Conclusions

This chapter has provided a brief overview of the growth, demographic characteristics and geographical distribution of ethnic minority groups resident in Great Britain in 1991, covering a wide range of topics which are explored in greater detail elsewhere in this and the other three volumes. It has illustrated the marked contrasts which exist both between White and all other ethnic groups, and also between each of the ethnic minority groups. The ethnic minority population has grown rapidly throughout the last 40 years or so, but the rate of growth now shows signs of slowing. The ethnic composition of the minority population has evolved over time, being initially dominated by Caribbean people, who were overtaken in size by the main South Asian ethnic groups. The rapid growth of these three ethnic groups in the 1970s and 1980s will be followed by increasing numbers of people with parents from different ethnic groups, while the number of new migrants from Africa and the Far East has increased in recent years and may continue to do so into the future. Over the remainder of this decade, people of mixed parentage are likely to form a growing proportion of school-age children, while young South Asian people will form a growing percentage of the workforce and of students.

The earlier migrant groups (the Black–Caribbean, Indian and Chinese ethnic groups) tend to be older on average than those with more recent arrivals and the mixed ethnic groups, whose members are predominantly UK-born. The Bangladeshi, Pakistani, Black–Other and Other – Other ethnic groups (the first two of which continue to receive international migrants) are extremely youthful, and thus have the potential for continued rapid increase in the medium term. A major problem with the ethnic group classification used in 1991 was the grouping together of a highly diverse range of ethnic and national groups into the Other categories, and the loss of specific information on the characteristics of people of mixed parentage. Though the question was quite successful overall, it is clearly important that the ethnic group question used by the 2001 Census matches better the changing perceptions of ethnic identity.

While the 1991 Census broadly confirms the demographic patterns already identified by the Labour Force Survey (Coleman and Salt, 1992), its unique value is that it provides for the first time detailed demographic and socio-economic data on the structure of ethnic minority populations in small geographical areas. The majority of people from ethnic minority groups lived in the most populous regions of Britain in 1991, but the spatial distribution of some ethnic groups such as the Pakistanis and Chinese was quite distinctive. Though the geographical distribution of ethnic minority groups is similar to that identified by country-of-birth data from previous censuses, the ethnic group question enables the detailed geographical distribution of the British-born ethnic minority population to be studied for the first time. This has highlighted the increased relative concentration of ethnic minority groups in the larger cities and inner urban areas, as a result of their rapid growth *in situ* at a time when the population as a whole was tending to move from larger to smaller cities and towns, and from inner areas to suburbs and rural areas. When data from the 2001 Census become available, it will be possible to study whether ethnic minority groups are joining in these 'counter-urbanisation' and 'suburbanisation' processes, or are being left behind in the declining parts of the urban system. This chapter has also demonstrated that the SARs drawn for the first time in 1991 provide the potential to generate quite detailed information for ethnic minority groups, which can also be generated for smaller (but more populous) areas within Great Britain.

Clearly, the related questions of under-enumeration and data imputation add a degree of uncertainty to the census information on ethnic groups, compounded by the fact that ethnic minority groups tend to live in areas where the incidence of imputation is greatest. The uncertainty in the data is further complicated by the difficulties experienced by persons in the Other categories in completing the ethnic group question in accordance with the expectations of the Census Offices. While all the census data must be regarded as an estimate based on a 98 per cent sample of the population, the combined effect of the factors discussed in this sector is likely to be that data for the Black (particularly Black–Other) and Other – Other ethnic groups contain a greater degree of uncertainty than that for the White and Asian ethnic groups (see also Chapter 3). There is a strong case for applying appropriate local adjustment factors to the ethnic group data for areas in which the Black ethnic groups form a large percentage of the resident population, and for a particular effort towards improving census coverage in areas of significant ethnic minority group concentrations when the 2001 Census is taken.

References

Booth, H. (1992) *The Migration Process: Two Demographic Studies of Migrant Populations in Britain and West Germany*. Aldershot: Avebury.

Coleman, D. and Salt, J. (1992) *The British Population: Patterns, Trends and Processes*. Oxford: Oxford University Press.

Eversley, D. and Sukdeo, F. (1969) *The Dependants of the Coloured Commonwealth Population of England and Wales*. London, Oxford University Press for the Institute of Race Relations.

Howes, E. (1986) *Black and ethnic minority population estimates*. Research Note 10, Research & Intelligence Section, Chief Executive's Office, London Borough of Hackney.

OPCS Immigrant Statistics Unit (1976) Country of birth and colour 1971–4. *Population Trends*, 2, 2–8.

OPCS Immigrant Statistics Unit (1977) New Commonwealth and Pakistani population estimates. *Population Trends*, 9, 4–7.

OPCS Immigrant Statistics Unit (1979) Population of New Comonwealth and Pakistani ethnic origin: new projections. *Population Trends*, 16, 22–7.

OPCS Population Statistics Division (1986) Estimating the size of the ethnic minority populations in the 1980s. *Population Trends*, 44, 23–7.

OPCS (1994) *International migration*: London: HMSO.

OPCS/GRO (Scotland) (1994) *Undercoverage in Great Britain*. 1991 Census User Guide 58.

OPCS/GRO (Scotland) (1994b) 1991 Census Supplement to Report on Ethnic Group and Country of Birth (OPCS, London)

Owen. C. (1993) Using the Labour Force Survey to estimate Britain's ethnic minority populations. *Population Trends*, 72, 18–23.

Owen, D.W. (1994) Spatial variations in ethnic minority group populations in Great Britain. *Population Trends*, 78, 23–33.

Owen, D.W. (1995) The demography, geography and socio-economic characteristics of the 'Black–Other' ethnic group. In: G.C.K. Peach (ed.), *Ethnicity in the 1991 Census, Volume 2: The Ethnic Minority Populations of Britain*.

Peach, G.C.K. (1968) *West Indian Migration to Britain: A Social Geography*. London: Oxford University Press.

Peach, G.C.K. (1991) *The Caribbean in Europe: contrasting patterns of migration and settlement in Britain, France and the Netherlands*. Research Paper in Ethnic Relations no. 15, Centre for Research in Ethnic Relations, University of Warwick.

Peach, G.C.K. and Rossiter, D. (1995) Level and nature of spatial concentration and segregation. In: P. Ratcliffe (ed.), *Ethnicity in the 1991 Census, Volume 3: Social Geography in Britain: Geographical Spread, Spatial Concentration and Internal Migration*.

Peach, G.C.K. and Winchester, S.W.C. (1974) Birthplace, ethnicity and the under-enumeration of West Indians, Indians and Pakistanis in censuses of 1966 and 1971. *New Community*, 3, 386–93.

Rees, P. and Phillips, D. (1995) Geographical spread: the national picture. In: P. Ratcliffe (ed.), *Ethnicity in the 1991 Census, Volume 3: Social Geography in Britain: Geographical Spread, Spatial Concentration and Internal Migration.*

Rose, E.J.B., et al. (1969) *Colour and Citizenship: A Report on British Race Relations*. London: Institute of Race Relations.

Simpson, S. (1993) Measuring and coping with local under-enumeration in the 1991 Census. Paper presented to the joint conference of the British Society for Population Studies, IBG Population Geography Study Group, British Section, Regional Science Association and ESRC Census Analysis Group on 'Research on the 1991 Census', University of Newcastle, September 1993.

Sly, F. (1993) Estimating Britain's ethnic minority populations using the Labour Force Survey *Employment Gazette,* September, 429–431.

Storkey, M. and Lewis, R. (1995) London: A True Cosmopolis. In: P. Ratcliffe (ed.), *Ethnicity in the 1991 Census, Volume 3: Social Geography in Britain: Geographical Spread, Spatial Concentration and Internal Migration.*

Chapter 5
Immigration and ethnic group

John Salt

5.1 Introduction

This chapter focuses on information about the international migration of ethnic minority groups, derived from the 1991 Census. Given that this source allows analysis for one year only (1990–91), the first part of the chapter provides a broader statistical context, indicating sources and the various types and levels of international migration to the UK, including some trend analysis.

As Chapter 2 indicates, the ethnic group question is not about immigration *per se*. Indeed, there is no concept of 'immigration' in UK legislation. Despite this, much academic and media comment sees immigrants and settled ethnic minority groups as one and the same, so that 'immigration' is presented by most commentators largely as a movement for settlement purposes of visible minority groups. The resulting confusion tends to obscure the complex nature of immigration to the UK, which involves a wide range of migrant types and motivation: labour, family reunion, settlement, asylum seeking, students, and a plethora of temporary moves. In this chapter the term 'immigrant', based mainly on the definitions used in the various official statistics, refers to those who have recently arrived in the UK (usually within the last year).

One of the few things that migrant and minority groups have in common, is that they are generally poorly captured in the official statistics – which in turn originate from a diversity of sources. Hence, the migration of ethnic groups measured by the census must be seen as only part of the contemporary UK immigration story (albeit an important and visible one), and by no means its entirety. Nevertheless, it has been the immigration of ethnic minority groups, particularly from New Commonwealth sources, that has largely driven UK immigration policy during the last half century.

The period since the Second World War has seen a slow but inevitable shift in British immigration policy. During the late 1940s and 1950s an open door was extended to hundreds of millions of citizens of the Empire and Commonwealth, and to hundreds of thousands of displaced persons from Europe. In the 1960s the door began to close, but not before immigration had set the UK well on course towards a mixed culture society. Legislation in 1962, 1968 and 1971 fundamentally changed the immigration relationship between the mother country and its Commonwealth, though questions of nationality remained unresolved until 1981. On the eve of the British Nationality Act of 1981 some 950 million people worldwide were entitled to some form of British citizenship, if not to the right of abode in the UK. In the 1980s and 1990s new legislation has been designed to control entry still further, and government policy is to bring settlement immigration down to an irreducible minimum.

While the level of the irreducible minimum is debatable, there can be little doubt that in their own terms the policies of successive governments in controlling entry for settlement have been largely successful. In the 1990s its geographical position has allowed the UK largely to avoid the immediate migration pressures from Eastern Europe, from across the Mediterranean basin, and more recently from the former Yugoslavia, that have confronted some European states. The most recent data for the UK show conflicting trends (Salt, 1995). In 1992 and 1993 there was a net loss of population by migration recorded in the statistics from the International Passenger Survey (but see the comment in section 5.2 about the need to adjust the total net flow figure), after nearly a decade of increase, but 1994 again saw a rise. Labour immigration rose during the 1980s, drifted down in the early 1990s in response to the recession before rising again in 1994. Numbers of accept-ances for settlement have been broadly stable for several years, variations from year to year principally reflecting administrative changes. Naturalisa-tion has also fallen. Asylum applications rose dramatically in the late 1980s, peaked in 1991, fell in the next two years, but rose again in 1994 and 1995. It is in this general context that the pattern of international immigration picked up by the 1991 Census has to be viewed.

5.2 Sources of international migration data for the UK

Sources of international migration data for the UK are both partial and complex (Coleman, 1987; Bulusu, 1991). This is a reflection of the rather haphazard way in which the present system has evolved in response to the development of immigration control during the 20th century. Most of the data are based on administrative systems, related to control rather than migrant numbers and characteristics. With the exception of the Interna-tional Passenger Survey, they record only inward movement.

Stock data

The census is one of two sources from which some data on 'migrant' stock may be derived. The definition is by birthplace, though in the absence of year of entry the census data are of little help in providing an estimate except in the broadest terms. Ethnic origin was asked for the first time in 1991, and can be related to birthplace. Because only cross-sectional data are available, the deeper insights that come from trend analysis are missing. Increasing numbers of people in ethnic minority groups are British Citizens. Many were born in the UK, so the ethnic question is of limited use as a migration source. In 1991, 2.14 million people were recorded with a country of birth outside the UK.

The sample Labour Force Survey is the second source of data on migrant stocks. Like the International Passenger Survey (see below) it is voluntary. It was first conducted in 1973, was biennial until 1983 and has been annual since 1984. It is now a quarterly sample survey of about 60 thousand private households and people living in National Health Service accommodation. Each person in the survey is given a weight, or 'grossing factor', but because of the small size of the sample, small numbers may be inaccurate: in an individual quarter the 95 per cent confidence interval for LFS estimates of 10,000 is $\pm$ 4,000. (The use of the LFS in the study of the foreign population and labour force in the UK, together with appropriate technical information, is described in Salt (1995).) Since its inception it has been used increasingly by government departments to obtain information useful in framing social and economic policy. During the 1980s it became widely used as a source of information on the labour force generally, and on the characteristics of ethnic minority groups in particular.

The survey includes all UK and foreign citizens. The nationality question means that all foreigners are included, and the LFS provides the only source of data on EU nationals working in the UK. The application of grossing factors means that one sample interviewee is aggregated up to about 300 people in total. This constitutes a major problem when dealing with foreign nationals, and with specific groups like ethnic minorities. Both flow and stock figures may be below this threshold for individual groups, particularly when any disaggregation into migrant characteristics is attempted. Data are available on nationality, age, sex, occupation, industry, region of destination and ethnicity. Its frequency makes the LFS a useful source for assessing trends. With the exception of ethnicity, most of the tables relating to international migration are unpublished. In 1991, the LFS recorded 1.75 million foreign nationals living in the UK.

A problem with establishing the total number of foreign nationals before 1992 was the large category (commonly 500–600 thousand) recorded with nationality not stated. From 1992 new methods of conducting the LFS have reduced the 'not stated' group to under 10 thousand. One consequence of this change is that the time series of nationality data from the LFS is broken between 1991 and 1992.

Flow data

Migrant flow data come from more varied sources. The International Passenger Survey is a continuing voluntary sample survey conducted by the Office of Population Censuses and Surveys which covers the principal air and sea routes between the UK and overseas, but excludes those between the UK and Eire. It is the only demographic source giving both immigration and emigration statistics, thus it has considerable value. Its results, with a lag of about 18 months, are published annually in OPCS Series MN *International Migration*.

Most of those surveyed are short-term travellers, but a sub-sample of 'migrants' is identified. A migrant into the UK is a person who has resided abroad for a year or more and on entering has declared the intention to stay in the UK for a year or more. A migrant from the UK is a person who has resided in the UK for a year or more and on leaving has declared the intention to reside abroad for a year or more. These definitions are coincidental with those of the United Nations. In 1991, the IPS recorded 267 thousand immigrants.

Data are available on citizenship, country of origin, destination region, age, sex, occupational status, but not ethnicity. Unfortunately, the sample size of migrants is small, around 2,500 in all, giving an overall standard error of around 5 per cent after grossing up. Hence, any breakdown by particular variables, such as country of origin or region of destination, becomes almost impossible because the standard errors are too high. Thus its use as an indicator of the characteristics of migrants is very limited. Also, the definition of migrant is based on intention to stay, and there is no guarantee that those recorded as migrants do actually come or go for the specified period. For example, it is likely that the data exclude persons seeking asylum after entering the country and other persons admitted as short-term visitors who are subsequently granted an extension of stay for a year or longer, perhaps as students or after marriage. It is estimated that there were around 50 thousand such persons in 1991 and in 1992, net of persons leaving the UK for a short-term period who stayed overseas for longer than originally intended. This adjustment needs to be added to the IPS migration data to give a better estimate of *actual* net migration, i.e. a net inflow of 40 thousand persons in 1992. Similar estimated adjustments ranging from around 10 thousand in 1982 to 50 thousand in 1991, and averaging around 20 thousand a year, should be made to the IPS data for 1982–91 (Home Office, 1994, 27). Unfortunately, there is no way of allocating the adjustment to flow origins or composition.

Both the LFS and the census provide transition data on immigrants to the UK, by asking for address one year ago. They do not provide full flow data. Because of the small sample size in the LFS, breakdowns showing the characteristics of individual nationalities or ethnic groups are rarely possible. In 1991, the LFS recorded 269 thousand immigrants, a similar number to that provided by the IPS.

There is a question in the census about place of residence a year ago, but none on nationality, nor year in which foreign nationals settled in the UK, nor country from which they came. Data for migrants are available by age, sex, ethnic group and country of birth. In 1991, the census recorded 326,398 migrants to Great Britain, a figure substantially larger than those of the LFS and IPS. The reasons for these discrepancies are several. The census figure can be expected to be larger than that of the IPS because of the definitional difference (the IPS figure includes only those intending to stay for a year or more) and because it includes those coming across the Irish Sea. The difference with the LFS is less obvious, but is likely to be related to the fact that the census is mandatory while the LFS is voluntary, the inclusion in the LFS (prior to 1992) of only those in private households, and the survey method.

There are some other sources of flow data relating to specific groups. Home Office statistics result primarily from enquiries made in the process of immigration control. Data on foreign nationals accepted for settlement are a by-product of immigration control and are popularly regarded as the main measure of longer-term (settlement) immigration. They are published annually in the Home Office's *Control of Immigration Statistics*. The National Health Service Central Register allocates a new NHS number and prepares a migration record for all new patients with a place of birth stated to be abroad. No information on the actual resident status of the person is available. The data may include some short-stay visitors, and settled immigrants who have been in the UK for some years.

There are some data relating only to those foreigners entering for employment, most notably from the issue (by the Department of Employment) of work permits, and the record (by the DSS) of national insurance contributions. In 1991, work permit issues totalled 28,978, and 117,597 newly entering foreign workers paid at least one national insurance contribution.

A recent review and evaluation of UK international migration data is in Salt, Singleton and Hogarth (1994).

Comparison of sources

It is apparent from the discussion above that no direct comparison may be made of the estimates of stocks and flows from the census and other sources, since concepts and definitions differ. The measurement of 'migrant' stock based on birthplace (census) gives a figure for 1991, 22 per cent higher than that based on nationality (from the LFS). The flow figure derived from the census is a similar percentage higher than those from the IPS and LFS. Thus, estimates of 'international migration' derived from the census are higher than those from the other major sources, but they are measuring different things.

The picture of international migration by ethnicity that may be derived from the census is partial in many respects. It is not possible to relate ethnicity to nationality through the census, nor to country of origin and destination. Nor do the data allow a distinction between those entering Britain for the first time and those who have been resident before, and are returning after a period abroad. This inability to distinguish the characteristics of those involved, and their origins and destinations, severely limits the use that may be made of census data as a source for international migration analysis. Although the LFS in theory allows ethnicity and nationality to be related, the small sample size leads mostly to blank cells.

5.3 Recent trends in international migration

Immigration and emigration from the UK

In recent years, the pattern of overall inflow has fluctuated around a rising trend. Inflows of non-nationals have consistently run ahead of those of British citizens (a group that would include substantial numbers of the ethnic minority population), especially from the mid-1980s onwards (Figure 5.1). The trend in outflows (Figure 5.2) is less clear. The large increase in outflow during the 1979–83 recession, mainly by British nationals, was

Figure 5.1 *International migration; inflow by citizenship, 1975-92, United Kingdom*

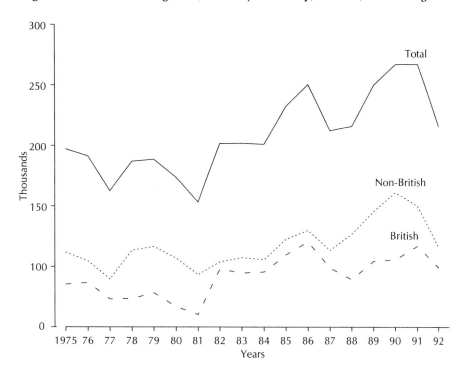

Figure 5.2 *International migration; outflow by citizenship, 1975-92, United Kingdom*

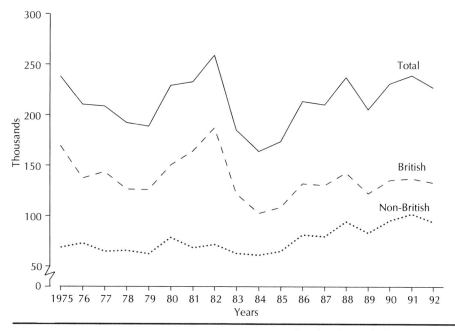

Figure 5.3 *International migration; net flow by citizenship, 1975-92, United Kingdom*

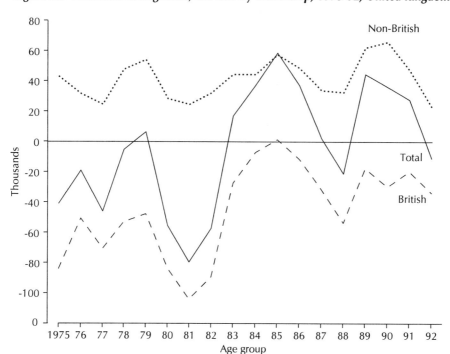

succeeded by comparatively low emigration levels in the middle 1980s. Since then outflows have increased steadily, among both nationals and non-nationals, though it is mainly the former who leave. Net flows were negative for the period 1975–83 (with the brief exception of 1979), then largely positive, except for 1988 and 1992 (Figure 5.3). The fluctuations depicted in Figure 5.3 reflect for the most part emigration by British people, among whom there was a net outflow for the whole period, apart from the break-even year of 1985. Net flows of non-nationals were positive throughout the period, the pattern broadly reflecting economic conditions, but with the amplitude of fluctuation much less than that of British people.

Acceptances for settlement

During the last two decades the number of acceptances for settlement steadily declined from over 70 thousand to a trough of 46 thousand in 1987, since when numbers have drifted slowly upwards (to 55.6 thousand in 1993) (Home Office, 1994). The vast majority of those granted settlement now are already resident in the UK. Most of the fluctuations in numbers of acceptances in recent years reflect technical and administrative changes in entry criteria and procedures, recorded in successive volumes of *Control of Immigration Statistics.*

A quarter of acceptances in 1993 were from the Indian subcontinent (ISC), a fifth from elsewhere in Asia, 19 per cent from Africa and 14 per cent from the Americas. The importance of Commonwealth links is still strong: 50 per cent of acceptances in 1993 were from the New Commonwealth, 6 per cent from the Old. In recent years acceptances from the latter have fallen (they were 16 per cent of the total in 1989), reflecting the fall in acceptances of Commonwealth citizens with UK-born grandparents.

Trends in recent years show some major changes in origins. The proportion of acceptances from the ISC has fallen from nearly a third to a quarter since 1983, while that from Africa has risen significantly. Acceptances from Africa have more than doubled from the annual average of 4.4 thousand in the years 1980–86. The Other – Asia group has also increased, from 16 to 20 per cent. Eastern Europe's proportion has doubled, but only to 2 per cent, while that from Western Europe has declined, along with that from Australasia.

Labour migration

It is not easy to establish the scale of foreign labour inflows on to the UK labour market, because different sources give different answers. Table 5.1 summarises foreign worker flows from the four available sources: work permits, the LFS, the IPS, and DSS national insurance statistics. These measure different groups. Work permits exclude EU nationals, so the numbers are low. DSS figures are high, partly because they encompass many people who work for short periods only (including EU nationals), perhaps on a casual basis. IPS data exclude the Irish, and should therefore be lower than those from the LFS, but they are not; the reasons for this are not known.

There is some evidence that EU sources have become less important in the 1990s, though the IPS figures are distorted by the absence of the Irish. The LFS and DSS both suggest that around 40 per cent of incoming foreign workers are from other EU countries.

Asylum

The number of applications for asylum ran at 4 to 5 thousand per annum during most of the 1980s, rose steeply in 1989, and peaked at almost 45

Table 5.1 *Flows of foreign national workers, 1986-94*

	1986	1987	1988	1989	1990	1991	1992	1993	1994
Work Permits (1)	18,688	20,348	25,974	29,730	34,627	28,978	30,051	29,329	30,092
Labour Force Survey (2)	34,953	40,317	45,459	53,400	54,995	50,500	35,400	37,100	45,652
International Passenger Survey (3)	61,400	53,900	65,000	68,600	85,500	75,000	54,300	51,600	65,700
Social Security (4)	109,897	93,847	106,008	108,839	105,466	114,521	117,597	107,972	125,773

Sources: (1) Department for Education and Employment, unpublished.
(2) Central Statistical Office, unpublished
(3) OPCS, *Population Trends*, quarterly
(4) Department of Social Security, unpublished

thousand in 1991. The following year it almost halved, and it fell again in 1993, to 22.4 thousand. However, data for 1994 show a steep rise in applications to 32.8 thousand, and, provisionally, over 40 thousand in 1995.

Only a small proportion of applicants receive full refugee status (4 per cent of all decisions in 1994), though more (17 per cent in 1994) are granted extended leave to remain. These two groups are allowed to stay in the UK, though there are no data on how long they ultimately remain. Of those refused asylum, it is thought that most manage to stay in the country illegally.

5.4   Immigrants and ethnic minority groups

The immigrations associated with the regimes of movement described above have contributed enormously to the contemporary diversity of the British population. In so far as they have maintained their own cultural characteristics, and transmitted them through the generations, they have created the multicultural society part of which is measured demographically in the ethnic tables of the census.

A distinction needs to be made between 'immigrants' and 'ethnic minority groups' (Coleman and Salt, 1992). British legislation does not recognise the concept of 'immigrant' (or 'emigrant'), though conventionally the term refers to a person who has recently moved home for a defined period (normally anything from 3 to 12 months – the latter in the case of the UK International Passenger Survey). In this section, the definition of immigrant is that from the census, namely someone who was living abroad a year before. An ethnic minority is a culturally defined group, defined on such bases as religion, language, social or family structure, or value systems. Its members may not have been recently (or ever) mobile internationally. Conceptually, therefore, immigrants and ethnic minority groups are very different, and certainly not coterminous groups. Hence, study of the migration patterns of ethnic groups tells us more about the latter than about the national patterns and processes of international migration.

Population by ethnic group and country of birth

The census records an ethnic minority population of 3.02 million, 5.5 per cent of the total GB population (54.8 million) (Table 5.2 (a)). Altogether about 3.7 million persons were born outside the UK, of whom 2.14 million (57.2 per cent) were White, and 1.6 million were from an ethnic minority group. While only 4.1 per cent of the White population were born outside the UK, this was the case for over half (53 per cent) of the ethnic minority population. Overall, 45 per cent of those born outside the UK were from the New Commonwealth and 34 per cent from Europe (including the Irish Republic).

There are considerable differences between the ethnic minority groups in the proportions born inside and outside the UK. Around three quarters of Asians and Chinese, and nearly two thirds of Bangladeshis were born outside the UK. In contrast, over half of the Black–Caribbean group (53.7 per cent), and most (84.5 per cent) of the Black–Other group were born in the UK. These variations principally reflect recency of immigration. The proportion of the Black–Other group born outside the UK is particularly low because it represents the fruits of mixed marriages, most of which will have occurred between persons already resident in the UK.

Analysis of ethnic groups by country of birth shows the expected pattern of most Black–Africans, Black–Caribbeans, and those from the Indian subcontinent, who were not born in the UK, being born in the New Commonwealth (Table 5.2 (a) to (c)). This was also the case for the Chinese and Asians, but with substantial proportions born in non-Commonwealth Asia (probably from the People's Republic of China via Hong Kong for many Chinese). The Other ethnic group, not surprisingly, shows the widest dispersion of birthplaces.

There was a slight preponderance of females (52 per cent) over males among those born outside the UK; however, the split was 50:50 among the ethnic minority population. Analysis of the male:female ratio for each country of birth group reveals little variation by ethnicity. The main differences occur in Bangladeshis and Asians from the New Commonwealth, among whom males are relatively more important. In contrast, Asians and Others, born in non-Commonwealth Asia, contain relatively more women.

Immigration by country of birth

Of the total number of immigrants who moved to live in Great Britain in the year before the 1991 Census (326,398), 59 per cent were born outside the UK (Table 5.3 (a)). As nationality is not recorded in the census, there can be no indication of how many of these are returning Britons. However, the proportion is broadly similar to the 56 per cent of immigrants to the UK who were foreign nationals, recorded in the IPS.

Europe was the main source region (54,124), accounting for 28 per cent of all immigrants. This is considerably less than European representation by nationality in flow figures derived from the LFS (54 per cent). About 22 per cent of those born in Europe were from the Irish Republic. Countries of the New Commonwealth provided 24 per cent (45,757) of those born outside the UK, those from the Old Commonwealth just under half that number. Overall, the Commonwealth as a whole was the birthplace of just over a third of all immigrants.

Analysis by age shows the dominance of the younger workforce group (aged 20–44), though there are some variations by country of birth. This is a particularly dominant group among those from the Old Commonwealth, in contrast to those from Africa. Africans, Asians, Americans and those from the rest of the world (ROW) have above average proportions of children, though not of 'students' (aged 16–19). The New Commonwealth and the former USSR, and to a lesser extent the Irish Republic, have above average proportions of entrants (for those born outside the UK) in the older (over 60) category. Overall, the age profile of those born outside the UK is younger than those from within.

Text continues page 140

Table 5.2(a) *Total population by country of birth and ethnic group*

Country of birth	Great Britain - Total numbers		Ethnic group			
	White	Non White	Black-Caribbean	Black-African	Black-Other	Indian
Total persons	51,873,794	3,015,050	499,964	212,362	178,401	840,255
United Kingdom	49,732,161	1,410,561	268,337	77,333	150,662	352,473
Outside UK	2,141,633	1,604,489	231,627	135,029	27,739	487,782
Irish Republic	587,011	5,539	1,060	638	913	980
EU (excl. UK and Ireland)	485,752	8,138	847	827	1,419	705
Rest of Europe	172,184	1,962	121	274	261	316
Old Commonwealth	173,635	3,720	171	350	435	538
New Commonwealth	340,555	1,347,841	226,496	100,758	13,418	475,391
Turkey	24,088	2,509	62	40	445	28
USSR	26,567	444	20	64	52	17
Africa (excluding above)	94,973	51,896	382	28,928	1,364	3,969
America (excluding above)	161,375	23,658	2,102	2,016	7,728	549
Asia (excluding above)	74,555	156,490	305	1,126	1,591	4,036
Rest of World	938	2,292	61	8	113	1,253
Total	51,873,794	3,015,050	499,964	212,362	174,401	840,255
% Columns						
United Kingdom	95.9	46.8	53.7	36.4	84.5	41.9
Outside UK	4.1	53.2	46.3	63.6	15.5	58.1
Irish Republic	1.1	0.2	0.2	0.3	0.5	0.1
EU (excl. UK and Ireland)	0.9	0.3	0.2	0.4	0.8	0.1
Rest of Europe	0.3	0.1	0.0	0.1	0.1	0.0
Old Commonwealth	0.3	0.1	0.0	0.2	0.2	0.1
New Commonwealth	0.7	44.7	45.3	47.4	7.5	56.6
Turkey	0.0	0.1	0.0	0.0	0.2	0.0
USSR	0.1	0.0	0.0	0.0	0.0	0.0
Africa (excluding above)	0.2	1.7	0.1	13.6	0.8	0.5
America (excluding above)	0.3	0.8	0.4	0.9	4.3	0.1
Asia (excluding above)	0.1	5.2	0.1	0.5	0.9	0.5
Rest of World	0.0	0.1	0.0	0.0	0.1	0.1
Total	100	100	100	100	100	100
% Rows						
United Kingdom	97.2	2.8	0.5	0.2	0.3	0.7
Outside UK	57.2	42.8	6.2	3.6	0.7	13.0
Irish Republic	99.1	0.9	0.2	0.1	0.2	0.2
EU (excl. UK and Ireland)	98.4	1.6	0.2	0.2	0.3	0.1
Rest of Europe	98.9	1.1	0.1	0.2	0.1	0.2
Old Commonwealth	97.9	2.1	0.1	0.2	0.2	0.3
New Commonwealth	20.2	79.8	13.4	6.0	0.8	28.2
Turkey	90.6	9.4	0.2	0.2	1.7	0.1
USSR	98.4	1.6	0.1	0.2	0.2	0.1
Africa (excluding above)	64.7	35.3	0.3	19.7	0.9	2.7
America (excluding above)	87.2	12.8	1.1	1.1	4.2	0.3
Asia (excluding above)	32.3	67.7	0.1	0.5	0.7	1.7
Rest of World	29.0	71.0	1.9	0.2	3.5	38.8
Total	94.5	5.5	0.9	0.4	0.3	1.5

Source: OPCS (1993) 1991 Census, and Ethnic group country of birth, Great Britain Vol 1. Table 5.

Pakistani	Bangladeshi	Chinese	Other Asian	Other	Total	
476,555	162,835	156,938	197,534	290,206	54,888,844	Total persons
240,558	59,679	44,676	43,269	173,574	51,142,722	United Kingdom
235,997	103,156	112,262	154,265	116,632	3,746,122	Outside UK
352	125	239	328	904	592,550	Irish Republic
705	88	521	651	2,375	493,890	EU (excl. UK and Ireland)
100	18	63	106	70	174,146	Rest of Europe
56	26	391	197	1,556	177,355	Old Commonwealth
233,509	102,679	77,691	78,665	39,234	1,688,396	New Commonwealth
25	21	14	194	1,680	26,597	Turkey
4	4	32	70	181	27,011	USSR
179	40	325	1,129	15,580	146,869	Africa (excluding above)
142	27	364	977	9,753	185,033	America (excluding above)
900	126	32,593	71,528	44,285	231,045	Asia (excluding above)
25	2	29	420	381	3,230	Rest of World
476,555	162,835	156,938	197,534	290,206	54,888,844	Total
						% Columns
50.5	36.6	28.5	21.9	59.8	93.2	United Kingdom
49.5	63.4	71.5	78.1	40.2	6.8	Outside UK
0.1	0.1	0.2	0.2	0.3	1.1	Irish Republic
0.1	0.1	0.3	0.3	0.8	0.9	EU (excl. UK and Ireland)
0.0	0.0	0.0	0.1	0.2	0.3	Rest of Europe
0.0	0.0	0.2	0.1	0.5	0.3	Old Commonwealth
49.0	63.1	49.5	39.8	13.5	3.1	New Commonwealth
0.0	0.0	0.0	0.1	0.6	0.0	Turkey
0.0	0.0	0.0	0.0	0.1	0.0	USSR
0.0	0.0	0.2	0.6	5.4	0.3	Africa (excluding above)
0.0	0.0	0.2	0.5	3.4	0.3	America (excluding above)
0.2	0.1	20.8	36.2	15.3	0.4	Asia (excluding above)
0.0	0.0	0.0	0.2	0.1	0.0	Rest of World
100	100	100	100	100	100	Total
						% Rows
0.5	0.1	0.1	0.1	0.3	100	United Kingdom
6.3	2.8	3.0	4.1	3.1	100	Outside UK
0.1	0.0	0.0	0.1	0.2	100	Irish Republic
0.1	0.0	0.1	0.1	0.5	100	EU (excl. UK and Ireland)
0.1	0.0	0.0	0.1	0.4	100	Rest of Europe
0.0	0.0	0.2	0.1	0.9	100	Old Commonwealth
13.8	6.1	4.6	4.7	2.3	100	New Commonwealth
0.1	0.1	0.1	0.7	6.3	100	Turkey
0.0	0.0	0.1	0.3	0.7	100	USSR
0.1	0.0	0.2	0.8	10.6	100	Africa (excluding above)
0.1	0.0	0.2	0.5	5.3	100	America (excluding above)
0.4	0.1	14.1	31.0	19.2	100	Asia (excluding above)
0.8	0.1	0.9	13.0	11.8	100	Rest of World
0.9	0.3	0.3	0.4	0.5	100	Total

Table 5.2(b) *Male population by country of birth and ethnic group*

Country of birth	Great Britain - Males		Ethnic group			
	White	Non White	Black-Caribbean	Black-African	Black-Other	Indian
Total Males	25,066,379	1,508,575	239,484	106,800	87,513	422,891
United Kingdom	24,073,295	702,822	128,378	38,339	73,618	178,871
Outside UK	993,084	805,753	111,106	68,461	13,895	244,020
Irish Republic	271,568	2,770	550	327	467	481
EU (excl. UK and Ireland)	204,889	3,949	388	414	674	355
Rest of Europe	81,368	953	57	134	146	150
Old Commonwealth	79,004	1,814	89	159	237	247
New Commonwealth	165,213	676,420	108,616	49,687	6,258	237,922
Turkey	13,575	1,495	40	25	265	9
USSR	16,771	224	15	23	27	8
Africa (excluding above)	45,467	29,285	197	15,979	696	1,747
America (excluding above)	77,366	11,800	966	1,121	4,302	254
Asia (excluding above)	37,414	75,911	155	590	753	2,267
Rest of World	449	1,132	33	2	70	580
Total	25,066,379	1,508,575	239,484	106,800	87,513	422,891
% Columns						
United Kingdom	96.0	46.6	53.6	35.9	84.1	42.3
Outside UK	4.0	53.4	46.4	64.12	15.9	57.7
Irish Republic	1.1	0.2	0.2	0.3	0.5	0.1
EU (excl. UK and Ireland)	0.8	0.3	0.2	0.4	0.8	0.1
Rest of Europe	0.3	0.1	0.0	0.1	0.2	0.0
Old Commonwealth	0.3	0.1	0.0	0.1	0.3	0.1
New Commonwealth	0.7	44.8	45.3	45.4	7.2	56.3
Turkey	0.1	0.1	0.0	0.0	0.3	0.0
USSR	0.1	0.0	0.0	0.0	0.0	0.0
Africa (excluding above)	0.2	1.9	0.1	15.0	0.8	0.4
America (excluding above)	0.3	0.8	0.4	1.0	4.9	0.1
Asia (excluding above)	0.1	5.0	0.1	0.6	0.9	0.5
Rest of World	0.0	0.1	0.0	0.0	0.1	0.1
Total	100	100	100	100	100	100
% Rows						
United Kingdom	97.2	2.8	0.5	0.2	0.3	0.7
Outside UK	55.2	44.8	6.2	3.8	0.8	13.6
Irish Republic	99.0	1.0	0.2	0.1	0.2	0.2
EU (excl. UK and Ireland)	98.1	1.9	0.2	0.2	0.3	0.2
Rest of Europe	98.8	1.2	0.1	0.2	0.2	0.2
Old Commonwealth	97.8	2.2	0.1	0.2	0.3	0.3
New Commonwealth	19.6	80.4	12.9	5.9	0.7	28.3
Turkey	90.1	9.9	0.3	0.2	1.8	0.1
USSR	98.7	1.3	0.1	0.1	0.2	0.0
Africa (excluding above)	60.8	39.2	0.3	21.4	0.9	2.3
America (excluding above)	86.8	13.2	1.1	1.3	4.8	0.3
Asia (excluding above)	33.0	67.0	0.1	0.5	0.7	2.0
Rest of World	28.4	71.6	2.1	0.1	4.4	36.7
Total	94.3	5.7	0.9	0.4	0.3	1.6

Source: OPCS (1993) 1991 Census, Ethnic group and country of birth, Great Britain Vol 1. Table 5.

Pakistani	Bangladeshi	Chinese	Other Asian	Other	Total	
245,572	84,944	77,669	93,605	150,097	26,574,954	Total persons
122,808	30,131	22,876	21,547	86,254	24,776,117	United Kingdom
122,764		54,813	54,793	72,058	63,843	1,798,837 Outside UK
176	62	112	148	447	274,338	Irish Republic
385	46	269	296	1,122	208,838	EU (excl. UK and Ireland)
54	9	36	44	323	82,321	Rest of Europe
37	14	183	99	749	80,818	Old Commonwealth
121,454	54,570	38,507	40,646	18,760	841,633	New Commonwealth
15	9	8	123	1,001	15,070	Turkey
4	4	13	37	93	16,995	USSR
77	19	155	543	9,872	74,752	Africa (excluding above)
77	15	144	468	4,453	89,166	America (excluding above)
472	63	15,359	29,429	26,823	113,325	Asia (excluding above)
13	2	7	225	200	1,581	Rest of World
245,572	84,944	77,669	93,605	150,097	26,574,954	Total
					% Columns	
50.0	35.5	29.5	23.0	57.5	93.2	United Kingdom
50.0	64.5	70.5	77.0	42.5	6.8	Outside UK
0.1	0.1	0.1	0.2	0.3	1.0	Irish Republic
0.2	0.1	0.3	0.3	0.7	0.8	EU (excl. UK and Ireland)
0.0	0.0	0.0	0.0	0.2	0.3	Rest of Europe
0.0	0.0	0.2	0.1	0.5	0.3	Old Commonwealth
49.5	64.2	49.6	43.4	12.5	3.2	New Commonwealth
0.0	0.0	0.0	0.1	0.7	0.1	Turkey
0.0	0.0	0.0	0.0	0.1	0.1	USSR
0.0	0.0	0.2	0.6	6.6	0.3	Africa (excluding above)
0.0	0.0	0.2	0.5	3.0	0.3	America (excluding above)
0.2	0.1	19.8	31.4	17.9	0.4	Asia (excluding above)
0.0	0.0	0.0	0.2	0.1	0.0	Rest of World
100	100	100	100	100	100	Total
					% Row	
0.5	0.1	0.1	0.1	0.3	100	United Kingdom
6.8	3.0	3.0	4.0	3.5	100	Outside UK
0.1	0.0	0.0	0.1	0.2	100	Irish Republic
0.2	0.0	0.1	0.1	0.5	100	EU (excl. UK and Ireland)
0.1	0.0	0.0	0.1	0.4	100	Rest of Europe
0.0	0.0	0.2	0.1	0.9	100	Old Commonwealth
14.4	6.5	4.6	4.8	2.2	100	New Commonwealth
0.1	0.1	0.1	0.8	6.6	100	Turkey
0.0	0.0	0.1	0.2	0.5	100	USSR
0.1	0.0	0.2	0.7	13.2	100	Africa (excluding above)
0.1	0.0	0.2	0.5	5.0	100	America (excluding above)
0.4	0.1	13.6	26.0	23.7	100	Asia (excluding above)
0.8	0.1	0.4	14.2	12.7	100	Rest of World
0.9	0.3	0.3	0.4	0.6	100	Total

Table 5.2(c)   *Female population by country of birth and ethnic group*

Country of birth	Great Britain - Females		Ethnic group			
	White	Non White	Black-Caribbean	Black-African	Black-Other	Indian
Total Females	26,807,415	1,506,475	260,480	105,562	90,888	417,364
United Kingdom	25,658,866	707,739	139,959	38,994	77,044	173,602
Outside UK	1,148,549	798,736	120,521	66,568	13,844	243,762
Irish Republic	315,443	2,769	510	311	446	499
EU (excl. UK and Ireland)	280,863	4,189	459	413	745	350
Rest of Europe	90,816	1,009	64	140	115	166
Old Commonwealth	94,631	1,906	82	191	198	291
New Commonwealth	175,342	671,421	117,880	51,071	7,160	237,469
Turkey	10,513	1,014	22	15	180	19
USSR	9,796	220	5	41	25	9
Africa (excluding above)	49,506	22,611	185	12,949	668	2,222
America (excluding above)	84,009	11,858	1,136	895	3,426	295
Asia (excluding above)	37,141	80,579	150	536	838	1,769
Rest of World	489	1,160	28	6	43	673
Total	26,807,415	1,506,475	260,480	105,562	90,888	417,364
% Columns						
United Kingdom	95.7	47.0	53.7	36.9	84.8	41.6
Outside UK	4.3	53.0	46.3	63.1	15.2	58.4
Irish Republic	1.2	0.2	0.2	0.3	0.5	0.1
EU (excl. UK and Ireland)	1.0	0.3	0.2	0.4	0.8	0.1
Rest of Europe	0.3	0.1	0.0	0.1	0.1	0.0
Old Commonwealth	0.4	0.1	0.0	0.2	0.2	0.1
New Commonwealth	0.7	44.6	45.3	48.4	7.9	56.9
Turkey	0.0	0.1	0.0	0.0	0.2	0.0
USSR	0.0	0.0	0.0	0.0	0.0	0.0
Africa (excluding above)	0.2	1.5	0.1	12.3	0.7	0.5
America (excluding above)	0.3	0.8	0.4	0.8	3.8	0.1
Asia (excluding above)	0.1	5.3	0.1	0.5	0.9	0.4
Rest of World	0.0	0.1	0.0	0.0	0.0	0.2
Total	100	100	100	100	100	100
% Rows						
United Kingdom	97.3	2.7	0.5	0.1	0.3	0.7
Outside UK	59.0	41.0	6.2	3.4	0.7	12.5
Irish Republic	99.1	0.9	0.2	0.1	0.1	0.2
EU (excl. UK and Ireland)	98.5	1.5	0.2	0.1	0.3	0.1
Rest of Europe	98.9	1.1	0.1	0.2	0.1	0.2
Old Commonwealth	98.0	2.0	0.1	0.2	0.2	0.3
New Commonwealth	20.7	79.3	13.9	6.0	0.8	28.0
Turkey	92.2	8.8	0.2	0.1	1.6	0.2
USSR	97.8	2.2	0.0	0.4	0.2	0.1
Africa (excluding above)	68.6	31.4	0.3	18.0	0.9	3.1
America (excluding above)	87.6	12.4	1.2	0.9	3.6	0.3
Asia (excluding above)	31.6	68.4	0.1	0.5	0.7	1.5
Rest of World	29.7	70.3	1.7	0.4	2.6	40.8
Total	94.7	5.3	0.9	0.4	0.3	1.5

Source: OPCS (1993) 1991 Census, Ethnic group and country of birth, Great Britain Vol 1. Table 5.

Pakistani	Bangladeshi	Chinese	Other Asian	Other	Total	
230.983	77,891	79,269	103,929	140,109	28,313,890	Total persons
117,750	29,548	21,800	21,722	87,320	26,366,605	United Kingdom
113,233	48,343	57,469	82,207	52,789	1,947,285	Outside UK
176	63	127	180	457	318,212	Irish Republic
320	42	252	355	1,253	285,052	EU (excl. UK and Ireland)
46	9	27	62	380	91,825	Rest of Europe
319	12	208	98	807	96,537	Old Commonwealth
112,055	48,109	39,184	38,019	20,474	846,763	New Commonwealth
10	12	6	71	679	11,527	Turkey
0	0	19	33	88	10,016	USSR
102	21	170	586	5,708	72,117	Africa (excluding above)
65	12	220	509	5,300	95,867	America (excluding above)
428	63	17,234	42,099	17,462	117,720	Asia (excluding above)
12	0	22	195	181	1,649	Rest of World
23,983	77,891	79,269	103,929	140,109	28,313,890	Total
						% Columns
51.0	37.9	27.5	20.9	62.3	93.1	United Kingdom
49.0	62.1	72.5	79.1	37.7	6.9	Outside UK
0.1	0.1	0.2	0.2	0.3	1.1	Irish Republic
0.1	0.1	0.3	0.3	0.9	1.0	EU (excl. UK and Ireland)
0.0	0.0	0.0	0.1	0.3	0.3	Rest of Europe
0.0	0.0	0.3	0.1	0.6	0.3	Old Commonwealth
48.5	61.8	49.4	36.6	14.6	3.0	New Commonwealth
0.0	0.0	0.0	0.1	0.5	0.0	Turkey
0.0	0.0	0.0	0.0	0.1	0.1	USSR
0.0	0.0	0.2	0.6	4.1	0.3	Africa (excluding above)
0.0	0.0	0.3	0.5	3.8	0.3	America (excluding above)
0.2	0.1	21.7	40.5	12.5	0.4	Asia (excluding above)
0.0	0.0	0.0	0.2	0.1	0.0	Rest of World
100	100	100	100	100	100	Total
						% Rows
0.4	0.1	0.1	0.1	0.3	100	United Kingdom
5.8	2.5	3.0	4.2	2.7	100	Outside UK
0.1	0.0	0.0	0.1	0.1	100	Irish Republic
0.1	0.0	0.1	0.1	0.4	100	EU (excl. UK and Ireland)
0.1	0.0	0.0	0.1	0.4	100	Rest of Europe
0.0	0.0	0.2	0.1	0.8	100	Old Commonwealth
13.2	5.7	4.6	4.5	2.4	100	New Commonwealth
0.1	0.1	0.1	0.6	5.9	100	Turkey
0.0	0.0	0.2	0.3	0.9	100	USSR
0.1	0.0	0.2	0.8	7.9	100	Africa (excluding above)
0.1	0.0	0.2	0.5	5.0	100	America (excluding above)
0.4	0.1	14.6	35.8	24.8	100	Asia (excluding above)
0.7	0.0	0.3	11.8	11.0	100	Rest of World
0.8	0.3	0.3	0.4	0.5	100	Total

The breakdown by sex shows an almost 50:50 split among total immigrants (Table 5.3 (b) and (c)). This is replicated in both the 'born in UK' and 'born outside UK' groups, though the latter group contains slightly more women than men. Indeed, for most of the countries of birth listed there was a slight preponderance of women, the principal exceptions being Europe and the Old Commonwealth. For those born outside the UK, there were more female migrants than male in most age-groups (except 45–59).

Immigrants 1990–91 by ethnic group

According to the census, three quarters (246,067) of all immigrants in 1990–91 were White, and a quarter (80,331) were from ethnic minority groups (Table 5.4). Among the latter, the largest group was the Asians (18,160, 5.6 per cent of all immigrants) and Black–Africans (15,536, 4.8 per cent). The comparatively small numbers of immigrants describing themselves as Black–Caribbean reflects their long establishment in Britain, and indicates that the group is not involved in significant chain migration. The numbers of Black–Other are also low, reflecting the UK birthplace of most of this group, and low chain migration. The general age breakdown shows a predictable pattern. The majority of immigrants were aged between 20 and 44, with a slightly higher percentage for White ethnic groups (66.4 per cent) than for ethnic minority groups (60 per cent). There were considerable differences in the age structure of immigrants between the ethnic groups. Ethnic minority group immigrants are more likely than White immigrants to be children (aged 1–15) and students (16–19), less likely to be late middle-aged (45–59), and slightly more likely to be elderly (60 and over). On the face of it, immigration of the ethnic minority population would seem to have a demographic rejuvenating effect, but this cannot be confirmed in the absence of emigration data. Murphy (1995) concludes that there is no noticeable rejuvenating effect.

Some ethnic minority groups contain considerably above average proportions of young people. This is particularly the case for Bangladeshis, Other, Black–Other and Pakistanis. In contrast, Chinese, Indian and Black–Caribbean immigrants contain relatively low proportions of children. In general these differences reflect the recency of the immigration stream, but it is also a consequence of events overseas that have encouraged immigration towards Britain, including the growth in numbers of asylum seekers. At the opposite end of the age spectrum, several groups have relatively high proportions of elderly immigrants, particularly Indians, but also Pakistanis, Bangladeshis and Black–Caribbeans. Black–Africans and Asians, in contrast, have a low grey-haired immigrant representation.

The variations at the end of the age spectrum have their implications for its middle. Bangladeshis and Pakistanis are comparatively ill-represented in the younger workforce group (20–44) , in marked contrast to Black–Africans, Asians and especially Chinese.

In the main, the differences in age structure by ethnic group for the population as a whole are replicated by the two sexes, though there are some differences in detail. Immigrant Indian, Pakistani and Bangladeshi children

Table 5.3(a) *Immigration 1990-91 by country of birth and broad age group: total population*

Country of birth	Great Britain - Total numbers			Age		
	1-15	16-19	20-44	45-59	60+	Total
Total Persons	62,856	18,413	211,630	23,083	10,416	326,398
United Kingdom	21,522	5,910	88,335	12,065	5,431	133,263
Outside UK	41,334	12,503	123,295	11,018	4,985	193,135
Irish Republic	1,399	1,218	8,657	775	380	12,429
EU (excl. UK and Ireland)	7,539	2,424	21,360	1,325	498	33,146
Rest of Europe	1,481	702	5,573	588	205	8,549
Old Commonwealth	3,259	987	15,959	754	234	21,193
New Commonwealth	8,913	3,397	27,752	3,449	2,246	45,757
Turkey	599	200	1,975	89	51	2,914
USSR	130	18	432	67	33	680
Africa (excluding above)	3,390	804	7,244	558	286	12,282
America (excluding above)	7,797	1,558	18,863	1,847	479	30,544
Asia (excluding above)	6,792	1,187	15,402	1,556	572	25,509
Rest of World	35	8	78	10	1	132
Total	62,856	18,413	211,630	23,083	10,416	326,398
% Columns						
United Kingdom	34.2	32.1	41.7	52.3	52.1	40.8
Outside UK	65.8	67.9	58.3	47.7	47.9	59.2
Irish Republic	2.2	6.6	4.1	3.4	3.6	3.8
EU (excl. UK and Ireland)	12.0	13.2	10.1	5.7	4.8	10.2
Rest of Europe	2.4	3.8	2.6	2.5	2.0	2.6
Old Commonwealth	5.2	5.4	7.5	3.3	2.2	6.5
New Commonwealth	14.2	18.4	13.1	14.9	21.6	14.0
Turkey	1.0	1.1	0.9	0.4	0.5	0.9
USSR	0.2	0.1	0.2	0.3	0.3	0.2
Africa (excluding above)	5.4	4.4	3.4	2.4	2.7	3.8
America (excluding above)	12.4	8.5	8.9	8.0	4.6	9.4
Asia (excluding above)	10.8	6.4	7.3	6.7	5.5	7.8
Rest of World	0.1	0.0	0.0	0.0	0.0	0.0
Total	100	100	100	100	100	100
% Rows						
United Kingdom	16.2	4.4	66.3	9.1	4.1	100
Outside UK	21.4	6.5	63.8	5.7	2.6	100
Irish Republic	11.3	9.8	69.7	6.2	3.1	100
EU (excl. UK and Ireland)	22.7	7.3	64.4	4.0	1.5	100
Rest of Europe	17.3	8.2	65.2	6.9	2.4	100
Old Commonwealth	15.4	4.7	75.3	3.6	1.1	100
New Commonwealth	19.5	7.4	60.7	7.5	4.9	100
Turkey	20.6	6.9	67.8	3.1	1.8	100
USSR	19.1	2.6	63.5	9.9	4.9	100
Africa (excluding above)	27.6	6.5	59.0	4.5	2.3	100
America (excluding above)	25.5	5.1	61.8	6.0	1.6	100
Asia (excluding above)	26.6	4.7	60.4	6.1	2.2	100
Rest of World	26.5	6.1	59.1	7.6	0.8	100
Total	19.3	5.6	64.8	7.1	3.2	100

Source: OPCS (1993) 1991 Census, Ethnic group and country of birth, Great Britain Vol 1. Table 4.

Table 5.3(b) *Immigration: 1990-91 by country of birth and broad age group: males*

Country of birth	Great Britain - Males	Age				
	1-15	16-19	20-44	45-59	60+	Total
Total Males	32.133	7,969	104,817	12,542	4,850	162,311
United Kingdom	10,945	2,803	44,967	6,754	2,659	68,128
Outside UK	21,188	5,166	59,850	5,788	2,191	94,183
Irish Republic	727	469	4,018	416	147	5,777
EU (excl. UK and Ireland)	3,931	829	9,645	711	183	15,299
Rest of Europe	748	139	2,428	317	94	3,726
Old Commonwealth	1,684	383	7,246	389	102	9,804
New Commonwealth	4,659	1,468	14,205	1,719	986	23,037
Turkey	328	100	1,105	54	18	1,605
USSR	66	9	174	28	17	294
Africa (excluding above)	1,751	424	4,071	294	129	6,669
America (excluding above)	3,868	829	9,482	978	253	15,410
Asia (excluding above)	3,407	512	7,442	879	261	12,501
Rest of World	19	4	34	3	1	61
Total	32,133	7,969	104,817	12,542	4,850	162,311
% Columns						
United Kingdom	34.1	35.2	42.9	53.9	54.8	42.0
Outside UK	65.9	64.8	57.1	46.1	45.2	58.0
Irish Republic	2.3	5.9	3.8	3.3	3.0	3.6
EU (excl. UK and Ireland)	12.2	10.4	9.2	5.7	3.8	9.4
Rest of Europe	2.3	1.7	2.3	2.5	1.9	2.3
Old Commonwealth	5.2	4.8	6.9	3.1	2.1	6.0
New Commonwealth	14.5	18.4	13.6	13.7	20.3	14.2
Turkey	1.0	1.3	1.1	0.4	0.4	1.0
USSR	0.2	0.1	0.2	0.2	0.4	0.2
Africa (excluding above)	5.4	5.3	3.9	2.3	2.7	4.1
America (excluding above)	12.0	10.4	9.0	7.8	5.2	9.5
Asia (excluding above)	10.6	6.4	7.1	7.0	5.4	7.7
Rest of World	0.1	0.1	0.0	0.0	0.0	0.0
Total	100	100	100	100	100	100
% Rows						
United Kingdom	16.1	4.1	66.0	9.9	3.9	100
Outside UK	22.5	5.5	63.5	6.1	2.3	100
Irish Republic	12.6	8.1	69.6	7.2	2.5	100
EU (excl. UK and Ireland)	25.7	5.4	63.0	4.6	1.2	100
Rest of Europe	20.1	3.7	65.2	8.5	2.5	100
Old Commonwealth	17.2	3.9	73.9	4.0	1.0	100
New Commonwealth	20.2	6.4	61.7	7.5	4.3	100
Turkey	20.4	6.2	68.8	3.4	1.1	100
USSR	22.4	3.1	59.2	9.5	5.8	100
Africa (excluding above)	26.3	6.4	61.0	4.4	1.9	100
America (excluding above)	25.1	5.4	61.5	6.3	1.6	100
Asia (excluding above)	27.3	4.1	59.5	7.0	2.1	100
Rest of World	31.1	6.6	55.7	4.9	1.6	100
Total	19.8	4.9	64.6	7.7	3.0	100

Source: OPCS (1993) 1991 Census, Ethnic group and country of birth, Great Britain Vol 1. Table 4.

Table 5.3(c) *Immigration 1990-91 by country of birth and broad age group: females*

Country of birth	Great Britain - Females	Age				
	1-15	16-19	20-44	45-59	60+	Total
Total Females	30,723	10,444	106,813	10,541	5,566	164,087
United Kingdom	10,577	3,107	43,468	5,311	2,772	65,135
Outside UK	20,146	7,337	63,445	5,230	2,794	98,952
Irish Republic	672	749	4,639	359	233	6,652
EU (excl. UK and Ireland)	3,608	1,595	11,715	614	315	17,847
Rest of Europe	733	563	3,145	271	111	4,823
Old Commonwealth	1,575	604	8,713	365	132	11,389
New Commonwealth	4,254	1,929	13,547	1,730	1,260	22,720
Turkey	271	100	870	35	33	1,309
USSR	64	9	258	39	16	386
Africa (excluding above)	1,639	380	3,173	264	157	5,613
America (excluding above)	3,929	729	9,381	869	226	15,134
Asia (excluding above)	3,385	675	7,960	677	311	13,008
Rest of World	16	4	44	7	0	71
Total	30,723	10,444	106,813	10,541	5,566	164,087
% Columns						
United Kingdom	34.4	29.7	40.6	50.4	49.8	39.7
Outside UK	65.6	70.3	59.4	49.6	50.2	60.3
Irish Republic	2.2	7.2	4.3	3.4	4.2	4.1
EU (excl. UK and Ireland)	11.7	15.3	11.0	5.8	5.7	10.9
Rest of Europe	2.4	5.4	2.9	2.6	2.0	2.9
Old Commonwealth	5.1	5.8	8.2	3.5	2.4	6.9
New Commonwealth	13.8	18.5	12.7	16.4	22.6	13.8
Turkey	0.9	1.0	0.8	0.3	0.6	0.8
USSR	0.2	0.1	0.2	0.4	0.3	0.2
Africa (excluding above)	5.3	3.6	3.0	2.5	2.8	3.4
America (excluding above)	12.8	7.0	8.8	8.2	4.1	9.2
Asia (excluding above)	11.0	6.5	7.5	6.4	5.6	7.9
Rest of World	0.1	0.0	0.0	0.1	0.0	0.0
Total	100	100	100	100	100	100
% Rows						
United Kingdom	16.2	4.8	66.6	8.2	4.3	100
Outside UK	20.4	7.4	64.1	5.3	2.8	100
Irish Republic	10.1	11.3	69.7	5.4	3.5	100
EU (excl. UK and Ireland)	20.2	8.9	65.6	3.4	1.8	100
Rest of Europe	15.2	11.7	65.2	5.6	2.3	100
Old Commonwealth	13.8	5.3	76.5	3.2	1.2	100
New Commonwealth	18.7	8.5	59.6	7.6	5.5	100
Turkey	20.7	7.6	66.5	2.7	2.5	100
USSR	16.6	2.3	66.8	10.1	4.1	100
Africa (excluding above)	29.2	6.8	56.5	4.7	2.8	100
America (excluding above)	26.0	4.8	62.0	5.7	1.5	100
Asia (excluding above)	26.0	5.2	61.2	5.2	2.4	100
Rest of World	22.5	5.6	62.0	9.9	0.0	100
Total	18.7	6.4	65.1	6.4	3.4	100

Source: OPCS (1993) 1991 Census, Ethnic group and country of birth, Great Britain Vol 1. Table 4.

Table 5.4 Immigration 1990-91 by ethnic group and region

Aggregate tables

	Great Britain	England	Scotland	Wales	Northern region	Yorkshire & Humberside	East Midlands	East Anglia	South East	South West	West Midlands	North West	Total
Total persons	326,398	294,773	22,923	8,702	8,012	17,867	14,243	18,867	175,573	24,205	16,147	19,8599	47,569
White	246,067	220,080	19,237	6,750	6,263	13,182	11,113	15,681	126,180	21,891	10,999	14,771	712,214
All ethnic minority groups	80,331	74,693	3,686	1,952	1,749	4,685	3,130	3,186	49,393	2,314	5,148	5,088	235,355
Black-Caribbean	3,056	2,979	46	31	18	131	118	106	2,118	136	236	116	9,091
Black-African	15,536	14,711	509	316	161	552	288	386	11,925	372	446	581	45,783
Black-Other	3,042	2,808	192	42	37	76	109	854	1,425	116	81	110	8,892
Indian	9,995	9,476	319	200	183	424	894	166	6,105	196	969	539	29,466
Pakistani	7,746	7,253	339	154	136	1,309	240	98	3,041	79	1,235	1,115	22,745
Bangladeshi	3,375	3,249	68	58	141	171	91	44	1,965	69	344	424	9,999
Chinese	8,057	7,154	666	237	276	523	436	311	3,869	350	636	753	23,268
Other-Asian	18,160	16,653	864	643	516	936	576	604	11,944	552	776	749	52,973
Other	11,364	10,410	683	271	281	563	378	617	7,001	444	425	701	33,138
Total	326,398	294,773	22,923	8,702	8,012	17,867	14,243	18,867	175,573	24,205	16,147	19,8599	47,569
% Columns													
White	75.4	74.7	83.9	77.6	78.2	73.8	78.0	83.1	71.9	90.4	68.1	74.4	75.2
All ethnic minority groups	24.6	25.3	16.1	22.4	21.8	26.2	22.0	16.9	28.1	9.6	31.9	25.6	24.8
Black-Caribbean	0.9	1.0	0.2	0.4	0.2	0.7	0.8	0.6	1.2	0.6	1.5	0.6	1.0
Black-African	4.8	5.0	2.2	3.6	2.0	3.1	2.0	2.0	6.8	1.5	2.8	2.9	4.8
Black-Other	0.9	1.0	0.8	0.5	0.5	0.4	0.8	4.5	0.8	0.5	0.5	0.6	0.9
Indian	3.1	3.2	1.4	2.3	2.3	2.4	6.3	0.9	3.5	0.8	6.0	2.7	3.1
Pakistani	2.4	2.5	1.5	1.8	1.7	7.3	1.7	0.5	1.7	0.3	7.6	5.6	2.4
Bangladeshi	1.0	1.1	0.3	0.7	1.8	1.0	0.6	0.2	1.1	0.3	2.1	2.1	1.1
Chinese	2.5	2.4	2.9	2.7	3.4	2.9	3.1	1.6	2.2	1.4	3.9	3.8	2.5
Other Asian	5.6	5.6	3.8	7.4	6.4	5.2	4.0	3.2	6.8	2.3	4.8	3.8	5.6
Other	3.5	3.5	3.0	3.1	3.5	3.2	2.7	3.3	4.0	1.8	2.6	3.5	3.5
Total	100	100	100	100	100	100	100	100	100	100	100	100	100

are more likely to be male than female; this is also true of Black–Caribbeans, but not the other two Black groups. Among the over-60 ethnic minority population, males are a smaller proportion than females, except for Bangladeshis, where the reverse is the case.

The dominance of the South East as a destination region is clear. It received 54 per cent (175,573) of all immigrants, and was an even bigger focus for ethnic minority groups (61.5 per cent). This dominance was true for all ethnic groups. The importance of ethnic minority groups in total regional immigration varied. They were relatively less important in Scotland (16.1 per cent of all immigrants), East Anglia (16.9 per cent) and especially in the South West (9.6 per cent), but more important in Yorkshire and Humberside (26.2 per cent), the South East (28.1 per cent), and especially in the West Midlands. With the exception of the South East, the absolute numbers of immigrants into other regions among the different ethnic groups were low, frequently less than 100.

Immigration rates

In order to compare the patterns of immigration by region and by ethnic group, immigration rates have been calculated as follows:

$$\frac{\text{number of immigrants (living abroad a year ago) by region and ethnic group}}{\text{total population by region and ethnic group}} \times 1000).$$

The results are presented in Table 5.5 and Figure 5.4.

The overall immigration rate into Great Britain was 6 per thousand, but the variation between ethnic groups was considerable. The rate for ethnic minority groups as a whole (26.6 per thousand) was over five times higher than that for White ethnic groups.

Table 5.5 *Immigration rate 1990-1991 by ethnic group*

Ethnic group	Per thousand of total population		
	Total	Males	Females
Total persons	6.0	6.1	5.8
White	4.7	4.9	4.6
All ethnic minority groups	26.6	26.7	26.6
Black–Caribbean	6.1	5.9	6.3
Black–African	73.2	79.2	67.0
Black–Other	17.1	17.8	16.4
Indian	11.9	11.1	12.7
Pakistani	16.3	15.7	16.9
Bangladeshi	20.7	19.1	22.6
Chinese	51.3	51.8	50.9
Asian	91.9	93.4	90.7
Other	39.2	39.7	38.5

Source: OPCS (1993) 1991 Census, Ethnic group and country of birth, Great Britain Vols 1 & 2. Tables 5 & 9.

Figure 5.4 *Regional immigration rates 1990-91: total population and ethnic minorities*

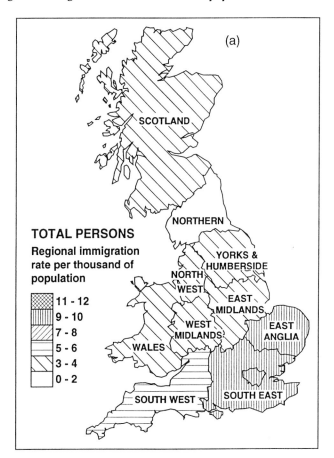

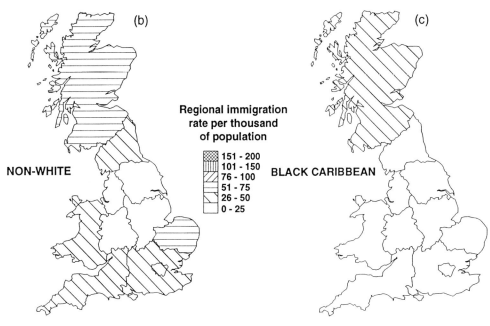

Variations between ethnic minority groups reflect both the recency of the immigration stream, and the size of the stock in that group. Asians had the highest immigration rate (91.9), Black–Caribbeans the lowest (6.1). The rates for Black–Africans and Chinese were also high, far more so than for those of Indian subcontinental (ISC) origin. Even among this last group, however, there were major differences: the rate for Indians was not much more than half that of Bangladeshis.

There were also some variations in immigration rate by sex. For all immigrants, the rate for males was slightly higher than that for females. Male rates were higher for the Black–African, Black–Other and Asian groups, but the reverse was the case for the groups with ISC origins.

Regional immigration rates for the total population (Figure 5.4a) show a broad south–north gradient, with the highest rates in the South East and East Anglia, and the lowest in the Northern region. The pattern for individual groups is more variable, as suggested in Figures 5.4b-k (the scale is constant to allow direct comparison). The rate of immigration for the ethnic minority population as a whole is highest in East Anglia and Scotland, two relatively new overseas immigration regions. It seems likely that this results from the presence in these regions of bases for US Armed Forces (see Chapter 7 by Owen in Volume 3). There are relatively low regional rates for Black–Caribbean, Indian and Pakistani groups, the highest being in Scotland and Wales. Bangladeshis show more regional variation, Scotland having the highest immigration rate for them. Rates for Black–Africans and Asians are universally high, but with very wide regional variations: the former group ranges from 62 per thousand in the North West to 184 per thousand in Scotland, the latter from 68 per thousand in the West Midlands to 188 per thousand in Scotland.

An attempt to explain these patterns is beyond the scope of this chapter. The maps represent a complex interplay between the size and location of the existing ethnic stocks and the number and characteristics of immigrants. In large measure the distributions of immigrants reflect the spread of ethnic minorities across British space, from the regions of their early settlement (especially the South East) into relatively new ones. This process has created a growing stock of population which serves as an attraction for immigration from abroad. Analysis of the extent to which internal migration by individual ethnic minorities is associated with international immigration streams is particularly overdue (see, for example, Salt and Kitching, 1992).

5.5 Conclusions

The future pattern of immigration by ethnic minority groups will depend on several major forces. New flows by foreigners will be heavily influenced by the evolution of government policy. At the moment this shows little sign of major change, and would probably survive a change of government in more or less its present form. Major new initiatives from Brussels may yet bring substantial change, most notably in extending the provisions of free movement to non-Community nationals. The major effects in this regard would probably come initially from Eastern European nationals working in the West, but numbers will probably be modest.

Much will depend, too, on how the ethnic minority groups now settled in Britain evolve. Patterns of family reunion are beginning to stabilise, at least among the older settled groups, but family formation which entails choosing marriage partners from the ethnic origin area prolongs immigration chains.

We must not assume, however, that the immigration of particular ethnic groups is necessarily for settlement purposes. Quite the contrary. As former immigrant groups become settled, particularly from the second generation, many of their members will adopt a similar pattern of international migration to the host population. This will involve periods spent working abroad, from which return migration, as distinct from 'new' immigration is to be expected. This trend is likely to increase as fewer people generally opt for permanent emigration, and temporary movements become the norm.

Finally, any analysis of patterns of immigration by ethnic groups inevitably focuses on the ethnic minority groups. The White population is in many respects just as diverse in its class, cultural and migration characteristics (for example, between Irish construction workers, American senior executives, and Australian youth holidaymakers). This postscript serves to emphasise that ethnicity provides only a partial basis for the study of Britain's international migration.

References

Bulusu, L.(1991) *A review of migration data sources.* Occasional Paper 39. London: OPCS.

Coleman, D.A.(1987/8) United Kingdom statistics on immigration: development and limitations. *International Migration Review*, 21, 1138–69.

Coleman, D.A. and Salt, J.(1992) *The British Population*: patterns, trends and processes. Oxford: Oxford University Press.

Home Office (1994) *Control of Immigration Statistics*. London:HMSO.

Murphy, M. (1995) The impact of migration on population composition: the British case. In Voets, S., Schoorl, J. and B. de Bruijn (eds) *Demographic Consequences of International Migration*. The Hague: Netherlands Interdisciplinary Demographic Institute, 207–224.

Salt, J.(1995) *International migration and the United Kingdom. Report of the UK SOPEMI Correspondent to the OECD.* Migration Research Unit, Department of Geography, University College London.

Salt, J. (1995) Foreign workers in the United Kingdom: evidence from the Labour Force Survey. *Employment Gazette*, January, 11-19.

Salt, J. and Kitching, R.T.(1992) The relationship between international and internal migration. In: A. Champion and A. Fielding (eds), *Migration Processes and Patterns, Volume 1: Research Progress and Prospects*. London: Belhaven, 148–62

Salt, J. and Singleton, A.(1994) *Report on the Extension of the Historical Series of Statistics on International Migration held in the MIGRAT Database.* London: Migration Research Unit, University College London.

Salt, J., Singleton, A. and Hogarth, J.(1994) *Europe's International Migrants.* London: HMSO.

Chapter 6
The age structure and ageing of the ethnic groups

Tony Warnes

6.1 Introduction

This chapter contributes to the understanding of the changing population structure of Britain's contemporary minority ethnic groups, first by examining their age structures in 1991, and second through a theoretical discussion of the processes that are conditioning these structures.

Without exception the ethnic minority populations of Great Britain are presently young, but almost certainly each has seen an increase in the average age and a slight rise in the proportion aged 60 years or more over the past decade (actual figures can be calculated only for birthplace groups because only birthplace is given in previous censuses). Most of the British ethnic minority groups have formed over the last four decades and were, to a large extent, initially attracted as migrant labour, with the usual characteristics of such populations, i.e. strong over-representation of the youngest adult age groups, few elderly people, and unbalanced sex ratios (Coleman, 1982). The latter feature has been variable, however, with the strong male over-representation in the early large migration flows (1950–69) diminishing and, among Caribbean migrants being replaced with female over-representation, partly reflecting employment opportunities and partly family completion (Diamond and Clarke, 1989, Figure 11.1).

As the decades have passed, the settlement of successive cohorts, immigration restrictions and the multiplication of British-born descendents have produced a general demographic tendency for the 'labour migrant' characteristics to weaken and for less atypical age structures to form. Many in the 1950s migrant cohorts, mainly from the West Indies, are now around or approaching the statutory retirement age: for the next few decades there will be substantial increases in the population of elderly ethnic minority people. In addition, the decline in fertility in some ethnic groups (that will be marginally reinforced by improvements in longevity) has produced a tendency for 'demographic ageing'. Projected child shares in these populations will be lower than they would have been had fertility remained at the higher level, and the share of the populations that are elderly will grow more quickly than would have been the case. More importantly for the family and social situation of ethnic minority elderly people, over a period of several decades there will be a reduction in the proportions who came to this country late in life, with neither the English language nor a knowledge of our health and welfare institutions, and who as adult migrants found themselves with an attenuated social network of siblings, cousins and juvenile acquaintances. On the other hand, there will be an increase in the proportion who have raised families in this country, have full citizenship in legal and practical terms, have extended kin networks here and associates from all stages of life.

With 'normalisation' of the age and sex structure, the social concerns and problems of the groups change. The problems of the 'pioneer' migrants included high dependency on marginal occupations with low wage rates, often menial tasks in low-profit industries, and what to do when, as frequently occurred, these jobs were extinguished. At such times a pervasive difficulty becomes acute: how to resolve dual allegiances to the native country and to Britain. One difficult choice was whether to minimise housing expenditure here in anticipation of return, or alternatively to commit one's family and resources to a home in this country. Gradually, one suspects, the initially high rates have declined of transient residence in this country and of 'turnover' or replacement of the individual members of the ethnic groups. The idea of returning is steadily eroded, except for some in association with retirement, and becomes inapplicable to later generations (Tizard and Phoenix, 1993). As commitment to this country strengthens, so concerns will grow about, for example, the education of children, their employment prospects and support when they establish their own homes and begin families, the difficulties of those made redundant in middle life, and not least, the well-being and care of retired and frail elderly people (Cameron *et al.*, 1989; Donaldson, 1986; McCalman, 1990).

This chapter attempts to promote understanding of the socio-economic implications of age structure change in Britain's ethnic minority populations. It first examines the age structures of each male and female ethnic group population (as recognised through the 1991 Census question). Each age structure is compared with all others and with the Great Britain aggregate population. The Other – Other category employed in the tenfold ethnic group output classification is treated as a residual, mainly because it includes people who refused to provide information on their ethnic group. Little value could be seen in close study of these 290,000 people (0.5 per cent of the Great Britain population) and they have been pooled with the 94.5 per cent who described themselves as White (which term henceforth describes the amalgam). The comparisons are therefore of the resident populations among 18 sex-specific ethnic groups.

A detailed examination of under-enumeration has not been undertaken here. The 1991 Census Validation Survey, and more successfully birth records and electoral rolls, point to differential under-enumeration of the ethnic minority groups compared to the White population, partly because of the concentration of ethnic minority groups in inner-city areas where the count was least comprehensive (Heady, Smith and Avery, 1994; Simpson and Dorling, 1994; see also Chapter 3). The evidence on differential age–sex specific enumeration among the ethnic minority groups is, however, incomplete. Simpson found that in Bradford in 1991, the census undercounted young Pakistani children far more than those of other ethnic minority groups (Chapter 3, Table 3.2). Comparisons for England and Wales of (a) the 1991 Census counts of children aged 0, 0–4 and 0–9 years by origin of mother with (b) the number of registered births in the appropriate prior intervals finds large deficits in many New and Old Commonwealth groups and also in those with United States-born mothers (Chapter 3, Table 3.3). Complex net migration and turnover dynamics appear to be involved. Unless the age concentrations of high under-enumeration, as among young adult men and elderly people living in institutions, are strongly structured by ethnic group membership, their effects on the age structure comparisons set out in this chapter will be modest.

While the current and prospective circumstances of ethnic minority elderly people cause concern and require careful examination, it would be simplistic to argue that all future age structure change in the ethnic minority groups is encapsulated in the term 'demographic ageing'. Certainly both the ageing of the original migrants, and the spreading age distribution of their British-born progeny would progressively bring about a more 'normal' age structure. But other processes modify the age structures of self-ascribed groups over time, including not only the familiar demographic controls of fertility and mortality but also, and potentially of large consequence, the more elusive cultural dynamics of changing identities. Detailed examination of the 1991 age structures provides a window onto the likely processes of change. Idiosyncrasies in the age structure of an ethnic group are often related to the history of the immigration flow and its secondary characteristics, i.e. the number entering in different years, the rate of turnover by age and sex, sex differences in net flows related to marriage, and later returns, including those by people reaching retirement age (Brown, 1984; Diamond and Clarke, 1989).

It will also be seen that the age structure of the Black–Other ethnic group is a consequence more of social and cultural than demographic processes. Detailed examination of their age structure throws some light on the age-selectivity of these cultural processes. As the social demography of an individual ethnic group is best covered by the specialist chapters of the second volume in this series, the focus here is on the reported age distributions in 1991, broad age structure comparisons and interactive changes, e.g. the extent to which the formation of a Black–Other (or Black–British) group is complemented by change among Black–Caribbeans.

6.2   The age structures of Britain's ethnic groups in 1991

Variations in the age distribution and the average age

The briefest study of the age structures of Britain's ethnic groups in 1991 shows that the White population, comprising 95 per cent of the total, had an age structure very similar to the aggregate, and that all other groups had much younger profiles (Table 6.1). In particular, the minority groups were characterised by both a dearth of elderly people and large shares in childhood. The simplest comparative indicator of the age structures of the ethnic groups is the average age. This has been approximated by assuming that the mean age in 17 five-year age-groups from 0–4 to 80–84 years is the central age, i.e. 82.5 years for the last, and that the mean age of those aged 85+ years is 90. For the Great Britain population in 1991, the average ages were 36.8 years for males and 39.8 years for females. The means of the individual

Table 6.1 *Age–sex structure of ethnic group populations, Great Britain 1991*

Age group	White		Indian		Pakistani		Bangladeshi		Chinese	
	Males	Females	Males	Females	Males	Females	Males	Females	Males	Females
0–4	1,713,030	1,633,238	37,790	36,252	31,914	30,662	12,368	12,158	5,700	5,429
5–9	1,616,934	1,538,221	41,520	40,426	34,313	32,885	12,841	12,068	6,020	5,556
10–14	1,559,956	1,481,864	40,068	38,375	32,974	30,501	12,184	11,032	5,920	5,544
15–19	1,688,895	1,621,766	35,264	34,125	25,384	22,873	10,493	9,268	6,886	6,393
20–24	1,905,378	**1,942,066**	35,004	**37,053**	21,519	**23,491**	6,057	**7,108**	8,900	8,313
25–29	2,023,518	**2,069,605**	34,012	**39,024**	14,273	**16,930**	4,430	**4,839**	9,303	9,210
30–34	1,861,466	**1,880,460**	39,312	**41,319**	17,834	**18,902**	5,479	4,449	8,711	**9,249**
35–39	1,708,778	**1,724,851**	39,705	37,826	18,339	15,881	3,967	**5,059**	6,970	**8,681**
40–44	1,930,171	**1,933,718**	29,850	29,733	9,883	**10,879**	1,412	**3,683**	5,427	**7,063**
45–49	1,627,531	1,623,939	21,128	**21,475**	7,650	7,600	2,283	**2,611**	3,418	**3,494**
50–54	1,427,027	**1,443,481**	21,962	19,346	11,164	7,650	5,248	2,783	3,491	3,135
55–59	1,346,667	**1,387,352**	17,621	14,669	9,401	6,085	4,099	1,618	2,806	2,415
60–64	1,317,907	**1,432,909**	12,514	10,798	5,834	3,478	2,721	629	1,852	1,754
65–69	1,240,356	**1,454,626**	7,883	7,128	3,011	1,390	830	251	1,113	**1,165**
70–74	937,577	**1,246,859**	4,757	4,649	1,217	789	336	160	620	**808**
75–79	704,096	**1,103,003**	2,416	**2,838**	455	448	116	78	321	**518**
80–84	404,617	**805,331**	1,194	**1,457**	212	**308**	54	**55**	141	**320**
85+	202,572	**624,235**	891	**871**	195	**231**	26	**42**	70	**222**
0+	25,216	26,948	422,891	417,364	245,572	230,983	84,944	77,891	77,669	79,269
Average	37.3	40.5	29.5	29.2	24.3	23.1	23.5	21.2	29.2	30.4
male/ female ratio	0.94		1.01		1.06		1.09		0.97	

Note: Figures in bold mark age groups in which females are more numerous than males. The totals for the aggregate and the White populations are given in thousands. Average age is the approximate mean age (years), as explained in the text.

Source: OPCS (1993a), volume 2, Table 6.

Asian–Other		Black–African		Black–Caribbean		Black–Other		All ethnic groups			Age group
Males	Females	Males	Females	Males	Females	Males	Females	Males	Females	Males + Females	
7,908	**7,934**	12,609	12,506	18,957	18,829	18,308	17,870	1,858,584	1,774,878	3,633,462	0-4
8,121	7,808	9,753	9,479	18,200	17,586	14,392	14,149	1,762,094	1,678,178	3,440,272	5-9
7,062	6,914	7,648	7,529	15,266	14,873	10,998	10,764	1,692,076	1,607,396	3,299,472	10-14
6,786	6,408	7,051	**7,248**	15,326	**15,708**	8,765	**8,952**	1,804,850	1,732,741	3,537,591	15-19
9,085	**9,268**	11,257	**12,491**	22,599	**26,406**	9,143	**10,750**	2,028,942	2,076,946	4,105,888	20-24
9,243	**11,429**	15,453	**17,445**	28,419	**35,392**	9,507	**11,515**	2,148,158	2,215,389	4,363,547	25-29
10,221	**12,479**	14,017	13,362	21,308	**27,367**	5,669	**6,312**	1,984,017	2,013,899	3,997,916	30-34
9,725	**12,364**	9,080	8,198	13,068	**17,547**	3,032	**3,047**	1,812,664	1,833,454	3,646,118	35-39
8,777	**11,641**	5,909	**6,089**	8,103	**12,496**	2,032	2,017	2,001,564	2,017,319	4,018,883	40-44
5,798	**6,512**	4,014	**4,416**	10,881	**15,041**	1,598	**1,671**	1,684,301	1,686,759	3,371,060	45-49
4,421	4,216	4,022	3,115	18,635	**18,694**	1,253	1,092	1,497,223	1,503,512	3,000,735	50-54
2,825	2,542	2,497	1,492	18,553	16,402	976	893	1,405,445	1,433,468	2,838,913	55-59
1,630	**1,762**	1,597	939	14,595	11,449	712	677	1,359,362	1,464,395	2,823,757	60-64
946	**1,136**	984	500	8,693	6,353	548	494	1,264,364	1,473,043	2,737,407	65-69
551	**703**	530	328	4,185	3,232	287	**299**	950,060	1,257,827	2,207,887	70-74
301	**457**	215	191	1,786	**1,790**	170	**182**	709,876	1,109,505	1,819,381	75-79
142	**207**	88	**126**	654	**791**	64	**116**	407,166	808,711	1,215,877	80-84
63	**149**	76	**108**	256	**524**	59	88	204,208	626,470	830,678	85+
93,605	103,929	106,800	105,562	239,484	260,480	87,513	90,888	26,575	28,314	54,889	0+
29.2	30.3	26.5	25.5	33.6	32.8	18.5	19.0	36.8	39.8		Average age
0.90		1.01		0.91		0.96		0.94			Male/ Female ratio

ethnic groups ranged from 18.5 to 40.5 years. Only the White population had average ages above the GB figures; all others varied in their degree of youthfulness and in the comparative ages of males and females.

The various age structures differ in detail as well as in the 'slopes' of the population pyramid for each ethnic group (Figure 6.1). Simplified pyramids, using 15-year age-groups and an open-ended 75+ years category, show clearly that only the White population has the senescent profile of the aggregate population, with substantial shares in the two oldest age groups. The Pakistani, Bangladeshi and Black–Other groups are distinctive for very high proportions of children; the Black–African and Other – Asian groups have exceptionally large proportions in the 15–29 years and 30–44 years age groups respectively. The Chinese have relatively high proportions in both these age groups but are most distinctive among the minority groups for the relatively high proportions of people aged 75 years or more. The Indian population is unusual for its similar proportions in the first three age groups, and the Black–Caribbean group for an exceptional enumerated female preponderance (see Chapters 2, 3 and 4).

More detailed comparisons are aided in Table 6.2 by the visual prominence of the quinquennial age-groups with 10 per cent or more of the total. The oldest non-White ethnic group was the Black–Caribbean with a mean of 33 years, males being slightly older than females. They had a higher share in the elderly age-groups than any other ethnic minority group, particularly among men in their sixties, but also had comparatively few people in the youngest four quinquennial age-groups. In comparison to the proportion in the Great Britain population, a deficit of 6 per cent among males aged 15–19 years was reported, which may be substantially down to differential under-enumeration at these ages in this ethnic group (Table 6.3) (OPCS, 1993b; Hall and Hall, 1995). The next youngest were males and females of the Chinese, Other – Asian and Indian ethnic groups with average ages of 29–30 years. In comparison to the Chinese, the Indians had relatively more elderly people and children, while the Other – Asians had relatively fewer elderly people, a higher proportion aged 30–49 years, and lower proportions aged 20–29 years and in childhood.

Proceeding to younger groups, the Black–Africans had a mean age of 26 years. Unusually high proportions of this population were aged 25–34 years, and there were relatively more children and exceptionally few people over 50 years. The high child proportions were mainly in the two youngest age groups and, like the Black–Caribbean male distribution, the 15–19 year age-group was in deficit. Pakistani males and females and Bangladeshi males all had mean ages around 23.5 years. All three had high proportions in the first four age groups, but also irregularities of over- and under-representation through middle age. Bangladeshi females were markedly younger again, with a mean age of 21.2 years produced by very high proportions aged up to 20 years and very small numbers aged 60 years or more. The youngest ethnic minority group by some distance was the Black–Other group, with an average age of under 19 years. This age structure was remarkable for a 'developed' nation, with more than one-fifth aged less than 5 years, and just under one half less than 15 years. Fewer than 9 per cent were aged 40 years or more.

Figure 6.1 *Population structure of the White population and the ethnic minority populations*

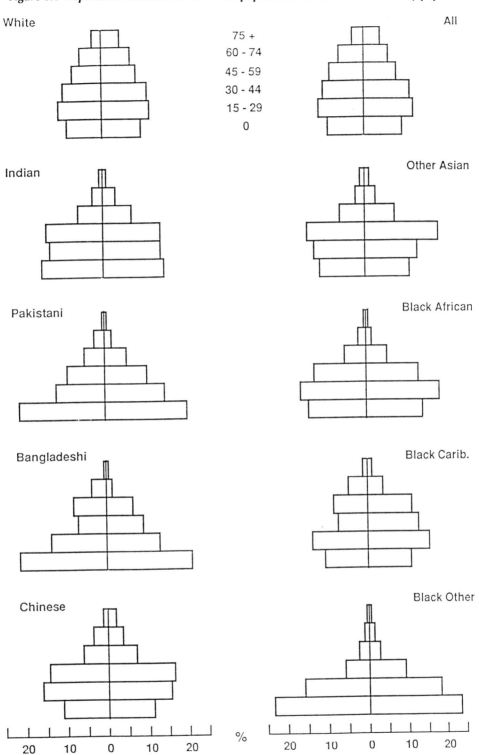

Table 6.2 Age structure of ethnic groups by sex, Great Britain, 1991 (percentage distributions)

Age group	White Males	White Females	Indian Males	Indian Females	Pakistani Males	Pakistani Females	Bangladeshi Males	Bangladeshi Females	Chinese Males	Chinese Females	Other–Asian Males	Other–Asian Females	Black–African Males	Black–African Females	Black–Caribbean Males	Black–Caribbean Females	Black–Other Males	Black–Other Females	All Groups Males	All Groups Females
0–4	6.8	6.1	8.9	8.7	13.0	13.3	14.6	15.6	7.3	6.8	8.4	7.6	11.8	11.8	7.9	7.2	20.9	19.7	7.0	6.3
5–9	6.4	5.7	9.8	9.7	14.0	14.2	15.1	15.5	7.8	7.0	8.7	7.5	9.1	9.0	7.6	6.8	16.4	15.6	6.6	5.9
10–14	6.2	5.5	9.5	9.2	13.4	13.2	14.3	14.2	7.6	7.0	7.5	6.7	7.2	7.1	6.4	5.7	12.6	11.8	6.4	5.7
15–19	6.7	6.0	8.3	8.2	10.3	9.9	12.4	11.9	8.9	8.1	7.2	6.2	6.6	6.9	6.4	6.0	10.0	9.8	6.8	6.1
20–24	7.6	7.2	8.3	8.9	8.8	10.2	7.1	9.1	11.5	10.5	9.7	8.9	10.5	11.8	9.4	10.1	10.4	11.8	7.6	7.3
25–29	8.0	7.7	8.0	9.4	5.8	7.3	5.2	6.2	12.0	11.6	9.9	11.0	14.5	16.5	11.9	13.6	10.9	12.7	8.1	7.8
30–34	7.4	7.0	9.3	9.9	7.3	8.2	6.5	5.7	11.2	11.7	10.9	12.0	13.1	12.7	8.9	10.5	6.5	6.9	7.5	7.1
35–39	6.8	6.4	9.4	9.1	7.5	6.9	4.7	6.5	9.0	11.0	10.4	11.9	8.5	7.8	5.5	6.7	3.5	3.4	6.8	6.5
40–44	7.7	7.2	7.1	7.1	4.0	4.7	1.7	4.7	7.0	8.9	9.4	11.2	5.5	5.8	3.4	4.8	2.3	2.2	7.5	7.1
45–49	6.5	6.0	5.0	5.1	3.1	3.3	2.7	3.4	4.4	4.4	6.2	6.3	3.8	4.2	4.5	5.8	1.8	1.8	6.3	6.0
50–54	5.7	5.4	5.2	4.6	4.5	3.3	6.2	3.6	4.5	4.0	4.7	4.1	3.8	3.0	7.8	7.2	1.4	1.2	5.6	5.3
55–59	5.3	5.1	4.2	3.5	3.8	2.6	4.8	2.1	3.6	3.0	3.0	2.4	2.3	1.4	7.7	6.3	1.1	1.0	5.3	5.1
60–64	5.2	5.3	3.0	2.6	2.4	1.5	3.2	0.8	2.4	2.2	1.7	1.7	1.5	0.9	6.1	4.4	0.8	0.7	5.1	5.2
65–69	4.9	5.4	1.9	1.7	1.2	0.6	1.0	0.3	1.4	1.5	1.0	1.1	0.9	0.5	3.6	2.4	0.6	0.5	4.8	5.2
70–74	3.7	4.6	1.1	1.1	0.5	0.3	0.4	0.2	0.8	1.0	0.6	0.7	0.5	0.3	1.7	1.2	0.3	0.3	3.6	4.4
75–79	2.8	4.1	0.6	0.7	0.2	0.2	0.1	0.1	0.4	0.7	0.3	0.4	0.2	0.2	0.7	0.7	0.2	0.2	2.7	3.9
80–84	1.6	3.0	0.3	0.3	0.1	0.1	0.1	0.1	0.2	0.4	0.2	0.2	0.1	0.1	0.3	0.3	0.1	0.1	1.5	2.9
85+	0.8	2.3	0.2	0.2	0.1	0.1	0.0	0.1	0.1	0.3	0.1	0.1	0.1	0.1	0.1	0.2	0.1	0.1	0.8	2.2

Source: Calculated from data in Table 6.1.

Age-group proportions above and below the national figures

The exceptional age structure of the Black–Other ethnic group draws attention to the ages of pronounced over- and under-representation in each ethnic minority group. A full matrix of the ratios of the age-groups of the ethnic groups relative to those of the GB population is given in Table 6.3. The general picture is of broad waves of surpluses and deficits extending over several adjacent age-groups. Among Whites, for example, a clear gradient is found from under-representation in childhood to over-representation at the oldest ages. The gradient was much steeper for females than males. In all other ethnic groups, the reverse gradient applied but with markedly different slopes and with perturbations. Distinctive features revealed by these data are that: (a) among Black–Africans the over-representation peaked at ages 25–29 years; (b) the equivalent peaks in the Chinese and Other –Asian populations were among people in their thirties; (c) the greatest relative ratios in the age structure of the Black–Caribbeans were at ages 50–59 years; (d) a trough in over-representation at ages 20–29 years occurred in the Indian population and, to a lesser degree, in the Pakistani and Bangladeshi distributions.

The mean ratio over 18 age-groups shows that some ethnic groups have high proportions of their populations in particular age-groups and few proportions in others, compared with the national population. If only one age-group had an excess, the mean ratio would tend to be low. The summary statistics of the distributions of the ratios for each ethnic–sex group are presented in Table 6.4. Only the White group's means were above the means for all groups, and the female figure was in a class apart, because the very high relative ratios in the older, less populous age-groups (particularly the female ratio of 3.01 at 85+ years) outweighed the relatively low ratios in the younger half of the age distribution. Among the other eight ethnic groups, the means were all within 0.81–0.90. These means had only a weak association with the average age, for only a minority of the variance in one is statistically associated with the other (Pearson's correlations: males r^2 = 0.33, females r^2 = 0.43).

The maximum and minimum relative age-group shares vary considerably, and so also do the ranges and variances (Table 6.4). The extreme ratios are sometimes at the youngest and oldest ages and sometimes in early-adult ages (Table 6.3). The frequency of large deviations also varies between none and 17 age-groups. Three ethnic groups were exceptional on these measures. Most distinctive were Black–Other males and females, with the greatest range of values, from around three times the GB share aged 0–4 years, to only 0.05 of the national percentage at 85+ years. Moreover, the group had the highest variances and the series of age-group ratios for both males and females were the only cases of uninterrupted (monotonic) decline with increasing age. The age structure of White males was exceptional in respect of the opposite characteristics. The Indians, Chinese and Other–Asian group had age structures which differed from both the aggregate and the dissimilar patterns of the Black–Others, Pakistanis, Bangladeshis and Black–Africans. Among all the ethnic–sex groups a strong and significant relationship was found between the average age and the concentration of the population

Table 6.3 Ratios of age-group representation* for sex-specific ethnic groups, Great Britain, 1991

Age group	White Males	White Females	Indian Males	Indian Females	Pakistani Males	Pakistani Females	Bangladeshi Males	Bangladeshi Females	Chinese Males	Chinese Females	Other–Asian Males	Other–Asian Females	Black–African Males	Black–African Females	Black–Caribbean Males	Black–Caribbean Females	Black–Other Males	Black–Other Females
0–4	0.97	0.87	1.28	1.24	1.86	1.90	2.08	2.23	1.05	0.98	1.21	1.22	1.69	1.89	1.13	1.15	2.99	3.14
5–9	0.97	0.86	1.48	1.46	2.11	2.15	2.28	2.34	1.17	1.06	1.31	1.27	1.38	1.52	1.15	1.14	2.48	2.63
10–14	0.97	0.86	1.49	1.44	2.11	2.07	2.25	2.22	1.20	1.10	1.18	1.17	1.12	1.26	1.00	1.01	1.97	2.09
15–19	0.99	0.89	1.23	1.20	1.52	1.46	1.82	1.75	1.31	1.19	1.07	1.01	0.97	1.12	0.94	0.99	1.47	1.61
20–24	0.99	0.94	1.08	1.16	1.15	1.33	0.93	1.20	1.50	1.37	1.27	1.22	1.38	1.61	1.24	1.38	1.37	1.61
25–29	0.99	0.95	0.99	1.16	0.72	0.91	0.65	0.77	1.48	1.44	1.22	1.41	1.79	2.11	1.47	1.74	1.34	1.62
30–34	0.99	0.93	1.25	1.33	0.97	1.10	0.86	0.77	1.50	1.56	1.46	1.69	1.76	1.78	1.19	1.48	0.87	0.98
35–39	0.99	0.94	1.38	1.33	1.09	1.01	0.68	0.95	1.32	1.61	1.52	1.84	1.25	1.20	0.80	1.04	0.51	0.52
40–44	1.02	0.95	0.94	0.95	0.53	0.63	0.22	0.63	0.93	1.18	1.24	1.57	0.73	0.81	0.45	0.67	0.31	0.31
45–49	1.02	0.95	0.79	0.81	0.49	0.52	0.42	0.53	0.69	0.70	0.98	1.05	0.59	0.70	0.72	0.97	0.29	0.31
50–54	1.00	0.95	0.92	0.82	0.81	0.59	1.10	0.63	0.80	0.70	0.84	0.76	0.67	0.56	1.38	1.35	0.25	0.23
55–59	1.01	0.97	0.79	0.66	0.72	0.50	0.91	0.39	0.68	0.58	0.57	0.48	0.44	0.28	1.46	1.24	0.21	0.19
60–64	1.02	1.04	0.58	0.51	0.46	0.29	0.63	0.16	0.47	0.43	0.34	0.33	0.29	0.17	1.19	0.85	0.16	0.14
65–69	1.03	1.13	0.39	0.36	0.26	0.13	0.21	0.07	0.30	0.31	0.21	0.21	0.19	0.09	0.76	0.47	0.13	0.10
70–74	1.04	1.29	0.31	0.31	0.14	0.10	0.11	0.06	0.22	0.29	0.16	0.15	0.14	0.07	0.49	0.28	0.09	0.07
75–79	1.05	1.53	0.21	0.25	0.07	0.07	0.05	0.04	0.15	0.24	0.12	0.11	0.08	0.05	0.28	0.18	0.07	0.05
80–84	1.05	1.95	0.18	0.23	0.06	0.09	0.04	0.05	0.12	0.26	0.10	0.07	0.05	0.04	0.18	0.11	0.05	0.04
85+	1.05	3.01	0.27	0.27	0.10	0.13	0.04	0.07	0.12	0.36	0.09	0.06	0.09	0.05	0.14	0.09	0.09	0.04
± 0.25	0	4	10	11	15	15	14	14	13	13	11	12	15	15	9	10	17	17
± 0.50	0	0	5	5	11	9	11	11	6	8	7	10	10	12	5	6	13	16

Notes: * Ratios of the percentage of a sex-specific ethnic group population in an age group to the equivalent percentage in the Great Britain population.
± 0.25 - number of ratios more than 0.25 from 1.0.   ±0.50 - number of ratios more than 0.5 from 1.0.

Source: Calculated from data in Table 6.1.

into certain age-groups, as indexed by the standard deviation of the age-group share ratios (Table 6.4). Young populations were associated with high variation in age-group shares, while the older populations had lower variation.

There were substantial differences between the age structures of males and females in several of the ethnic groups. Taking the ethnic minority groups in 1991 collectively, females were more numerous but the sex ratio of 1.006 per cent was slight in comparison to the ratio of 1.069 in the White population (Table 6.1). Unexpectedly, the ratio was higher in the Other – Asian (1.11) and Black–Caribbean (1.09) populations than among the White population. The sex ratios at specific age-groups were highly variable. Among Black–Caribbeans, females exceeded males by at least 25 per cent through ages 25–49 years; in some age-groups the female excess wass massive, e.g. 54.2 per cent at ages 40–44 years. A similar but less pronounced pattern is found among the Other – Asian population, with a peak female excess of 32.6 per cent in the same age-group. The sex ratios of the Chinese and Black–Other ethnic groups were similar to those of the aggregate population, while males predominated in the three South Asian origin and the Black–African ethnic groups. This male over-representation was concentrated in late-working and early old ages, and was most pronounced among the Pakistanis

Table 6.4 *Summary statistics on the distribution of relative age-group shares* for sex-specific ethnic group populations, Great Britain,1991*

Sex and ethnic group	Mean	Minimum	Maximum	Standard deviation	Coefficient of variation
Females					
Black–Other	0.87	0.04	3.14	0.99	1.14
Bangladeshi	0.82	0.04	2.34	0.80	0.98
Black–African	0.85	0.04	2.11	0.73	0.86
Pakistani	0.83	0.07	2.15	0.70	0.84
Other–Asian	0.87	0.06	1.84	0.60	0.69
Chinese	0.85	0.24	1.61	0.48	0.56
Black–Caribbean	0.90	0.09	1.74	0.50	0.56
Indian	0.86	0.23	1.46	0.45	0.52
White	1.17	0.86	3.01	0.54	0.46
All ethnic groups	1.00	1.00	1.00	0.00	0.00
Males					
Black–Other	0.81	0.05	2.99	0.92	1.14
Bangladeshi	0.85	0.04	2.28	0.77	0.91
Pakistani	0.84	0.06	2.11	0.68	0.81
Black–African	0.81	0.05	1.79	0.62	0.77
Other–Asian	0.83	0.09	1.52	0.53	0.64
Chinese	0.83	0.12	1.50	0.51	0.61
Indian	0.86	0.18	1.49	0.45	0.52
Black–Caribbean	0.89	0.14	1.47	0.43	0.48
White	1.01	0.97	1.05	0.03	0.03
All ethnic groups	1.00	1.00	1.00	0.00	0.00

* For each ethnic–sex group, summary statistics of the 18 age-group ratios between the percentage of the population and the equivalent percentage in the Great Britain population.

and Bangladeshis. Through the age-groups from 50–54 to 70–74 years, the Pakistani male:female ratios were 1.5, 1.5, 1.7, 2.2 and 1.5, and the Bangladeshi 1.9, 2.5, 4.3, 3.3 and 2.1.

6.3   Age structure similarities and dissimilarities

Similarities and differences between the various male and female age structures have been examined through correlation and a cluster analysis. Only six ethnic–sex groups had significantly different age structures from the GB sex-specific aggregate (Table 6.5). The most dissimilar were Bangladeshi males (r = +0.54, p[H_0]>0.01), and four others also met the requirments (p[H_0]>0.001): Bangladeshi females, Black–Other males and females, and Pakistani females. While the age structure of Pakistani males was significantly correlated with the GB array (r = +0.68, p[H_0]<0.001), the coefficient differed little from that for females (r = +0.63).

Table 6.5   *Product moment correlation matrix of quinquennial age-group percentages, ethnic groups in Great Britain, 1991*

	White	Indian	Pakis- tani	Bangla- deshi	Chinese	Other– Asian	Black– African	Black– Caribbean	Black– Other	All groups
Males										
White	1.00	0.87	*0.65 ***	*0.54 ***	0.88	0.89	0.80	0.82	*0.56 ***	1.00
Indian		1.00	0.90	0.80	0.93	0.95	0.89	0.77	0.77	0.89
Pakistani			1.00	0.97	0.74	0.75	0.75	*0.65 ***	0.91	0.69
Bangladeshi				1.00	*0.61 ***	*0.60 ***	*0.64 ***	*0.62 ***	0.90	*0.58 ***
Chinese					1.00	0.96	0.95	0.83	*0.67 ***	0.89
Other–Asian						1.00	0.92	0.73	*0.66 ***	0.90
Black–African							1.00	0.82	0.78	0.83
Black–Caribbean								1.00	*0.62 ***	0.83
Black–Other									1.00	*0.59 ***
All ethnic groups										1.00
Significant *r***	3	0	2	5	2	2	1	3	5	2
Females										
White	1.00	0.82	*0.57 ***	**0.48 *****	0.87	0.86	0.79	0.85	**0.51 *****	1.00
Indian		1.00	0.90	0.83	0.94	0.92	0.90	0.83	0.79	0.86
Pakistani			1.00	0.98	0.72	0.68	0.79	*0.64 ***	0.93	0.63
Bangladeshi				1.00	*0.62 ***	*0.59 ***	0.70	**0.52 *****	0.92	**0.54 *****
Chinese					1.00	0.97	0.91	0.86	*0.63 ***	0.90
Other–Asian						1.00	0.87	0.80	*0.57 ***	0.88
Black–African							1.00	0.89	0.82	0.83
Black–Caribbean								1.00	*0.63 ***	0.87
Black–Other									1.00	*0.57 ***
All ethnic groups										1.00
Significant *r***	3	0	3	5	2	2	0	3	5	3
significant *r***	2	0	0	3	0	0	0	1	1	1

Notes: All coefficients are positive.   Statistical significance: ** p(H_0) > 0.001,   *** p(H_0) > 0.01.

Turning to the ethnic sex-specific age structures most similar to that of the GB population, White females (r = +0.99) and males (r = 1.00) were hardly distinguishable, and Indian, Chinese and Other – Asian males and females, and Black–Caribbean females, all gave correlations in the range +0.87–0.90. Two age-structure sets are therefore observed, one similar to the GB distribution, with at least 75 per cent of the age-group variation being related to the national pattern ($r^2 \geq 0.75$); and the dissimilar set, with no group having more than 46 per cent of its age-group variation associated with the national profile.

The age structure of each sex-specific group has also been compared with all others. The most dissimilar pairs were Bangladeshi males and, first, White females (r = +0.40) and, second, Other – Asian females (r = +0.45), followed closely by the differences between White females and Black–Other males (r = +0.47) and Bangladeshi females (r = +0.48). The number of significantly different correlations for each ethnic–sex group is displayed at the foot of Table 6.5. These confirm that the Bangladeshi and Black–Other populations had the most distinctive age structures, with Black–Caribbeans and Whites in a second group. Perhaps surprisingly, in comparison with the total population, the Indians (not the Whites) and Black–African females have the least distinctive age structures.

A cluster analysis works with quantitative measures of differences in variable scores, here being the 18 age group percentages for each of the 18 ethnic–sex groups (giving at the outset 153 pairs for comparison). It proceeds iteratively, successively amalgamating the most similar groups, and at each stage recalculating the measures of difference for the reduced number of groups or clusters. Its early steps therefore associate the ethnic-sex groups with the most similar age structures into sets or clusters. The comparison of these sets clarifies the main contrasts in age structures among all groups, and the minority ethnic group membership of each set indicates their similarity or difference according to multiple criteria, namely 18 age-group percentages, an improvement on a taxonomy based exclusively on the mean age. Among the most instructive results of a cluster analysis are those which indicate how much of the total information (or variance) is 'lost' at each successive step.

Of most interest are the groupings arrived at *after* a sequence of amalgamations of highly similar cases and *before* a long step, which implies the amalgamation of relatively dissimilar cases and the loss of much detail. Cluster analyses do not give single best solutions; they need careful interpretation but provide considerable insights into the structures of similarity and difference among cases. The criterion of dissimilarity employed in the SPSS agglomerative procedure is the Euclidean distance of separation, the sum of the squared differences for all 18 age-group percentage comparisons (Norusis, 1990, Section B, 161).

Figure 6.2 illustrates the progressive merging of the different ethnic groups, taking the two sexes separately. The first eight amalgamations or steps link males and females of the same ethnic group, but at the ninth, Bangladeshi males are grouped with the Pakistanis. The Chinese are then grouped with the Other – Asian group, and then the Indians. Next, the Bangladeshi female distribution is linked with the male distribution. After this twelfth step six clusters remain, three of which are single ethnic groups: the Whites, Black–Caribbeans and Black–Others. The relative dissimilarity of these six clusters is marked by the increase in the stage coefficient from 42.7 to 82.1 before a further amalgamation. Thereafter the Black–Caribbeans are amalgamated with the Indian, Chinese and Other – Asian groups, and then the Whites associate with the Black–Caribbeans. These four clusters precede another large step in the sequence and repay comparative description.

The contrasts in the age distributions of the four clusters are shown by the over- and under-representations of each age-group from 0–4 to 85+ years (Table 6.6). Ratios to the national representation of over 1.2 are in bold characters, and if over 1.5 also underlined; ratios below 0.8 are italicised, and if below 0.5 also underlined. Cluster 1 (Whites and Black–Caribbeans) had moderate over-representations of people aged 20–34 years and in their fifties, moderate under-representations of people aged 70+ years and (unexpected for the birth years 1945/46–1950/51) 40–44 years, but only one extreme ratio, the excess at 25–29 years. The other three clusters were all young but to differing degrees and with notable differences in (a) the gradient from childhood excesses to elderly deficits, and (b) the ages of the highest over-representations.

Figure 6.2 *Cluster analysis dendrogram: ethnic-sex groups, Great Britain 1991*

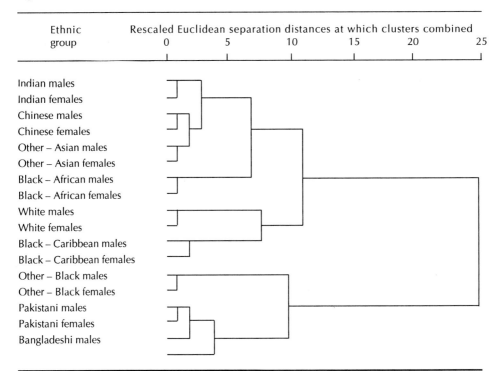

Table 6.6 *Relative age structure ratios for four and two clusters of ethnic-sex groups,*
Great Britain, 1991

Age group	Four cluster solution				Two clusters	
	1	2	3	4	Set 1 & 2	Set 3 & 4
0–4	1.06	**1.35**	<u>**2.13**</u>	<u>**3.07**</u>	**1.25**	<u>**2.44**</u>
5–9	1.06	**1.37**	<u>**2.35**</u>	<u>**2.55**</u>	**1.26**	<u>**2.42**</u>
10–14	0.99	**1.28**	<u>**2.29**</u>	<u>**2.03**</u>	1.19	<u>**2.21**</u>
15–19	0.98	1.17	<u>**1.73**</u>	<u>**1.54**</u>	1.11	<u>**1.66**</u>
20–24	1.15	**1.34**	1.18	**1.49**	**1.27**	**1.28**
25–29	**1.29**	**1.46**	*0.77*	1.48	1.40	1.01
30–34	1.16	<u>**1.56**</u>	0.95	0.92	**1.43**	0.94
35–39	0.95	**1.45**	0.96	*0.51*	**1.28**	0.81
40–44	*0.79*	1.06	*0.52*	<u>*0.31*</u>	0.97	<u>*0.45*</u>
45–49	0.93	0.80	*0.51*	<u>*0.30*</u>	0.84	<u>*0.44*</u>
50–54	1.19	*0.77*	0.81	<u>*0.24*</u>	0.91	0.62
55–59	1.19	*0.57*	0.65	<u>*0.20*</u>	*0.77*	0.50
60–64	1.02	<u>*0.39*</u>	<u>*0.38*</u>	<u>*0.15*</u>	0.60	<u>*0.31*</u>
65–69	0.82	<u>*0.25*</u>	<u>*0.16*</u>	<u>*0.12*</u>	<u>*0.44*</u>	<u>*0.14*</u>
70–74	*0.70*	<u>*0.19*</u>	<u>*0.09*</u>	<u>*0.08*</u>	<u>*0.36*</u>	<u>*0.09*</u>
75–79	*0.63*	<u>*0.13*</u>	<u>*0.05*</u>	<u>*0.06*</u>	<u>*0.30*</u>	<u>*0.05*</u>
80–84	*0.58*	<u>*0.10*</u>	<u>*0.04*</u>	<u>*0.05*</u>	<u>*0.26*</u>	<u>*0.04*</u>
85+	*0.57*	<u>*0.10*</u>	<u>*0.04*</u>	<u>*0.05*</u>	<u>*0.25*</u>	<u>*0.05*</u>

Note: The data are ratios of the percentage of a cluster population in an age-group, as determined by the
means of the member ethnic groups, to the equivalent percentage in the Great Britain population. Ratios
of less than 0.8 are italicised and if less than 0.5 underlined; ratios of more than 1.2 are in bold and if
more than 1.5 underlined. The member groups of the clusters are; 1 Whites and Black Caribbeans; 2
Indians, Chineses, Other–Asians and Black–Africans; 3 Pakistanis and Bangladeshis; 4 Black–Others.

Cluster 2 (Indians, Chinese, Other – Asians and Black–Africans) had moderate deficits of people in their fifties and substantial deficits in all older age-
groups. Its greatest over-representations were distinctively among people
in their twenties and thirties. Cluster 3 (Pakistanis and Bangladeshis) was
similar to Cluster 2 in its under-representations of the older age-groups but
had much stronger over-representations of children and juveniles. It also
had fluctuations of considerable amplitude through the working ages, with
the moderate deficits at 25–29, 40–49 and 55+ years dovetailed with higher
shares at the intervening ages. Cluster 4, the Black–Others alone, had
substantial deficits not just of elderly people but of all age-groups above 40
years, and greater excesses than the other Clusters of children aged 0–9
years and of people in their early twenties.

With further aggregation of these four clusters, the analysis takes a long
stride to the next amalgamation and a short penultimate step to two groups
(to minimise confusion, described here as sets). The prior Clusters 1 and 2
form Set 1&2 with 12 ethnic–sex groups, and Set 3&4 has prior Clusters 3 and
4 with just the Bangladeshis, Pakistanis and Black–Others. Set 1&2 had
substantial deficits of elderly people aged from 65–69 years upwards, but
the under-representation was minor compared to the scanty presence of
people aged 70+ years in Set 3&4. This was not however the only or the most
marked distinction between the sets. Set 1&2 had a bimodal distribution of
surpluses: the dominant wave extended through ages 20–39 with a peak

ratio of 1.43 at 30–34 years, and the subordinate peak was at 5–9 years. On the other hand, Set 3&4 almost reproduced the monotonic decline of the relative shares seen in the Black–Other ethnic group. From a zenith of 2.44 at 0–4 years, the ratios reduced to 0.05 at 85+ years. The steepest declines occurred first between 10–14 and 25–29 years, to the extent that the set had under-representations from 30 years upwards, and second after 35–39 years.

6.4 Empirical synthesis

This extended exercise in the description and analysis of comparative age structures has not turned every stone. Neither single years of age nor available breakdowns by marital status or household type have been examined. The principal findings are that the most distinctive age structures are those of the Black–Other and White female populations, the first because of its exceptional youthfulness, the latter because of its exceptional proportions (when compared to males and females combined in Great Britain) of people aged 75+ years. Lest it be thought that an exceptionally high number in advanced old age is a trivial disturbance in comparison to a surplus of children, it is worth emphasising the comparative sizes of the ethnic group populations.

Among Black–Others, the shares that were double or more the national equivalents occurred at ages 0–14 years in both sexes. The population of these ages above the expected national representation in 1991 was 52,750. Comparable over-representations in the White female population occurred only at 80+ years, but totalled no less than 809,188 people. Even the modest surplus of White males at these advanced ages, of just 5 per cent, totalled 28,914 people.

The Black–Others were the youngest ethnic group, the average age of females falling just below one half of the national female mean, and the Bangladeshi population was little older. On the other hand, the Black–Caribbean group was distinctly older than any other ethnic minority group, the average age of males being 0.91 of the national mean. The most instructive results from this exercise are the details of under- and over-representation through the complete age range. The Other – Asian population had its highest age-group concentration among people in their thirties, but the Black–African and Black–Caribbean ethnic groups had their highest populations among people in their twenties. While the distribution for Chinese males matched that of the Black–African and Black–Caribbean groups, that of Chinese females was closer to the Other – Asian distribution.

The exploration of similarities and dissimilarities attracted attention to the levels and ages of over- and under-representation. Differences in the ages at which substantial deficits of older people set in, or after which the substantial excesses of children end, become distinguishing marks. So in the four cluster taxonomy, the Black–Other ethnic group is set apart as eccentrically dominated by children and juveniles. Another cluster unites only the Pakistani and Bangladeshi ethnic groups, also with substantial childhood over-representation, but with near normal shares of people in their thirties and fifties. The third cluster comprises only the White and Black–Caribbean ethnic groups which, along with the lowest deviations from the aggregate pattern of age-groups, had its strongest over-representations among people in their twenties and fifties.

The remaining Indian, Chinese, Other – Asian and Black–African ethnic groups comprise the fourth cluster: its strongest over-representations were in early working ages, but in comparison to the Black–Other and Pakistani–Bangladeshi clusters, the deviations of its proportions from the national standard were low, particularly at the youngest and oldest ages. With only moderate surpluses of children and more than negligible numbers in old age, its age structure was intermediate, neither showing extreme youthfulness nor the national aged profile.

6.5 Processes of age structure change

Understanding the dynamics of age structure change in self-ascribed ethnic minority groups involves more complex issues than the projection of the age structure of a homogeneous national population. For the latter, the only operative processes are described by the current levels and trends in mortality, fertility and external migration. For the ethnic minority groups, questions of the acceptability of the proffered labels and of identity come into play, particularly in connection with generational succession.

Although some ethnic minority groups have been represented in Great Britain for centuries, today's populations have developed from substantial immigration flows that began no earlier than the 1950s and which, in most cases, peaked during the following two decades (see Chapter 5). Each ethnic group has had a distinctive immigration and settlement history. Already at least one is preponderantly UK born. In 1991, 84 per cent of those describing themselves as Black–Other were born in the United Kingdom (OPCS, 1993a, Table 5).

Not only have the dates and duration of the highest inflows differed intricately, the dynamics of change in cultural identities, and their manifestation in people's choices from the constrained list of identities offered by the 1991 Census have been complex and variable processes. For some individuals and groups, the self-description requested by the census form will have been especially difficult because of either or both mixed parentage and multi-national lineage. This may have been a particular conundrum for people of Asian origin with a strong affiliation to one of its national cultures and previous residence in Africa or the Caribbean. The classification offered in 1991 used both race (or more precisely skin colour) and the geography of ancestry (sometimes citing nation and sometimes region). Some respondents doubtless would have preferred to stress their own nativity or a religious affiliation.

Sufficient points have been made to demonstrate the complexity of the processes of identity formation and change: some of these are documented more fully in the companion volumes in this series. As one turns from the current age structure to the prospects for age structure change in a minority ethnic group, it becomes apparent that many paths are possible. We assume that most groups will age, but how else might the age distributions change? The age structure of any recently arrived minority group is likely to change more swiftly than those of general or national populations. This general effect arises from the age-selectivity of migrants, temporal fluctuations of the migration flow, inherited differentials in fertility and mortality from national levels, and subsequent convergence towards them.

While many of these factors have characterised British ethnic minority groups, it is not inevitable that the age structure of an ethnic group changes rapidly, one prominent example being that of the contemporary American black population. Paradoxically, in special cases the age structure of an ethnic group can be unusually rigid, brought about by processes which apply to the extreme cases of selected or special populations of boarding schools and nursing homes. To understand the possible trajectories, it has been found useful to consider the matter abstractly, by describing extreme and ideal age structures and their temporal change. In the following section, these ideal types are described and their relevance to the contrasting age structures among Britain's ethnic groups in 1991 is considered.

6.6   Models of age structure and age structure change

The greatest possible contrast in ethnic minority group age structures is between a highly age-selective pattern that does not change over time, and a near-normal age structure that loses any irregularities over a relatively short time. While the polarised extremes of this dichotomy may be rare, elements of the contrast are variously present among Britain's minority ethnic groups, and help in explaining their current age structures as well as providing indications of the likely directions of change.

Constantly atypical age structures

A constant atypical age structure occurs whenever members of one sex of an ethnic minority group enter a nation to fill defined positions, whether jobs, student places or indeed those of an encamped army, with two key conditions: restricted eligibility for residence, and continuous or periodic replacement of the population (Table 6.7). The temporary residents have restricted social roles. They enter the territory by permits, which may limit the eligible ages or duration of residence. When the licences expire, the immigrants leave and are replaced by others. In some cases no reproduction takes place, and while a few deaths will occur, the 'vacancies' would be filled by others of the eligible ages, so mortality has no effect on the age structure. The size of the ethnic group and its age structure are virtually constant: the mean age fluctuates within only a narrow range related to the duration or the eligible ages of residence. The age structure is artificially tidy, with substantial over-representations in the licensed age-groups and an absence of others, very often including children and retired people.

Table 6.7 Emblematic minority group age structures

Characteristic	Atypicality and normality of age structure and pace and extent of change		Contrast in initial size, change in mean age, and equilibrium age structure	
	Guest workers (Antarctic)	Mass migration (Mass repatriation)	First generation (Creoles)	Last generation (Exiles)
Ages commonly over-represented	Young working adults	Young working-age adults and children	Initially infants, then progressively to older groups	Progressively older age groups
Ages commonly under-represented	Children and elderly people	Elderly people	Initially all apart from infants,	Initially children, then progressively to older people
Turnover	Substantial or total	Variable, often initially high but slows	Reversion and exits to other groups	By definition inoperative
Reproduction	None	Normal	Initially members too young, then varies with rate of within-group unions	By definition inoperative
Age structure change in short term	Negligible	Minor to negligible	Rapid increase of mean age, and rising age of eldest	Rapid increase of mean age, and rising age of youngest
Age structure change in long term	None	Changes as national population	Slowing change, group distinctive-ness retained	Dies out

Such situations are not only abstract. The description fits well the human populations of weapons-testing ranges, the artificial territories of oil rigs and, more surprisingly, the entire continent of the Antarctic. While it is unlikely that any ethnic group in a contemporary open society is so tightly constrained, the model approximates the age structures of, say, African students in Moscow and of special cases of ethnic minority group 'guest' workers. Comparable patterns have been described for the modern pioneer settlement of Indian seaman in British ports during the first half of this century: 'Some became labourers in heavy industry, while others established themselves in self-employment ... Often, however, migrants did not stop in Britain for more than three or four years, although on their return to India many were replaced overseas by close relatives in a system of rotating transience' (Robinson, 1986, 26).

In contemporary Britain, the ethnic minority groups that are most affected by these processes are probably those with the highest proportions in Britain for higher educational, training and career advancement reasons. Successful projections of the ageing of the Black–African and Other – Asian ethnic minority groups, among whom students and corporate employees are numerous, should give close attention to turnover through the age-specific rates of in- and out-migration.

Ephemerally distinctive age structures

If the Antarctic age structure is one of persistent peculiarities, the antithesis is clearly one of minor and ephemeral special features. The probability of a newly settled ethnic group having exactly the same age structure as the indigenous population is, however, extremely low. The nearest approximations are likely to result from mass deportations (or other forced migrations) of ethnic groups who return *in toto* to an ancestral nation. But the majority of mass migrations are selective of relatively young adults in their reproductive years. Normally their nuptiality, fertility and mortality differ from the national schedules. Over time, the vital rate schedules tend to modify, often converging towards the patterns of the host community. Such convergence is likely to be encouraged by acculturation and assimilation but it is not dependent upon it. Morbidity and mortality schedules might, for example, converge with those of the indigenous community for reasons associated with hygiene, nutrition, preventive medicine and health care, and without appreciable change in the group's cultural, linguistic or religious identity.

A recent examination of mortality differentials and their trends over the period 1970/71 to1979/83 found that among men, the African and Caribbean-born had among the highest mortality rates at the beginning of the period and the largest percentage declines over the decade, while 'women born in the African and Caribbean Commonwealth ... showed the greatest improvement over the period' (Balarajan and Bulusu, 1990).

Age structure change in a first-generation population

A second dichotomous contrast in minority population histories and age structures can be recognised. This is between a new population group, one that existed nowhere before a migration or settlement, and a population that does not or cannot reproduce. When a population group moves from its native territory to another, by that act it distinguishes itself. The experience cannot be undone, as native Japanese who return from a lengthy period of voluntary residence overseas discover. Even more defining is to be born in the new territory of the migrant settlement group. The progeny are defined by a particular combination of ancestry and birthplace and sometimes become the first generation of a previously non-existent minority group. The group may define itself, or its identity may be ascribed by the containing society. The age structure of the resulting population is, by definition, initially extremely young. As the decades pass, the first-generation population ages while the ages of their descendants progressively spread.

While the extreme types are again mainly abstractions, interesting approximations are found in the population record. The formation of the Mestizo and Creole ethnic groups of the American continent, or of the Boer population in South Africa, are notable cases. Taking United States citizens of, say, Swiss descent, the age structure in the last quarter of the nineteenth century would have been exceptionally young. The same applies today to those descended from Cambodian-born parents, and to the more diffuse Latino ethnic group which is forming from Latin American parentage (Hayes-Bautista, Schink and Chapa, 1988; Minkler and Robertson, 1991).

Among British ethnic groups, the inspected data strongly suggest that the age structure of the Black–Other group is a product of this first-generation process. While not forgetting that some of the Black–Others recorded in 1991 would have been temporarily resident natives of the United States (especially on US Air Force bases), the extreme youthfulness of this ethnic group is consistent both with a large fraction being descendants of Caribbean-born and African-born Black British citizen parents, and with the self-ascription of the Black–Other designation by many adolescents and young adults. Put another way, the data support a hypothesis that the adoption of the Black–British or Black–Other designation at the expense of Black–Caribbean, Black–African and Asian labels is most likely in adolescence, on marriage, or by parental proxy on the birth of a child. The relative contributions of births and adult adoptions are, however, unclear. Consequently any prognosis concerning the pace of formation of a Black–British group, of people who willingly accept that designation, will be extremely difficult until a good understanding is achieved of the propensities to retain or reject the labels which describe the areas of parental origin. The problem is compounded by ambivalence about the label 'Black' among people of Asian descent (Hiro, 1992, viii–xi).

Age structure change in a last-generation group

If the Black–Other group is substantially a first-generation population, then its evolution will be directly associated with age structure change in the ethnic groups of its parents. It is a matter of both cultural and logical identity that if the progeny of an ethnic group create a new identity, the replacement of the parents' group ceases. If also the immigration flow stops, then the parents become the last generation. Over time, that population will progressively age and die. Evidence for this process will first be shortfalls in children, and then in successively older age-groups. There may be other signs in marriage and fertility patterns. With reference to the British ethnic minority groups, the intriguing questions are the extent to which this scenario is already moulding the age structure and vital statistics of the Black–Caribbean ethnic group and might face several others.

The question may throw light on the downward trend of fertility among women born in the Caribbean, which by 1991 was 0.81 of the England and Wales level. During the 1980s this proportion was itself reducing by 0.028 points each year. Some part of this decline may result from the increasing average age of the Caribbean-born population, but the contribution of identity switching should be considered. If when young Black–Africans and Black–Caribbeans have a child, the event increases their propensity to describe themselves as Black–Other or Black–British, then the result would be a reallocation of births from the Black–African and Black–Caribbean populations to Black–Others. In such cases, a birth might add not only a child but also one or two parents to the population of Black–Others. A fertility rate for that population would appear insupportably high.

Four extreme situations have been considered. None capture certain pervasive aspects of ethnic identity change. In a multi-ethnic population in an evolving society, identities evolve through mixed marriages and the intricate processes of acculturation and assimilation, including changes in religious affiliation and shifting attachments to racial, ancestral, religious and situational facets of identity (Coleman, 1985; Tizard and Pheonix, 1993). On this reasoning, the major problem in understanding the future age structure (and indeed future population size) of an ethnic group is that of understanding the influences on ethnic identity. This is a taxonomic problem of unusual sensitivity. Students of population must proceed carefully in applying conventional projection methods based solely on fertility, mortality and net migration. Even short-term projections related to the ageing of the extant population can in special circumstances be upset by altered identities and self-ascription.

6.7 Conclusions

This examination of the age structure of Britain's ethnic minority groups in 1991 has detailed variations around their common youthfulness sufficient to challenge assertions of homogeneity among them. The age structure of Black–Others is so distinct that (as in the cluster analysis) it resists association with any other ethnic minority group. On the other hand, the Black–Caribbeans have a relatively high average age and an age distribution that is quite similar to that of the White population. Not only do the average ages vary, so also do the ages of under- and over-representation. These differences reflect not only the ethnic groups' distinctive settlement histories, but also contrasts in the contemporary social and demographic processes that affect them.

The Black–African and Other – Asian populations have relatively few children and may still have a substantial turnover of people in their over-represented young working age-groups. The Black–Caribbeans also have relatively few children, partly as a result of low fertility but probably also associated with parents' ascription of their children as Black–Other. The latter population has a remarkably high proportion in the childhood ages: higher fertility is inadequate and probably inappropriate as the explanation, rather the operative process involves a substantial element of first-generation formation. On the other hand, the high proportion of children in the Pakistani and Bangladeshi populations are more likely to be accounted for by high fertility.

What signs and signals of prospective change come from this detailed inspection of the age distributions on census night? For the majority of Britain's ethnic minority groups, a pervasive trend for some decades will be progressive ageing and the spread of their age distributions. The extent to which relative youthfulness is preserved will depend on two factors: the level of net in-migration and the level of fertility. While in-migration flows may still be substantial, for the foreseeable future they are unlikely to be as high as previously. The highest current flows, for the Bangladeshi and Pakistani groups, may remain high but are unlikely to halt the relative ageing of the groups. Relatively high fertility among the Islamic ethnic groups will sustain high proportions of children for at least a decade, but the long-term prospects are uncertain.

Demographic ageing does not result exclusively in higher relative and absolute numbers of elderly people. The 1991 age distributions indicate that one manifestation over the next decade among most of the ethnic minority populations, particularly those originating from South Asia, will be a moderation of the under-representation of people in late working age. The strong social changes in the characteristics of these populations that this implies will include rapidly growing numbers of parents with adult children, of three-generation families, and of wider kinship networks within Britain. It may be that the growth of the well-established middle-aged population will promote the development of the voluntary sector within several ethnic minorities. Just as the Jewish community in Britain has often been 'regarded as a good example of how groups can help to meet the needs of its members by provision of voluntary services' (Bowling and Farquhar, 1993, 214; Schweitzer, 1991), several of the more recent ethnic minority groups, particularly those with strong religious traditions, may repeat that course.

The more commonly anticipated increase in the number of elderly people will in numerical terms be dominated by the Indian and Black–Caribbean groups. In 1991, these two groups accounted for 62 per cent of the ethnic minority population aged 50–59 years. The Pakistani population made up another 14.6 per cent, but no other group accounted for as much as 6 per cent. Moreover, in 1991 the Indian and Black–Caribbean minority group populations aged 75+ years totalled 15,468, 70 per cent of the ethnic minority total. It is therefore in these groups that some of the most problematic issues concerning incomes and poverty and the provision of primary care, community health, social service and residential care support will first manifest and require resolution.

As specialist commentaries have emphasised, the British elderly population has to date been little affected by the post-1950 settlement of ethnic minority groups but during the next decade the ethnic profile will change. Of the 8.8 million people aged 65+ years in Great Britain in 1991, only 87,958, or just under 1 per cent, were in the ethnic minority groups; and they comprised just 3,871 (0.5 per cent) of the 830,678 persons aged 85+ years. Research on the social, health and welfare characteristics of the older members of the ethnic minority groups is now gathering momentum (Ananthanarayanan, 1994; Atkin and Rollins, 1993; Blakemore and Boneham, 1994; Karmi, 1993). It remains the case that as many presumptions as well-founded statements circulate even among the professionals. Some urgency is required to increase our knowledge in these areas, for the early studies have revealed many unmet needs and, an incentive to the funding agencies, that many social and health care contacts are ineffectual, sometimes because of mutual communication difficulties and sometimes a result of misunderstanding about Britain's health and welfare institutions.

Many elderly people in Britain with origins in the Indian subcontinent live with their children in multi-generational households. A survey in 1987 of Asian elderly patients (55+ years) of five general medical practices in Central Birmingham Health Authority found that, of 84 people of Asian origin, 3.6 per cent lived alone, 8.3 per cent with a spouse only, and 88.1 per cent with others. The comparable percentages among a sample (n=66) of White patients were 43.9, 22.7 and 33.3 (Cameron *et al.*,1989, Table 13.5).

One should be wary, however, of simplicities about the strength of Asian family structures and of the family support that is available within them. Today's complex households may reflect primarily low income, and the older people who have migrated to join their children may be selective of strong kin ties. As material, housing and educational standards rise, family structures in the Asian-origin populations may change quickly (Walker and Ahmed, 1994). Elderly people originating from the Caribbean have living arrangements much closer to national norms. In some ethnic groups, there are large numbers of multiply-deprived elderly people, and their situation will be worsened by histories of low pay and incomplete histories of employment and National Insurance contributions. Some groups will also be disadvantaged, particularly with respect to their health and health care, by poor childhood nutritional and educational standards, ignorance of British institutions and entitlements, and poor reading or conversational ability in the English language (Ebrahim *et al.*, 1991; Ebrahim, 1992).

The educational, welfare and health institutions of this country are not necessarily adapted or receptive to the needs of ethnic minority populations. Initially questions of adjustment arise in the workplace, then in schools and vocational and higher educational institutions, and last in the services for frail and dependant elderly people. More than a decade ago, Blakemore (1982) found a high incidence of GP consultations among ethnic minority groups but remarkably low contacts with community health services and personal social services, particularly the meals-on-wheels and home-help domiciliary services. The same pattern has been found more recently (Balarajan *et al*, 1989; Boneham, 1989; Pharoah, 1995). Several researchers have suggested that it is the attitudes of general practitioners that are an important contributor to their own low referral rate of elderly people from ethnic minority groups to community health services (Cameron, Badger and Evers, 1989). This represents a special challenge to the purchasers and providers of community care under the post-1993 legislation, particularly for inner city community health service NHS trusts and local authority social services departments, for in these areas the independent and voluntary sectors are under-developed and poorly placed to respond to the retrenchment of direct local authority provision (Karmi, 1993).

There is clearly much that this country's institutions and professions can and should do in the way of advice, encouragement, practical support and direct provision in the support of ethnic minority elderly people (Askham *et al.*, 1995; Pharoah, 1995). Even within primary care, where a large proportion (possibly a majority in the London Boroughs) of general practitioners are themselves of Asian origin and the issues have been recognised for many years, high levels of ignorance and misinformation on the part of providers and patients are found. Among GPs there is a disappointing level of awareness of the special services provided by FHSAs and social service departments (Pharoah, 1995, 70–2). Pharoah's 1991 survey of 44 family health survey authority managers found that the most commonly cited need was for translation services and needs surveys (as echoed in evaluations of social service provision), and 'only two initiatives were seen as having been targeted specifically at elderly people from ethnic minority communities' (Pharoah, 1995, Chapter 2). Asian GPs were less likely than White GPs to see special needs in the elderly Asian-origin population, and were less likely to believe that family support is available. On the other hand, 'one-third of Asian service users but only one-in-ten of Caribbeans said they had problems with (health and social) services. For the Asians most of these problems were perceived as to do with ... ethnicity. When asked to say how services could be improved ... the main two were more interpreters and more Asian staff' (Askham *et al.*, 1995, 107).

It is disappointing that linguistic difficulties and a lack of knowledge of services are still identified as important barriers to service access among Asian-origin elderly people. The deficiencies will not be easily removed, for self-reinforcing cycles are described. The ignorance of services is associated with a lack of demand, which in turn relaxes pressure on the health and welfare agencies to appoint ethnic minority staff. That in turn contributes to the low profile and lack of awareness among the ethnic minority communities of the nature of the nation's health and welfare services. Once again, the case for more energetic study is reinforced by the heterogeneity and cultural diversity of Britain's ethnic minority populations.

With respect to needs and services, it is probably inadequate to generalise for Asians or for Blacks. As this detailed examination of age structure differences has suggested, it is close study of numerous and many quite small ethnic groups that will generate substantial improvements in our understanding of their needs and of the social and welfare consequences of their demographic evolution.

References

Ananthanarayanan, T.S. (1994) Epidemiology of mental illness among Asians in the United Kingdom. *British Journal of Hospital Medicine*, 52(10), 500–6.

Askham, J., Henshaw, L. and Tarpey, M. (1995) *Social and Health Authority Services for Elderly People from Black and Minority Ethnic Communities.* London: HMSO.

Atkin, K. and Rollins, J. (1993) *Community Care in a Multi-Racial Britain: A Critical Review of the Literature.* London: HMSO.

Balarajan, R., Yuen, P. and Soni Raleigh, V. (1989) Ethnic differences in general practitioner consultations. *British Medical Journal*, 299, 958–60.

Balarajan, R. and Bulusu, L. (1990) Mortality among immigrants in England and Wales, 1979–83. In: M. Britton (ed.), *Mortality and Geography: A Review in the Mid-1980s*, OPCS DS No. 9. London: HMSO.

Blakemore, K. and Boneham, M. (1994) *Age, Race and Ethnicity: A Comparative Approach.* Buckingham: Open University Press.

Boneham, M. (1989) Ageing and ethnicity in Britain: the case of elderly Sikh women in a Midlands town. *New Community*, 15(3), 447–59.

Bowling, A. and Farquhar, M. (1993) The health and well-being of Jewish people aged 65 to 85 years living at home in the East End of London. *Ageing and Society*, 13(2), 213–45.

Brown, C. (1984) *Black and White Britain: The Third PSI Survey*. Aldershot: Gower.

Cameron, E., Badger, F. and Evers, H. (1989) District nursing, the disabled and the elderly: who are the black patients? *Journal of Advanced Nursing*, 14(5), 376–82.

Cameron, E., Evers, H., Badger, F. and Atkin, K. (1989) Black old women, disability and health carers. In: M. Jefferys (ed.), *Growing Old in the Twentieth Century*. London: Routledge, pp. 230–48.

Coleman, D.A. (ed.) (1982) *Demography of Immigrant and Minority Groups in the United Kingdom*. London: Academic Press.

Coleman, D.A. (1985) Ethnic intermarriage in Great Britain. *Population Trends*, 40, 4–9.

Diamond, I. and Clarke, S. (1989) Demographic patterns among Britain's ethnic groups. In: H. Joshi (ed.), *The Changing Population of Britain*. Oxford: Basil Blackwell, pp. 177–98.

Donaldson, L. (1986) Health and social status of elderly Asians: a community survey. *British Medical Journal*, 293, 1079–82.

Ebrahim, S. (1992) Health and ageing within ethnic minorities. In: K. Morgan (ed.), *Gerontology: Responding to an Ageing Society*. London: Jessica Kingsley, pp. 50–62.

Ebrahim, S., Patel, N. and Coats, M. (1991) Prevalence and severity of morbidity among Gujarati Asian elderly: a controlled comparison. *Family Practice*, 8, 57–62.

Hall, R. and Hall J. (1995) Missing in the 1991 census: a million persons and £millions in grants. *Area*, 27(1), 53–61.

Hayes-Bautista, David E., Schink, W.O. and Chapa, J (1988) *The Burden of Support: Young Latinos in an Aging Society*. Stanford, CA: Stanford University Press.

Heady, P., Smith, S. and Avery, V. (1994) *The 1991 Census Validation Survey: Coverage Report*, OPCS Social Survey Report No. SS1334. London: HMSO.

Hiro, D. (1992) *Black British, White British: A History of Race Relations in Britain*. London: Paladin.

Karmi, G. (1993) Equity and health of ethnic minorities. *Quality in Health Care*, 2(2), 100–3.

McCalman, J.A. (1990) *The Forgotten People: Carers in Three Ethnic Minority Communities in Southwark*. London: King's Fund Centre.

Minkler, M. and Robertson, A. (1991) The ideology of age/race wars: deconstructing a social problem. *Ageing and Society*, 11(1), 1–22.

Norusis, M.J. (1990) *SPSS/PC+ Statistics 4.0 for the IBM PC/XT/AT and PS/2*. Chicago: SPSS Inc.

OPCS/GRO(S) (1993a) *1991 Census: Ethnic Group and Country of Birth, Great Britain*. London: HMSO.

OPCS (1993b) How complete was the 1991 Census?. *Population Trends*, 71, 22–5.

Pharoah, C. (1995) *Primary Care for Elderly People in Ethnic Minorities*. London: HMSO.

Robinson, V. (1986) *Transients, Settlers and Refugees: Asians in Britain*. Oxford: Clarendon.

Schweitzer, P. (1991) A place to stay: growing old away from home. In: A.J. Squires (ed.), *Multicultural Health Care and Rehabilitation*. London: Edward Arnold.

Simpson, S. and Dorling, D. (1994) Those missing millions: implications for social statistics of non-response to the 1991 census. *Journal of Social Policy*, 23(4), 543–67.

Tizard, B. and Phoenix, A. (1993) *Black, White or Mixed Race*. London: Routledge.

Walker, R. and Ahmed, W. (1994) Asian and Black elders and community care: a survey of care providers. *New Community*, 20(4), 635–46.

Chapter 7
Marriage patterns and inter-ethnic unions

Ann Berrington

7.1 Introduction

Marriage and family formation are areas in which ethnic diversity can be clearly seen. Cultural and religious preferences and beliefs as to if, when, and whom one is expected to marry vary between (but also within) the ethnic groups as identified in the census. At the same time these preferences are modified by the socio-economic opportunities and constraints facing individuals in contemporary Britain, for example the availability of a suitable spouse, the opportunity for women to continue into higher education before commencing marriage and family formation, and so on. The investigation of marriage patterns among ethnic minority groups in Britain is made complex by the fact that some will have married before arriving in Britain and the process of marriage and family formation is itself likely to have been affected by the process of migration.

There are a number of reasons for the interest in analysing ethnic differences in marriage patterns. First, traditional patterns of marriage in the original populations from which ethnic minority individuals in Britain come, are often very different to those customary in Britain. Therefore the extent to which traditional patterns of marriage among ethnic minority populations are attenuated into those of the host population have been seen by some as evidence of assimilation. Indeed, the number of inter-ethnic unions is clearly an indicator of the extent of integration and mixing between ethnic groups (Gordon, 1964; Coleman, 1985). However, it must be noted that demographic convergence is not necessarily associated with assimilation and equality in other spheres of life, such as education and employment.

Second, patterns of entry into, and exit from marriage have important implications for family and household formation (Berrington, 1994; Murphy, Chapter 8). For some individuals age at first marriage remains an important indicator of entry into regular sexual intercourse and hence exposure to childbearing. For others, informal unions are likely to occur before and outside of marriage. Fortunately data on informal cohabiting unions are also available from the census.

Finally, much attention has focused on the documented rise in age at first marriage among women in South Asia, as an indication of increasing levels of female status (McDonald 1985; Casterline *et al.*, 1986; Duza, 1989; Singh, 1989; Alam and Leete, 1993). Interest lies therefore in identifying trends and differentials in the age at first marriage among South Asian women in Britain. Similarly, large spousal age differences traditionally found among patriarchal societies in South Asia and Africa have also been seen as an indication of a lack of female status (Casterline *et al.* 1986; Cain 1993) and have important consequences for widowhood and household formation in later years. Given that it is important to analyse ethnic patterns of marriage and family formation, what data are available which allow us to do so?

Data sources for investigating marriage patterns among ethnic minority groups

Since neither country of birth nor ethnicity is recorded at marriage registration, patterns of marriage formation and dissolution among ethnic minority groups must be deduced from data provided in censuses and sample surveys. At present no data are available to study the dynamics of entry into and out of marriage among ethnic minority groups. While retrospective marriage histories are collected within the General Household Survey, the sample size (10,000 households per annum) is not sufficient to analyse marriage and family formation patterns among individual ethnic minority groups. Some longitudinal information on changes in marital status, for example between censuses or successive births, is available from the Office of Population Censuses and Survey's Longitudinal Study (LS), but only by country of birth. More useful data on ethnicity will be available from the LS in the future once the 1991 Census information has been linked.

In the meanwhile in order to compare marriage patterns among ethnic groups, we have to look to cross-sectional data, which provide us with a 'snapshot' picture of an individual's marital status at the time of the census or survey. Previous work in this area has used data collected within the Labour Force Survey, which has a sample size of around 60,000 households per annum (Berrington, 1994). This chapter uses the 1991 Census to compare ethnic differences in current marital status, the prevalence of cohabiting unions, spousal age differences, and the propensity to form inter-ethnic unions. In all these analyses the data refer to the total (private and institutional) resident population of Great Britain. Information on ethnicity is obtained from the census ethnic group question, where answers to the precoded tick boxes together with written in answers, are used to assign individuals to one of 35 ethnic groups, which have then been collapsed into a ten-fold output classification released in the Samples of Anonymised Records. For further details of the coding of the ethnic group question see Chapter 2 and OPCS/GRO (Scotland) (1992).

7.2 Information on marital status from the 1991 Census

Legal marital status

Question four of the 1991 Census household form collects information on legal marital status (Box 7.1). The marital status question has remained unchanged in England and Wales since 1981, though in Scotland in 1981 the question did not distinguish between first and subsequent marriages. These census data are then processed for 100 per cent of the population and tables

published in the census volume *1991 Census Sex Age and Marital Status.*
(OPCS/GRO(S) 1993)

The distinction between married (first marriage) and remarried provides an
additional index of the level of marital dissolution among different ethnic
groups. Comparison of the size of the remarried population as compared
with the population of currently divorced and widowed provides an indication of the level of remarriage. However, in many of the published tables
(including that for marital status by ethnic group), the two married groups
are amalgamated and this additional information is lost. In order to retain
this information and analyse the full marital status distribution for each
ethnic group (as shown in Appendix 7.1) it is necessary to use the two per
cent Sample of Anonymised Records (SAR).

The census marital status question does not allow individuals to describe
themselves as separated, and it seems likely that some people who have
experienced marriage breakdown but have not completed their legal divorce proceedings will report themselves as divorced as opposed to legally
married. In fact, data from the 1991 Census Validation Survey suggest that
4.2 per cent of those who reported themselves as divorced in the census
should have been reported as married (first marriage). Other discrepancies
are much smaller and include a slight under-reporting of remarriages and
overstatement of first marriages (OPCS, 1994). Cohabiters are categorised
within this question in a number of ways depending upon their legal marital
status. Never-married cohabiters would theoretically be described as single,
while individuals who are legally married but currently cohabiting with
someone who is not their spouse should be classified as married, but may
have described themselves as divorced or even remarried.

Cohabitation

The 1991 Census is the first UK census which collected reliable information
on *de facto* cohabiting relationships. Cohabiting couples can be derived from
question five – relationship in household – whereby each individual is asked
to specify their relationship to a reference individual. The question attempts
to identify cohabiting partnerships by means of a stated category on the
census form. The list of relationship codes differs from that in 1981 in that
'cohabitant' replaces *'de facto* spouse' (derived from write-in answers) and

that 'child of cohabitant' and 'cohabitant of son/daughter' are included in an attempt to identify hidden families within households. A computer algorithm was then used by the OPCS to allocate individuals within households into family units of which four main types are identified in the SAR (Box 7.2). Because families, as defined in the census, may only contain two generations if the younger generation is single (never married) and has no partner or offspring, we can assume that the oldest male and oldest female in cohabiting couple families are themselves the cohabiting couple[1].

Estimates of the proportions currently cohabiting derived from the census in this way are similar to those from the General Household Survey and the Labour Force Survey in 1991 (Table 7.1).

To summarise then, the following analyses use census data from a variety of sources and at different levels of aggregation. Legal marital status can be obtained for the 10 summary ethnic groups by sex and five-year age-groups from the published 100 per cent tables. Further information on legal marital status including *remarriage* by ethnic group can be obtained using cross-tabulations from the two per cent individual SAR. However, analyses of *cohabitation* require information on all household members, at the individual level, which can be obtained from the one per cent household SAR. In each analysis the largest data source within which the investigation is possible has been used so as to maximise sample size.

Box 7.2 *Family unit type*

1. **Married couple family:** a married couple with or without their never-married child(ren) including a childless married couple

2. **Cohabiting couple family:** two persons of the opposite sex living together as a couple with or without their never-married child(ren) – including a childless cohabiting couple.

3. **Lone parent family:** a father or mother together with his or her never married child(ren).

4. **No family person:** an individual member of a household not assigned with other members to a family.

Table 7.1 *Comparison of estimates of cohabitation from 1991 Census, 1991 Labour Force Survey, 1991/2 General Household Survey[1]. Men and women aged 16-24, Great Britain*

Sex	Percentage cohabiting		
	1991 Census	1991 LFS	1991/2 GHS[1]
Men	6.8	6.7	7.6
Women	10.6	10.5	11.7

[1]GHS estimate derived from information collected in the Family Information   Section.
Source: 1991 Census One Per Cent Household SAR (ESRC/JISC purchase). Crown Copyright. 1991 Labour Force Survey. 1991/2 General Household Survey.

7.3 Entry into marriage

Age at first marriage

It is usual in situations where there is no direct information on age at first marriage for the proportions single within each sex and five-year age-group to be used to estimate a 'singulate mean age at marriage' (SMAM) (Table 7.2). The SMAM, derived by Hajnal (1953), is an estimate of the average number of years spent single by those who ultimately marry. The calculation procedure is shown in Box 7.3. Caution is required in the interpretation of this measure in situations where patterns of entry into first marriage are changing rapidly over time. If the age at first marriage has been rising over the past years, as is likely for most of the ethnic groups, the SMAM will tend to underestimate the current true mean age at first marriage. Despite this the SMAM remains a useful summary measure to describe the very different patterns of entry into first marriage shown for some of the ethnic groups in Figures 7.1 (a) and (b).

As Table 7.2 shows, the singulate mean age at marriage is generally lower among women than men. The exception is among the Black–Caribbean and Black–Other ethnic groups where the SMAM is very similar for men and women or even slightly higher among women, (though the value of measuring age of entry into 'legal marriage' is questionable for these groups as stable sexual unions are likely to take place outside this formal framework).

Among women, the lowest SMAMs are reported among the South Asian ethnic minority groups, particularly Bangladeshi (21 years) and Pakistani women (22 years). Indian ethnic minority women delay marriage until somewhat later. Higher ages at first marriage are found among the White (27 years) and Black populations (28–33 years). The same general trend is found among men, though the range is somewhat smaller: from 25 years among Pakistani and Bangladeshi men, to 31 years among Black–Caribbean men.

Table 7.2 *Singulate mean age at marriage by sex and ethnic group. Resident population, Great Britain, 1991*

Ethnic group	Men	N	Women	N
White	28.3	25066,379	26.7	26807,415
Black–Caribbean	31.3	239,484	33.3	260,480
Black–African	29.7	106,800	28.4	105,562
Black–Other	29.6	87,513	29.8	90,888
Indian	26.3	422,891	23.7	417,364
Pakistani	24.5	246,572	22.3	230,983
Bangladeshi	25.2	84,944	21.2	77,891
Chinese	28.9	77,669	26.4	79,269
Other–Asian	28.9	93,605	23.8	103,929
Other	28.6	150,097	27.1	140,109

Source: Derived from Table 6, 1991 Census Sex Age and Marital Status. London: HMSO

Box 7.3

The singulate Mean Age At Marriage (SMAM), (Hajnal, 1953) is an indirect measure of age at marriage used in circumstances where no direct information on age at marriage are collected. The SMAM uses the percentage single at each age at the time of the census to estimate the average number of years spent single by those who marry.

It assumes:
1) That all those who marry do so before age 50
2) That first marriage patterns have been constant in the past

Example – following Newell (1988)

Indian ethnic minority women in Britain

Age	Percentage Single		
		Years of singleness before age 50	= 2454.76
		Percentage single at age 50	= 2.79
16–19	94.37		
20–24	56.35	Number of years spent single by those	
25–29	19.66	who never marry	= 139.25
30–34	8.02		
35–39	4.73	Number of years spent single by those	
40–44	3.71	who marry	= 2315.51
45–49	2.99		
50–54	2.58	Percentage married by age 50	= 97.21
		Average number of years spent single by those who marry	= 23.82

The earlier and near universal entry of South Asian men and women into marriage can be seen clearly in Figures 7.1 (a) and (b), where the proportion married rises quickly such that by their early thirties around nine out of ten men are married, in comparison with only three quarters of White men, two thirds of Black–African men, and only half of Black–Caribbean and Black–Other men. The pattern for women is similar with the vast majority of Bangladeshi women married by their early thirties, in comparison with 83 per cent of White women, two thirds of Black–African women and just four out of ten Black–Caribbean women. These very different marriage patterns have important implications for household and family formation as discussed further in Berrington (1994) and Murphy (Chapter 8, this volume).

Trends in age at first marriage — comparison with the 1981 Census

Since the early 1970s, first marriage rates and the proportions ever-married by each age have decreased substantially for England and Wales as a whole. Comparison of the proportions single by sex and age according to country of birth (ethnicity was not collected in the 1981 Census), using data from the 1981 and 1991 Censuses, allows us to determine whether this delay in marriage was confined to particular ethnic groups. The data published in Table 7 of the 1981 Census report *Sex, Age and Marital Status* refer to just six age-groups: 0–15, 16–19, 20–24, 25–29, 30–44, and 45 and over. We are unable therefore to compute and compare SMAMs for each country of birth in 1981 and 1991, but can replicate the 1981 published table for 1991 by using the two per cent individual SAR (Table 7.3).

Figure 7.1(a) *Percentage ever married by ethnic group, men, Great Britain, 1991*

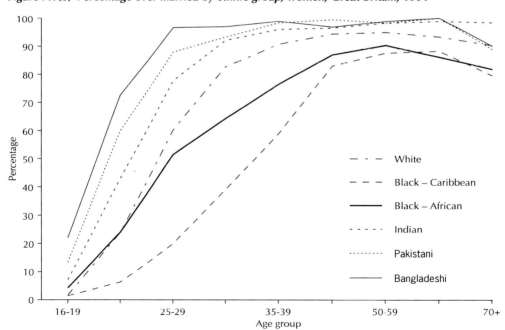

Source: 1991 Census Two Per Cent Individual SAR

Figure 7.1(b) *Percentage ever married by ethnic group, women, Great Britain, 1991*

Source: 1991 Census Two Per Cent Individual SAR

Table 7.3 *Percentage single in 1981 and 1991 according to sex, age and country of birth. Resident population, Great Britain*

Country of birth	Men			Women		
	1981	1991	Relative percentage change	1981	1991	Relative percentage change
Age group 20-24						
UK	74.3	88.6	**19***	53.6	76.1	**42***
Caribbean New Commonwealth[1]	87.0	94.7	**9**	55.3	54.0	**-1**
India	49.1	75.0	**53***	21.9	33.3	**52***
Pakistan	51.8	59.2	**14**	17.0	19.9	**17**
Bangladesh	61.1	73.1	**20***	9.8	22.5	**130***
Age group 25-29						
UK	33.4	53.6	**47***	18.5	38.0	**105***
Caribbean New Commonwealth	55.3	54.0	**-2**	54.7	54.6	**0**
India	15.9	23.8	**50***	6.6	12.5	**91***
Pakistan	15.5	20.7	**34***	4.5	7.6	**67***
Bangladesh	19.8	27.6	**39**	2.5	2.3	**-8**

[1] Includes Barbados, Jamaica, Trinidad Tobago, Other independent States, Caribbean Dependent States.
* Statistically significant difference at the five per cent level.

Source: Table 7 1981 Census: Sex Age Marital Status. London:HMSO and 1991 Census: Two Per Cent Individual SAR (ESRC/JISC purchase). Crown copyright.

While it is difficult to compare changes over this period when the baseline proportions of individuals who were single in 1981 are so different, it seems that (apart from the Caribbean-born population), all groups have seen a significant increase in the proportions remaining single by their mid- and late-twenties. The relative percentage change is particularly great among Bangladeshi-born women in their early twenties, and even more notable among Indian-born men and women *throughout* their twenties.

Comparison of 'first-' and 'second-generation' individuals

One might expect ethnic minority individuals who have spent all, or a considerable part of their lives growing up in Britain to have marriage patterns intermediate between those traditionally found in the country of origin and those of the dominant White culture. Previous analyses using Labour Force Survey data (Berrington, 1994) suggested that 'second-generation' South Asians were indeed delaying marriage to a later age than their 'first-generation' counterparts. In those analyses, individuals who had arrived in the UK under the age of five were included as 'second-generation'. Year of entry is not collected in the census and so 'second-generation' in these analyses refers to those born inside the United Kingdom.

The concentrated time span of the main migration streams to Britain during the 1960s and 1970s has resulted in little overlap between cohorts born outside the UK and the UK-born. As a result, it is not possible to summarise the patterns of entry into marriage in terms of a singulate mean age at marriage which requires information from age 15 to 50, but one can compare those age-groups for which there is a sufficient sample size (Table 7.4). The small number of non-UK-born Black–Caribbean and Black–Other individuals in the two per cent SAR means that the Black–Caribbean, Black–African and Black–Other ethnic groups have been combined, while the lack of UK-born Bangladeshis requires them to be combined with the Pakistani population. Small sample sizes have also meant that the Chinese population is included within Other–Asian.

Table 7.4 *Percentage of men and women who are single according to whether 'first -' or 'second ' generation Resident population, Great Britain, 1991*

	Men				Women			
	% Single		N		% Single		N	
	Generation				Generation			
	'Second-'	'First-'	'Second-'	'First-'	'Second-'	'First-'	'Second-'	'First-'
Age group 20-24								
White	88.6	88.0*	36,796	1,515	76.1	80.0*	36,909	1,792
Black	95.9	87.6*	681	153	91.9	71.3*	681	188
Indian	82.0	82.6	471	258	61.6	51.1*	385	282
Pakistani/Bangladeshi	76.2	64.6*	286	285	57.4	21.4*	251	323
Other–Asian[1]	92.5	93.8	93	307	78.8	77.1	80	288
Other	85.7	94.5	42	164	88.4	68.8*	189	80
Age group 25-29								
White	53.2	58.2*	38,182	1,878	37.1	46.2*	38,550	1,999
Black	80.9	58.2*	729	256	79.7	46.5*	859	357
Indian	32.0	32.1	178	499	27.5	21.0	153	628
Pakistani/Bangladeshi	32.8	22.8	64	338	29.2	6.5*	65	338
Other–Asian	73.0	50.4*	37	341	(48.3)	31.3	29	376
Other	69.1	46.9*	139	147	62.5	38.5*	136	121

[1] Includes Chinese
* Statistically significant difference at the five per cent level

Source: 1991 Census Two Per Cent Individual SAR (ESRC/JISC purchase). Crown Copyright.

Inspection of Table 7.4 suggests that, apart from the White ethnic group, UK-born individuals are generally more likely to be single than their non-UK-born counterparts. The very low levels of marriage among the UK-born Black population, most of whom are Black–Caribbean or Black–Other, is particularly striking. While no differences are found between 'first-' and 'second-generation' Indian ethnic minority men, there is some evidence, at least among the younger age-group, that 'second-generation' Indian women delay marriage to a later age than their 'first-generation' counterparts. This trend is seen more clearly among men and women of Pakistani and Bangladeshi ethnic origin. For example, over three quarters of UK-born Pakistani and Bangladeshi men aged 20–24 are single, compared with less than two thirds of non-UK-born men. Similarly over half of UK-born Pakistani and

Bangladeshi women in their early twenties are currently single, compared with only one in five non-UK-born women. Similar findings have recently been made by Heath and Dale (1994). Interpretation of these results is somewhat difficult however as some young South Asians born outside the UK will have migrated to Britain for the purpose of marriage. Migration of spouses from the Indian subcontinent is discussed further in section 7.6.

The cultural context of marriage among the South Asian population in Britain

The traditional pattern of earlier and near universal marriage among the South Asian ethnic minorities seems to be continuing in contemporary Britain, though all ethnic groups have seen some delay in marriage and increase in the age at marriage over the last decade, as have the populations of South Asia. Age at first marriage has often been seen as an indicator of female status and much attention has focused upon the steady rise in age at first marriage in South Asia (McDonald, 1985; Casterline *et al.*, 1986; Duza, 1989; Singh, 1989; Alam and Leete, 1993). For example, the SMAM for women in India has risen steadily, from 13 at the beginning of the century, to 19.7 years in 1991 (Alam and Leete, 1993; Office of the Registrar General, India, 1994). Similarly, age at marriage has increased in Bangladesh where estimates from the 1989 Bangladesh Fertility Survey suggest SMAMs of 25.5 and 18.0 years respectively, compared with estimates from the 1961 Census of 22.9 and 13.9 (National Institute of Population Research and Training, 1993). Data from the 1991 Pakistan Demographic and Health Survey provide SMAMs of 26.5 and 21.7 years for men and women (Pakistan Demographic and Health Survey, 1992).

Bearing in mind the pronounced regional variations in age at marriage hidden within these national level data, it seems that age at marriage among South Asian women in Britain, is higher than for women in South Asia. But among South Asian men, age at marriage is if anything lower among those living in Britain.

The UK census data highlight important differences within the South Asian ethnic minority population, in particular the higher age at marriage among Indian ethnic minority men and women, emphasising the importance of examining (as far as sample sizes will permit) each ethnic group separately. Further work is required to investigate the extent to which this delay in marriage is associated with an increase in higher eduction, and the growth in labour force participation, especially among non-Muslim South Asian women. Estimates from the 1989–91 Labour Force Surveys suggest that while two thirds of Indian ethnic minority women aged 25–34 are economically active (roughly the same percentage as for White women), the figures for Pakistani and Bangladeshi women are much lower at 22 per cent and 10 per cent respectively (Berrington, 1994).

Qualitative research has shown how the entry of many Asian women into (often full-time) work outside the home, albeit in relatively low-paid, insecure jobs, can modify their roles as wife and mother. For example, the increased importance of women's wage labour in supporting household income among Asian families in Britain, has meant some renegotiation of household roles (Bhachu, 1985; Warrier, 1988; Westwood, 1988). The entry of women into the labour market also has important implications for the marriage process itself. As Westwood (1988) argues 'for young women coming to Britain and some British Asians, the issue of dowry has become enmeshed with the notion of the bride as a wage labourer capable of realizing wages through the exchange of labour power in the market'. Bhachu (1985) describes how the increased earning power of many young Sikh women means that they are now able to make significant contributions to their own *daajs* (dowry) and hence may demand more control over them.

Among the relatively successful East African Sikh community increasing importance is being placed upon the *individual* assets of the potential spouses (home ownership of the groom, educational qualifications, etc.) such that the marriage is becoming more 'couple-orientated' and less of an alliance between two families (Bhachu, 1985). Further differences in marriage patterns within the South Asian ethnic minorities are likely, according to religion, caste and geographical region of origin (Bhachu, 1985; Westwood, 1988; Ballard, 1990).

Table 7.5 *Percentage of men and women aged 25–29 who are single according to higher educational qualifications.[1] Resident population, Great Britain, 1991*

Ethnic group	Men				Women			
	% Single		N		% Single		N	
	Diploma or above	None	Diploma or above	None	Diploma or above	None	Diploma or above	None
White	61.5	51.5*	7,724	32,336	50.4	34.7*	7,445	33,104
Black	73.3	75.3	135	850	68.9	70.2	177	1,039
Indian	50.6	25.3*	182	495	45.1	17.1*	144	637
Pakistani/Bangladeshi	54.2	19.2*	59	343	(56.3)	8.3*	16	387
Chinese	53.0	58.0	83	112	44.1	32.8	59	116
Other–Asian	60.4	44.6	53	130	31.4	28.5	51	179
Other	68.5	52.8*	89	197	56.3	49.5	71	182

* Statistically significant difference at the 5 per cent level.
[1] The census only collected information on educational qualifications at or above diploma level. Individuals who did not report their educational qualifications are included in the group with no, or below diploma level qualifications.

Source: 1991 Census Two Per Cent Individual SAR (ESRC/JISC purchase). Crown copyright.

In addition to these traditional cultural variations in marriage patterns we are also likely to find differences related to education, social class and other attributes associated with contemporary Britain (Heath and Dale, 1994). Table 7.5 demonstrates the large variation in the proportions married in their late twenties according to educational qualification. It is immediately clear that education is an important factor delaying the age at marriage among all ethnic groups (except the Black ethnic groups where the percentage married among both educational groups is relatively low). The differential between those with higher level qualifications and those with none is much larger than the differentials between 'first-' and 'second-generation' men and women shown previously in Table 7.4. For example, among Indian ethnic minority men, half of those with higher qualifications are single, compared with a quarter of those without. Among Indian ethnic minority women the percentage single among those with higher qualifications (45 per cent) is almost as high as that for White ethnic minority women with higher qualifications and is much higher than White women without higher qualifications. The same pattern is found among Pakistani and Bangladeshi women, where over half of those with higher level qualifications are single, compared with just 8 per cent of those without. However caution must be used in interpreting these estimates as precise figures, as the sample of women with higher level qualifications is small. We can see then that cultural preferences as to age at marriage are to some extent modified by the socio-economic opportunities and constraints facing individuals.

Marriage patterns among Black–Caribbean, Black–African and Black–Other ethnic minorities

In contrast to the South Asian ethnic groups, the Black–Caribbean, Black–African and Black–Other populations in Britain are much less likely to be currently married and are much more likely to be single. As Figure 7.1 shows, even by their late thirties just less than half of Black–Caribbean men and under two thirds of Black–African men are married. Most researchers have tended to assume that these patterns result from the customary marriage and family formation processes found in the Caribbean, where unions are likely to take place outside formal marriage.

Traditionally in the Caribbean, couples may live together without being legally married in a 'common-law' marriage, or they may be in a regular sexual partnership but not living together as a couple, in a 'visiting union'. Hence childbearing frequently takes place outside formal marriage, and there is an emphasis on the mother–child bond and a lack of emphasis upon the conjugal bond (Clarke, 1957; Smith, 1956). Recent data from the Trinidad and Tobago Demographic and Health Survey demonstrate the continuation of these traditional union formation patterns (Heath *et al.*, 1988).

Unfortunately relatively little recent empirical research has been undertaken to investigate the development of Afro-Caribbean marriage and family structure in Britain, though Driver (1982) and Barrow (1982) both provide some insight into the impact of migration on traditional patterns of West Indian domestic organisation, and the qualitative research undertaken by Goody and Groothues (1979) highlights ways in which traditional marital roles among West African couples are adapted to life in London. More recently, national level data from the Labour Force Survey suggest that cohabitation remains commonplace among both 'first-' and 'second-generation' Afro-Caribbeans in Britain (Berrington, 1994), and the proportion of births to Caribbean-born women which occur outside marriage has remained at around one half (OPCS, 1993a).

The delay and/or rejection of marriage by Black women has lead to much debate particularly in the United States where the differentials in marriage and family formation between White and Black women has increased recently (Farley, 1988; DaVanzo and Rahman, 1993). Explanations, both in the United States and Britain, generally focus on the structural constraints faced by Black women in finding a suitable spouse, both historically as a result of colonialism and slavery, and currently given the higher levels of unemployment, and lower levels of education among Black men (Smith, 1957; Staples, 1985; Farley, 1988; Stone, 1983; Phoenix, 1987). Other researchers have argued that there is less economic incentive for Black women to marry given their high labour force participation rates and the small wage differential between Black men and women (Stone, 1983; Farley, 1988). More recently, attitudinal data from the United States have revealed racial differences in the desire to marry, and in individuals' economic and romantic expectations and perceived benefits of marriage (Bulcroft and Bulcroft, 1993; South, 1993). As Table 7.5 shows, the low levels of marriage among Black–Caribbean, Black–African and Black–Other men and women in Britain are found among both those with and without higher levels of education.

7.4 Marital breakdown and remarriage among ethnic minority groups

Divorce

The census provides us with the proportions currently divorced (decree absolute) by ethnic group, sex and age (Appendix 7.1). By comparing those in a particular age-group, say those in their forties, it is immediately obvious that the proportions currently divorced are highest among the Black–Caribbean and Black–Other populations (around 13 per cent of men and 20 per cent of women) and slightly lower among the White population (9 per cent of men and 12 per cent of women). Higher levels of marital dissolution among the Black as compared with the White population are also found in the United States (Staples, 1985; DaVanzo and Rahman, 1993); a trend which persists once other structural and compositional factors have been controlled (Castro-Martin and Bumpass, 1989). Again researchers in both the United States and Britain have highlighted the greater economic independence of Black women compared with their White counterparts, as a factor facilitating divorce and separation (Foner, 1979; Staples, 1985).

In contrast, divorce is relatively uncommon within the South Asian ethnic minorities, the proportion currently divorced reaching 2 per cent among Indian men, but less than 2 per cent among Pakistani and Bangladeshi men. The proportions divorced among South Asian women were similarly low at around 3 per cent, though as shown more clearly in Figure 7.2 (b), divorce is more common among young Indian women. Although permitted under Islam and within Hindu and Sikh culture under certain circumstances, divorce is very strongly discouraged. Indeed a divorced women may have no role outside of her husbands family and may not be able to rejoin her own extended family. According to Booth (1992) potential deportation may also be a factor discouraging men and women who have recently arrived in the UK for the purpose of marriage to separate.

Remarriage

The size of the currently divorced population will be affected not only by the rates of entry into marriage and rates of breakdown of these marriages, but also by rates of remarriage. By combining the percentage who are currently divorced and widowed with those who are remarried we arrive at the percentage who have ever experienced marital breakdown. Figures 7.2 (a) and (b) show, for a selection of ethnic groups, the percentage of ever-married men and women up to age 50–59 who have experienced marital dissolution. Confining attention to the ever-married population controls for the size of the population which is actually at risk of marital breakdown.

Examination of Figures 7.2 (a) and (b) demonstrates the much higher levels of marital dissolution among Black–Caribbean, Black–African and White men and women compared with South Asian men and women. At the same time however, there is some divergence among the South Asian populations such that young Indians, particularly Indian women, are more likely to experience divorce than young Pakistani or Bangladeshis.

The relative size of the remarried group in comparison with the size of the divorced population gives some indication of the likelihood of remarriage among the different ethnic groups. As seen in Appendix 7.1, the remarried population is much larger as a percentage of the population which has experienced marital breakdown among the White and South Asian ethnic minorities, and much smaller among the Black population. For example, among White women in their forties roughly the same percentage (around 12 per cent) are currently divorced as are currently remarried. Among Black–Caribbean, Black–African and Black–Other women however, the ratio is much lower. For example, among Black–Caribbean women in their forties, 20 per cent are currently divorced and 6 per cent are currently remarried. These data suggest that the propensity to remarry following divorce is much lower among the Black ethnic minorities, as is the case in the United States (Staples, 1985; DaVanzo and Rahman, 1993).

Widowhood

The prevalence of widowhood in any society depends upon the general level of mortality in that society, the average difference in age between spouses, the relative mortality levels of men and women in the society and, finally, the level of remarriage among widows. As shown in Appendix 7.1 the size of the widowed population increases particularly rapidly with age among the South Asian populations such that one in three women in their sixties are currently widowed, compared with one in four White women. This higher level of widowhood is likely to be due to large spousal age differences (especially within the Bangladeshi community (see section 6), combined with a cultural tradition found among most South Asian societies for widows not to remarry, but to remain supported within their husband's lineage

Figure 7.2(a) *Percentage of ever married men who have experienced marital dissolution, Great Britain, 1991*

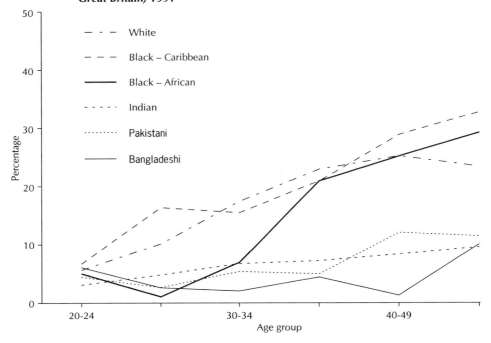

Source: 1991 Census Two Per Cent Individual SAR

Figure 7.2(b) *Percentage of ever married women who have experienced marital dissolution, Great Britain, 1991*

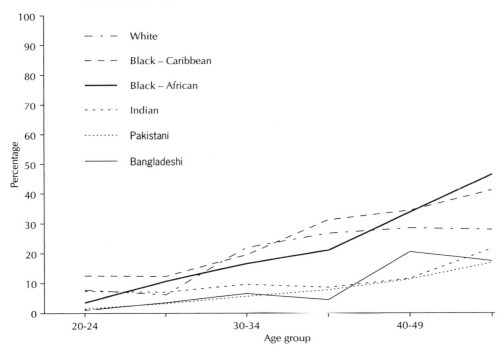

Source: 1991 Census Two Per Cent Individual SAR

Demographic characteristics of the ethnic minority populations

(McDonald, 1985). It also seems likely that some of these widowed women have migrated as widows from the Indian subcontinent (where mortality levels are much higher and hence widowhood more common) to join sons and daughters settled in the UK.

7.5 The prevalence of cohabitation among ethnic minority groups

In Britain as a whole, cohabitation is becoming an increasingly important part of individuals' life courses. For example, among first marriages taking place in the late 1980s, half of couples lived together before marriage (OPCS, 1993b). Table 7.6 shows the proportions currently cohabiting by sex and ethnic group for those age-groups where cohabitation is most prevalent. Women enter into cohabitation at a younger age than men. Proportions cohabiting are generally similar among the White population and the Black ethnic minority population, with Black–Africans being consistently less likely to cohabit than Black–Caribbean or Black–Other groups (a feature related to their earlier and higher levels of marriage). Among those aged 16–24, 7 per cent and 11 per cent of White men and women respectively were reported to be cohabiting in comparison with 6 per cent of Black–Caribbean men and women, and 4 per cent of Black–African men and women. Indian, Pakistani and Bangladeshi ethnic minority men and women are much less likely to be in a cohabiting union (less than 1 per cent). Further work is required to investigate the duration and stability of cohabiting unions and their relationship with childbearing and rearing within the different ethnic minority groups.

Table 7.6 *Proportions currently cohabiting by sex, age and ethnic group. Resident population, Great Britain, 1991*

Ethnic group	Age group 16–24				Age group 25–39			
	Men		Women		Men		Women	
	%	N	%	N	%	N	%	N
White	7.1	31,405	11.2	31,337	11.2	53,745	9.9	55,065
Black–Caribbean	6.1	343	6.1	345	18.5	617	9.0	733
Black–African	3.7	162	4.3	140	5.6	337	5.7	354
Black–Other	6.6	152	5.0	161	14.5	145	9.7	207
Indian	0.5	600	0.7	606	2.4	1,091	0.8	1,082
Pakistani/Bangladeshi	0.4	501	0.2	481	1.4	576	1.0	594
Other–Asian	1.6	257	3.8	261	1.7	460	2.1	570
Other	2.0	199	6.4	218	7.7	353	7.6	317

Source: 1991 Census One Per Cent Houshold SAR (ESRC/JISC purchase). Crown Copyright.

Further interest lies in predicting future trends in cohabiting unions: will they become more prevalent among the South Asians ethnic minorities? Some clues may be found in Table 7.7, where 'first-' and 'second-generation' individuals are compared. Among all groups (except Pakistani and Bangladeshi women) the data suggest that those born in the UK are more likely to cohabit, though relatively small sample sizes mean that the results are statistically significant for only Indian and Other ethnic minority men and Other–Asian women (2). The large difference seen among the residual Other ethnic group largely results from the different ethnicities of those making up the UK-, and non-UK-born populations (the former include individuals of mixed race and the latter include Arab, North African and Iranian ethnic groups).

Table 7.7 *Comparison of percentage currently cohabiting among 'first-' and 'second-generation, men and women aged 25–34. Resident population, Great Britain, 1991*

Ethnic group	Men				Women			
	'Second-'		'First-generation'		'Second-'		'First-generation'	
	%	N	%	N	%	N	%	N
White	11.2	51,375	10.8	2,370	9.9	52,418	10.5	2,647
Black–Caribbean	19.8	384	16.3	233	10.3	416	7.3	317
Black–African	7.1	56	5.3	281	9.0	78	4.7	276
Black–Other	18.2	99	6.5	46	10.1	149	8.6	58
Indian	5.6	126	2.0	965*	1.7	120	0.7	962
Pakistani/Bangladeshi	1.7	58	1.4	518	0	61	1.1	533
Other–Asian	(3.9)	26	1.6	434	(11.1)	27	1.7	543*
Other	13.6	132	4.1	221*	10.5	143	5.2	174

* Statistically significant difference at the 5 per cent level.

Source: 1991 Census One Per Cent Houshold SAR (ESRC/JISC purchase). Crown Copyright.

7.6   Spousal age differences and the marriage market

Spousal age differences

Previous analyses have highlighted cross-national variations in spousal age differences (Casterline *et al*, 1986) and variations between ethnic groups in Britain (Airey, 1985; Berrington, 1994). The analysis of spousal age differences is complex. The age difference between partners will differ according to the ages of couples included in the analyses and according to the type of union (first-marriage, remarriage, etc.) and marital status of the individual involved. It is well known that spousal age differences are smaller among remarried women compared with those marrying for the first time.

For the purpose of this analysis all married and cohabiting unions are included in the analysis (Figure 7.3 and Table 7.8). Of particular note are the larger age differences between South Asian, and especially Bangladeshi, wives and their husbands, with one third being 10 years or more apart in age (Figure 7.3). Much smaller age differences exist between couples of White, Black and Other ethnicity; around one in five Black–Caribbean and Black–Other women are older than their partner. Note once again the divergence within the Black population, Black–Africans having somewhat larger spousal age differences (16 per cent of men being 10 or more years older than their partners). Among all ethnic groups the age differences are larger among older couples (Table 7.8).

Figure 7.3 *Spousal age difference for selected ethnic groups, Great Britain, 1991*

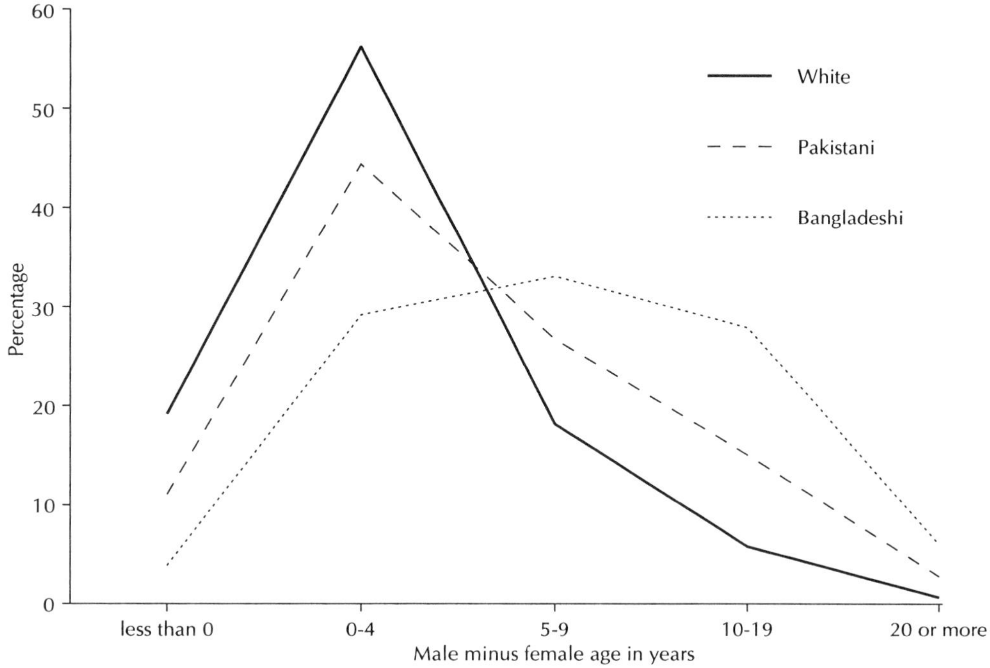

Source: 1991 Census One Per Cent Household SAR

Large spousal age differences have important demographic and socio-economic consequences. The chances of widowhood are obviously increased for women married to men who are much older than themselves. This can be seen clearly among the older Bangladeshi women in Appendix 7.1 and Figure 7.2. The large spousal age difference found among the Bangladeshi population has also had important consequences for the age–sex structure of

Table 7.8 *Spousal age difference distribution by ethnic group. Married and cohabiting couples where male partner is aged 16–34 and 35-59, Great Britain 1991*

Ethnic group of male partner	Age of male partner									
	16–34					35–59				
	Less 0	1–4	5–9	10+	N	Less 0	1–4	5–9	10+	N
White	25.0	61.9	12.1	1.0	28,104	17.6	57.0	18.5	7.0	64,288
Black–Caribbean	30.4	55.5	14.8	0.8	263	19.8	42.6	23.3	14.3	420
Black–African	23.1	60.6	12.5	3.9	104	10.5	38.9	29.6	21.0	162
Black–Other	33.8	52.5	12.5	1.3	80	10.5	43.9	33.3	12.3	57
Indian	14.8	62.2	21.4	1.6	556	10.0	49.5	31.6	8.8	1,141
Pakistani	18.7	54.2	23.8	3.3	273	8.0	40.7	28.3	23.1	477
Bangladeshi	8.0	33.3	46.7	12.0	75	2.5	28.7	27.1	41.2	122
Chinese	14.5	63.2	21.1	1.3	76	16.0	38.5	31.4	14.2	169
Other–Asian	15.7	70.8	13.5	0.0	89	11.6	48.1	30.6	9.7	258
Other	26.2	49.0	20.8	4.0	149	16.2	39.7	25.2	18.8	234

Source: 1991 Census One Per Cent Household SAR (ESRC/JISC) purchase). Crown Copyright.

the Bangladeshi population in Britain. It seems likely that the very low sex ratios (number of males/number of females, multiplied by 100) found among Bangladeshis aged in their forties, and the much higher sex ratios in the age-group 50–59, to some extent results from the original male migrant population, now aged in their fifties, being joined in the 1970s and 1980s by their wives currently aged in their forties. A similar suggestion has recently been put forward by Ballard and Kalra Singh (1994).

Ethnic minorities and the marriage market

The extent to which these marriage patterns result from differences in 'desired spousal age difference' and to what extent they result from structural constraints in the availability of potential partners is unclear. In the case of the Bangladeshi population, large spousal age differences are a traditional feature among marriages in Bangladesh, while small age differences have been found in the Caribbean and Latin America (Casterline *et al.*, 1986). Casterline and colleagues (1986) suggest that large spousal age differences are likely to be more common in patriarchal societies such as those found in South Asia and Africa, especially where patrilocality is the rule, and much smaller in bilateral kinship societies where neolocal residence is more common.

The impact of the marriage market on spousal age differences is complex and difficult to quantify (Casterline *et al.*, 1986). This is especially the case for ethnic minority populations in Britain, where the marriage market extends outside the UK (subject to immigration controls), and there are strong preferences among many South Asians for caste endogamy, and hypergamy for women (Ballard and Ballard, 1977; Saifullah Khan, 1977; Bhachu, 1985; Westwood; 1988). The complex requirements of some South Asians in Britain, in terms of the religion, caste and socio-economic status of potential marriage partners, combined with a relatively restricted choice of eligible kin (especially in the early stages of settlement in the UK), has meant that they have looked overseas for suitable marriage partners (Ballard and Ballard, 1977; Saifullah Khan, 1977; Bhachu, 1985; Westwood, 1988). Among many Sikh and Gujarati Indians there is a continued preference for arranged marriages to take place between members of the same caste and many East African Sikhs have strong preferences to marry Sikhs who are also migrants from East Africa (Bhachu, 1985).

The importance of marriage and kinship rules in influencing the processes of migration to Britain are highlighted by Ballard (1990). Comparison of Muslim Mirpuris and Sikh Jullunduris both of Punjabi origin demonstrates how the preference for marriages between close relatives (ideally cousins) found among the Muslim Mirpuris encourages greater ties between British Mirpuris and their siblings who remain in the Punjab. Mirpuri brothers and sisters generally expect to be given first-refusal in offers of marriage with each others' children and as a result marriages between British- and Punjabi-based partners are more common than among the Punjabi Sikh population where no such prior obligations between British- and Punjabi-based kin exist (Ballard, 1990).

Migration of spouses from the Indian subcontinent

Data arising from immigration clearance control procedures and admittance to the UK for settlement show that currently around 15,000 individuals are accepted for settlement annually from the Indian subcontinent, just under two thirds of whom are spouses (Home Office, 1994). In the 1960s, males, often already married, were accepted as primary migrants and only later applied for their wives and other dependants to join them in the UK. Information on length of marriage and year of husband's entry for wives applying to join their husbands already settled in the UK, suggest that in comparison with 10 years ago, a much higher proportion of men are themselves born in the UK, and that the marriages are of relatively short duration.

Figure 7.4 shows the cumulative number of persons accepted as a spouse for settlement in the UK according to the country of origin. The number of husbands accepted has increased in recent years, partially as a result of changes in legislation allowing husbands to apply to join wives currently in the UK under the same restrictions as wives arriving to join husbands, and partially as a result of increases in the number of single Asian women in Britain. Apart from this legislative change giving husbands the same right of entry to join their spouse as wives, succeeding immigration legislation and practice has generally made it increasingly difficult for partners to enter the UK. For example, fiance(e)s, and recently married couples must now serve a probationary period in order to prove that marriage was the primary purpose of migration. For further details of changes in legislation see Booth

Figure 7.4 *Spouses accepted for settlement in the UK from India, Pakistan and Bangladesh*

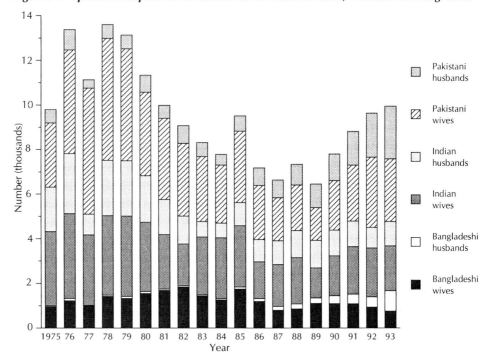

Source: Home Office Control of Immigration Statistics, United Kingdom.

(1992), and The Home Office annual Command Paper *Control of Immigration Statistics United Kingdom*.

7.7 Inter-ethnic unions

Trends in inter-ethnic marriage

The formation of inter-ethnic unions has been seen as an important indicator of the degree of assimilation or integration of an ethnic minority into a host society (Gordon, 1964). As Coleman (1994) points out, inter-ethnic unions clearly indicate the extent to which individuals are able to mix in the marriage market, and inter-marriage itself promotes further breakdown of separate identities and barriers between ethnic minorities by the creation of a mixed ethnicity population.

Since the late 1970s, when the 1977/78 National Dwelling and Household Survey and later the annual UK Labour Force Survey routinely included an ethnic group question, it has been possible to cross-tabulate the ethnic group of partners and calculate the percentage of men and women in each ethnic group who are married to a White partner (Jones, 1982 and 1984; Airey, 1985; Coleman, 1985 and 1994; Saggar, 1987; Berrington, 1994). Over the last decade a consistent picture has emerged whereby ethnic minority men are more likely than ethnic minority women to be married to a White partner, and for inter-ethnic unions to be most common among those of mixed and Afro-Caribbean ethnicity, and least common among those of South Asian ethnic origin. Recent analyses using 1989–91 Labour Force Survey data suggest that among the Caribbean population, levels of inter-ethnic unions have increased over the late 1980s, though no such increase was found among the South Asian populations. However, there was some evidence to suggest that inter-ethnic unions may be more common among 'second-generation' Indian and Pakistani men (Berrington, 1994).

The different wording of the ethnic group question in the census compared with the earlier Labour Force Surveys makes further analysis of time trends very difficult, especially for the Black–Caribbean, Black–African and Black–Other populations. Estimates of the level of inter-ethnic among the South Asian and Chinese populations from the census are similar to those from the 1989–91 Labour Force Survey.

Evidence from the 1991 Census

An analysis of ethnic origin for couples in the 1991 Census (one per cent SAR) is shown in Table 7.9, while Table 7.10 shows the percentage of men and women in each ethnic group married to, or cohabiting with, a White partner. The vast majority of couples contain individuals of the same ethnic group. Overall only 1.3 per cent are inter-ethnic unions, the majority of which are between an ethnic minority individual and a White individual. There is little mixing within the Asian ethnic minorities and only a very modest number of unions between the different Black ethnic minorities

(Table 7.9). However this is perhaps not surprising given the relatively small size, and often different geographical locations, of these ethnic minority populations. The larger size of the White population means that we should expect, through chance alone, a higher number of partnerships between one White and one ethnic minority individual, than those between two different ethnic minority individuals.

Table 7.9 *Inter-ethnic unions. All married and cohabiting men and women. Resident population, Great Britain, 1991*

Ethnic group of male partner	Ethnic group of female partner										
	White	Black–Carib-bean	Black–African	Black–Other	Indian	Pakis-tani	Bangla-deshi	Chinese	Other–Asian	Other	Total
White	**126,150**	102	41	63	71	10	0	79	148	139	126,803
Black–Caribbean	225	**559**	8	10	4	2	0	2	3	12	865
Black–African	48	16	**208**	4	2	1	0	0	0	2	281
Black–Other	76	3	2	**62**	1	0	0	0	2	1	147
Indian	134	2	4	1	**1,762**	18	0	5	4	5	1,935
Pakistani	42	0	0	1	6	**775**	0	0	4	3	831
Bangladeshi	7	0	2	0	4	1	**217**	0	0	2	233
Chinese	34	0	0	0	2	0	0	**234**	0	0	270
Other–Asian	55	4	1	1	4	4	1	2	**296**	6	374
Other	218	2	1	2	7	4	0	2	5	**191**	432
Total	126,989	728	267	144	1,863	815	218	324	462	361	132,171

Source: 1991 Census One Per Cent Household SAR (ESRC/JISC purchase). Crown copyright.

As found in previous analyses, inter-ethnic unions are generally more common among ethnic minority men than among ethnic minority women and are more common among the Black than the South Asian ethnic minority populations (Table 7.10). For example, 40 per cent of Black–Caribbean men aged 16–34 and 20 per cent of Black–Caribbean women aged 16–34 are currently living with a White partner, compared with just 7 and 4 per cent of Indian men and women. However, as found in earlier analyses of Labour Force Survey data, Chinese and Other Asian women are more likely to be married to a White partner compared with their male counterparts. Levels of inter-ethnic unions among the Black–African, Chinese and Other–Asian populations, are intermediate between those of the Black–Caribbean population, and those of the South Asian populations.

Unsurprisingly, levels of inter-ethnic unions are particularly high among the mixed ethnicity populations who are classified as either Black–Other (if they reported themselves as Black–British or Black, Black/White mixed) or Other (if they reported themselves to be of mixed Asian–White descent). Over half of men and women classified as Black–Other are reported to be living with a White partner.

Table 7.10 *Percentage of married and cohabiting men and women aged 16–34 and 35–59 living with a White partner. Resident population, Great Britain 1991*

Ethnic group	Age group							
	16–34				35–59			
	Men		Women		Men		Women	
	% with White partner	N	% with White partner	N	% with White partner	N	% with White partner	N
Black–Caribbean	39.5	263	20.9	187	21.9	420	15.1	385
Black–African	19.2	104	8.9	90	13.0	162	17.8	163
Black–Other	60.0	80	51.9	77	42.1	57	33.9	56
Indian	7.0	556	4.1	537	7.6	1,141	3.8	1,089
Pakistani	6.2	273	2.2	271	3.6	477	0.6	470
Bangladeshi	4.0	75	0.0	68	1.6	122	0.0	116
Chinese	15.8	76	22.4	89	11.8	169	26.1	207
Other–Asian	18.0	89	38.3	115	13.6	258	30.4	316
Other	57.7	149	44.4	117	48.3	234	37.3	201

Source: 1991 Census One Per Cent Houshold SAR (ESRC/JISC purchase). Crown Copyright.

The proportion of couples who are ethnically mixed is higher among younger couples (Table 7.10) which suggests that ethnic minority individuals are increasingly choosing to form an inter-ethnic union. However, comparison of 'first-' and 'second-generation' men and women provides a less consistent picture. Among men, inter-ethnic unions seem to be more likely among those born in the UK ($p<0.05$ only for Pakistani and Bangladeshi men and Other men. There is no difference among Indian, Pakistani and Bangladeshi women according to generation (though over half of UK-born Other–Asian and Other women have a White partner in comparison with about 30 per cent of non-UK-born Other–Asian and Other women).

Inter-ethnic cohabitation

Inter-ethnic unions might be expected to be more common among cohabiting couples, who may hold less 'traditional' marriage views. It might also be the case that the couples' different ethnic backgrounds may themselves be factors in making legal marriage less likely. The small number of inter-ethnic cohabiting couples reported in the SAR means that our interpretation of results from the 1991 Census must at best be tentative. However the data, shown in Table 7.11, do suggest that inter-ethnic unions are significantly more common among young cohabiting couples than young married couples. For example, 4.5 per cent of married Indian men aged 16–34 have a White partner as compared with two thirds of cohabiting men ($p<0.05$). The corresponding figures for Indian women are 3.6 per cent and 33.3 per cent ($p<0.05$). This is not the case among the Black population however, where there was no difference.

Table 7.11 *Comparison of percentage with a White partner between 'first-' and 'second-generation' and between married and cohabiting men and women aged 16-34. Resident population, Great Britain, 1991*

Ethnic group	Men				Women			
	'Second-'		'First-generation		'Second-'		'First-generation'	
	%	N	%	N	%	N	%	N
Black–Caribbean	42.9	184	31.7	79	22.2	144	20.8	77
Black–African	(27.3)	22	17.1	82	9.7	31	13.8	109
Black–Other	64.8	54	(50.0)	26	54.9	51	44.1	34
Indian	10.7	103	6.2	453	4.1	146	4.3	606
Pakistani/Bangladeshi	13.2	53	4.4	295 *	0.0	86	1.2	419
Other–Asian	(28.6)	7	16.5	158	(55.6)	18	28.9	280*
Other	70.4	54	50.5	95 *	53.5	58	32.0	103*
	Married		Cohabiting		Married		Cohabiting	
	%	N	%	N	%	N	%	N
Black–Caribbean	31.0	142	49.6	121*	20.5	117	21.4	70
Black–African	19.0	79	(20.0)	25	9.2	65	(8.0)	25
Black–Other	52.0	50	73.3	30	43.1	52	(69.2)	26*
Indian	4.5	533	(65.2)	23*	3.6	528	(33.3)	9*
Pakistani/Bangladeshi	4.1	339	(66.7)	9*	1.8	333	(0.0)	6
Other–Asian	16.9	154	(18.2)	11	29.0	186	(55.6)	18*
Other	52.9	123	(80.8)	26*	33.7	86	74.2	31*

* Statistically significant difference at the five per cent level

Source: 1991 Census One Per Cent Houshold SAR (ESRC/JISC purchase). Crown Copyright.

Other socio-economic characteristics of inter-ethnic couples

Table 7.12 shows the percentage of ethnic minority men and women aged 16–39 married or cohabiting with a White partner by social class and whether or not they have higher educational qualifications. The analysis is confined to this age-group because of the relationship between both the propensity to have higher level qualifications, and the propensity to be in an inter-ethnic union, with age. Although caution in interpreting these results is required because of the small sample sizes involved, the data seem to provide a consistent pattern among both men and women whereby social class and educational differentials in the propensity to be married to, or cohabiting with, a White partner differ between the Black and South Asian ethnic groups. Among young Black men and women the proportions with a White partner are slightly higher among those in the lower social classes and among those with lower educational qualifications, while among young Indian, Pakistani and Bangladeshis the reverse is suggested. In particular, it is South Asians in professional and managerial occupations, and those with higher education, who are the most likely to be married to, or cohabiting with, a White partner. However small sample sizes mean that many of the differences seen in Table 7.12 are *not* statistically significant.

Table 7.12 *Percentage married or cohabiting with a White partner according to social class and educational qualification. Men and women aged 16–39. Resident population, Great Britain, 1991*

Ethnic group	Social class¹								Educational qualification²			
	I & II	[se]	IIIN	[se]	IIIM	[se]	IV & V	[se]	Lower than diploma	[se]	Diploma or above	[se]
Men												
Black	34.2	[3.8]	33.8	[5.4]	41.5	[3.7]	45.8	[5.1]	39.1	[2.2]	25.4	[3.8]*
Indian	10.7	[1.7]	5.9	[2.3]	2.1	[0.9]	5.1	[1.6]	4.6	[0.8]	14.1	[2.6]*
Pakistani/Bangladeshi	10.3	[2.8]	2.3	[2.3]	4.2	[1.7]	1.3	[0.9]	4.0	[0.9]	8.1	[3.5]
Other–Asian	16.8	[3.2]	17.1	[6.4]	10.9	[3.9]	13.9	[5.8]	13.3	[2.4]	17.8	[3.8]
Other	63.1	[4.8]	(50.0)	[11.2]	58.8	[8.4]	60.5	[7.9]	54.0	[4.2]	58.3	[5.4]
Women												
Black	28.8	[3.6]	25.7	[3.2]	(43.5)	[10.3]	27.5	[4.6]	23.4	[2.0]	22.1	[3.5]
Indian	12.2	[2.3]	1.8	[0.8]	3.2	[3.2]	2.0	[0.9]	2.9	[0.5]	11.5	[3.0]*
Pakistani/Bangladeshi	7.5	[4.2]	0.0	[-]	(0.0)	[-]	0.0	[-]	0.9	[0.4]	(3.6)	[3.5]
Other–Asian	35.3	[4.4]	36.1	[4.6]	(36.8)	[11.1]	30.3	[5.7]	27.9	[2.3]	35.7	[4.5]*
Other	52.5	[6.5]	56.0	[7.0]	(60.0)	[12.6]	50.0	[9.1]	38.0	[3.8]	49.2	[6.5]

se = standard error.

* Statistically significant difference between the two levels of education at the five per cent level

¹ Those in the armed forces or whose social class is missing or inadequately described are not included in this analysis

² The census only collected information on educational qualifications obtained after age18. Any individuals who did not report their educational qualifications are included in the group with no, or below diploma level qualifications.

Source:1991 Census One Per Cent Household SAR (ESRC/JISC purchase). Crown copyright.

Table 7.13, shows the social class and educational qualifications of White men and women are shown according to the ethnic group of their partner. The social class distribution and educational qualifications of those married to, or cohabiting with, partners who are also White, can be compared with those of individuals who are married to, or cohabiting with, a partner from an ethnic minority. The data suggest that White men with an ethnic minority partner are more likely to be in professional and managerial occupations, and to have higher level qualifications than White men married to. or cohabiting with White women. This is particularly the case among White men with Asian partners. Among White women, the patterns are slightly more complex. While White women married to, or cohabiting with Asian and Other ethnic minority men tend to have higher status occupations and to be more highly educated, the socio-economic characteristics of White women married to Black men are very similar to those of White women with White partners.

The overall picture then is one where among White men and women inter-ethnic unions are generally associated with more privileged socio-economic

Table 7.13 *Social class distribution of White men and women aged 16–39 according to ethnic group of partner. Resident population, Great Britain, 1991*

Ethnic group	Percentage social class distribution					Percentage with diploma or above qualification[2]		
	I & II	IIIN	IIIM	IV & V	N (100%)	Diploma or above	[se]	N
White men whose partner is								
White	36.0	10.4	35.1	18.5	39,195	19,6	[0.2]	41,029
Black	41.5	12.3	23.6	22.6	106	25.2	[4.0]	119
Indian	66.7	6.1	18.2	9.1	33	51.5	[8.7]	33*
Chinese	(64.3)	(14.3)	(14.3)	(7.1)	28	51.6	[9.0]	31*
Other–Asian	52.2	10.1	24.6	13.0	69	32.9	[5.4]	76*
Other	53.3	7.8	24.7	14.3	77	41.0	[5.6]	78*
Women whose partner is								
White	29.2	41.0	6.9	22.9	41,956	16.7	[0.2]	47,716
Black	29.1	36.2	12.7	22.1	213	16.7	[2.4]	246
Indian	55.2	24.1	10.3	10.3	58	36.8	[5.8]	68*
Pakistani/Bangladeshi	(39.1)	(30.4)	(0.0)	(30.4)	23	(24.0)	[8.5]	25
Chinese	(50.0)	(45.5)	(0.0)	(4.6)	22	(32.0)	[9.3]	25
Other–Asian	(48.2)	(29.6)	(3.7)	(18.5)	27	31.4	[7.8]	35
Other	47.5	32.0	4.9	15.6	122	33.3	[3.9]	147 *

* Statistically significant difference from those with a White partner at the five per cent level
[1] Those in the armed forces or whose social class is missing or inadequately described are not included in this analysis
[2] The census only collected information on educational qualifications obtained after age 18. Individuals who did not report their educational qualifications are included in the group with no, or below diploma level qualifications

Source: 1991 Census One Per Cent Household (SAR) (ESRC/JISC purchase). Crown Copyright.

status. White women married or cohabiting with Black ethnic minority men have similar socio-economic characteristics to White women married to, or cohabiting with White men. However, more data providing larger sample sizes are required for further investigation of the effect of these and other factors e.g. region of residence on the level of inter-ethnic unions, and how these factors vary for the different ethnic groups.

7.8 The mixed ethnicity population in Britain

One result of inter-ethnic unions is a population of mixed ethnicity. Up until 1991, the ethnic group question asked within the Labour Force Survey, allowed individuals to identify themselves as being of mixed ethnicity, and to provide further details in a write-in box. These data have allowed re- searchers to examine the size and socio-demographic structure of the mixed population as a distinct group (Coleman, 1985 and 1992; Owen, 1993; Berrington; 1994). Recent estimates suggest that there are about 309,000 individuals of mixed descent, who make up a significant proportion (12 per cent) of the ethnic minoriy population in Britain. Over three quarters of the mixed population are UK-born and over half are under age 15 (Berrington, 1994). As discussed by Coleman (1994) the increasing numerical importance of the mixed population, is most clearly visible within the youngest age-groups, where around one in five ethnic minority 0–4-year-olds is of mixed ethnicity. However, the change of the Labour Force Survey ethnic group question to become consistent with the 1991 Census ethnic group question has meant that this source of direct information about the mixed population is no longer available.

The 1991 Census ethnic group question invited those 'descended from more than on ethnic or racial group' to tick the group to which the person considers he/she belongs, or tick the 'Any Other Ethnic Group' box and describe their ancestry in the space provided. Individuals of mixed Black–Caribbean and White descent may have ticked Black–Other or Other Ethnic Group, but may have felt it more appropriate to tick Black–Caribbean or indeed White. As discussed further by Owen (Chapter 3 of Volume 2), individuals of Black/White parentage make up an important component of the Black–Other ethnic group. Further investigation, using the household SAR, of the reported ethnicities of the parent(s) and children in mixed ethnicity families may prove very illuminating.

7.9 Conclusions

There are large differences between ethnic groups in Britain in patterns of marriage formation and dissolution. The South Asian populations are char- acterised by earlier and near universal marriage, with age at marriage being lowest among Pakistani and Bangladeshi men and women and somewhat later for Indian men and women. Age at marriage is especially high among the Black–Caribbean and Black–Other ethnic groups. Comparison with 1981 Census data suggests that all ethnic groups have seen some increase in the proportions single among young men and women. Divorce is common among the White and Black–Caribbean, Black–African and Black–Other ethnic groups, and a substantial number of Black–Caribbean and Black–Other men and women report themselves as currently divorced as a result of low rates of remarriage. In contrast, the number of South Asian men and women who are currently divorced is very low, at around 3 per cent. Marital dissolution among the South Asian populations is largely through the death of a spouse. The large spousal age differences found among the South Asian and particularly Bangladeshi population contribute towards high rates of widowhood among older women.

Cohabiting unions are relatively common among young White, Black–Caribbean, Black–African and Black–Other men and women, but remain unusual among the South Asian populations, though the data suggest some increase among young 'second-generation' Indian men. Overall 1.3 per cent of all married and cohabiting unions are ethnically mixed. The majority of these are partnerships between individuals of White and Black–Caribbean, Black–African, Black–Other and Other groups. Ethnic minority men remain more likely to live with a White woman than ethnic minority women, apart from Chinese and Other Asian men who are less likely to be married or cohabiting with a White partner compared with Chinese and Other–Asian women. Inter-ethnic unions are more common among cohabiting than married couples and are more prevalent among younger couples. Further research into the socio-economic characteristics of inter-ethnic couples is required, in particular to investigate the way in which factors associated with having a White partner seem to differ between the Black populations on the one hand and the South Asian populations on the other.

Notes

(1) There are a very few cases where, as a result of family reconstitution following death or divorce, the oldest male or female is not the partner, but the child. However these cases are very unlikely to make a difference to the analyses and using this approach the analysis of marital status can be extended to include cohabiting unions, using the one per cent household SARs.

(2) Statistical significance has been calculated on the basis of a simple random sample. The sampling procedure for the SARs means that the standard errors should be multiplied by design factors. Preliminary work by Simpson et al. (1994), suggests design factors for the one per cent household SAR of around 2 for ethnic group variable (ranging from 1.5 for Black–Other, to 2.4 for Bangladeshi.

References

Airey, P. (1985) Who marries whom: an examination of the socio-economic characteristics of marriage partners with regard to an evaluation of the marriage market. Unpublished MSc thesis, University of London.

Alam, I. and Leete, R. (1993) Variations in fertility in India and Indonesia. In: Richard Leete and Iqbal Alam (eds), *The Revolution in Asian Fertility: Dimensions, Causes and Implications*. Oxford: Clarendon Press.

Ballard, R. and Ballard, C. (1977) The Sikhs: The development of South Asian settlements in Britain. In: J. Watson (ed.), *Between Two Cultures: Migrants and Minorities in Britain*. Oxford: Basil Blackwell.

Ballard, R. and Singh Kalra, V. (1994) *The ethnic dimensions of the 1991 Census: A preliminary report*. University of Manchester, Census Microdata Unit.

Ballard, R. (1990) Migration and kinship: the differential effect of marriage rules on the process of Punjabi migration to Britain. In: C. Clarke, C. Peach and S. Vertovec (eds), *South Asians Overseas*. Cambridge: Cambridge University Press, pp. 219–48.

Barrow, J. (1982) West Indian Families: an insiders perspective. In: R. Rapoport, M. Fogarty and R. Rapoport (eds), *Families In Britain*. London: Routledge and Kegan Paul, pp. 220–32.

Berrington, A. (1994) Marriage and family formation among the white and ethnic minority populations in Britain . *Ethnic and Racial Studies*, 17(3), 517–46.

Bhachu, P. (1985) *Twice Migrants: East African Sikh settlers in Britain*. London: Tavistock Publications.

Booth, H. (1992) *The Migration Process in Britain and West Germany*. Aldershot: Avebury.

Bulcroft, R. A. and Bulcroft, K. A. (1993) Race differences in attitudinal and motivational factors in the decision to marry. *Journal of Marriage and The Family*, 55, 338–55.

Cain, M. T. (1993) Patriarchal structure and demographic change. In: N. Federici, K. Mason and S. Sogner (eds), *Women's Position and Demographic Change*. Oxford: Clarendon Press.

Casterline, J. B., Williams, L. and McDonald, P. (1986) The age difference between spouses: variations among developing countries. *Population Studies*, 40, 353–74.

Castro-Martin, T. and Bumpass, L. (1989) Recent trends and differentials in marital disruption. *Demography*, 26(1), 37–51.

Clarke, E. (1957) *My Mother Who Fathered Me*. London: George Allen and Unwin.

Coleman, D. (1985) Inter-ethnic marriage in Great Britain. *Population Trends*, 40, 1–10.

Coleman, D. (1992) Ethnic Intermarriage. In: A. Bittles and D. F. Roberts (eds), *Minority Populations: Genetics, Demography and Health*. London: Macmillan, pp. 208–40.

Coleman, D. (1994) Trends in fertility and intermarriage among immigrant populations in Western Europe as measures of integration. *Journal of Biosocial Science*, 26, 107–36.

DaVanzo, J. and Rahman M. O. (1993) American families: trends and correlates. *Population Index*, 59(3), 350–86.

Driver, G. (1982) West Indian Families: an anthropological perspective In: R. Rapoport, M. Fogarty and R. Rapoport (eds), *Families in Britain*. London: Routledge and Kegan Paul, pp. 205–19.

Duza, A. (1989) Bangladesh Women in Transition: Dynamics and Issues. In: K Mahadevan (ed.), *Women and Population Dynamics: Perspectives from Asian Countries*. London: Sage Publications.

Farley, R. (1988) After the starting line: Blacks and women in an uphill race. *Demography*, 25(4), 477–95.

Foner, N. (1979) *Jamaica Farewell: Jamaican migrants in London*. London: Routledge and Kegan Paul.

Goody, E. and Muir Groothues, C. (1979) West African Couples In London. In: V. Saifullah Khan (ed.), *Minority Families In Britain*. London: The Macmillan Press, pp. 59–88.

Gordon, M. (1964) *Assimilation in American Life*. Oxford: Oxford University Press.

Hajnal, J. (1953) Age at marriage and proportions marrying. *Population Studies*, 7, 115–36.

Heath, K., Da Costa-Martinez, D. and Sheon, A. R. (1988) *Trinidad and Tobago Demographic and Health Survey 1987*. Family Planning Association of Trinidad and Tobago and Institute for Resource Development/ Westinghouse Columbia, Maryland USA.

Heath, S. and Dale, A. (1994) Household and family formation in Great Britain: the ethnic dimension. *Population Trends*, 77, 5–13.

Home Office (various years) *Control of Immigration: Statistics United Kingdom*. London: HMSO.

Jones, P. (1982) Ethnic intermarriage in Britain. *Ethnic and Racial Studies*, 5, 223–8.

Jones, P. (1984) Ethnic intermarriage in Britain: a further assessment. *Ethnic and Racial Studies*, 7(3), 398–405.

McDonald, P. (1985) Social Organization and Nuptiality in Developing Societies. In: J. Cleland, J. Hobcraft and B. Dinesen (eds), *Reproductive Change in Developing Countries Insights from the World Fertility Survey*. Oxford: Oxford University Press.

National Institute of Population Research and Training (1993) *Bangladesh Fertility Survey 1989: Secondary Analysis*. Dhaka: NIPORT.

Newell, C. (1988) *Methods and Models In Demography*. London: Belhavan Press.

OPCS (1993a) *Birth Statistics 1991*. Table 9.9 Series FM1 no 20. London: HMSO.

OPCS (1993b) *General Household Survey 1991*. Table 11.10. Series GHS no 22. London: HMSO.

OPCS (1994) *First results from the quality check element of the 1991 Census Validation Survey*. OPCS Monitor, SS94/2. London: HMSO.

OPCS/GRO (Scotland) (1992) *1991 Census: Definitions Great Britain*. Ref CEN91 DEF. London: HMSO.

OPCS/GRO(Scotland) (1993) *1991 Census: sex, age and marital status: Great Britain*. Ref CEN91 SAM. London: HMSO.

Office of the Registrar General, India (1994) *Sample Registration System Fertility and Mortality Indicator, 1991*, Table 2.

Owen, C. (1993) Using the Labour Force Survey to estimate Britain's ethnic minority populations. *Population Trends*, 72, 8–23.

Owen, D. (1996) The demography, geography and socio-economic characteristics of the 'Black–Other' ethnic group. *Ethnicity in the 1991 Census*, Volume 2. London: HMSO.

Pakistan Demographic and Health Survey 1990/91 (1992). National Institute of Population Studies Islamabad, Pakistan. IRD/Macro International Inc.

Phoenix, A. (1987) Theories of gender and Black families. In: G. Weiner and M. Arnot (eds), *Gender Under Scrutiny*. London: Hutchison and The Open University Press.

Saggar, S. (1987) The 1984 Labour Force Survey and Britain's 'Asian' population. *New Community*, 13(3), 395–411.

Saifullah Khan, V. (1977) The Pakistanis: Mirpuri villagers at home and in Bradford. In: Watson James (ed.), *Between Two Cultures: Migrants and Minorities in Britain*. Oxford: Basil Blackwell.

Simpson, S., Fieldhouse E. and Sandhu A. (1994) *Bias, Sampling Error and Coverage: the preliminary validation of the Sample of Anonymized Records from the 1991 Census*. Census Microdata Unit Occasional Paper no. 2. Manchester University.

Singh, K. P. (1989) Status of women in Punjab and Haryana. In: K Mahadevan (ed.), *Women and Population Dynamics: Perspectives from Asian Countries*. London:Sage Publications.

Smith, R. T. (1956) *The Negro Family In British Guiana*. London: Routledge and Kegan Paul.

South, S. J. (1993) Racial and ethnic differences in the desire to marry. *Journal of Marriage and The Family*, 55, 357–70.

Staples, R. (1985) Changes in Black Family Structure: the conflict between family ideology and structural conditions. *Journal of Marriage and The Family*, 47, 1005–13.

Stone, K. (1983) Motherhood and waged work: West Indian, Asian and white mothers compared. In A. Phizacklea (ed.), *One Way Ticket*. London: Routledge and Kegan Paul.

Warrier, S. (1988) Marriage, maternity and female economic activity: Gujarati mothers in Britain. In: S. Westwood and P. Bhachu (eds), *Enterprising Women: Ethnicity, economy and gender relations*. London: Routledge.

Westwood, S. (1988) Workers and wives: Continuities and discontinuities in the lives of Gujarati women. In: S. Westwood and P. Bhachu (eds), *Enterprising Women: Ethnicity, economy and gender relations*. London: Routledge.

Acknowledgements

Much of this work is based upon the SARs provided through the Census Microdata Unit of the University of Manchester with support of the ESRC/JISC. Thanks are due to the Office of Population Censuses and Surveys for providing access to the Labour Force Survey and General Household Survey, which are used with the permission of Her Majesty's Stationery Office, and the ESRC Data Archive for supplying these data. The author is also grateful to Ian Diamond and the editors for their comments on earlier drafts of this chapter.

Appendix 7.1 *Current marital status distribution by sex, age and ethnic group. Resident population, Britain, 1991*

Sex, ethnic group and age group	Per cent					
	Single	First marriage	Remarried	Divorced	Widowed	N
Men						
White						
16–19	99.4	0.5	0.0	0.0	0.0	28,214
20–24	88.6	10.8	0.1	0.6	0.0	38,311
25–26	53.4	41.9	1.3	3.3	0.0	40,060
30–34	27.9	59.5	5.4	7.0	0.1	36,361
35–39	16.2	64.5	10.0	9.0	0.3	33,619
40–49	10.3	67.1	12.7	9.2	0.7	70,635
50–59	8.1	70.4	11.5	7.9	2.1	54,882
60–69	8.1	71.0	9.0	4.9	7.0	50,583
70+	6.8	59.0	8.8	2.3	23.1	44,953
Black–Caribbean						
16–19	98.5	0.7	0.4	0.4	0.0	271
20–24	96.9	2.9	0.0	0.2	0.0	477
25–26	80.3	16.5	0.6	2.7	0.0	527
30–34	53.0	39.7	2.9	4.4	0.0	413
35–39	37.3	49.6	4.1	7.8	1.2	244
40–49	26.0	52.6	6.4	12.9	2.0	342
50–59	12.8	58.6	12.2	13.6	2.7	711
60–69	12.4	59.5	9.2	13.8	5.1	435
70+	12.7	54.2	11.0	7.6	14.4	118
Black–African						
16–19	99.2	0.8	0.0	0.0	0.0	124
20–24	89.7	9.7	0.5	0.0	0.0	195
25–26	65.9	33.7	0.4	0.0	0.0	276
30–34	37.5	58.1	2.0	2.3	0.0	301
35–39	37.3	49.6	4.1	7.9	1.2	198
40–49	15.6	63.1	12.8	7.3	1.1	179
50–59	9.2	64.2	14.3	11.2	1.0	98
60–69	13.0	54.3	15.2	8.7	8.7	46
70+	(15.0)	(50.0)	(5.0)	(15.0)	(15.0)	20
Black–Other						
16–19	99.1	0.9	0.0	0.0	0.0	115
20–24	92.6	6.8	0.0	0.6	0.0	162
25–26	73.6	24.7	1.1	0.5	0.0	182
30–34	60.0	32.5	3.3	4.2	0.0	120
35–39	24.5	55.1	12.2	8.2	0.0	49
40–49	12.7	60.6	12.7	14.1	0.0	71
50–59	10.9	50.0	21.7	17.4	0.0	46
60–69	(27.8)	(44.4)	(16.7)	(5.6)	(5.6)	18
70+	(33.3)	(66.7)	(0.0)	(0.0)	(0.0)	9
Indian						
16–19	98.9	1.1	0.0	0.0	0.0	540
20–24	82.2	17.3	0.1	0.4	0.0	729
25–26	32.1	64.7	1.3	1.9	0.0	677
30–34	9.3	84.7	3.7	2.4	0.0	756
35–39	5.9	87.3	4.1	2.5	0.1	826
40–49	3.1	88.8	5.2	2.4	0.5	965
50–59	3.3	87.4	4.8	2.3	2.2	790
60–69	4.1	84.2	3.9	1.6	6.2	386
70+	5.1	67.0	2.5	0.5	34.9	197

Sex, ethnic group and age group	Per cent					
	Single	First marriage	Remarried	Divorced	Widowed	N
Men						
Pakistani						
16–19	93.4	6.6	0.0	0.0	0.0	380
20–24	69.2	29.4	0.9	0.5	0.0	442
25–26	22.8	75.2	0.7	1.4	0.0	294
30–34	11.9	83.3	3.1	1.7	0.0	360
35–39	5.8	89.5	4.1	0.6	0.0	343
40–49	5.4	83.2	8.7	1.5	1.2	333
50–59	1.2	87.5	9.0	1.4	0.9	433
60–69	1.8	89.0	6.1	0.6	2.4	164
70+	5.7	69.8	1.9	0.0	22.6	53
Bangladeshi						
16–19	97.6	2.4	0.0	0.0	0.0	166
20–24	74.4	24.0	0.0	1.6	0.0	129
25–26	28.7	69.4	0.9	0.9	0.0	108
30–34	8.4	89.7	1.9	0.0	0.0	107
35–39	2.9	92.9	2.9	0.0	1.4	70
40–49	2.5	96.3	1.3	0.0	0.0	80
50–59	1.4	88.7	7.5	1.4	0.9	212
60–69	4.1	82.4	10.8	1.4	1.4	74
70+	(8.3)	(58.3)	(16.7)	(0.0)	(16.7)	12
Chinese						
16–19	100	0.0	0.0	0.0	0.0	149
20–24	94.3	5.7	0.0	0.0	0.0	194
25–26	55.9	43.1	0.5	0.5	0.0	195
30–34	24.5	69.9	3.1	1.8	0.6	163
35–39	13.8	81.9	1.4	2.9	0.0	138
40–49	5.7	85.3	4.5	3.8	0.6	157
50–59	2.2	88.1	3.7	5.9	0.0	135
60–69	9.8	78.7	6.6	3.3	1.6	61
70+	(12.5)	(70.8)	(4.2)	(0.0)	(12.5)	24
Other–Asian						
16–19	99.3	0.7	0.0	0.0	0.0	141
20–24	92.7	7.3	0.0	0.0	0.0	206
25–26	49.2	47.5	0.0	3.3	0.0	183
30–34	24.4	72.0	1.3	2.2	0.0	225
35–39	12.3	81.0	2.6	4.1	0.0	195
40–49	5.8	86.3	6.1	1.9	0.0	313
50–59	7.3	82.8	5.3	3.3	1.3	151
60–69	7.4	77.8	9.3	1.9	3.7	54
70+	(4.2)	(79.2)	(4.2)	(0.0)	(12.5)	24
Other–Other						
16–19	98.5	1.5	0.0	0.0	0.0	196
20–24	90.3	9.4	0.0	0.4	0.0	267
25–26	57.7	39.1	1.7	1.4	0.0	286
30–34	34.6	57.2	4.8	3.3	0.0	269
35–39	12.7	70.0	5.9	11.4	0.0	220
40–45	13.2	65.7	8.9	11.8	0.4	280
50–55	12.3	67.2	8.2	10.7	1.6	122
60–65	11.0	69.5	8.5	9.8	1.2	82
70+	3.7	55.6	7.4	13.0	20.4	54

Sex, ethnic group and age group	Per cent					
	Single	First marriage	Remarried	Divorced	Widowed	N
Women						
White						
16–19	98.3	1.6	0.0	0.1	0.0	27,127
20–24	76.2	21.9	0.3	1.5	0.1	38,701
25–26	39.8	56.5	2.9	0.7	0.2	38,249
30–34	17.3	64.5	7.8	10.1	0.4	36,896
35–39	9.3	66.4	11.5	12.0	0.8	34.425
40–49	5.6	67.5	13.0	12.0	2.0	70,321
50–59	5.1	68.3	9.9	8.7	7.9	56.126
60–69	6.7	57.4	6.3	5.4	24.2	57,284
70+	9.8	27.1	3.6	2.3	57.3	75,523
Black–Caribbean						
16–19	98.5	0.4	0.0	0.8	0.4	268
20–24	93.7	5.5	0.0	0.6	0.2	506
25–26	80.1	17.4	0.2	2.3	0.0	654
30–34	61.0	31.4	0.9	5.9	0.7	539
35–39	41.1	40.5	3.2	14.9	0.3	348
40–49	17.0	54.5	6.3	19.5	2.7	512
50–59	12.4	51.5	5.5	25.3	5.2	652
60–69	11.8	49.7	4.4	19.7	14.4	340
70+	20.5	30.7	2.4	4.7	41.7	127
Black–African						
16–19	95.7	3.5	0.0	0.0	0.9	116
20–24	76.1	23.1	0.0	0.4	0.4	238
25–26	48.6	46.0	1.5	3.5	0.6	346
30–34	35.7	53.6	1.3	6.8	2.6	235
35–39	23.5	60.4	5.4	8.1	2.7	149
40–49	13.0	57.6	5.4	17.9	6.0	184
50–59	9.7	48.4	7.5	23.7	10.8	93
60–69	13.9	30.6	2.8	25.0	27.8	36
70+	(18.2)	(27.3)	(9.1)	(9.1)	(36.4)	11
Black–Other						
16–19	98.5	1.5	0.0	0.0	0.0	133
20–24	87.2	11.9	0.5	0.5	0.0	218
25–26	73.6	22.7	1.4	2.3	0.0	216
30–34	53.6	34.4	5.6	6.4	0.0	125
35–39	30.7	41.9	12.9	12.9	1.6	62
40–45	11.3	57.5	8.8	20.0	2.5	80
50–55	6.3	46.9	18.8	21.9	6.3	32
60–65	(20.0)	(35.0)	(5.0)	(30.0)	(10.0)	20
70+	(7.1)	(14.3)	(0.0)	(14.3)	(64.3)	14
Indian						
16–19	92.8	7.0	0.2	0.0	0.0	570
20–24	57.1	39.7	0.3	2.7	0.2	667
25–26	22.3	72.2	1.8	3.3	0.4	781
30–34	7.9	83.2	3.3	4.7	0.9	809
35–39	4.0	87.7	4.0	3.1	1.2	747
40–49	3.5	85.3	2.6	3.4	5.2	1,020
50–59	1.8	76.9	1.9	3.0	16.4	676
60–69	1.2	58.8	0.9	1.7	37.5	347
70+	1.6	27.9	0.5	0.0	70.0	190

Appendix 7.1-*continued*

Sex, ethnic group and age group	Per cent					
	Single	First marriage	Remarried	Divorced	Widowed	N
Women						
Pakistani						
16–19	86.5	13.2	0.3	0.0	0.0	379
20–24	40.1	59.0	0.5	0.5	0.0	439
25–26	12.1	85.1	0.3	1.9	0.6	315
30–34	6.8	87.9	3.2	1.5	0.6	340
35–39	1.7	90.6	2.7	4.0	1.0	299
40–49	0.5	88.2	2.9	2.6	5.8	382
50–59	1.7	81.7	0.7	1.0	14.9	295
60–69	0.0	62.8	0.0	2.3	34.9	86
70+	(11.1)	(11.1)	(3.7)	(3.7)	(70.4)	27
Bangladeshi						
16–19	78.0	20.8	0.0	0.0	1.2	168
20–24	27.4	71.9	0.0	0.7	0.0	135
25–26	3.4	93.2	0.0	2.3	1.1	88
30–34	1.1	92.4	4.4	1.1	1.1	92
35–39	1.1	94.4	2.2	2.2	0.0	90
40–49	3.2	77.0	4.8	3.2	11.9	126
50–59	1.2	81.6	3.5	1.2	12.6	87
60–69	(0.0)	(61.1)	(0.0)	(0.0)	(38.9)	18
70+	(10.0)	(30.0)	(0.0)	(0.0)	(60.0)	10
Chinese						
16–19	98.6	1.5	0.0	0.0	0.0	138
20–24	87.4	11.5	0.0	1.1	0.0	182
25–26	36.6	62.3	0.0	1.1	0.0	175
30–34	15.8	77.2	3.5	2.3	1.2	171
35–39	12.1	79.4	4.2	2.4	1.8	165
40–49	10.1	75.8	4.0	8.6	1.5	198
50–59	4.4	73.5	3.7	5.2	13.2	136
60–69	4.3	58.6	7.1	4.3	25.7	70
70+	2.3	18.6	2.3	0.0	76.7	43
Other–Asian						
16–19	93.1	6.2	0.0	0.8	0.0	130
20–24	67.7	32.3	0.0	0.0	0.0	186
25–26	29.1	67.8	0.4	2.6	0.0	230
30–34	13.4	77.7	5.5	2.4	1.0	291
35–39	12.5	76.4	5.6	4.7	0.9	233
40–45	11.5	74.3	4.8	6.4	2.9	374
50–55	10.7	60.7	7.9	10.0	10.7	140
60–65	3.6	62.5	3.6	1.8	28.6	56
70+	(7.4)	(18.5)	(7.4)	(3.7)	(63.0)	27
Other–Other						
16–19	96.1	3.9	0.0	0.0	0.0	181
20–24	82.5	16.7	0.0	0.7	0.0	269
25–26	51.4	42.7	2.4	3.6	0.0	253
30–34	24.2	63.1	3.5	9.1	0.0	198
35–39	15.9	60.3	9.9	13.9	0.0	151
40–49	13.6	64.9	10.1	8.8	2.6	228
50–59	6.7	60.0	8.2	13.3	11.9	135
60–69	10.9	45.3	9.4	9.4	25.0	64
70+	15.5	22.4	1.7	5.2	55.2	58

Source: 1991 Census Two Per Cent Individual SAR (ESCR/JISC purchase). Crown copyright.

Chapter 8
Household and family structure among ethnic minority groups

Mike Murphy

8.1 Introduction

Distinctive patterns of family and household sizes and structures for different ethnic groups can be of long-standing. For example, in the United States, data from the 1910 Census showed the existence of substantial racial differences in family and household structure at that time. Compared with Whites, African–American households were less likely to consist of a single nuclear family and more likely to be headed by women, as is still the case in the USA today. Such continuities in living arrangements within ethnic groups indicate that the economic, cultural and demographic factors which underpin these patterns remain important (Morgan *et al.*, 1993).

Comparable data for Britain do not exist, most obviously because there were no large, ethnic minority groups in Britain until recent decades. Even during this period, data on ethnic minority groups have only been available in large-scale official surveys such as the Labour Force Survey (LFS) and National Dwelling and Housing Survey (NDHS) since the late 1970s (though there have also been specialised surveys (Brown, 1984)). While such sources have provided insights about the living arrangements of ethnic groups (Haskey, 1989; Berrington, 1994; Commission for Racial Equality, 1988; Department of the Environment, 1993), the availability of census data on ethnic groups allows this area to be analysed in more detail, in part because the data sets available for analysis are larger than those from sample surveys and the census is often considered to be the most 'authoritative' data source (see Chapter 1).

This chapter considers the living arrangements of various ethnic groups in Britain. One general problem is that there are many different aspects to people's living arrangements. For example there are differences in size of households and families; the roles which men and women play; and the extent to which households comprise one person or family, or more complex units. There are a number of specific difficulties in the interpretation of results for ethnic groups. One arises from the very different age structures of ethnic minority populations, which are generally much younger than average (see Chapter 4).

As average household and family size and structure varies substantially across the life course, the question arises of how far the observed overall differences among ethnic groups reflect such demographic factors rather than the choices and constraints which they face. In later sections an attempt will be made to allow for differences in sex and age structures of the ethnic groups in order to assess the extent of underlying differentials in living arrangements. Before doing this, we need to consider the idea of an ethnic minority household.

8.2 Classification of ethnic minorities and households

Even to define an 'ethnic minority household' is problematic if the household comprises members of more than one ethnic group (as is indeed the case for virtually any classification based on *individuals*). The ethnic composition of a given household could be defined as that of a single individual in the household, such as the designated 'head of household'. The 'head of household' as used here and in 1991 Census reports is the first person ('reference individual') entered on the census household form, who is usually resident and aged 16 or over. The relationship to that person is given for all other persons on the form.

Alternatively, the individual rather than the household may be used as the basis of analysis, which overcomes the difficulty in the allocation of households to a unique ethnic minority category. However, this will lead to results which may appear to be rather different to the more conventional ones, such as published Census tables, which are based on the *household* as the unit of analysis and the ethnic classification solely on that of the head of household (or less commonly the *family*) (see, for example, OPCS, 1993, Table 4 and various tables in OPCS, 1994).

In order to facilitate comparisons with such sources, a number of household-level analyses will also be presented. One example of these different perspectives is that the average size of households in the SAR 1% household sample was 2.48 people. However, the same sample members lived in households with an average size of 3.20 people. This reflects the fact that those living in larger households are counted once each in the latter case, but only once overall in the former case. Box 8.1 gives a simple example: if half of households comprised one person and half comprised three people, the average household size would be two people, but three quarters of people would live in three-person households so the average size of the household people lived in would be 2.5 persons. This is a general point with respect to the analysis of households and families, rather than specific to ethnic groups and similar considerations hold for other aspects of living arrangements such as the fact that 11 per cent of people live alone, but 26 per cent of households contain one person only (see also King and Preston, 1990).

Since the focus of this chapter is on families and households, the subsequent analysis will be based mainly on the 1% Household SAR file (Census Microdata Unit, 1993). Although large by most standards, for more detailed analysis even by such basic variables as age and sex, the numbers in the ethnic minority groups quickly become small and therefore results are statistically unreliable due to sampling variation. Of the nine ethnic minority groups available for analysis in this SAR sample, there are fewer than 100 people aged 60 and over in five groups. Therefore some of these groups have been combined, both to increase sample sizes and to facilitate comparisons between groups in those cases where the sample sizes would otherwise have been inadequate.

Instead of using an a *priori* aggregation of groups, discriminant analysis was used to identify those combinations of ethnic groups which were the most similar in their family and household structures within the various age and sex categories. Overall, it was found that the five collapsed 'natural' groups identified by this technique were intuitively plausible in the groups they contained. The Black (and Other–Other) group comprises four groups, the three Black groups plus the Other–Other group, over half of whom are Black–Caribbean. Although these groups have different characteristics (see Volume 2), with respect to their living arrangements they are closer to each other than to other groups in the SAR classification. The other collapsed groups were a Pakistani/Bangladeshi group (the former accounting for about three quarters of the group), and an Other–Asian (including Chinese) group. The numbers are shown in Table 8.1.

In some of the later tables in this chapter, when sample sizes permit, the full set of nine groups is shown. Other ways of presenting these data could be selected. For example, Heath and Dale (1994) in their analysis of 16–35-year-

---

Box 8.1

Illustrative calculation of alternative household size measures

Household size	Number of house-holds	Number of people living in given household type	Number of people with whom an individual lives (including self) in household
1	50	50	50
3	50	150	450
Total	100	200	500

Average household size:

$$\frac{\text{Total number of people}}{\text{Total number of households}}$$
$$= \frac{200}{100}$$
$$= 2.0$$

Average number of people which a person lives with (including self):

$$\frac{\text{Total household sizes of people living in household}}{\text{Total number of people}}$$
$$= \frac{500}{200}$$
$$= 2.5$$

Table 8.1 *Classification of collapsed ethnic groups*

Collapsed ethnic classification			SAR ethnic classification		
Group	Sample size		Group	Sample size	
	Heads of household	People		Heads of household	People
White	206,197	503,094	White	206,197	503,094
Black (& Other–Other)	3,815	11,079	Black–Caribbean	2,020	4,590
			Black –African	681	1,904
			Black–Other	367	1,711
			Other–Other	747	2,874
Indian	2,148	7,985	Indian	2,148	7,985
Pakistan/Bangladeshi	1,227	5,853	Pakistani	961	4,505
			Bangladeshi	266	1,348
Other Asian (including Chinese)	982	3,159	Chinese	424	1,317
			Other Asian	558	1,842
Unclassified	28	-	Unclassified	28	-
Total	214,369	531,170	Total	214,369	531,170

de jure numbers, people columns exclude members of 28 households in sample with 12 or more people for whom information on individual-level characteristics is unavailable. In 7 cases, there were two or more joint heads identified; in these cases, the head was taken as the oldest male in the household.

old ethnic groups combined the Other–Asian group with the South Asian groups, and they excluded the Chinese and Other–Other groups; the former on the grounds that it was not clear how it could be combined with another group. It is not stated if this classification was derived empirically or theoretically.

As pointed out in Chapter 2 of this volume, even the nine-fold classification available in the SAR is by no means precise. For example, those describing themselves as Arab were included in Other–Other group rather than Other–Asian group. The Other–Other group is clearly very heterogeneous with over half being British-born, though the remainder are distributed over a wide variety of birthplaces, with the largest group, 13 per cent of the total, born in the Middle-East. However, nearly half of those who are not heads of household have a Black head of household.

Table 8.2 *Age above which 25 or fewer people are in SAR 1% household sample by ethnic group and sex*

	White	Black (& Other–Other)	Indian	Pakistani/ Bangladeshi	Other Asian (including Chinese)
Men	Over 95	77	78	69	69
Women	Over 95	81	79	64	72

Although reallocation of some members of the Other–Other group could have been done on the basis of country of birth or of the reported ethnic group of relations, especially parents, some arbitrary decisions would have been required and therefore in the rest of this chapter the empirically-derived collapsed classification will be used. The choice of level of aggregation of ethnic groups will affect some analyses more than others. Clearly the proportion of multi-ethnic households — those containing members of more than one ethnic group — will increase with the fineness of the classification used.

Even with this aggregation, the sample sizes of ethnic minority groups are relatively small, especially for older age groups, therefore it was necessary to smooth the age patterns to facilitate comparisons between groups. This was done by fitting cubic spline curves to the data of the figures in this chapter. Moreover, for each group shown in the figures, the values have been truncated around the age above which there are 25 or fewer men or women in the sample (corresponding to an overall population in Great Britain of about 2,500 individuals). The age cut-offs are as given in Table 8.2.

Some variables analysed here are also available in the 2% individual SAR. Comparison of these results shows that differences are generally small and the interpretation of the results of this chapter remain essentially unaltered. For an extended discussion, including the methodology of smoothing and estimation of standard errors, see Murphy and Grundy (1995).

However before examining detailed patterns, the overall results will be considered, starting with the most basic indicator — household size — though even here the situation is not straightforward. The pattern of living arrangements found will be compared with that of the White group, which in practice is very similar to that of the overall population because of its numerical dominance.

8.3   Household size

There are a number of ways of computing average household size. In the SAR 1% Household file, the overall average *de jure* household size was 2.48 people. (Unless otherwise stated, all analyses in this chapter are based on de jure populations, i.e. excluding visitors and including household members who were absent on census night. Of the 215,789 households in the SAR 1% Household file, 1,392 households contained no permanent resident, only visitors. These households have been excluded from the calculations of average household size). This is the usual household-level average referred to earlier. Unfortunately the characteristics of those living in households of size 12 people and over are not available for analysis for reasons of confidentiality. There were 28 such households (about 1 in 8,000). While their exclusion does not alter the overall figure to the level of accuracy quoted here, and is not considered to be a general problem (Heath and Dale, 1994), it could be important for the South Asian ethnic groups. For example, if the distribution of ethnic composition of these 28 households were to be the same as those of households of size 11, and it was assumed that their average

Table 8.3   *Average household size by ethnic group of head of household and average number of people lived with by ethnic group*

Ethnic group	(a) Average household size by ethnic group of head of household			(b) Average number of people in household by ethnic group of individual		
	Adults[1]	Children[1]	Total	Adults[1]	Children[1]	Total
White	1.96	0.48	2.44	2.29	0.84	3.13
Black (& Other–Other)	1.90	0.73	2.63	2.28	1.25	3.53
Black–Caribbean	1.90	0.63	2.53	2.31	0.90	3.20
Black–African	1.97	0.87	2.85	2.45	1.48	3.93
Black–Other	1.68	0.83	2.50	2.05	1.54	3.58
Other–Other	1.95	0.81	2.76	2.27	1.48	3.76
Indian	2.68	1.15	3.83	3.10	1.52	4.62
Pakistani/Bangladeshi	2.72	2.17	4.89	3.08	2.94	6.03
Pakistani	2.73	2.08	4.81	3.11	2.86	5.97
Bangladeshi	2.69	2.48	5.18	2.98	3.22	6.20
Other Asian						
(including Chinese)	2.31	0.82	3.13	2.78	1.20	3.98
Chinese	2.29	0.73	3.02	2.77	1.12	3.89
Other Asian	2.33	0.88	3.21	2.79	1.25	4.04
All ethnic groups	1.97	0.51	2.48	2.31	0.88	3.20

[1] Adults aged 16 and over; children aged 15 or under.

size was 13 people, then the average household size of the Pakistani/Bangladeshi group would increase from 4.89 to 4.97; the increase in the Indian group would be 0.025; and the other groups would remain essentially unaltered.

As noted earlier, though a convenient and common way of analysing households by individual-level characteristics is to use those of the 'head of household' (as shown in Table 8.3 panel (a)), this will not show, for example, whether ethnic group non-heads are living in large or small households. More detailed analysis shows that this does lead to biases in interpretation especially for the Black (and Other–Other) groups (see Appendix 8.1, p. 237). Nevertheless households headed by members of all ethnic minority groups have above-average sizes, offset by the slightly lower than average value for those with White heads. The four groups comprising the three Black groups and Other–Other group have values between 2.50 and 2.85; the Other–Asian group (including Chinese), around 3.1; the Indian group, 3.83; and the highest household size of all is among the Pakistani and Bangladeshi groups, with the latter having a value of 5.18.

A similar pattern is found by considering the size of household in which people live (the individual-level definition referred to earlier), where the overall average is higher at 3.20 people. A comparison of these alternative measures is given in Table 8.3. Since the average size of households in which White people live is 3.13 people, the average number of people lived with is one fewer, i.e. 2.13 people. For the Pakistani and Bangladeshi group, the

Figure 8.1 *Average number of people in household, Great Britain, 1991*

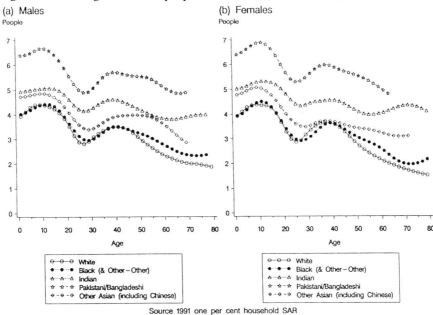

(a) Males   (b) Females

People   People

Legend:
- ⊖⊖⊖ White
- ●●● Black (& Other – Other)
- △△△ Indian
- ☆☆☆ Pakistani/Bangladeshi
- ◇◇◇ Other Asian (including Chinese)

Source 1991 one per cent household SAR

corresponding figure is nearly two and a half times as large, over five people.

Thus it can be seen that the average household size, however defined, is largest among the South Asian (Indian subcontinent) groups, especially the Pakistani/Bangladeshi group and smallest among Whites. Large household sizes are due both to larger numbers of adults and of children, though principally to children. The maximum difference in average number of adults per household in the collapsed classification is only 0.8 adults, but over twice that figure for children. At least part of these observed differences are due to the different age structures of the various ethnic group populations. Old people tend to live in small units and those with dependent children are in the largest households (Murphy, 1983).

In order to control for these factors, Figure 8.1 shows values for individual age and sex groups. The crude differences shown in Table 8.3 panel (b) remain largely unaltered and tend to be replicated for each age and sex group. The Pakistani/Bangladeshi group consistently has the highest values, about two and a half people more on average at every age compared with the White group (which is very close to that of the overall value), whereas the crude overall gap in Table 8.3 panel (b) is just under three people. Thus the difference between groups remains relatively constant with age, apart from the Indian group where the trend is rather flatter than the other groups. This means that though the values for Indian children are closer to those for White children than for Pakistani/Bangladeshi children, for older people, the values are closer to those of the Pakistani/Bangladeshi group. However, such constant differences as shown in Figure 8.1 will lead to very different living arrangements for older people. For example, the average number of other people with whom a White person aged 65 or over

Table 8.4 *Household size distribution (per cent) by ethnic group*

Ethnic group	Number in household			
	1	2–4	5–8	9–11
White	11.0	73.6	15.3	0.1
Black (& Other–Other)	9.3	66.6	22.8	1.3
Indian	2.5	48.9	44.6	4.0
Pakistani/Bangladeshi	1.8	22.9	62.1	13.2
Other Asian (including Chinese)	6.3	60.2	31.7	1.8
All ethnic groups	10.7	72.5	16.5	0.4

lives is 0.8, whereas the corresponding figure for a South Asian person is 3.3 people. Thus the typical living experience of the South Asian groups is markedly different from the other groups.

Presentation of average household size understates the concentration of ethnic minority groups in the largest households, such as those comprising 9 to 11 people (Table 8.4). While there are only 0.4 per cent of people overall living in households of size 9 to 11, the figure for the Pakistani/Bangladeshi group is 13 per cent. This group accounts for only 1.1 per cent of the population, but for 40 per cent of these large households and they have 100 times the probability of a White person of living in such a household. The consequences of such large household sizes are found in a number of associated areas such as the extent of overcrowding among certain ethnic groups (see Volume 4).

More detailed aspects of household structure will be considered later. However, one obvious factor related to the difference in household size is the average number of children present, which is determined mainly by fertility patterns (discussed in Chapter 4) as well as the propensity of adults to live in large or small households, the subject that forms the main focus of this chapter. This analysis of living arrangements will be done initially by considering headship rates.

8.4 Headship rates

Although it has been subject to criticism in recent decades (Murphy, 1991a), one of the most common ways of summarising household patterns is by the use of headship rates — the proportion of those in a particular age, sex or other group who are designated as 'head of household' ('reference individual'). The overall headship rate — the ratio of numbers of household heads to the total private household population — is simply the reciprocal of the average household size. However, to allow for different demographic structures, headship rates by age and sex are shown in Figure 8.2.

There are a number of differences between ethnic groups. Among teenagers, the lowest rates are found among the Indian group (0.4 per cent), and the highest (7 per cent) among Black women. For adult men, the patterns appear broadly similar at younger ages, though there are still some substantial

Figure 8.2 *Headship rates, Great Britain, 1991*

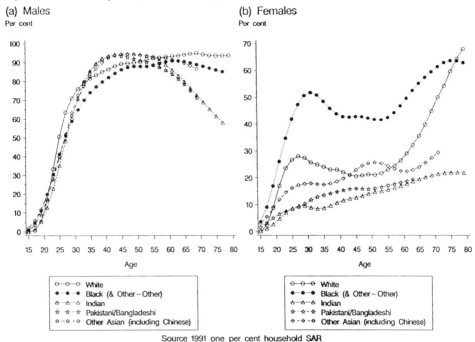

(a) Males
Per cent

(b) Females
Per cent

Age

Age

⊖–⊖–⊖	White
●–●–●	Black (& Other – Other)
⋄⃘⋯⋄⃘⋯⋄⃘	Indian
☆ ☆–☆	Pakistani/Bangladeshi
⋄–⋄–⋄	Other Asian (including Chinese)

⊖–⊖–⊖	White
●–●–●	Black (& Other – Other)
⋄⃘⋯⋄⃘⋯⋄⃘	Indian
☆ ☆–☆	Pakistani/Bangladeshi
⋄–⋄–⋄	Other Asian (including Chinese)

Source 1991 one per cent household SAR

differences. At younger ages the White group tends to have the highest rates: at age 25 the estimated value was about 50 per cent, while most other groups had values about 10 points lower, apart from the Indian group which was about 15 points lower.

In the middle working years, Black and — to a lesser extent — White men have lower rates than all the Asian ethnic groups. This is linked in part to marriage differences (see Chapter 7, Table 7.1), in that a much higher proportion of men in the South Asian ethnic group tend to be married at these ages. However, at older ages, the pattern is completely reversed so that around age 75, about 90 per cent of Black and White men, but only about half of South Asian ethnic group men are household heads, with headship rates starting to decline in this latter group before age 50. The reasons for these patterns will be discussed later, but they are clearly associated with reasons other than marriage.

For women, patterns of headship rates are broadly similar for the three Asian ethnic groups on the one hand, and Black and White women on the other, though the levels differ within these two sets. White and — to an even greater extent — Black women have much higher headship rates, with a tendency for initial high rates to decline until about age 50 and then increase. Among the Asian groups, the levels are generally lower, especially for the South Asian groups, and the rates tend to exhibit a fairly steady rise with age. This reflects the different marriage patterns of the various groups; substantial differences in the propensity of non-married women to head their own household; and differences in the likelihood of married women being the designated 'head of household'. Thus about half of Black women in their thirties are heads of household compared with about one in ten South Asian women.

Table 8.5 *Headship rates (per cent) by age, sex, selected[1] marital statuses, and ethnic group*

Ethnic group	Age 15–29		Age 30–44		Age 45–59	Age 60 and over	
	Single	Married	Single	Married	Married	Married	Widowed/ divorced
Men							
White	18	85	53	91	95	96	89
Black							
(& Other–Other)	24	69	53	83	90	88	94
Indian	8	60	54	88	94	78	45
Pakistani/Bangladeshi	8	51	62	86	90	82	42
Other Asian							
(including Chinese)	20	71	72	87	94	94	56
All ethnic groups	18	84	53	91	95	96	89
Women							
White	18	14	54	11	7	6	91
Black							
(& Other–Other)	35	20	78	19	17	18	84
Indian	5	6	40	4	5	4	32
Pakistani/Bangladeshi	4	8	55	8	9	2	52
Other Asian							
(including Chinese)	15	9	57	10	12	11	41
All ethnic groups	18	14	55	11	7	6	91

[1] Values have not been given for marital status categories where numbers are small.

Table 8.6 *Ratio of observed to expected average household size if overall headship rates obtained by ethnic group of head of household*

Ethnic group	Ratio
White	99.9
Black (& Other–Other)	86.6
Black–Caribbean	83.4
Black–African	88.6
Black–Other	80.9
Other–Other	96.4
Indian	120.6
Pakistani/Bangladeshi	114.8
Pakistani	115.1
Bangladeshi	113.5
Other Asian (including Chinese)	107.2
Chinese	104.9
Other–Asian	109.0
All ethnic groups	100.0

Headship rates for women by marital status are highest for Black women in all cases shown in Table 8.5, apart from elderly women. For men, Whites generally have the highest values. The low rates for Black married men are noteworthy (though this is offset by the particularly high rates for married Black women). For those under age 30, the headship rates for single Black men are three times those for South Asian men, and for single Black women they are about eight times those for South Asian women. Indeed even for married South Asian men, nearly half of this age group are not heads of their own household, compared with 15 per cent of White married men. Possible indicators about the role and status of women may be inferred from the fact that about one in five Black married women are the reference individual ('head of household'), compared with one in 20 South Asian women, with White women in an intermediate position.

For older people, substantial differences are also found. While about 90 per cent of both Black and White men and women who were formerly married head their own households, the figures are far lower among the Asian ethnic groups, with, for example, just under one third of Indian ethnic group widows heading their own household.

Part of the overall differences in household size is due to the different age structures of the ethnic group populations and use of age-specific headship rates can control for this to some extent. In order to try and show the sorts of differences which would exist if age and sex effects could be eliminated, an indirect standardisation technique was employed. The overall national headship rates by age and sex were applied to each ethnic population age and sex structure to estimate how many heads of household would be expected within each group if these rates applied. The ratio of the observed to the expected numbers is shown in Table 8.6. (It is not possible to produce directly-standardised results with the total population as standard because the headship rates for the ethnic minority groups at individual ages are subject to wide margins of error). The values in Table 8.6 show the ratio of average household size which would be found if the particular ethnic group had the same headship rates as the overall population to the observed value for that group. These results should be regarded as illustrative only since the pattern of headship rates is in part a consequence of the population age and sex distribution, and in the light of the problems in defining an unambiguous concept of an 'ethnic minority household' referred to earlier.

As in Table 8.3, the largest values are found for the South Asian groups, though on this basis, the Indian group has relatively fewer heads (and therefore larger standardised household size) than the Pakistani and Bangladeshi groups. The Other–Asian and Chinese groups retain their relative positions. The groups which have the lowest average household size, after controlling for age and sex structure, are those that comprise the Black (and Other–Other) groups, about 13 per cent below the expected value, thus reversing the above-average values shown in Table 8.3 and Appendix 8.1. This is associated with the very high rates of headship among Black women not being offset by the slightly below average values for Black men. These differences will be relevant to making household projections for ethnic groups, and there are a number of Housing Associations that concentrate on particular ethnic groups.

So far, discussion has been confined to basic indicators of household size and headship. Some of these reflect the patterns of *family* living arrangements within households, and these will now be considered.

8.5 Type of family lived in

Households are made up of family units. The statistical definition of a family is a nuclear family-based one consisting of a couple (married or cohabiting) with or without never-married child(ren), or a lone parent with never-married child(ren) (see also Chapter 7, Box 7.2; and Dale and Marsh (1993)). Grandparent(s) with never-married grandchild(ren) comprise a family unit if there is a 'missing middle generation'. In the case of a three-generation group consisting of the grandparent(s), never-married child and grandchild(ren), the last two form the family unit. There may also be people living in a household, but not in a family as defined above, who may or may not be related to any other household members. These will be referred to as 'monos', to distinguish them from those living alone ('solos'). Thus the primary classification of family types is by whether or not it contains a

Table 8.7 *Family types in which individuals live (per cent), by ethnic group*

Ethnic group	Family type				Sample size (= 100%)
	Couple with child(ren)[1]	Couple without child(ren)[1]	Lone parent[2]	Not family	
White	51.6	23.4	9.6	15.4	503,094
Black (& Other–Other)	44.4	9.7	28.1	17.9	11,079
Black–Caribbean	38.9	11.7	30.0	19.4	4,590
Black–African	42.4	9.0	21.9	26.7	1,904
Black–Other	43.4	5.9	38.7	11.9	1,711
Other–Other	54.9	9.3	22.8	13.1	2,784
Indian	74.4	11.2	6.6	7.8	7,985
Pakistani/Bangladeshi	79.4	5.3	8.3	7.0	5,853
Pakistani	78.3	5.9	8.6	7.2	4,505
Bangladeshi	83.1	3.0	7.4	6.5	1,348
Other–Asian (including Chinese)	60.4	12.9	7.8	18.8	3,159
Chinese	58.9	14.1	7.0	20.0	1,317
Other–Asian	65.1	12.1	8.4	18.0	1,842
All ethnic groups	52.2	22.7	9.9	15.3	531,170

[1] Never-married child(ren) of any age, 'couple' includes married and cohabiting partnerships.
[2] Includes both those with and without dependent children.

couple, and whether or not it contains children. The distributions are shown in Table 8.7.

The most noteworthy feature is the very high prevalence of lone parenthood among the Black and Other–Other groups, over one quarter of whom are living in such families, compared with under 10 per cent in all of the other groups. Lone parenthood refers not only to those with dependent children, but any lone parent with never-married children in the household. It would therefore also include, for example, an elderly widowed parent living with an unmarried child. If lone parents with *dependent* children are considered, the proportion for the Black group is 22.7 per cent compared with an overall figure of 6.5 per cent, and with no other group exceeding 7 per cent. The highest proportion of lone parenthood in the Black and Other–Other groups is found among the Black–Other group (nearly 40 per cent), and the lowest among the Black–African and Other–Other groups (with values around 22 per cent). For other types of family living arrangements, the main distinction is between the South Asian groups who are much more likely to be living as part of a couple with children, and much less likely to be living outside a family unit than all other groups.

The fact that these patterns are not artefacts of the different demographic structures is confirmed by Figure 8.3 which shows how the patterns of family living change with age for the different ethnic groups. For those living outside a family, there are high rates for the Other–Asian (including Chinese) group among young adults, many of whom are students. At older working ages, the Black group generally has the highest rates (above 25 per cent), especially among men (Figure 8.3 (g)). For children, the association of lone parenthood with the Black ethnic group is clear, with over 40 per cent being in this family type, compared with well under 10 per cent of South Asian groups and just over 15 per cent of Whites (Figures 8.3 (e) and (f)).

Although these data refer to a given point in time rather than to a given group of people followed through time, they do show the experiences which different groups might expect if no substantial changes occur in years to come. The data for men and women are most dissimilar for the Black group, because of the overwhelming likelihood of the woman taking on the role of lone parent. Moreover, the lifetime experiences of groups would be very different. For example, while one third of White men might expect to be in the 'empty nest' phase of a couple without children around age 50, for Pakistani/Bangladeshi men, this point would only occur about age 70, by which time about two thirds of White men would be in this situation (Figures 8.3 (c) and (d)). For women, there is no age where more than one third of the Black ethnic group are in this phase of the 'conventional life' cycle, a fact which tends to emphasise the inapplicability of such frameworks for the analysis of non-Western groups (Collver, 1963; Murphy, 1995). The above examples could be repeated for many other aspects of the diversity of life-course experiences of various ethnic groups.

Figure 8.3 *Family living arrangements, Great Britain 1991*

(a) Males in couple with children family
Per cent

(b) Females in couple with children family
Per cent

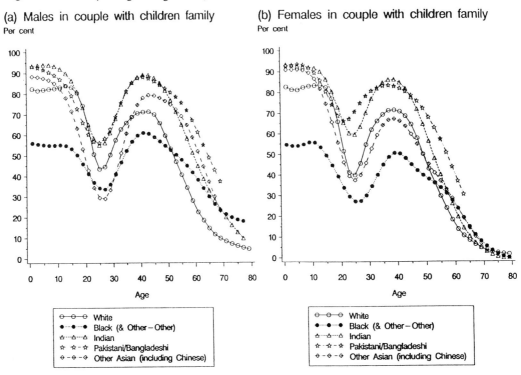

(c) Males in couple without children family
Per cent

(d) Females in couple without children family
Per cent

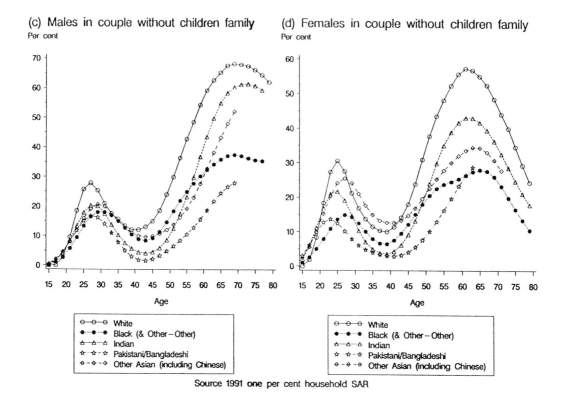

Source 1991 one per cent household SAR

Figure 8.3 - *continued*

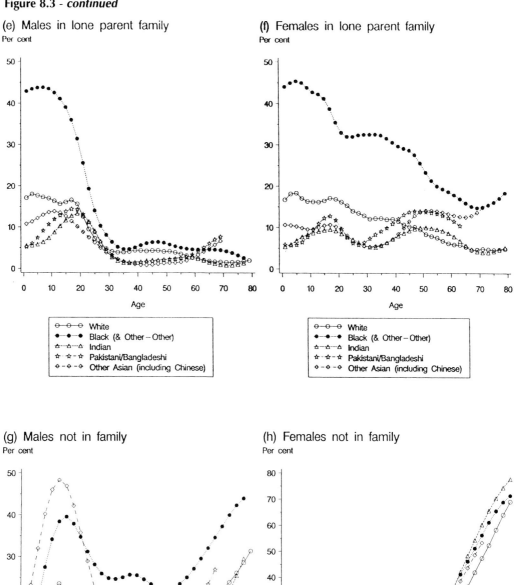

(e) Males in lone parent family

(f) Females in lone parent family

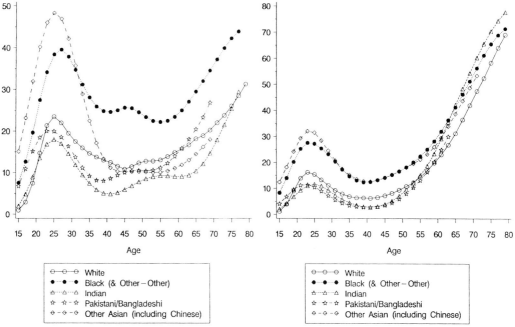

(g) Males not in family

(h) Females not in family

Source 1991 one per cent household SAR

8.6 Families within households

While the great majority of people live in households consisting of a single family (over three quarters) or one person (11 per cent), the remaining one in eight comprises groups of particular interest because they are unusual; they reflect substantial differences between ethnic groups; and they may have policy implications such as overcrowded households consisting of more than one family (Table 8.8). These 'unconventional' groups include, in declining proportions:

1 *One family and mono(s)* (which could include a nuclear family living with a relative such as an aged, widowed parent, a divorced child, or a non-relative). Such arrangements are much more common among all the ethnic minority groups than among White people.

2 *Two or more monos,* which could include a variety of possibilities such as (non-cohabiting) flat sharers, gay couples, and certain related groups not defined as a 'family', such as two elderly sisters living together.

3 *One-person households,* in which distinctly fewer of the South Asian groups live, as is also the case for the other household type above containing no family.

4 *Complex households* comprising at least two distinct families. These

Table 8.8 *Sharing arrangements of individuals (per cent) by ethnic group*

Ethnic group	Sharing type					Sample size (= 100%)
	One family only	One family & mono(s)	Two or more monos	One person only	At least two families	
White	79.5	5.1	3.0	11.0	1.5	503,094
Black (& Other–Other)	72.0	9.9	5.7	9.3	3.0	11,079
Black–Caribbean	71.6	7.6	4.6	12.4	3.8	4,590
Black–African	60.3	15.5	12.4	9.5	2.2	1,904
Black–Other	80.4	7.8	3.8	6.0	2.1	1,711
Other–Other	75.5	11.0	4.2	6.4	2.8	2,784
Indian	66.5	14.3	1.5	2.5	15.2	7,985
Pakistani/Bangladeshi	68.8	14.0	1.5	1.8	14.0	5,853
Pakistani	67.3	14.5	1.3	1.9	15.1	4,505
Bangladeshi	73.8	12.4	2.2	1.4	10.2	1,348
Other–Asian (including Chinese)	65.3	15.9	7.0	6.3	5.4	3,159
Chinese	65.6	13.3	8.4	7.2	5.5	1,317
Other–Asian	65.1	17.8	6.0	5.7	5.4	1,842
All ethnic groups	78.9	5.5	3.0	10.7	1.9	531,170

exhibit the sharpest differentiation between ethnic groups in that the overall figure is about 2 per cent of people living in such households, but about 15 per cent of the South Asian group.

Comparison of groups is complicated by the very different age structures of the ethnic group populations, but the small proportion of the White population living in one of these four unconventional household types is not an artefact. All the ethnic minority groups are more likely than the White group to have a non-family member living with them, though this is much less marked for the Black and Other–Other groups than for the South Asian ones. About one third of the South Asian groups are living in a household containing a nuclear family but with other permanent residents as well. In particular, South Asians are much more likely to live in households containing at least two family units — about 15 per cent do so, compared to 5 per cent of Other–Asian and Chinese groups, about 3 per cent of the Black (and Other–Other) groups, and about 1.5 per cent of the White group. Conversely, the South Asian groups have few households containing no family.

While the prevalence of extended family living is relatively low, even among those groups most likely to do so, it should be remembered that the census data are cross-sectional and refer to the situation at one particular day in April 1991. Such living arrangements are likely to be experienced at some stage by much higher proportions of the population. For example, in a 15-year study of middle-aged women in the US, between a quarter and a third of White women had lived in an extended family at some stage, and two thirds of Black women had done so (Beck and Beck, 1989).

The patterns by sex and age for what might be regarded as the extremes of the distribution, living alone and in complex households, are shown in Figure 8.4. Whereas well over 90 per cent of White children are in a one-family household, only just over two thirds of South Asian groups start off in such a household (Figures 8.4 (a) and (b)). For family plus mono(s) households, the White group is under-represented, so that by about age 80, while about 5 per cent of White women live in such households, the corresponding figure for Indian women is over 50 per cent (Figure 8.4 (d)).

Among all groups, the majority of monos sharing with a family are related to the head of household, but the proportions differ: for Whites, the value is about two thirds, compared with over 90 per cent for the Indian group, which has the highest value. The much greater propensity of Black men to live alone is evident at all ages, while the patterns for Black and White women are very similar (Figures 8.4 (g) and (h)). At older ages the differences between the Asian and non-Asian groups is striking: the proportions living alone among the Black and White groups are about three times that of the Asian groups, so that around age 75, about half of the Black and White groups live alone compared with only about 15 per cent of the South Asian group (this analysis excludes the institutional populations, which is discussed in Murphy and Grundy, 1995).

In general, living in complex households is more common at certain stages of the life cycle: as young children, young adults and among older people,

Figure 8.4 *Household sharing arrangements, Great Britain ,1991*

(a) Males in one family household
Per cent

(b) Females in one family household
Per cent

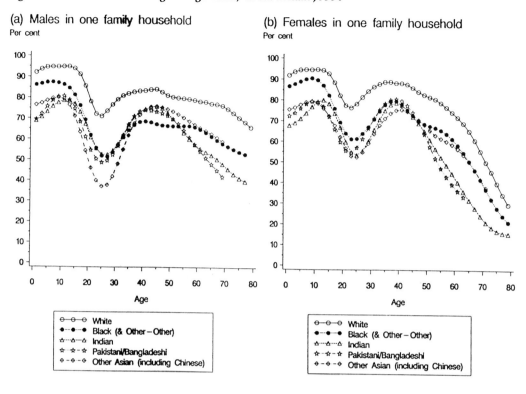

(c) Males in family and mono(s) household
Per cent

(d) Females in family and mono(s) household
Per cent

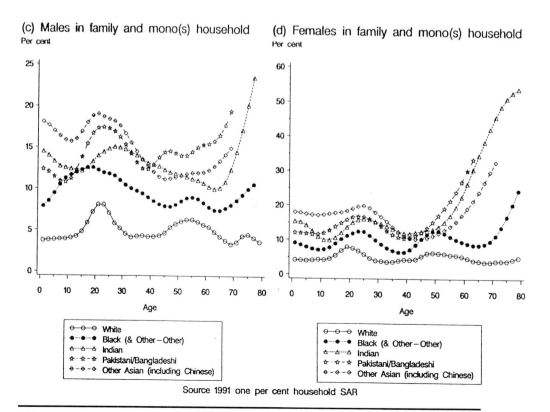

Source 1991 one per cent household SAR

Demographic characteristics of the ethnic minority populations

Figure 8.4 - *continued*

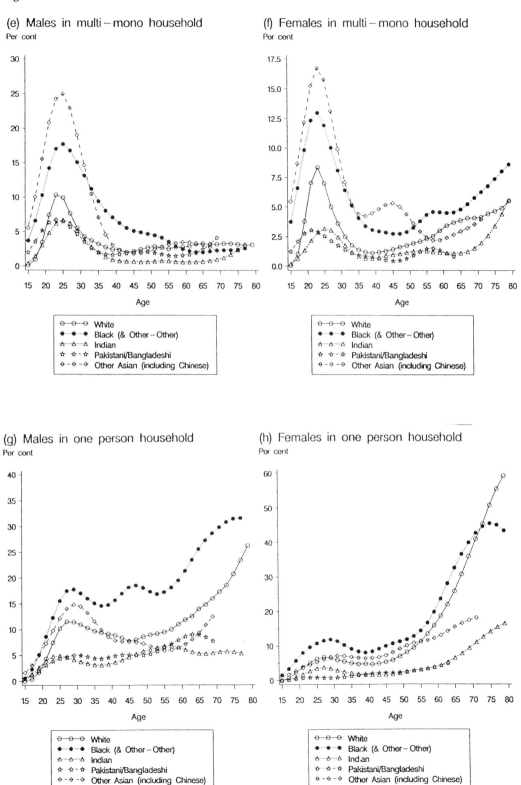

(e) Males in multi—mono household

Per cent

(f) Females in multi—mono household

Per cent

(g) Males in one person household

Per cent

(h) Females in one person household

Per cent

Source 1991 one per cent household SAR

Figure 8.4 - *continued*

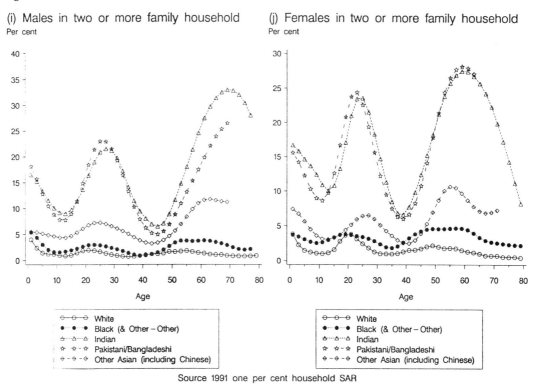

(i) Males in two or more family household
Per cent

(j) Females in two or more family household
Per cent

Source 1991 one per cent household SAR

but the levels differ between groups (Figures 8.4 (i) and (j)). For South Asian groups, between 10 and 20 per cent of all age groups are likely to be living in complex households, whereas for the non-Asian groups, at no stage are more than 5 per cent living in such a household.

Two particular partially-overlapping types of complex household will now be considered, those containing at least two families and three-generation households.

8.7 Complex households

The proportion of complex households has been declining over time in Britain (Wall, 1983), with an apparently accelerating fall in the 1980s (Murphy and Berrington, 1993), even though the classical north-western European pattern has tended to be relatively simple for many centuries (Hajnal, 1982). Ethnic minorities, especially those originating in South Asia, are heavily over-represented among complex households (and even more so when the relative scarcity of elderly people to form such complex households is taken into account). Because the prevalence of complex households among South Asian groups is so high, the question arises as to how far this is a preferred form of living arrangement and how far it is due to 'constraint' factors such as inadequate housing.

Table 8.9 shows how the pattern of the Pakistani/Bangladeshi group compares with that of England and Wales in 1851 and with the pattern among the White population in Britain in 1991. The similarity with the historical population is clear, apart from the numbers of non-relatives (mainly servants and lodgers in the earlier period). A similar pattern emerges with the average household size in 1851, 4.6 persons as compared with the values of 4.9 for the Pakistani/Bangladeshi and 2.4 for the White group in 1991. While this does not imply the mechanisms which lead to these similarities are the same, or that it represents some trend in household structure progression, the fact that South Asian household structures are broadly similar to those which have long since passed in Britain once more emphasises their distinctive nature.

Among households comprising more than a single family unit, ethnic minority groups are more likely to share with relatives than are White groups (Haskey, 1989). Of course any discussion of ethnic groups in Britain must acknowledge their migrant as well as ethnic status and recognise that some of the observed patterns will reflect their recent arrival and the typical patterns arising from assistance provided within such groups to more recent arrivals. Thus, some of the household complexity will be transient as recent arrivals receive temporary help from relatives. However, given that the relatively long-established Indian group (Chapter 4 in Volume 2) tends to exhibit the greatest complexity, other more long-lasting influences are also at work, though data such as those in the census can only suggest some explanations.

The first type of extended household to be considered is the three-generation household, defined here as either a household containing the parent and/or parent-in-law *and* child/child-in-law of the head of household. (This 'middle-head' group also contains a very small number of households with the parent/parent-in-law and grandchild of the head) or those with the child/child-in-law and grandchild of the head of household ('upper-head'). In theory, other forms of three-generation households could also exist, for example if this descent group did not contain the head of household. Such groups could not be identified in the SAR, but the numbers could only be tiny.

Table 8.9 *Relation of household member to head of household, England and Wales 1851, and Great Britain 1991, Pakistani/Bangladeshi and White groups*

Relationship	Percent		
	England and Wales 1851[1]	Pakistani/Bangladeshi group GB 1991	White group GB 1991
Head	22	21	41
Spouse	15	16	25
Child	44	53	30
Other relation	7	9	2
Non-relation	13	1	2

[1] Wall, 1983.

Table 8.10 shows the distribution of such three-generation households. Overall, about one in six of the Indian group live in such households compared with one in 40 of the White group. The patterns of who is the head in such households tends to differ in that for the three Asian groups, the head is most likely to be in the middle generation, whereas for the White and Black groups, the head is most likely to be in the upper level (especially among Black ethnic groups, where the head is about twice as likely to be in the upper level). Blacks have also the highest proportion of households containing a grandparent and grandchild with the intervening generation not in the household. The typical three-generation Asian household comprises a couple with children living with an elderly parent or parents, whereas for the Black ethnic group, the majority consist of a young lone mother living with her parent(s).

Table 8.10 *Proportion of people living in three-generation households by ethnic group*

Ethnic group	Type of three-generation household			Sample size (=100%)
	Upper[1]	Middle[2]	Not in such household	
White	1.4	1.1	97.4	503,094
Blacks (& Other–Other)	2.6	1.4	96.0	11,079
Indian	6.9	10.6	82.5	7,985
Pakistani/Bangladeshi	5.3	5.9	88.8	5,853
Other Asian (including Chinese)	1.3	4.5	94.2	3,159
All ethnic groups	1.6	1.3	97.1	531,170

[1] Head in oldest of three generations.
[2] Head in middle generation.

A particularly clear difference between families living in another's household for Asian and non-Asian ethnic groups is seen in Table 8.11. Whereas about four fifths of such Asian families are married couples (with or without children) and about one fifth are lone parents, these figures are almost exactly reversed for both the White and Black ethnic groups, among whom the secondary families are predominantly lone-parent ones, and usually contain the daughter of the head of household. Thus the majority of sharing families are in direct descent with the head of household (or his/her spouse).

Table 8.11 *Family types of 'secondary'[1] families in three-generation households (per cent), by ethnic group*

Ethnic group	Family type			Sample size (families=100%)
	Married	Cohabiting	Lone parent	
White	23.3	3.7	73.0	1,691
Black (& Other–Other)	20.0	3.3	76.7	60
Indian	86.5	0.0	13.5	148
Pakistani/Bangladeshi	80.6	0.0	19.4	72
Other Asian (including Chinese)	84.6[2]	0.0[2]	15.4[2]	13
All ethnic groups	30.4	3.2	66.4	1,984

[1] Families which do not include the family of head of household.
[2] Based on sample fewer than 50 families.

Multi-family households are not necessarily three-generation households and *vice versa*. Ethnic minority groups are also more likely to have more distant relations living in their households than the White group. While vertically-extended three-generation households are most common among the Indian group, the Pakistani/Bangladeshi and the Other—Asian groups are more likely to be horizontally-extended, having more brothers and sisters living with the household head (Table 8.12).

Table 8.12 *Relationship of heads[1] of 'secondary' family units in 2+ family households to the head of household (per cent), by ethnic group*

Ethnic group	Child/ child-in- law	Parent/ parent- in-law	Sib/sib- in-law	Other relation	Other	Sample size (=100%)
White	79.9	10.5	3.0	1.4	5.1	1,542
Black (& Other–Other)	76.6	4.7	4.7	1.6	12.5	64
Indian	58.7	25.0	11.5	1.4	3.4	208
Pakistani/Bangladeshi	44.2	27.4	19.5	4.4	4.4	113
Other Asian (including Chinese)	53.3[2]	20.0[2]	20.2[2]	6.7[2]	0.0[2]	30
All ethnic groups	75.1	13.0	5.2	1.7	5.1	1,957

[1] The head of family is generally taken to be the head of household if the family contains the head of household; otherwise, in a couple, the head of family is the first member of the couple on the form. In a lone parent family, the head of family is the lone parent.
[2] Based on sample fewer than 50 people.

The evidence presented here suggests that among non-Asian groups, household extension will frequently be a non-preferred type of arrangement, typically associated with a younger lone parent daughter living with her parents, rather than a type of living arrangement actively sought by those involved. However, the situation for South Asian groups is less clear cut. If it is assumed that those with the greatest command over resources will be in the best position to achieve their preferences, then the more these patterns reflect 'choice' the more common they should be among better-off groups and vice versa. Table 8.13 therefore compares the social class distribution of the heads of those in single family and two-plus family households. In every group, those higher up the social scale are more likely to be in a single-family home, with relatively little difference in the patterns between groups. Thus the overall greater propensity for South Asian groups to be extended appears to be similarly distributed across social classes as with other ethnic groups, though the overall level is much higher. Thus there is no evidence that higher social status groups are likely to seek extension.

8.8 Conclusions

The results above have shown that substantial differences exist between the household and family patterns of different ethnic minority groups in Britain, and these are generally much more marked than those found between other socio-economic subgroups within the population. In particular, there are higher proportions of female-headed, lone-parent families among Black

Table 8.13 *Social class of heads of household (per cent) by ethnic group of household head*

Ethnic group of household head	Social class of household head								Sample size (classified heads=100%)	
	I & II		IIIn		IIIm		IV & V			
	One family	Two+ families	One family	Two+ families	One family	Two+ families	One family	Two+ families	One family	Two+ families
White	37	27	13	10	30	35	20	28	112,932	1,214
Black (& Other–Other)	32	15[1]	20	15[1]	22	33[1]	26	36	1,762	39
Indian	40	27	13	14	26	27	21	31	1,270	157
Pakistani/ Bangladeshi	27	19	10	8	30	29	33	44	612	78
Other Asian (including Chinese)	44	29[1]	16	17[1]	24	38[1]	16	17[1]	492	24
All ethnic groups	37	26	13	11	30	34	20	28	117,068	1,512

[1] Based on sample size of fewer than 50 people.

people and more extended household structures among the South Asian groups. The fact that these particular aspects tend to be concentrated in distinct ethnic groups in Britain contrasts with the United States, where they are both relatively common among both of the major ethnic minority groups, Blacks and Hispanics (Tienda and Angel, 1982).

The living arrangements of elderly people exhibit major differences between ethnic groups. While the existence of cultural norms and socio-economic factors are important, their relative impact is unclear. In the US, it has been suggested that for the elderly population, if the distributions of income for minority groups were the same as for Whites, most of the variations in living arrangements would disappear (Soldo and Lauriat, 1976). Other studies have emphasised the existence of a strong independent 'ethnic group effect' for the differing propensities among various ethnic groups to form particular types of living arrangements (Angel and Tienda, 1982; Wolf, 1984) though these may also partially represent a 'coping strategy'.

The ethnic group classification in Britain is related essentially to skin colour, with the Irish-born sometimes included as an honorary ethnic minority. The reasons for having a relatively detailed classification for ethnic minority groups, but none for the White group is discussed in Chapter 2 of this volume. Nevertheless, more detailed breakdowns of ethnic affiliation elsewhere have shown interesting differences. For example, analyses in Canada showed that ethnicity — British/French or Jewish/Italian — was a more powerful determinant of whether elderly women lived alone than variables such as income, education or age (Kausar and Wister, 1984). Even within a particular county or group, cultural traditions may also have a role in determining household structures (Bartiaux, 1991).

What a single snapshot such as the 1991 Census cannot do is to show how these trends are evolving over time, in particular the extent to which British-born ethnic minorities are likely to move towards patterns which are more typical of the population as a whole. The relatively little overlap at a given age among those who are UK-born or overseas-born within all ethnic minority groups (Berrington, 1994), and the magnitude of age-related changes in living arrangements means that it is not possible to address this question with data from a single census. Moreover, the selective nature of the operation of the immigration system is likely to have an independent influence. For example, marriage is one of the reasons for which acceptance for settlement is permitted. Following the condemnation of the British Government's immigration policy by the European Court of Human Rights on the ground of discrimination against women, the rules were amended in 1985. Although there is now in theory no legal or administrative difference in the treatment of men and women, in practice there are substantial differences in the patterns of acceptance for settlement between the sexes, with many more women admitted (Home Office, 1995, Tables 2.1 and 2.2).It is therefore unsurprising that non-UK born ethnic minority women in their 20s are more likely to be married than their UK-born contemporaries, whereas for White women, who are not subject to the same restrictions in many cases, the reverse is the case. For men, there is also an excess pattern, but the magnitude is much less. Thus it does not seem possible to establish the magnitude of any 'assimilation effect' associated simply with place of birth (this implicitly acting as a proxy for childhood circumstances) without simultaneously considering the political system which determines migration policy. As a result we cannot answer the question of how far the distinctive living arrangements of these ethnic minority groups which have been identified in numerous studies are due to factors such as recent arrival in many cases; short-term and longer-term socio-economic disadvantage and racial discrimination and harrassment; the political context; and cultural preferences. What is obvious, however, is that it is extremely unhelpful to treat these ethnic minorities as a single group. Even though they may have common experiences of discrimination, the responses have often been completely different, in that these groups are often concentrated at both ends of the distributions, rather than showing similar patterns.

For these reasons also, it is not possible to predict how the living arrangements of these ethnic minority groups are likely to change over time. As the proportion of British-born ethnic minorities increases, some convergence towards overall average patterns might be expected, as appears to be the case for fertility. However, some emerging trends such as towards more lone parenthood may impact disproportionately on certain ethnic minority groups. This was the case in the US, where birthplace effects are largely irrelevant but where shifts away from 'traditional' family living arrangements have been greater for Blacks than for Whites, so tending to increase rather than to decrease these differences (Bianchi and Farley, 1979). There is evidence that British-born Blacks are more dissimilar to the overall pattern than are those born overseas (Heath and Dale, 1994).

While characteristic patterns of living arrangements among different ethnic groups explain some of the differences in other socio-economic areas such as housing, and thus consideration of the ethnic dimension is an important mechanism for improving understanding of differences in such other areas, at a deeper level it raises the question of how far change can occur in these other areas without changes in the fundamental aspects of living arrangements discussed here. (The living arrangements are a consequence of a variety of influences including the cultural background, migrant status, demographic structure, socio-economic characteristics of the ethnic groups as well as political, social and economic situation in Britain.) On balance, an approach that acknowledges a number of distinctive demographic regimes which are subject to similar influences but respond to them with different degrees of sensitivity as in the case of various European countries (van de Kaa, 1987; Coleman, 1993) would seem to be the appropriate one, rather than one that concentrates on the effect of birthplace *per se*.

Following on from discussion in the US, in recent years there have been a number of critical statements about non-traditional family and household living arrangements such as lone parenthood and cohabitation from some politicians, commentators and academics. In Britain, unlike in the US, little connection has so far been made with the specific patterns of different ethnic minority groups, especially the Black group. While living arrangements are assumed to be within the calculus of individual choice, the same is not true for skin colour which forms the primary basis of the ethnic group classification.

Given the dramatically different patterns of living arrangements between groups, the concept of a generalised notion of 'choice' as an abstract concept is probably unhelpful in this context. The ways in which preferences are formed is unlikely to be the same. For example, among groups where extra-marital childbearing is common, and where potential husbands have very poor economic expectations, the conventional Western model of childbearing within a marital union by a couple able to set up an independent household with the husband providing for his family will not be an option in many cases. These comments are not meant to disguise the range of problems associated with some non-traditional living arrangements, and other chapters in these volumes show how they are associated with many wider aspects of society and social policy. However, the central role of the family and household environment for the socialisation of children means that there is also the problem when negative images are applied to certain non-traditional living arrangements of 'self-fulfilling prophesies' for those involved, especially for the future of their children. If this is compounded with the distinctiveness visibly associated with membership of particular ethnic groups, the effects are likely to be even more substantial for those concerned. The development of living arrangements among ethnic minority groups, and wider societal reactions to these is likely to be a sensitive issue in decades to come.

References

Angel, R. and Tienda, M. (1982) Determinants of extended household structure: cultural pattern or economic need? *American Journal of Sociology*, 87(6), 1360–83.

Bartiaux, F. (1991) Household composition of the elderly in Italy (1981). *European Journal of Population*, 7(1), 59–98.

Beck, W. and Beck, S.H. (1989) The incidence of extended households among middle-aged Black and White women: estimates from a 15-year panel study. *Journal of Family Issues*, 10(2), 147–68.

Berrington, A. (1994) Marriage and family formation among the white and ethnic minority populations in Britain. *Ethnic and Racial Studies*, 17(3), 517–46.

Bianchi, S.M. and Farley, R. 1(979) Racial differences in family living arrangements and economic well-being: an analysis of recent trends. *Journal of Marriage and the Family*, 41(3), 537–51.

Brown, C. (1984) *Black and White Britain*. London: Policy Studies Institute.

Census Microdata Unit. (1993) *User Guide to the SARs*. Manchester: Census Microdata Unit.

Coleman, D.A. (1993) Britain in Europe: international and regional comparisons of fertility levels and trends. In: M. Ní Bhrolcháín (ed.), *New Perspectives on Fertility in Britain*. OPCS Studies on Medical and Population Subjects No 55. London: HMSO, pp. 67–93.

Collver, A. (1963) The family cycle in India and the United States. *American Sociological Review*, 28, 86–96.

Commission for Racial Equality (1988) *Housing and ethnic minorities: Statistical Information*. London: Commission for Racial Equality.

Dale, A. and Marsh, C. (eds) (1993) *The 1991 Census Users Guide*. London: HMSO.

Department of the Environment (1993) *Housing in England: Housing Trailers to the 1988 and 1991 Labour Force Surveys*. London: HMSO.

Hajnal, J. (1982) Two kind of preindustrial household formation systems. *Population and Development Review*, 8, 449–94.

Haskey, J. (1989) Families and households of the ethnic minority and white populations of Great Britain. *Population Trends*, 57, 8–19.

Heath, S. and Dale, A. (1994) Household and family formation in Great Britain: the ethnic dimension. *Population Trends*, 77, 5–13.

Home Office (1995) *Control of Immigration Statistics UK Third and Fourth Quarters and Year 1994. Home Office Statistical Bulletin 9/95*. London: Home Office.

Jones, T. (1993) *Britain's Ethnic Minorities*. London: Policy Studies Institute.

Kausar, T. and Wister, A. (1984) Living arrangements of older women: the ethnic dimension. *Journal of Marriage and the Family*, 46(2), 301–11.

King, M. and Preston, S.H .(1990) Who lives with whom? Individual versus household measures. *Journal of Family History*, 15(2),117–32.

Morgan, S.P., McDaniel, A., Miller, A.T. and Preston, S.H. (1993) Racial differences in household and family structure at the turn of the century. *American Journal of Sociology*, 98(4), 799–828.

Murphy, M. (1983) The life course of individuals in families: describing static and dynamic aspects of the contemporary family. In: *The Family:*

Proceedings of the British Society for Population Studies Conference, 1983, OPCS Occasional Paper 31. London: OPCS, pp. 50–70 .

Murphy, M. (1991a) Household modelling and forecasting: dynamic approaches with use of linked census data. *Environment and Planning A*, 23, 885–902.

Murphy, M. (1991b) Modelling households: a synthesis. In M. Murphy and J. Hobcraft (eds), *Population Research in Britain: Supplement to Population Studies 45*. London: Population Investigation Committee, pp. 157–76.

Murphy, M. (1995) The family life cycle. In: G. Wunsch and J. Duchêne (eds), *Collect et comparabilité des données démographiques et sociales en Europe*, Chair Quetelet Seminar, 1991. Louvain-la-Neuve: UCL Academia, pp149-82.

Murphy, M. and Berrington, A. (1993) Household change in the 1980s: a review. *Population Trends*, 73, 18–26.

Murphy, M. and Grundy, E. (1995) Living arrangements of elderly ethnic group members in Britain. London School of Economics, unpublished [mime]

OPCS/GRO (Scotland) (1993) *1991 Census Report for Great Britain*. London: HMSO.

OPCS/GRO (Scotland) (1994) *1991 Census: Ethnic Group and Country of Birth*: Great Britain. London: HMSO.

Soldo, B. and Lauriat, P. (1976) Living arrangements among the elderly in the United States: a loglinear approach. *Journal of Comparative Family Studies*, 7(2), 351–66.

Tienda, M. and Angel, R. (1982) Headship and household composition among Blacks, Hispanics, and other Whites. *Social Forces*, 61(2), 508–31.

Van de Kaa, D. (1987) Europe's second demographic transition. *Population Bulletin*, 42, 1.

Wall, R. (1983) The household: demographic and economic change in England 1650–1970. In: R. Wall, J. Robin and P. Laslett (eds), *Family Forms in Historic Europe*. Cambridge: Cambridge University Press.

Wolf, D.A. (1984) Kin availability and the living arrangements of older women. *Social Science Research*, 13(1), 72–89.

Acknowledgements

Thanks are due to OPCS for making available data from the Sample of Anonymised Records (SAR); the Census Microdata Unit at Manchester University; the University of Manchester Computing Centre; and (with the support of ESRC/JISC/DENI) to the editors for useful comments. This chapter represents the author's views and not those of OPCS or the Home Office.

Appendix 8.1

There are two problems in considering relative sizes of ethnic minority households (or families). The first is the general problem of whether one uses the individual or the household as the unit of analysis, which is not specific to this case. The second arises directly from the fact that ethnic classification is inherently individual in nature. If all households were ethnically homogeneous, there would be no additional problems. However, since this is not the case, further complications arise and a number of alternative approaches may be adopted.

To allow for the ethnic group of all household members, while using households rather than individuals as the basis for comparison (to facilitate comparisons with the usual case), a scheme was constructed whereby each individual in the household contributes equally and the sum of weights for each household was one (for further details of the method, see Murphy, 1991b). In this calculation, for a household of size N, a value of $1/N$ is given to each member, and these values are allocated to the ethnic group of the individual concerned. Thus the overall average value is 2.48 as in the usual calculation of average household size, but it is possible now to define a similar quantity for each ethnic group. The results obtained and shown in Table A8.1 were very similar to those in Table 8.3 (a).

Apart from the values given in both panels of Table 8.4, an alternative calculation would simply be to divide the numbers in a particular ethnic group by the number of heads of household in the same group, using the figures in Table 8.1. This would give, for example, a figure of 2.90 for the Black ethnic group — substantially greater than the figure of 2.63 from Table 8.3 (a) (Table A8.1).

If all households comprised only a single ethnic group, all the average values would be identical (as, of course, is the total figure). Thus the 'average Black household size' could be 6 or 17 per cent above average depending on the calculation used, even if the calculation is based on the ethnic group of the head of household. The reason for this is illustrated in Table A8.2. It can be seen that for 'mixed' households, Blacks are substantially under-represented as heads, in that they comprise over half of non-heads, whereas they account for only about one third of heads. While this gives the arithmetic reconciliation between the figure, discussion of why such patterns exist will have to be deferred.

It should be noted that the headship rate analysis is based on disaggregated calculations used to produce the first row of values in Table A8.1. This is relevant to the discussion of Table 8.6 in that the appropriate unstandardised values for comparison are those of the first row Table A8.1, rather than any of the other values quoted here.

Table A8.1 *Average household size on alternative assumptions*

	White	Black (& Other–Other)	Indian	Pakistani/ Bangladeshi	Other Asian (including Chinese)
Ratio population to heads	2.44	2.90	3.72	4.77	3.22
Contribution function[1]	2.44	2.69	3.82	4.90	3.08

[1] See Murphy, 1991b for details.

Table A8.2 *Household distribution (people) by ethnic group[1] of heads and non-heads*

Households with	Numbers of			
	Black heads	Non-Black heads	Black non-heads	Non-Black non-heads
Blacks only	3,119	0	4,578	0
Blacks and non-Blacks	696	1,357	2,686	2,259
Non-Blacks only	0	209,197	0	307,278

[1] 'Black' includes 'Other–Other' group.

Chapter 9
Indigenous and older minorities

Paul Compton

9.1 Introduction

In focusing its inquiry on the ethnic minority population, the 1991 Census question on ethnic origin fails to capture the full heterogeneity of the resident population of Britain. This is, of course, perfectly understandable given that the census is undertaken as an aid to the good administration of the country and not as a data source for social scientists. Since the ethnic minority populations raise particular issues, government policy needs to be informed by the hard factual information that a population census supplies. None the less, it is important to recognise that the category White as used in the census covers a wide range of peoples coming from a variety of cultural backgrounds, who are just as worthy of demographic study as the ethnic minority population.

First and foremost, we have the indigenous peoples of the four constituent parts of the United Kingdom — the English, Scots, Welsh and Northern Irish. Although the differences that separate them are small by international standards, these identities can be deeply felt and surface in the form of national rivalries, specific institutional structures and even differences in demographic characteristics. Moreover, they also constitute substantial minorities in each other's territories at least in a statistical sense — the English in Wales, the Northern Irish in Scotland, the Scots in England etc. In other multinational states, this degree of diversity might well be explicitly recognised by designating the smaller groups as national minorities, especially in circumstances where the largest group is as numerically dominant as the English.

Yet, this four-fold categorisation is a very broad brush grouping and the potential for diversity within the indigenous populations also needs to be recognised. This is clearest in the case of Northern Ireland where the Catholic minority is culturally and, more significantly from the point of view of this volume, demographically distinct from the Protestant majority. As for the British mainland, there is an explicit assumption that, apart from the recognised ethnic minority groups, religious and other culturally-based differentials are no longer significant; the Jews, for instance, would be a case in point. But though this may well be true in most cases, it is certainly not proven and is an area that might be usefully investigated. For instance, an indigenous 'Celtic' culture still survives in Wales and Scotland among those who those who speak Welsh and Scots Gaelic, but we can only guess at the extent to which such cultural distinctiveness might also be reflected in demographic distinctiveness. Or again, it is not unreasonable to hypothesise that the overtly pro-natalist stance of many Christian groups might be reflected in the appearance of significant fertility differentials between them and the secular majority.

Of the older White minority groups originating from outside the present boundaries of the United Kingdom, the Southern Irish are numerically the most significant. The first large-scale Irish immigration into Great Britain occurred around the middle of last century (though an Irish presence in Britain dates from long before that) and the influx has continued more or less unabated since that time. Although assimilation is constantly whittling away at its numbers, cultural distinctiveness and tendency to geographical localisation (the Catholic Irish much more so than the Protestant Anglo-Irish) has meant that the Irish remain the most visible of the older UK minority populations.

Other older minority populations originate from the countries of the Old Commonwealth, the United States and Europe. Taken together they are about as numerous as the Irish, but their heterogeneity — composed of more than 25 different nationalities — means fragmentation and virtual invisibility. They also differ somewhat from the Irish in comprising substantial expatriate elements (many of the Irish, of course, are also expatriates in the sense of intending to return home at some future time) who are not necessarily in Britain for permanent settlement. In addition to these, one might also mention the White component in the population originating from the New Commonwealth. Cypriots and Maltese make up about a third of these but the number of White minority group members from India, Singapore, Kenya and Zimbabwe is also substantial.

Like the other contributions to this volume, the objective here is to outline the main demographic features of these traditional minorities. The chapter is divided into three distinct and separate sections. After an opening discussion of general issues, the first section draws on census and vital statistical data to highlight the principal demographic features of England, Scotland, Wales and Northern Ireland. These are intended as surrogates for the demographies of the English, Scots, Welsh and Northern Irish and the emphasis is on differentiation.

The second section focuses on the main demographic characteristics of the indigenous and older White UK minorities. Census place of birth data are used to describe the numerical breakdown of these minorities in 1991, and to highlight temporal trends, compositional aspects (age and sex profiles) and geographical distribution. The picture is incomplete, however, in that we know little about the fertility and mortality characteristics of each individual minority group.

The third section is devoted to the particular circumstances of Northern Ireland and its double minority situation — the Protestant minority within the whole of Ireland and the Catholic minority within Northern Ireland. The demographic contrasts between the Catholic and Protestant populations are sharply defined and though tending to narrow, continue to be of wider socio-economic and political significance. The section focuses particularly on the problems that arise from the unreliability of recent censuses. An assessment is also made of how the denominational balance within the population may be expected to change in the future. The discussion is possible because, unlike the censuses of England and Wales and Scotland, the Northern Ireland census inquires into religious affiliation (Compton, 1993).

9.2   General issues

The specific demographic interest in minority groups lies in the way they are differentiated from the majority population in respect of features like geographical distribution, age and sex composition, fertility, mortality and migration characteristics. Such differences pose questions about the extent to which immigrant minority populations retain the demographic features of the populations from which they originate, the nature and process of demographic convergence between minority and majority populations and so on.

These are also interesting questions from the point of view of demographic theory, but the empirical data for the UK are not in a form that facilitates comprehensive investigation. For this, we require a full range of demographic information, in which majority and minority populations are clearly identified. Otherwise interpretations are tentative and open to ambiguity. As far as the objectives of this chapter are concerned, there is no particular problem in describing the specific demographies of England, Scotland, Wales and Northern Ireland. These are described in a straightforward manner in the census and vital statistical records. The problem lies in the fact that they are not precisely the populations of interest.

In most circumstances, it would be sufficient to use the demography of England as a surrogate for the demography of the English, that of Scotland as a surrogate for the Scottish, etc. But though closely overlapping, they are not identical; at the risk of appearing pedantic the demography of England consists of the aggregation of the demographies of the majority White English population plus those of the various minority populations — the Scots, Welsh and Irish living in England, together with the ethnic minority groups and other minority populations. To study these different elements, census and vital statistical data needs to be broken down in such a way that national origins can be identified, but these data are not always available. In addition to this, the situation is a dynamic as opposed to static one in which the populations of the constituent parts of the UK are continually augmented through the assimilation of minority groups through intermarriage and the progression of generations, notwithstanding the current trend towards multi-culturalism and the preservation of cultural identity. The latter exemplifies itself in the attempts to foster the indigenous Celtic tongues in Wales and Scotland and, more controversially, in Northern Ireland, as well as in institutional recognition of minority groups in general. Hence, though the different components are readily identified, attaching precise quantitative estimates to them is beyond the scope of the chapter.

When it comes to investigating the indigenous and older UK minority populations there is no option other than to rely on place-of-birth statistics. Persons born 'abroad' must have migrated to the country of current residence at some time during their lifetime. Hence, at first sight, birth-place data would appear to provide a satisfactory way of identifying minorities. For instance, on the face of it, one might reasonably assume that a person born in Austria would be of Austrian national origin and so on. But, it has long been recognised that this is not the case; in fact, birth-place data are no clear indicator of national origin and are a relatively poor estimator of the size of minority communities.

It should not necessarily be assumed that all persons born and resident in Britain would regard themselves as British; for instance, if of non-British parentage such individuals might well identify with and be citizens of their parents' country of origin (citizenship was last enumerated in the 1961 Census). Similarly, it is equally misleading to count all residents born abroad as non-British; if born to British parents or of British ancestry such individuals might well regard themselves as British and possibly also be British citizens. In the past, birth-place data have been used in combination with nationality, as in the estimation of the alien population at the end of last century, or in combination with surnames to establish the size of the different ethnic groups (Immigrant Statistics Unit, 1977; Waterman and Kosmin, 1986), or with parents' birth-place in the case of the population of New Commonwealth and Pakistan (NCWP) origin in 1971, in attempts to resolve these difficulties.

The range of possibilities is not only exceedingly large, but also complicated by the legal complexities surrounding who is and who is not British. But most crucially, birth-place data fail to capture the second- and third-generation members of minority populations. Hence, while they may well be a satisfactory indicator in the case of recently formed minority groups, i.e. when the majority of members have been born outside the country, place-of birth data understate the size of long-established minority groups and are also misleading about specific aspects of composition. Since the long-established minority populations are arguably the most interesting from the point of view of demographic theory, this drawback constitutes a serious limitation. The matter is further complicated by the question of when — after how many generations in this country — minority groups cease to be minority groups *per se* and become part of the indigenous population.

None the less, within these limitations birth-place data can provide a useful guide to some aspects of the demography of minority groups, the most obvious recent example being their use in the estimation of the size of the NCWP population in 1961 and 1971 (summarised in Coleman and Salt, 1992). The discussion about the indigenous and older minority groups that follows is based wholly on birth-place data and is subject to all the caveats mentioned above. It is most seriously deficient when it comes to estimating the true size of Britain's oldest minority group originating from Ireland. The inclusion of the second- and third-generations of that population would more than double the birth-place total of just over half a million. Against that, the discussion of the rapidly growing minority groups from Europe, where a much higher proportion have been born abroad, is less biased.

9.3 The demographies of England, Scotland, Wales and Northern Ireland

Recent decades have seen a gradual blurring of traditional demographic differentials in the UK. Regional populations, especially in respect of birth rates, natural change and age composition, now appear less heterogeneous than in the past. This has gone hand in hand with the decline of traditional institutions and the emergence of a mass culture that reaches into every part of the country. The economic enfranchisement of women has been an integral part of these changes, and the essential mechanism of 'demographic convergence' has been fertility decline.

Yet, notwithstanding this trend towards uniformity, England, Wales, Scotland and Northern Ireland still exhibit individual demographic traits that should not be glossed over. Even though fertility differentials are less pronounced than in the past they have not altogether disappeared, while if anything, mortality disparities may well have increased. As for migration, while it obviously serves along with intermarriage to promote population mixing, its selectiveness by age and other demographic traits also helps create disparities between recipient and donor areas.

At the level of constituent countries, it is Northern Ireland and Scotland that are most distinct demographically, while Wales and England, if only for reasons of population size, are closest to the national average. The Welsh, the Scots and the Northern Irish all pride themselves on being different from the English. They have their own separatist movements, most obviously in the case of Northern Ireland, and the latter two have their own education and legal systems. The Scots and Northern Irish cling more tenaciously to traditional attitudes and values than do the English, and also possibly more so than the Welsh. Moreover, they are similar in their broad population composition, each being comprised of a mix of Catholic Irish and Scots Presbyterian. In other words, notwithstanding the broad societal shift towards greater uniformity, a certain demographic distinctiveness would seem to be a natural consequence of these deviations from the UK norm. The demographic profiles of each of the four countries as shown in the vital statistical record and by recent census data are presented in Table 9.1.

Northern Ireland stands out most clearly from the rest of the country. Up to 1986, natural increase was running at around 0.7 per cent per annum due to a combination of relatively high crude birth rate (17 per 1,000 per annum) and lower than average crude death rate. Two factors in particular distinguish the province from the rest of the country — namely, an adherence to traditional values and the depth of intercommunity antagonism between Protestants and Catholics bound up in conflicting national aspirations. In these circumstances, it is not altogether surprising that Northern Ireland is the one part of the UK where the traditional disparity between Catholic and

Table 9.1 *Demographic profiles of UK constituent countries*

	UK	England	Wales	Scotland	Northern Ireland
Fertility (1992)					
Crude birth rate (per 1,000 pop)	13.5	13.5	12.9	12.9	15.9
Total fertility rate	1.8	1.8	1.9	1.7	2.2
% births illegitimate	30.8	31.1	34.1	31.4	21.9
Mortality/expectation of life (1990/1992)					
Crude death rate (per 1,000 pop)	11.0	10.9	11.7	12.0	9.3
expectation of life, males (years)	73.0	73.2	73.2	71.1	71.8
expectation of life, females (years)	78.5	78.7	78.7	76.7	77.6
Infant mortality rate (per 1,000 live births)	6.6	6.5	6.0	6.8	6.0
Population change (1981-91)					
Natural change (per 1,000)[1]	-	18	9	5	75
Actual change (per 1,000)[1]	-	-1	6	-34	26
Net migration (per 1,000)[1]	-	-20	-2	-40	-45
Population composition (according to 1991 censuses)					
% aged 0–15	20.1	20.0	20.7	20.2	26.0
% of pensionable age	18.7	18.7	20.1	18.2	14.9
Sex ratio	1065	1063	1069	1090	1052
Married (%)	46.6	46.6	47.4	46.5	43.0
Divorced (%)	4.9	5.0	5.0	4.2	1.8
Ethnic composition (% White)	94.7	94.5	98.5	98.7	99.8

[1] Resident population base as opposed to population present base.
Source: Population Trends, OPCS, various.

Protestant fertility still persists (Catholics account for 40 per cent of the reproductively active population but contribute around 50 per cent of live births) and where overall fertility, as a consequence, is well above the national average — currently a total fertility rate of 2.2 compared with 1.8 nationally. But even here these traditional patterns are now under considerable pressure. The province's birth rate is, in fact, dropping sharply down from 18.0 per 1,000 in 1986 to 15.1 per 1,000 in 1993 and, judging from the available evidence, the Catholic/Protestant birth rate differential could soon disappear. These and other related issues are considered in more detail in the third section of this chapter.

Scotland, on the other hand, records the lowest total fertility rate in the country, and a birth rate as low as that of Wales. Because the death rate is also relatively high, natural increase is low. In fact, the high death rate is not just an age composition effect, but reflects significantly higher mortality than in the other constituent countries, with life expectancy at birth currently standing at two years below England and Wales. Thus, despite having a similar population make-up and also similar vital rates up to the 1960s, Scotland and Northern Ireland in many respects now lie at the opposite ends of the UK demographic spectrum. (Scotland may well be a model for Northern Ireland's demographic future.) They share a history of net out-migration, but whereas in Northern Ireland natural increase more than offsets the net outflow of people to give growth of 2.7 per cent over the last intercensal period, in Scotland population actually fell by 0.7 per cent between 1981 and 1991. (The net migration gains recorded by both areas after 1989 reflect the depth of the latest economic downturn and probably only represent a temporary reversal of the traditional pattern (OPCS 1994).)

In view of its numerical dominance (with 83.5 per cent of the UK population), the English vital rates are to all intents and purposes a reflection of the national average. In recent years the birth rate has tended to climb and the death rate to remain stable. Because a moderate net inflow of population was also recorded through most of the 1980s, the outcome was a 2.8 per cent growth in the population of England between 1981 and 1991. The birth rate in Wales is a little lower and the death rate a little higher than in England. Natural increase, as a consequence, has been lower, but because there has been a greater net inflow, actual population growth over the last intercensal period was marginally higher at 3.1 per cent. Welsh birth and death rates are, however, affected by age structure and when controlled for age, fertility is actually higher than in England.

As age and sex composition are a consequence of these different vital rates and migration flows, the population structures of the four constituent countries also vary in a predictable manner. In terms of age composition, Northern Ireland's population is clearly the youngest, the 1991 Census recording 26 per cent of people under the age of 16. The Welsh population is the oldest in terms of the percentage of individuals of pensionable age, though England records the lowest proportion of under-16-year-olds. The sharply lower birth rates now compared with 30 years ago are reflected in the way each country's profile tapers at the base (Figure 9.1). Sex ratios vary mainly as a function of migration patterns and levels of life expectancy. Hence, the greater than expected female surplus in Scotland has been generated by a greater net outflow of males to other parts of the UK. Northern Ireland, by contrast, records the smallest female surplus because the province has lost relatively fewer males over the longer term, while the marginally greater female surplus in Wales compared with England is essentially a function of retirement mobility.

All parts of the UK have seen a shift towards more divorce, more remarriage and more informal unions. The 1991 Census and other sources show that these processes have developed fairly uniformly in England and Wales, though judging from the level of illegitimacy, informal unions may be

Figure 9.1 *Age profiles for England-, Scotland-, Wales-, and Northern Ireland-born populations based on the 1991 Censuses of Population*

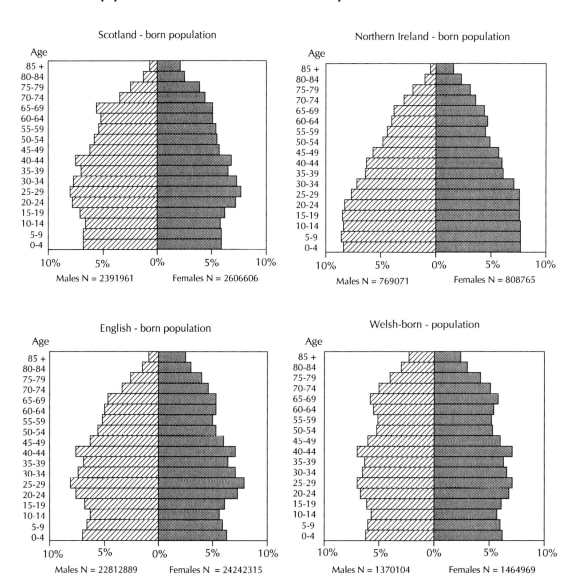

Source: 1991 Census - Ethnic group and country of birth, volume 1

somewhat more prevalent in Wales. Scotland records a lower percentage of divorces than England and Wales, though this is still substantially above the Northern Ireland level. In terms of ethnic composition, Scotland, Wales and Northern Ireland are virtually homogeneous. The ethnic minority element in Scotland and Wales amounts to around 1.5 per cent of the respective totals. In Northern Ireland the proportion is even lower than this; though there are no exactly equivalent data, the census breakdown by religious affiliation suggests a figure of no more than 0.25 per cent.

The 1991 Censuses also enquired into knowledge of the Welsh, Gaelic and Irish languages and provides some measure of the cultural diversity of the indigenous populations of Wales, Scotland and Northern Ireland. The specific wording of the question for each jurisdiction, together with the religion question in Northern Ireland, is reproduced in Table 9.2.

In Scotland the numbers speaking Gaelic were rather low at just under 66,000 or 1.4 per cent of those aged 3 and over (Table 9.3). In Northern Ireland and Wales the equivalent populations are significantly larger; hence, the 1991 Census enumerated 131,974 Irish-speakers in Northern Ireland — that is 8.8 per cent of the equivalent population — and 508,098 Welsh-speakers in Wales, or 18.7 per cent of those aged 3 and over. Full fluency in these minority languages as reflected in the numbers able to speak, read and

Table 9.2. *The Gaelic, Irish and Welsh language questions used in the 1991 Censuses plus the wording of the religion question for Northern Ireland*

For Scotland
Scottish Gaelic
Can the person speak, read or write Scottish Gaelic?   Can speak Gaelic
Please tick the appropriate box(es)   Can read Gaelic
                                                          Can write Gaelic
                                                          Does not know Gaelic

For Wales
Welsh language
Can the person speak, read or write Welsh?   Can speak Welsh
Please tick the appropriate box(es)   Can read Welsh
                                                          Can write Welsh
                                                          Does not know Welsh

For Northern Ireland
Irish Language
Can the person speak, read or write Irish?   Can speak Irish
Please tick the appropriate box(es)   Can read Irish
                                                          Can write Irish
                                                          Does not know Irish

Religion
Please state the Religion, Religious Denomination or Body   Religion
to which the person belongs. The general term 'Protestant'
should not be used alone and the denomination should be
given as precisely as possible.

If none write NONE

Sources: 1991 Census Gaelic Language, GRO for Scotland, page 3; 1991 Census Welsh Language, OPCS, page 3; the Northern Ireland Census 1991, Irish Language Report, DHSS and RG Northern Ireland, enumeration schedule, question 14.

Table 9.3. *Gaelic, Welsh and Irish Speakers in Scotland, Wales and Northern Ireland*

	1931	1951	1971	1991	Percent change 1931-91
Gaelic speakers enumerated in Scotland	136,135	95,447	84,580	65,978	-51.5
Welsh speakers enumerated in Wales1	909,300	714,700	542,400	508,098	-44.1
Irish speakers enumerated in Northern Ireland	-	-	-	124,358	-

[1] The figures for 1931, 1951 and 1971 are Welsh Office estimates.
Sources: 1991 Census Gaelic Language, GRO for Scotland, Table 1; 1991 Census Welsh Language, OPCS, Table 1; the Northern Ireland Census 1991, Irish Language Report, DHSS and RG Northern Ireland, Table 1.

write is, however, lower at 13.6 per cent in Wales, 5.3 per cent in Northern Ireland and 0.6 per cent in Scotland. Equivalent data from earlier censuses are not available for Northern Ireland and reliable information about the recent trend in the number of Irish-speakers in the province does not therefore exist. For Scotland and Wales though, the regular census inquiries into Gaelic- and Welsh-speakers have recorded persistent downward trends. Hence, the number of Gaelic speakers in 1991 was down by 30 per cent compared with 1951, and if anything this decline is accelerating. Welsh-speakers were similarly down by around 30 per cent over the same period, though here the rate of decline has been decelerating with numbers more or less holding their own during the 1980s (Table 9.3).

9.4   Indigenous and older UK minorities

This section uses place-of-birth data to examine the main characteristics of the indigenous and older White minority groups. Where possible, equal weight is given to each of the four constituent countries, but the limited availability of data in the published record means that Northern Ireland cannot be treated on the same basis as England, Scotland and Wales. This will have to await the publication of the 1991 Northern Ireland small area statistics (SAS). While birth-place data have been used extensively in the context of New Commonwealth immigrants, there is no significant literature to act as a backdrop to what follows about the White minority populations. The last comprehensive description appeared in the 1951 Census General Report (General Register Office, 1958) but the practice of publishing census commentaries was discontinued after 1961.

General distribution

The breakdown of birth-places in 1991 for UK constituent countries is summarised in Table 9.4. Expressed in terms of the proportion of residents born elsewhere, the Welsh population is more heterogeneous (22.8 per cent born elsewhere) than either England or Scotland (just over 10 per cent born elsewhere), while Northern Ireland is the least heterogeneous of the UK constituent countries. The heterogeneity of Wales, however, is a wholly internal UK characteristic and is attributable to the high proportion of English in the principality rather than to a substantial foreign-born population. Similarly, most of the heterogeneity of the Scottish and Northern Irish populations comes from the presence of residents born in other parts of the UK. In fact, defining heterogeneity solely in terms of non-UK-born residents shows that the Welsh, Scottish and Northern Irish populations are remarkably uniform, containing at most 3 per cent non-indigenous elements. Indeed, in the case of Northern Ireland, we are left with a people virtually homogeneous in respect of birthplace if we exclude those born in the Irish Republic as well as those born in Great Britain to Northern Irish parents. In other words, of the four constituent countries, it is only the English population that contains substantial admixtures of residents born outside the UK.

A related aspect concerns the dispersal of indigenous groups away from their own parts of the UK. If this is expressed as the proportion born in a given constituent part residing elsewhere in the UK, the level of dispersal is highest in the case of the Welsh, with 20.5 per cent residing outside Wales in

Table 9.4   *Composition of the population of UK constituent countries by place of birth, 1991*

Place of birth	Place of residence							
	England No. (000s)	%	Scotland No. (000s)	%	Wales No. (000s)	%	N. Ireland No. (000s)	%
England	42,003	89.3	354	7.1	540	19.0	65	4.1
Scotland	744	1.6	4,454	89.1	23	0.8		
Wales	545	1.2	15	0.3	2,188	77.2		
N. Ireland	211	0.4	26	0.5	7	0.3	1,453	92.1
Total UK	43,503	92.5	4,850	97.0	2,758	97.3		
Other British Isles	582	1.2	24	0.5	15	0.5	36	2.3
Other European Union	452	1.0	26	0.5	16	0.6		
Rest of Europe, USSR & Turkey	213	0.5	9	0.2	5	0.2	25	1.6
Old Commonwealth & USA	286	0.6	28	0.6	7	0.2		
Elsewhere	2,019	4.3	63	1.3	34	1.2		
All White minorities	3,033	6.4	482	9.6	613	21.6	-	-
From which:								
Indigenous UK minorities	1,500	3.2	395	7.9	570	20.1	-	-
Older White minorities	1,533	3.3	87	1.7	43	1.5	-	-
All birth-places	47,055	100.0	4,999	100.0	2,835	100.0	1,578	100.0

Source: 1991 Census Ethnic Group and Country of Birth Great Britain, volume 1, OPCS and RG Scotland, Table ; the Northern Ireland Census 1991 Summary Report, DHSS and RG Northern Ireland, Table 7.

1991. The Scottish and Northern Irish record more modest dispersal levels of 15 and 14 per cent respectively, but only 2 per cent of those born in England live elsewhere in the UK. These are variations that largely reflect the basic geography of the UK and the size differences between England and the rest of the country. The other determinant is, of course, the space economy and its impact on life-time migration flows. The outcome is that whereas roughly as many Welsh-born live in England as English-born in Wales, the patterns involving the English, Scots and Northern Irish are highly asymmetrical, with the number of Scots and Northern Irish in England far exceeding the number of English in Scotland and Northern Ireland. Otherwise, there is a stronger Scottish presence in Wales than Welsh presence in Scotland, and more Northern Irish in Scotland than Scots in Northern Ireland.

The place-of-birth data reveal the wide range of national origins of the non-indigenous White minority groups (Table 9.5). Those originating from European Union countries make up the largest single group in each of the four countries, though the proportion is rather lower in Scotland than in either England or Wales. This dominance is very much a function of the size of the population originating from the Irish Republic, who account for roughly a third of the foreign-born White minority population in England and Wales, a little over a quarter of this total in Scotland, and more than four fifths in Northern Ireland. It reflects the close social and economic ties between Britain and Ireland and requires no further comment.

The German-born population ranks in second place. Although there is clearly a German minority population in the UK, e.g. refugees entering the country in the 1930s and 1940s, the German wives of British husbands etc., the birth-place data are inflated by the inclusion of children who happened to have been born in Germany to members of British Armed Forces temporarily stationed there. In effect, there is no reason why it should be materially different in size from minorities originating from other large EU countries.

Although there is no particular need to elaborate on most of the other figures in Table 9.4 there are a few points of note. The cultural and historical linkages within the English-speaking world are strong enough to generate large Australian, Canadian, New Zealand and US communities in Britain, but especially in Scotland in the case of those born in the US and Canada. The Italian and Polish communities with their origins in the immediate post-war years also stand out, particularly in Wales in the case of the Italians. Otherwise, one may note the comparatively new Turkish-born community that is forming in England, mainly in London, and the prominence in Scotland of Norwegians, whose presence is linked to geographical proximity and the North Sea oil industry.

Temporal trends

The discussion so far has focused on the static, cross-sectional patterns for 1991. This section concentrates on two aspects of recent temporal trends — the longer term trend obtained by comparing 1951 and 1991, and the shorter term trend revealed by change over the last intercensal period, 1981 to 1991.

Table 9.5 *Breakdown of the foreign born by birth-place and country of residence; 1991*

Country/area of birth	Place of residence					
	England No. (000s)	%	Scotland No. (000s)	%	Wales No. (000s)	%
European Union	1.008.4	65.8	48.5	56.5	29.5	70.3
Irish Republic	556.3	36.3	22.8	26.5	13.4	32.0
Germany	193.3	12.6	13.9	16.2	8.3	19.7
Italy	83.7	5.4	3.9	4.6	3.3	7.9
France	50.0	3.2	2.4	2.8	1.1	2.7
Spain	37.0	2.4	1.0	1.2	0.7	1.6
Netherlands	26.4	1.7	2.2	2.5	0.9	2.0
Portugal	19.2	1.3	0.2	0.3	0.4	0.9
Belgium	15.8	1.0	0.7	0.9	0.5	1.3
Greece	13.5	0.9	0.5	0.6	0.6	1.5
Denmark	13.2	0.9	0.8	1.0	0.2	0.5
Other Europe	213.0	13.9	9.4	11.0	5.3	12.5
Poland	68.0	4.4	3.6	4.2	2.1	4.9
Turkey	26.0	1.7	0.4	0.5	0.2	0.5
USSR	25.2	1.6	1.1	1.4	0.7	1.7
Austria	19.5	1.3	0.7	0.8	0.5	1.2
Yugoslavia	13.1	0.9	0.3	0.4	0.4	1.0
Hungary	11.9	0.8	0.2	0.2	0.3	0.8
Switzerland	11.9	0.8	0.5	0.6	0.2	0.6
Sweden	10.4	0.7	0.4	0.5	0.2	0.4
Czechoslovakia	8.2	0.5	0.3	0.4	0.2	0.5
Norway	7.4	0.5	1.1	1.3	0.2	0.4
Rest	11.3	0.7	0.5	0.6	0.1	0.3
Old Commonwealth & USA	285.6	18.6	28.0	32.6	7.2	17.2
Australia	66.3	4.3	5.0	5.9	1.9	4.5
Canada	53.2	3.5	8.0	9.3	2.0	4.8
New Zealand	37.9	2.5	2.4	2.7	0.8	1.8
USA	128.3	8.4	12.6	14.7	2.6	6.1
Total	**1.507.0**	**100.0**	**85.9**	**100.0**	**42.0**	**100.0**

Source: 1991 Census Ethnic Group and Country of Birth Great Britain. volume 1. OPCS and RG Scotland. Table 1.

Indigenous minority groups

The patterns are dynamic and varied (Table 9.6). Looking at the indigenous UK minority groups, the number of English-born residents in Scotland and Wales has risen by around 50 per cent since 1951, with one third of this increase occurring between 1981 and 1991. A similar trend is seen for Scottish- and Northern Irish-born residents in Wales, but not for Welsh- and Northern Irish-born residents in Scotland. As for England, the long-term drift of population to the South East might have led one to anticipate a general increase in the indigenous minority populations there over both periods. In fact, the number of Welsh-born has dropped continuously — by 16 per cent since 1951 and by almost 5 per cent since 1981 — with only marginal growth in the number of Scottish- and Northern Irish-born since

Table 9.6 *Percentage change in population by country of birth, 1951–91 and 1981–91*

Birth-place	Place of residence					
	England		Scotland		Wales	
	1951-91	1981-91	1951-91	1981-91	1951-91	1981-91
United Kingdom	10.9	-0.4	43.7	12.9	50.2	15.1
England	-	-	59.4	15.9	49.6	15.3
Scotland	31.7	1.7	-	-	54.3	11.6
Wales	-16.0	-4.8	52.7	1.4	-	-
N Ireland	52.2	4.4	-39.1	-28.5	81.5	8.4
European Union						
All countries	48.0	4.1	-21.1	-1.3	31.3	7.1
Excluding						
Irish Republic	118.4	13.4	62.5	14.1	91.3	13.6
Portugal	1386.4	20.3	200.0	15.8	407.0	-0.8
Spain	507.4	-4.2	151.1	24.7	46.5	11.1
Greece	209.3	22.0	105.9	23.4	70.7	-6.2
Italy	173.2	-6.0	-25.1	-21.3	32.9	-16.0
Denmark	127.3	54.4	61.7	6.2	42.3	32.0
Netherlands	109.2	22.8	162.7	28.1	110.0	24.3
Germany	107.6	18.4	98.0	18.3	154.0	30.6
France	68.4	36.4	88.8	31.2	72.8	38.5
Irish Republic	19.9	-1.9	-50.1	-18.7	-4.5	0.3
Belgium	6.2	12.2	-2.6	16.1	11.6	10.7
Other Europe	-31.4	-3.8	-54.9	-8.8	-49.7	-9.5
Turkey	697.1	126.4	327.0	28.7	175.3	131.0
Bulgaria	406.5	115.8	1342.1	93.1	83.3	50.0
Finland	271.3	25.1	109.3	31.4	20.8	20.8
Sweden	242.3	58.1	73.4	28.8	40.9	50.0
Norway	76.9	25.9	54.7	29.0	-18.5	1.1
Hungary	54.4	-12.5	22.8	-4.1	57.6	-9.3
Yugoslavia	33.9	1.4	-60.4	-10.4	-43.9	-15.8
Switzerland	-1.2	2.4	1.2	15.1	40.0	8.2
Romania	-32.7	16.2	-43.8	29.5	-29.0	2.7
Czechoslovakia	-34.5	-11.5	-25.6	-4.6	-50.3	-12.4
Austria	-34.7	-11.4	-35.0	-0.8	-18.3	-2.3
Poland	-53.3	-20.6	-65.8	-40.3	-66.1	-18.9
USSR	-66.0	-24.9	-81.5	-35.0	-54.1	-18.1
Old Commonwealth						
& USA	101.7	20.6	55.9	1.5	31.8	11.4
New Zealand	238.4	44.3	140.3	16.4	253.0	32.5
USA	128.2	23.9	82.1	2.9	-12.7	14.2
Australia	122.3	19.6	112.1	5.4	107.8	8.7
Canada	19.8	3.1	4.1	-7.4	41.2	4.3

Sources: 1991 Census Ethnic Group and Country of Birth Great Britain, volume 1, OPCS and RG Scotland, Table 1; Census 1981 Country of Birth Great Britain, OPCS and RG Scotland, Table 1: Census 1951 England and Wales General Tables, GRO, Tables 32 and 33.

1981. Northern Ireland, of course, is exceptional. The number of Northern Ireland residents born in Great Britain was around 5 per cent higher in 1991 than in 1951. It was marginally down on the 1981 figure, however, but because the latter was an under-enumeration, the real decline since then is actually understated; comparison with 1971 gives a 15 per cent drop in the British-born element in the province.

Whereas migration statistics are time specific, trends in place-of-birth data reflect the distributional outcomes of population movements aggregated over an indefinite time span. The interpretation of such trends, moreover, is complicated by the fact that birth-place statistics are a function not only of migration, but also of the mortality of migrants. Hence, a change in birth-place total from one period to another may simply reflect the fact that an earlier generation of migrants has fallen out of the statistics. None the less, it is still reasonably safe to conclude that the trends described above encapsulate the continuing dispersal and mixing of the British population.

Foreign-born populations

The pattern of change in the number of foreign-born residents is equally varied. Apart from the former Communist countries of Eastern Europe, numbers originating from the rest of Europe have generally increased. Although many individuals entered Britain from Eastern Europe in the aftermath of the Second World War, the erection of the Iron Curtain put a stop to these flows. As a consequence, natural depletions were not repaired by additional new-comers and the numbers originating from these countries have fallen at each successive census since 1951. For instance, the Polish-born population has declined from over 150,000 to 73,000 and the Russian-born population from 76,000 to 27,000. Likewise, the Czech and Romanian minority populations have fallen by around a third. Hungarians and Yugo-slavs constitute the principal exceptions; Hungarian numbers were boosted as a result of the 1956/57 uprising, but they too have declined in the most recent period. The Yugoslav authorities, on the other hand, adopted a more relaxed attitude to emigration after around 1963.

As a postscript, it would appear that the situation captured in the most recent census has probably already been superseded as far as the Balkans and the successor states to the USSR are concerned. The fall of Communism and the opening of frontiers has generated a substantial pressure to emigrate from these countries and, though not as strong as first anticipated in 1990, some is bound to be directed towards Britain. As this is essentially a post-1991 phenomenon it will only be fully captured in the next census, though the modest upturn in the number of Romanian-born residents in Britain after 1981, presumably concentrated in the two years after the Romanian revolution in 1989, is an indication of how the situation may change.

Austria is the only non-Communist country recording a substantially lower total in the birth-place statistics in 1991 than 1951. This, too, is probably related to the Second World War in that the 1951 figure is inflated by the presence of Austrian refugees. Other minority groups that have declined in more recent years are the Italian-born, because the immigration of the 1950s has not been maintained, and the Spanish-born, where an initial influx in the aftermath of the fall of Franco during the 1970s, has not been matched by subsequent immigration. Otherwise, the most significant of the recent declines is in the number persons born in the Irish Republic. This rose sharply during the 1950s and 1960s as Irish workers were drawn into the British labour market, peaked in 1971 at almost 700,000, but has since fallen back to under 600,000.

The largest increases in those born outside the UK have come from the countries of the European Union. Portugal, Spain and Greece, whose numbers were initially very small, head the list in terms of percentage change, but the numbers from Italy, Denmark, Holland and Germany have all doubled since 1951. When the period since 1951 is viewed as a whole, these groups have tended to grow significantly faster in England than in either Scotland or Wales, but a more even pace of change has established itself since 1981 as each constituent UK country begins to play a fuller role in European affairs.

Outside the European Union, growth has been most pronounced in the case of persons born in Turkey, Sweden and Finland. The numbers originating from New Zealand, the US and Australia have more than doubled since 1951 — much of this increase occurring during the 1980s. By contrast, the Canadian-born population in England and Wales has grown more modestly, and has actually fallen back a little in Scotland.

Age and sex composition

Age profiles

Place-of-birth data produce very different age profiles to those of naturally regenerating populations; whereas the latter are primarily a function of the temporal flux in the number of births, the former mainly reflect the processes of migration. Hence, when compared with the full resident population of an area, they generally show an under-representation of children and an over-representation of adults. The precise age patterns will, of course, vary with the magnitude and timing of migratory movements, being relatively smooth when migration flows have been continuous over time but irregular when movements have fluctuated.

The age distributions of the UK indigenous minority groups constitute good examples of smooth profiles: they are under-represented in each constituent country up to about the age of 20; there is a rough balance in the 20 to 34 age range, and over-representation thereafter (Table 9.7). Past migration trends do, however, generate a degree of variability around these norms. For instance, the Welsh in England are heavily concentrated in the 60 and over age-group, essentially because the influx has been tailing off over successive censuses. The proportions of children among the indigenous minority groups in England are somewhat lower than in either Wales or Scotland because relatively fewer family units with children move to England. And the Scots and Northern Irish in England and Wales are most over-represented in the 40 to 49 age range because of heavy in-migration 20 to 30 years ago.

Table 9.7 *Age breakdown of indigenous UK minorities in 1991*

Resident in **England**	England	Wales	Born in Scotland	Northern Ireland
0–19	27	8	10	8
20–34	22	20	24	25
35–59	30	36	41	43
60+	21	35	24	25

Resident in **Wales**	Wales	England	Born in Scotland	Northern Ireland
0–19	28	17	11	9
20–34	21	21	22	21
35–59	29	36	40	43
60+	22	26	27	26

Resident in **Scotland**	Scotland	England	Born in Wales	Northern Ireland
0–19	27	18	16	10
20–34	22	26	24	24
35–59	30	36	37	37
60+	21	20	23	29

Source: 1991 Census Ethnic Group and Country of Birth Great Britain, volume 1, OPCS and RG Scotland, Table 2.

The age profiles of non-indigenous White minority groups tend to vary as a function of their different migration histories (Figure 9.2). Some are strongly skewed towards the upper end of the age range, characteristic of minority populations with declining numbers. This type is most clearly seen in the case of those originating from Poland and the former USSR where some 75 per cent of individuals, mainly men, were of pensionable age in 1991. Both profiles result from the cessation of immigration in the immediate post-war years. Persons born in the Irish Republic constitute another good example of an ageing minority (only 4 per cent of the Irish-born in Britain are under the age of 20). Successive censuses record the progression of the large-scale immigration from the Republic during the 1950s and 1960s through the age profile (it accounts for more than a third of the Southern Irish-born population in Britain) to its present position at the upper end of the economically active age range. The Czech-, Yugoslav- and Hungarian-born elements of the population constitute the other main ageing minorities, with profiles not dissimilar to that of Poland.

The age profiles of growing minority populations are, by contrast, more symmetrical (Figure 9.2). These include the minority populations originating from continental EU countries, where the child-age component, though under-represented, is still substantial. Since the pensioner-age component is also generally under-represented, it is characteristic for these minorities to be predominantly of economically active age. They are a product of the normal age selectiveness of immigration in which family units with children are comparatively prominent. The French-born comprise such a profile. The

Figure 9.2 *Age profiles of selected minority populations based on birth-place data from the 1991 Census of Population*

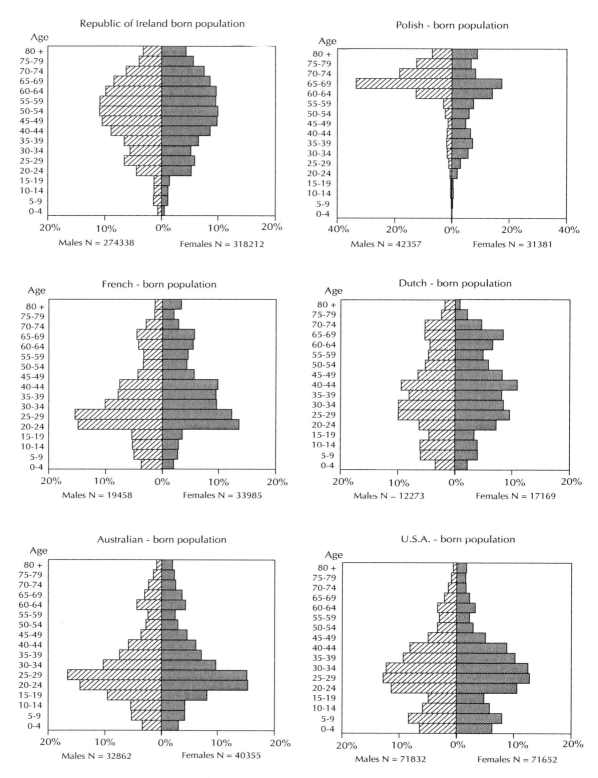

Source: 1991 Census - Ethnic group and country of birth, volume 2

20–34 age range is dominant; the under-19 age-group make up around 15 per cent of the total, and the proportion of pensionable age is substantially less than in the British population as a whole. The Danish, Spanish, Portuguese, German and Dutch profiles are similar, whereas the Italian profile (Italians came into the country in large numbers in the 1950s) is more like that of the Irish.

Of the remaining older minorities, those originating from Australia, New Zealand and the US have similar age profiles to those mentioned above. Indeed, the US profile is closest to that of the overall population. On the other hand, because the Canadian-born minority population has been in decline, its profile shows substantial ageing — 30 per cent were aged 60 and over in 1991. The rapidly growing Turkish-born population in Britain, a product of recent substantial immigration, also deserves comment; just under 45 per cent are aged 20–34 and only 5 per cent are 65 and over.

Sex composition

The sex composition of the various minority groups is also strongly differentiated (Tables 9.8 and 9.9). Of the indigenous UK minority groups, the Scottish- and Northern Irish-born are most divergent; because males leave Scotland in comparatively greater numbers than females, males predominate among Scottish-born residents in England and Wales. The natural consequence of this is that the female excess in the Scottish-born population of Scotland is greater than elsewhere in the UK. Northern Ireland, by contrast, is in many respects the obverse. Hence, there is a substantial excess of females among the Northern Ireland-born population in Wales and Scotland with the consequence that the female excess in Northern Ireland itself is less marked than elsewhere. Females are also over-represented among the English-born in Wales and the Welsh-born in England. Such disparities presumably result from the specific sex profiles of long-term migration flows together with the operation of differential mortality. For instance, males predominate in the Scottish-, Welsh- and Northern Irish-born populations of economically active age in England, because males are more likely to move permanently to England for work-related reasons, whereas the female excess in the older age groups arises from lower female mortality rates.

Table 9.8 *Sex ratios of indigenous minorities in 1991 (females per 1000 males)*

Country of residence	Country of birth			
	England	Wales	Scotland	Northern Ireland
England	1062	1093	977	1042
Wales	1100	1065	998	1123
Scotland	1046	1001	1094	1139
Northern Ireland		901		1045

Source: 1991 Census Ethnic Group and Country of Birth Great Britain, volume 1, OPCS and RG Scotland, Table 2.

Table 9.9 *Great Britain: Sex ratios by birth-place ranked by size of female surplus/deficit in 1991 (females per 1000 males)*

Birth-place	1991	1981	1951
Finland	3813	4783	3107
Austria	2702	2802	2326
Sweden	1974	2378	1463
Switzerland	1942	2227	1829
Belgium	1884	2145	2174
Denmark	1776	2020	1482
France	1744	2128	2220
Norway	1521	1774	1332
Germany	1458	1559	1913
Netherlands	1399	1450	1235
Spain	1348	1303	1027
Czechoslovakia	1235	1118	853
Australia	1227	1221	1346
Canada	1196	1102	950
Portugal	1171	1230	1486
Irish Republic	1160	1131	1120
New Zealand	1135	1189	1171
Scotland	1076	1061	1074
Wales	1070	1060	1062
England	1062	1059	1084
Northern Ireland	1055	1040	926
Italy	1016	1051	1700
USA	997	884	608
Yugoslavia	951	860	238
Greece	933	1090	1901
Romania	897	863	718
Bulgaria	853	1320	826
Turkey	765	753	1350
Hungary	710	684	1162
Albania	713	750	-
USSR	589	549	624

Sources: 1991 Census Ethnic Group and Country of Birth Great Britain, volume 1, OPCS and RG Scotland, Table 1; Census 1981 Country of Birth Great Britain, OPCS and RG Scotland, Table 1: Census 1951 England and Wales General Tables, GRO, tables 32 and 33.

The variability is sex ratios among the non-indigenous minority groups is even more marked. Most are female dominant, with some ratios exceeding 1,500 females per 1,000 males (France, Switzerland, Austria, etc.), but the groups originating from Central and Eastern Europe, and the US, are more typically male dominant. The reasons for this diversity are not always immediately apparent, though the census does provide a number of pointers. For instance, the female surpluses invariably arise from an excess of ever-married females, with the clear inference that the phenomenon is marriage-related, i.e. British men with foreign-born wives tend to settle in Britain, whereas British women with foreign-born husbands are more likely to settle abroad. The net effect is to boost the number of foreign-born women vis a vis foreign-born men. Furthermore, since a substantial part of the foreign inflow to Britain is connected with marriage, this process might be expected to produce a female surplus among the foreign-born, regardless of country of origin.

In other words, male dominant minorities may be considered atypical. In the case of those born in Poland, Romania, former Yugoslavia, and the former USSR, they are a product of the refugee movements to this country immediately before and in the aftermath of the Second World War. In the case of Hungary, the surplus derives from the disproportionate number of males who left during the 1956 uprising and who are now aged somewhere between 40 and 64. The male surplus among the Turkish-born population on the other hand, is most pronounced between the ages of 25 and 54; there are comparatively few married women in this age range, and the explanation may well be connected with the political situation in Turkish Kurdistan.

Sex ratios are not static quantities, however, and may vary over time (Table 9.9). For example, whereas strong female dominance has always been a feature of those born in Finland and Austria, in other cases this dominance has tended to lessen over time, e.g. with those born in France, Germany and Portugal. In yet other cases, male surpluses have given way to female surpluses as exemplified by those born in Czechoslovakia and Canada, or a male surplus has considerably diminished, e.g. with those born in the USA and Yugoslavia. A comprehensive discussion of these changes is clearly beyond the scope of this chapter. Two things are plain, however. First, the change in the sex ratio of those born in the USA is a function of the declining number of US servicemen in Britain. Second, the clear trend towards falling female surpluses among most of the minorities originating from EU countries is connected with greater European integration and the fact that people now come to this country for a wide range of different reasons. This in turn creates more balanced sex ratios within minority groups.

9.5   Geographical distribution

A geographical feature that virtually all minority populations share in common is an over-concentration in England (Table 9.10). Only in exceptional circumstances is this not true, for instance, Norwegians and Canadians in Scotland, and persons born in the Irish Republic in Northern Ireland. The spatial asymmetry can be very pronounced; for example, over 97 per cent of the Turkish-born and 96 per cent of the Hungarian-born populations resided in England in 1991. But, equally, there are other cases where the pattern is closer to the overall distribution of the population — for example the US-, Australian- and Dutch-born populations.

Table 9.10 *Great Britain: percentage distribution of selected foreign-born minorities by constituent country*

	GB	Ireland	Holland	Australia	Norway	USA	Canada	France	Poland	Hungary	Turkey
England	85.1	93.9	89.8	90.5	84.7	89.4	84.2	93.5	92.3	95.6	97.8
Scotland	9.5	3.8	7.3	6.9	13.2	8.8	12.6	4.4	4.9	1.8	1.4
Wales	5.4	2.3	2.9	2.6	2.1	1.8	3.2	2.1	2.8	2.6	0.8
Total	**100.0**	**100.0**	**100.0**	**100.0**	**100.0**	**100.0**	**100.0**	**100.0**	**100.0**	**100.0**	**100.0**

Source: 1991 Census Ethnic Group and Country of Birth Great Britain, volume 1, OPCS and RG Scotland, Table 1.

Given this degree of localisation, it is therefore not so much the Great Britain-wide patterns that are of significance as the specific distributional patterns in England. In fact, the foreign-born display a number of characteristic features. Like the ethnic minority groups, they tend to be over-concentrated in the south east of England, especially London. But unlike the ethnic minority groups, they are generally under-represented in other large centres of population — specifically in the metropolitan counties. They also tend to be under-represented in non-metropolitan areas — namely in the cities, towns and villages outside the conurbations — though there are exceptions to this.

Irish- and French-born minority groups

These and other distributional features are best examined by discussing a number of specific examples (Table 9.11). For example, well over half of the Irish-born population live in south east England, 38 per cent in Greater London alone. Compared with the population overall, Irish-born people are only about half as likely to live in non-metropolitan areas, but are well represented in the metropolitan counties, especially in the West Midlands and North West. The French-born population, by contrast, is rather more typical of the general schema above. Less than 10 per cent are found in the metropolitan counties, and there is also under-representation in non-metropolitan areas. Against that over 40 per cent reside in Greater London — more in inner than outer boroughs — and fully 80 per cent are found in the southern half of the country — the South East, East Anglia and the South West. The fact that the fastest rates of increase between 1981 and 1991 were also in the south has served to reinforce this pattern. The distributions of Spanish-, Portuguese-, Belgian- Dutch-, and Greek-born residents are similar to this.

Italian- and German-born minority groups

In contrast, the Italian- and German-born communities are rather more dispersed. Although Italians are still highly localised in the South East and Greater London, their representation in the Midlands and northern half of England is also relatively strong. The distribution of the German-born population, on the other hand, is nearer to that of the population at large. Under-representation in metropolitan counties is offset by over-representation in non-metropolitan areas so that the distribution by standard region more or less follows that of the overall population. This similarity is connected with the fact that a substantial part of this group is composed of the children of servicemen who were born in Germany.

The Italian-born population declined in every region between 1981 and 1991, more so for females than males, with the exception of the non-metropolitan parts of Yorkshire and Humberside. Decline was greater in metropolitan counties, especially the West Midlands and Greater Manchester, than in non-metropolitan counties. In marked contrast, the German-born population increased in each standard region. While there was little difference between males and females in terms of *absolute* growth, the

Table 9.11 *Geographical distribution of selected populations by country of birth and region of residence in England in 1991*

Region	Birth place									
	England	Ireland	Norway	Holland	France	Spain	Hungary	Poland	Germany	Italy
North	6.9	1.3	6.0	2.8	1.5	1.2	2.9	1.8	4.4	1.6
Yorks & Humberside	10.8	4.5	4.7	5.3	3.7	2.8	8.5	9.7	9.2	4.9
East Midlands	8.7	5.0	4.0	5.2	3.6	3.2	6.8	10.2	8.3	6.5
East Anglia	4.4	2.0	4.3	6.1	3.3	2.5	2.3	2.9	5.6	4.4
South East	34.4	58.1	60.9	58.1	70.6	76.1	58.2	48.6	44.8	63.1
South West	10.0	7.3	8.9	9.4	8.1	5.3	6.3	6.9	12.6	6.4
West Midlands	11.0	12.1	4.0	5.2	4.5	3.3	6.8	9.7	7.2	6.5
North West	13.7	11.9	7.2	8.0	4.8	5.5	8.3	10.2	8.0	6.6
Metropolitan Counties	23.7	22.1	12.2	9.3	7.8	7.2	17.4	20.8	13.1	11.4
Non-Met. Counties	64.4	39.4	59.0	68.1	50.3	41.3	45.4	47.1	70.3	52.7
Greater London	11.9	38.5	28.8	22.6	41.9	51.5	37.3	32.1	16.6	35.9

Region	England	Turkey	Australia	New Zealand	Canada	USA		Scotland	Wales	Northern Ireland
North West	6.9	0.7	2.7	1.8	3.7	1.4		8.4	2.0	4.2
Yorks & Humberside	10.8	2.0	4.8	3.2	6.0	3.7		8.9	4.3	7.3
East Midlands	8.7	1.7	4.4	3.3	5.9	4.3		8.9	5.7	6.9
East Anglia	4.4	1.1	4.0	3.4	4.7	24.2		4.3	3.1	3.6
South East	34.4	88.4	62.7	73.1	52.3	55.3		40.5	37.9	42.4
South West	10.0	2.4	12.5	8.0	12.1	15.2		9.3	19.6	8.9
West Midlands	11.0	1.6	5.0	3.2	6.4	2.8		8.1	16.4	11.5
North West	13.7	2.2	6.6	4.0	8.9	4.0		11.6	10.9	15.2
Metropolitan Countiess	23.7	4.2	9.4	5.7	12.4	5.4		16.8	13.8	21.9
Non-Met. Counties	64.4	17.4	55.4	45.7	65.8	69.2		68.0	73.2	58.1
Greater London	11.9	55.6	35.2	48.5	21.9	25.5		15.2	12.9	20.0

Source: 1991 Census Ethnic Group and Country of Birth Great Britain, volume 1, OPCS and RG Scotland, Table 1.

smaller base population meant that the percentage male increase was significantly higher everywhere. Otherwise growth was more pronounced in non-metropolitan than metropolitan counties. Regionally, it was fastest in East Anglia, the South West and non-metropolitan Yorkshire and Humberside, but was well down on the average in Greater London and the South East. In other words, the recent spatial change of the German-born population has broadly mirrored that of the general population.

Polish- and Hungarian-born populations

The Poles and Hungarians are broadly representative of minorities originating from Central and Eastern Europe (Table 9.11). As already explained these are long-established populations who have seen relatively little numerical accretion in recent decades. Like the Irish-born population, they are relatively numerous in the metropolitan areas of Yorkshire and Humberside, the West Midlands and the North West, but unlike the Irish population they are not as concentrated in Greater London and the South East. That there are marked differences between the respective male and female distributions is also a characteristic feature — females are more numerous in London and the South East but are under-represented in metropolitan counties. Recent change is similarly differentiated. Male numbers have decreased almost everywhere, whereas female numbers have increased in some regions, though still within the context of overall decline. The Turkish-born population also have a distinctive geography. This group more than doubled in size between 1981 and 1991 and is now the most localised of the White minority populations, with over half its number residing in Greater London and under 10 per cent located outside the South East.

Old Commonwealth- and USA-born minority groups

Residents born in the Old Commonwealth and USA also tend to avoid the metropolitan counties and are therefore under-represented in the West Midlands, the North West and the Northern region (Table 9.9). But against that they are quite widely dispersed in the southern half of the country. Australians and Canadians, for example, are not only over-represented in the South East but also in the South West, and to a lesser extent in East Anglia. The US-born population is also heavily concentrated in East Anglia, because of the presence of US military bases in the region. In addition, they are more localised in non-metropolitan areas than is generally the case, where they actually exceed the ratio recorded in the general population.

Recent growth patterns also vary. The New Zealand-born population has expanded most rapidly since 1981, especially in Greater London, the South West and East Anglia, where growth rates in excess of 25 per cent were recorded. So too has the US-born population, especially females, again notably in Greater London and the South West, but also in the East Midlands, and in the non metropolitan areas of Yorkshire and Humberside and the South East. By contrast, the number of Canadian-born people has undergone general decline in the North, North West and West Midlands, but has increased in the southern areas of the country largely due to rising numbers of females. The Australian pattern of change is similar. East Anglia, the South West and Greater London are the main growth regions, whereas the number of Australians has declined in the Greater Manchester, Merseyside and West Midlands metropolitan counties.

Indigenous minority groups

The geographical distribution of the indigenous Scots, Welsh and Northern Irish minority populations in England closely mirrors the distribution of the English population as a whole (Table 9.12). However, there are still significant divergences that may be noted. For example, the Scots and Welsh favour non-metropolitan areas and, aside from London, are under-represented in the conurbations, whereas the Northern Irish favour the large centres of population. Regionally, the Welsh are heavily concentrated in the South West and the West Midlands, and the Scots in the North West, reflecting geographical propinquity, whereas the Northern Irish favour the North West and South East, i.e the traditional points of access to Britain. None of these populations show any significant differences in distribution by sex. In overall terms, the Scottish-born distribution is more similar to that of the native English than those of either the Welsh or Northern Irish.

The patterns of change since 1981 are also strongly differentiated (Table 9.12). All three groups diminished in size in the metropolitan counties, particularly the Welsh-born population, but the Northern Irish- and Scottish-born populations continued their strong growth in non-metropolitan areas. Similarly, Welsh numbers dropped sharply in Greater London against continued increase in the number of Northern Irish- and Scottish-born. Regionally, the Scottish-born population increased most rapidly in East Anglia, the South West and the Outer South East, but declined in the East and West Midlands, and in the North West. The Welsh-born population declined in all regions bar East Anglia, the South West and the Outer South East, whereas those originating from Northern Ireland increased in all regions with the exception of the East and West Midlands, the North West and Yorkshire and Humberside. A degree of differentiation by sex is also apparent.

Table 9.12 *Geographical distribution of the indigenous minorities by region of residence in England in 1991 and change between 1981 and 1991.*

Region	Distribution			Percentage Change		
	Scottish-born	Welsh-born	Northern Irish-born	Scottish-born	Welsh-born	Northern Irish-born
North	8.4	2.0	4.2	2.4	-2.3	6.9
Yorks & Humberside	8.9	4.3	7.3	-5.2	-5.8	-0.3
East Midlands	8.9	5.7	6.9	-4.5	-1.3	-0.7
East Anglia	4.3	3.1	3.6	17.4	11.8	17.4
South East	40.5	37.9	42.4	3.1	-6.7	11.4
South West	9.3	19.6	8.9	14.7	2.8	14.4
West Midlands	8.1	16.4	11.5	-1.6	-7.1	-5.9
North West	11.6	10.9	15.2	-4.5	-12.5	-7.5
Metropolitan Counties	16.8	13.8	21.9	-10.7	-16.9	-9.8
Non-Metropolitan Counties	68.0	73.2	58.1	5.0	-1.0	7.0
Greater London	15.2	12.9	20.0	2.9	-10.7	16.3
Total	100.0	100.0	100.0	1.7	-4.8	4.4

Sources: 1991 Census Ethnic Group and Country of Birth Great Britain, volume 1, OPCS and RG Scotland, Table 1; Census 1981 Country of Birth Great Britain, OPCS and RG Scotland, Table 1:

9.6 Northern Ireland

Northern Ireland is the most clear-cut example of majority/minority demographic relationships in the UK. Reference has already been made to what in effect is the existence of a 'double minority' in the province — Catholics constituting the minority in Northern Ireland and Protestants the minority in the whole of Ireland. The demographic significance of this is two-fold. On the one hand, the concept of ethnocentrism (e.g Day, 1968; Kennedy, 1973)) suggests that it is their status as a minority in the province that has fuelled a higher Catholic rate of population growth; while on the other hand, a high rate of growth within an already large Catholic/nationalist minority has stoked up Protestant/unionist fears about being 'out-bred' and the consequence that Northern Ireland could eventually leave the United Kingdom. In effect, the Northern Ireland problem is one of conflicting nationalisms in which religion and demography are closely intertwined.

Charting the distinctive demographies of Catholics and Protestants is helped by the fact that religion has been an item of census inquiry since 1861. However, there are also fundamental gaps in our knowledge because births and deaths are not registered by parental denomination, nor is there much in the way of reliable information about religion and migration. Moreover, even census information has become more problematic since 1971 because of the refusal of substantial numbers of people to state their denomination (the census question on religion is a voluntary one). In 1971 and 1981 the bulk of those not responding were Catholic, whereas in 1991 most are thought to have been Protestants (Compton and Power, 1986; Jardine, forthcoming). Hence appropriate adjustments have to be made to the last three Northern Ireland censuses if proper sense is to be of recent denominational trends. To complicate matters further, the 1981 Census was the subject of a campaign of non-cooperation with the result that the population was seriously under-enumerated (Morris and Compton, 1985).

General trends

The answer to the question 'What is the current denominational breakdown of the Northern Ireland population?' is therefore crucially dependent on the nature of the adjustments to the census data that are made. (The breakdown by major denomination/religion as it was enumerated in 1991 is presented in Table 9.13 for information.) Because the answer to this question is a central political issue, there is a wide spread of opinion about what the breakdown is (Breen, 1994; Eversley and Heer, 1984; McKitterick, 1992, Macourt, forthcoming). In fact, all that can be determined with any degree of certainty is the range within which the Catholic and non-Catholic proportions lie. These ranges, together with what are considered to be the best estimates for 1971, 1981 and 1991, are presented in Table 9.14. The pre-1961 Northern Ireland census figures can be accepted at face value and are also shown in the table to complete the temporal trend. Interestingly, the estimated Catholic total for 1991 — at around 41.0 per cent — is almost exactly what it had been 130 years earlier in 1861.

Table 9.13. *Religious breakdown in Northern Ireland: 1991 (resident population)*

Religion/denomination	Number	Percent
Roman Catholic	605,639	38.4
Presbyterian	336,891	21.4
Church of Ireland	279,280	17.7
Methodist	59,517	3.8
Baptist	19,484	1.2
Brethren	12,446	0.8
Free Presbyterian	12,363	0.8
Congregational	8,176	0.5
Other Protestant denominations and sects	59,513	3.8
Hindu, Moslem, Sikh, Buddhist	2,141	0.1
Jew	410	0.0
Fringe Christian and Other Groups[1]	4,457	0.3
No religion, atheist, agnostic, indefinite answer	62,692	4.0
Not Stated	114,827	7.3
Total	1,577,836	100.0

[1]Jehovah's Witnesses, Church of the Latter day Saints, Baha'i World Faith, Seventh Day Adventist, Christian Scientist, Charismatic, Chistadelphian, British Israelite, Zoroastrians
Source: the Northern Ireland Census Religion Report, DHSS and RG Northern Ireland, Appendix.

Table 9.14 *Breakdown of the Northern Ireland population by religious denomination, 1861 and 1926 to 1991*

Census	Population (000s)	Catholic %	Range (%)	Non–Catholic %	Range (%)
1861	1,396	40.9	–	59.1	–
1926	1,257	33.5	–	66.5	–
1937	1,280	33.5	–	66.5	–
1951	1,371	34.4	–	65.6	–
1961	1,425	34.9	–	65.1	–
1971	1,520	36.8[1]	31.4–40.8	63.2[1]	59.2–68.6
1981	1,532	38.7[1]	28.0–46.5	61.3[1]	53.5–72.0
1991	1,578	41.5[1]	38.4–45.7	58.5[1]	54.3–61.6

[1] Best estimate.
Source: The Northern Ireland Census Religion Report, DHSS and RG Northern Ireland, modified version of Table 1.

In line with the all-Ireland trend, Catholic numbers dropped sharply after the Potato Famine, bottomed out in the first decades of this century, nudged upwards between 1937 and 1961, but more recently have been rising at around 2 percentage points per decade. If this rate of advance were to continue, the Catholic and Protestant populations would achieve virtual parity within 40 years and thereafter Catholics would move into the majority. It is this scenario that is the basis of Protestant/unionist fears that Northern Ireland will eventually leave the UK.

The components of change responsible for the demographic advance of the Catholic population are clear in outline, but difficult to quantify precisely. The reason for the advance has been the combination of a high level of Catholic natural increase with a considerable lessening of the traditional Catholic excess in net emigration. We can be reasonably certain that Catholic natural increase remained above 1 per cent per annum throughout the 1970s and 1980s. Although the evidence from baptismal data (Annuario Pontificio, various dates) and census age structure suggests that the Catholic birth rate has dropped significantly in recent years — down from around 25 per 1000 in 1980 to under 20 per 1000 in 1990 — this has occurred in the context of a death rate of no more than 9 per 1000 (Compton, 1995). With a non-Catholic birth rate in the range 14 to 15 per 1,000 and a death rate of around 11.5 per 1,000, there has been a situation over the last decade or so in which natural increase in the Catholic population has been some three times higher than that in the non-Catholic population.

Net external migration figures complete the picture. The evidence suggests that the last intercensal period saw roughly equal numbers of Catholics and Protestants leaving the province. From the Protestant side, there are disproportionate numbers of students going on to higher education in Britain, most of whom never return to the province, while the Catholic side contributes disproportionate numbers of economically active leavers. Combining all three components — births, deaths and net migration — gives the Catholic non-Catholic balance sheet presented in Table 9.15. The tentative, almost speculative, nature of the estimates presented in this table must be emphasised. The base populations for 1981 are themselves estimates that have been adjusted for non-statement and non-enumeration. Similarly, the 1991 base has been adjusted for non-statement. The birth and death estimates are derived indirectly, while the net migration estimates are a simple residual calculation.

Geographical patterns

These macro-level trends also extend down to the regional level. Hence, comparing the census figures for 1991 with those for 1971, after due adjust-

Table 9.15 *The demographic balance sheet for Catholics and Non–Catholics in Northern Ireland: 1981–1991*

			Catholics	non–Catholics
1)		Actual population 1981	593,300	939,100
2)		Estimated births 81–91	137,000	137,000
3)		Estimated deaths 81–91	52,000	107,500
4)	(2–3)	Natural increase 81–91	85,000	29,500
5)	(1+4)	Expected population 1991	678,300	968,600
6)		Observed population 1991	645,000	932,000
7)	(6–5)	Estimated net migration 81–91	–33,000	–36,600

Source: Author's calculations.

ment for non-statement, shows the general increase in the Catholic population replicated in most geographical areas. The western half of the province
— the West of Bann region (comprising the local government districts of
Armagh, Cookstown, Derry, Dungannon, Fermanagh, Limavady,
Maghcrafelt, Newry & Mourne, Omagh and Strabane) — has become substantially more Catholic. Here, the Catholic total has grown by 25 per cent
since 1971 and as the non-Catholic population declined by 4 per cent over
the same period, the Catholic proportion in the region's population has risen
from 58 to 64 per cent. A similar process may also be noted in the east. The
same 25 per cent growth in the Catholic population occurred in the East of
Bann region (comprising the local government districts of Ards, Antrim,
Ballymena, Ballymoney, Banbridge, Belfast, Carrickfergus, Castlereagh,
Craigavon, Coleraine, Down, Larne, Lisburn, Moyle, Newtonabbey and
North Down), though here the non-Catholic population also increased by 17
per cent, with the result that the relative Catholic advance from 28 to 30 per
cent of the region's total was rather less marked.

At the local government district level, in all but five of the 26 districts the
Catholic proportion was higher in 1991 than in 1971. (The five recording a
decline in the Catholic proportion were all located in the east and comprised
Ards, Banbridge, Carrickfergus, Larne, Newtownabbey and North Down.)
The greatest proportionate rises occurred in Belfast (although within an
overall declining population), Cookstown, Derry, Down, Limavady, Lisburn,
Newry & Mourne and Strabane. Belfast aside, the picture is therefore one of
greater geographical polarisation at the margins, with non-Catholics re-
treating from the west and Catholics evacuating some Protestant areas in the
east. Although there are obviously other districts that have become more
mixed, one would suspect that segregation at the locality level remains as
strong as ever. A definitive statement about this, however, will have to await
investigation on a more detailed geographical scale.

Mixed marriages

Geographical separation is but one instance of the pervasive polarisation
that runs through Northern Ireland society. It also occurs in employment
and education, and demographically in the individual choice of marriage
partners. In a population with an inter-community breakdown of roughly
four to six, one would expect about half of all marriages to be mixed
Catholic/Protestant if group membership did not effect the choice of marriage partners. While there is no doubt that the actual proportion is well
below this expected rate, there is a widespread perception that the number
of mixed marriages has risen significantly in recent years. However, the
precise level and trend have been difficult to quantify because the available
data are patchy and generally unreliable. In these circumstances, the census
provides the one comprehensive source of information in that an estimate
can be derived from the cross-tabulation of the religious denomination of
spouses.

Although the picture this gives is based on current religion rather than
religion at the time of marriage, and to that extent will understate the true
proportion (denomination at the time of marriage is obviously more exact),

the resulting estimate that only 2.3 per cent of marriages in 1991 involved Catholic/Protestant partners is still surprisingly low (special census tabulation). It is lower than the findings from most recent surveys, e.g. an estimated 3.6 per cent by the Northern Ireland Fertility Survey conducted in 1983 (Compton & Coward, 1989) and 4.5 per cent by Moxon-Browne in 1979 (Moxon-Browne, 1983). It is, however, comparable with the 2 per cent mixed marriages obtained from the 1971 Census. In effect, far from being on a rising trend, the picture is of a broadly static situation in which the various estimates probably lie within the error margins of the data. As for mixed marriage differentials, the 1991 Census findings show a flat social class profile, but a tendency for the rate to vary inversely with age at marriage. A degree of geographical variation is also indicated.

The census and survey figures can be reconciled if it is assumed that the census understates the true position. There are several reasons for believing this to be so. Because social and family pressures against mixed marriages remain strong, it may be supposed that the anecdotal evidence that couples in mixed marriages are more likely to leave the province, thereby escaping a census enumeration, is probably correct. Additionally, the census data suggest that partners from across the religious divide are more likely to cohabit than the population at large — in 1991, 12 per cent of cohabiting couples were in Catholic/Protestant unions (special census tabulation); their inclusion raises the proportion of mixed marriages from 2.3 to 2.5 per cent. It is also possible that one or both partners in a mixed marriage enumerated themselves as being of no religion; adding the Catholic/none and Protestant/none combinations to the 2.5 per cent above further raises the total to 3 per cent. Another adjustment would be to take account of the fact that some partners change denomination to that of the spouse subsequent to marriage. The Northern Ireland Fertility Survey suggested that this occurs in around 40 per cent of cases, therefore the 3 per cent above can probably be further inflated to an estimated 5 per cent of all couples living in a mixed Catholic/Protestant union in 1991. Although this in turn could be adjusted upwards to allow for higher levels of out migration by couples in mixed marriages, it still leaves the conclusion that mixed marriages are far below what would be expected from any normative criterion.

The future denominational balance

The other great issue in Northern Ireland's demography concerns future change in the denominational balance of the population. Although there is no exact relationship between denomination and constitutional preference, the perception is widespread that were a Catholic/nationalist majority to come about, the province might wish to leave the UK and join the Irish Republic. Because a Catholic majority will only come into existence through differential population growth, the speed and direction of demographic change is fundamental to Northern Ireland politics.

A straightforward view of the trends in recent decades points to an eventual Catholic majority. The Catholic proportion has been rising at about 2 percentage points per decade, up from 34.9 per cent in 1961 to 41–42 per cent in 1991, and a simple extrapolation of this trend would suggest a Catholic majority within the next 50 years. Similarly, projecting estimated rates of natural increase between 1981 and 1991 gives a Catholic majority some time between 2021 and 2031 and projecting the respective rates of intercensal change over the same period (8.7 and -0.7 per cent respectively) produces a Catholic majority around 2031.

However, more detailed evidence from the 1991 Census shows that the situation is complex. Of particular relevance in this regard are the inferences that can be drawn from the census age breakdown of the population by denomination, and the data on the number of children born to married women. Because the faster Catholic rate of growth is attributable to a higher birth rate, the progress towards a Catholic majority should be visible in the age breakdown of the population by denomination. A majority should appear first within the population aged 0 and thereafter emerge systematically in the age structure with the passage of time. The process will obviously be affected by the relative size of the birth rate disparity as well as by any differentials in mortality and external migration. The age breakdown of the Northern Ireland population by denomination therefore acts as a barometer of the future balance within the population as a whole.

The position in 1991 by single years of age up to the age of 19 is presented in Table 9.16. The salient points are that as far as the enumerated population is concerned, non-Catholics constitute a clear majority at all ages above 18. Below the age of 18, the situation is indeterminate because of non-statement; inspection of the table shows that Catholics were the largest enumerated group between ages 1 and 13 with a clear implication that they might already be a majority in this age range. It should be noted, however, that the percentage of Catholics peaks at the age of 9 (47.6 per cent) and not at age 0. Therefore, while the trend above the age of 9 is quite consistent with the eventual emergence of a Catholic majority, the trend in the population aged 9 and under is more consistent with demographic resurgence within the non-Catholic population.

The breakdown within the population, excluding those not stating a denomination from the calculation (columns 6 and 7 in Table 9.13), reveals non-Catholic majorities above age 14 and also at age 0. With confidence of a higher non-Catholic rate of non-statement it may be concluded that these are almost certainly real majorities and not artefacts of non-statement. Otherwise, there would be Catholic majorities between ages 1 and 14, though at ages 1, 2 and 3 they are only marginal and could just as easily be non-Catholic majorities.

Looking at the evidence that comes from apportioning the numbers not stating a denomination, while there are clear variations in the overall refusal rate, the breakdown by denomination was consistent across the whole age range. The correction can therefore be based on the overall aggregate rates of non-statement calibrated to the specific non-statement rate recorded at each age. The picture that now emerges is rather different (Table 9.16). This time there are only Catholic majorities between the ages of 6 and 10. The breakdowns at 4, 5 and 11 are evenly balanced, with non-Catholic majorities at all other ages. The clear inference that the falling proportion of births to non-Catholics may well have bottomed out in the mid-1980s is particularly significant.

Unlike Great Britain, the Northern Ireland census also included an inquiry into the number of children born to ever-married women. It is the number of children born in the year preceding the census that is of most interest in this particular context. Space precludes detailed analysis but, not unexpectedly, the breakdown of these births by denomination mirrors the denominational breakdown in the population aged 0 in 1991; 44.5 per cent were to Catholic mothers, 47.7 per cent to non-Catholic mothers and 7.8 per cent to mothers who did not state their denomination. The main difference lies in the lower percentage of births with non-stated denomination, which has the effect of raising the non-Catholic proportion and is consistent with the notion that non-statement was higher within the non-Catholic group. It is also consistent with the inference already drawn from the age data that there were more births to non-Catholics than to Catholics in 1990–91 — 51.5 to 48.5 per cent would seem to be in the right range.

None the less, it still has to be emphasised that even though Catholic marital fertility may well be falling, it is still substantially above the non-Catholic level. In the 20–34 age group, for example, which accounts for over 80 per cent of legitimate births in Northern Ireland, the marital fertility rates were

Table 9.16 *The 1991 age breakdown of the Northern Ireland Population by denomination (percent as enumerated, percent of stating population only and percent after apportionment)*

(1)	(2)	(3)	(4)	(5)	(6)	(7)	(8)	(9)
Age	Popul-ation	Catholic	¹Non Catholic	Not stated	Catholic	¹Non Catholic	Catholic	¹Non Catholic
		(% as enumerated)			(% of stating population)		(% after apportionment)	
0	24,747	44.3	45.0	10.7	49.6	50.4	48.5	51.5
1	25,239	45.2	45.1	9.6	50.1	49.9	49.2	50.8
2	25,465	45.5	45.0	9.5	50.2	49.8	49.4	50.6
3	26,082	45.5	45.3	9.2	50.1	49.9	49.4	50.6
4	26,720	46.6	44.6	8.7	51.1	48.9	50.0	50.0
5	26,278	46.4	44.7	8.9	50.9	49.1	50.0	50.0
6	25,856	46.7	44.9	8.4	51.0	49.0	50.2	49.8
7	26,073	47.2	44.4	8.4	51.6	48.8	50.6	49.4
8	25,495	47.3	44.5	8.2	51.5	48.5	50.8	49.2
9	25,451	47.6	44.5	7.9	51.7	48.3	51.0	49.0
10	26,699	47.1	45.1	7.8	51.1	48.9	50.3	49.7
11	26,772	46.8	46.2	7.1	50.3	49.7	50.0	50.0
12	25,330	46.8	46.2	7.1	50.3	49.7	49.5	50.5
13	24,711	46.6	46.0	7.4	50.3	49.7	49.4	50.6
14	24,357	46.5	46.5	7.0	50.0	50.0	49.1	50.9
15	24,623	45.4	47.5	7.0	48.9	51.1	48.0	52.0
16	25,075	44.9	48.1	6.7	48.4	51.6	47.6	52.4
17	25,642	43.5	49.2	6.8	48.1	51.9	46.4	53.6
18	26,273	42.8	51.0	6.2	45.6	54.4	45.0	55.0
19	25,968	43.0	50.6	6.4	45.9	54.1	45.3	54.7

Source: the Northern Ireland Census Religion Report, DHSS and RG Northern Ireland, Table 4.

177 and 139 for Catholics and non-Catholics respectively, giving a differential of 27 per cent. There is, of course, a caveat to be added here: the census figures refer to legitimate births only and exclude the 20 per cent born out of wedlock. The general tenor of the argument would only be invalidated, however, if the assumption about higher non-Catholic non-statement were wrong or if Catholic women accounted for most illegitimate births, a proposition for which there is no evidence.

In other words, the census evidence suggests that a Catholic majority in the province is by no means inevitable. Although the picture is complicated by the possible effect of differential migration, the census evidence points to a substantial fall in the Catholic birth rate in recent years, which is also borne out independently by the trend in Catholic baptisms. A useful way of conceptualising Northern Ireland's demography is to think of it as the place where the British and Irish demographic systems overlap — Protestants exhibiting an essentially British and Northern Catholics an essentially Irish demographic pattern. Although lagged in time, the fall in the birth rate of Northern Catholics postulated here may therefore be seen as an extension of the sharp decline in the Republic's birth rate since 1980. In this view the border does not act as a divide as far as Catholic demography is concerned. Moreover, following through this reasoning, the recent sharp fall in the overall Northern Ireland birth rate (down from 18.0 to 15.1 between 1986 and 1993) becomes mainly attributable to Catholic rather than non-Catholic birth rate decline. In effect, it is being suggested that the era of 'high' Catholic natural increase in Northern Ireland is now over (e.g. Fitzgerald, 1993). Indeed, given the experience of Catholic fertility decline in other European countries — the lowest rates are now found in the traditionally devout Catholic countries of Southern Europe — one cannot preclude the Northern Ireland rate dropping below that of non-Catholics in future years. Census- and baptismal-based estimates of the recent trend in crude birth rates by denomination are presented in Table 9.17.

Table 9.17 *Catholic and Non-Catholic birth rates estimated from census and baptismal data: 1980/81–1990/91*

Census-based estimates				Estimates derived from baptismal records				
Year	Catholic	Non-Catholic	All	Year	Number	Catholic (%)	Catholic	Non-Catholic
		(rates per 1000)					(rates per 1000)	
1980/81	23.8	14.8	18.3	1980	28,582	49.5	23.5	15.0
1981/82	23.2	14.2	17.7	1981	27,302	50.0	23.0	14.5
1982/83	22.9	14.3	17.7	1982	27,028	53.2	24.0	13.5
1983/84	22.9	14.5	17.8	1983	27,255	51.2	23.2	14.2
1984/85	22.6	14.8	17.8	1984	27,993	50.8	23.1	14.5
1985/86	22.6	14.9	17.8	1985	27,635	49.4	22.3	14.9
1986/87	22.6	14.9	17.8	1986	28,152	49.5	22.6	15.2
1987/88	21.8	15.0	17.6	1987	27,865	49.1	22.0	15.1
1988/89	21.0	14.7	17.0	1988	27,767	48.6	21.5	15.2
1989/90	20.2	14.5	16.6	1989	26,080	49.3	20.3	14.1
1990/91	19.8	14.6	16.6	1990	26,499	49.0	20.8	14.4
				1991	26,265	47.7	19.5	14.7
				1992	25,572	48.5	19.2	14.0

Source: the Northern Ireland Census Religion Report, DHSS and RG Northern Ireland, Table 4; Annuario Pontificio 1978 to 1994

Projection scenarios

Let us now examine how the population balance may be expected to evolve over future decades in the light of the foregoing discussion. Four projection scenarios are presented here based on a cohort survival model, with the following assumptions:

1. The corrected 1991 Catholic and non-Catholic populations broken down by five-year age-group and sex are used as the initial populations. Each projection moves forward in five steps — 1991, 1996, 2001 and so on.
2. Fertility assumptions are based on the estimated age-specific birth rates for 1991 (Table 9.18).
3. The 1990–92 Northern Ireland life table is used to model mortality; survivorship ratios are assumed to be identical for each denomination.
4. Net migration will continue at the levels estimated for the intercensal period 1981–91 allocated to age-group in the same ratios as the migration values imputed from the National Health Service Central Registry.

It is emphasised that the projections are designed to illustrate the impact of specific sets of demographic assumptions on future Catholic and non-Catholic numbers and should not be treated as forecasts. Using this approach, it is possible to produce a very large number of projections, given the wide range of plausible assumptions that can be made about future changes in the levels of fertility, mortality and net migration. However, this work is limited to reporting the results of what are regarded as the four most informative scenarios. The first two scenarios involve projecting natural increase only, in one as a constant and in the other assuming Catholic fertility decline. The other two scenarios include an assumption about net migration within the same framework. Altogether the four scenarios establish markers from which the effects of other combinations of assumptions are readily deduced. The results are given in Table 9.19.

Table 9.18 *Estimated age-specific birth rates by denomination for 1991 (rates per 1,000 population)*

Age group	Catholic	Non–Catholic	All
15–19	25	30	27
20–24	90	85	100
25–29	185	135	150
30–34	130	90	105
35–39	65	40	50
40–44	12	8	10
45–49	1	1	1
TFR	2.5	1.9	2.2

Source: Author's calculations

Table 9.19 *Projected numbers of Catholics and non-Catholics to year 2036 (numbers are given in 00s)*

Year	Projection 1 [1]		Projection 2 [2]		Projection 3 [3]		Projection 4 [4]	
	Non-Catholic	Catholic	Non-Catholic	Catholic	Non-Catholic	Catholic	Non-Catholic	Catholic
1996	943,3	683,8	943,3	681,8	924,2	665,5	924,2	663,4
2001	954,2	726,5	954,2	719,7	914,6	690,6	914,6	684,1
2006	962,5	771,0	962,5	753,8	899,1	714,4	899,1	698,5
2011	968,7	816,1	968,7	785,0	879,3	736,7	879,3	708,6
2016	973,7	860,3	973,7	813,6	856,2	756,6	856,2	715,5
2021	978,0	903,2	978,0	839,3	830,7	774,5	830,7	719,7
2026	980,5	945,1	980,5	862,4	801,4	788,4	801,4	719,4
2031	979,6	985,5	979,6	881,1	766,9	799,2	766,9	714,5
2036	975,4	1,025,2	975,4	895,1	727,0	807,1	727,0	704,7

[1] Constant birth and survivorship rates assumed. The rates for Catholics and non-Catholics are those estimated for the early 1990s (see text).
[2] Catholic age specific birth rates assumed to decline to non-Catholic level by 2011. Survivorship held constant as in projection 1.
[3] Constant birth and survivorship rates assumed as in projection 1. Catholic and non-Catholic net migration assumed to continue at the level estimated for the intercensal period 1981-91 and built into the projection as absolute numbers.
[4] Birth and survivorship rates as in projection 2. Net migration as in projection 3.

Source: Author's calculations.

Projection 1 holds age-specific birth and survivorship rates constant at the levels estimated for 1990–92, i.e. it is an extrapolation of current natural increase. It shows that if the current fertility differential persists, in the absence of differential out migration, a simple Catholic majority would come about around 2030. At that time, however, non-Catholics would still constitute a 52 per cent majority of the voting age population and this would not disappear until somewhere between 2046 and 2051. Unless non-Catholic migration increases significantly relative to Catholic migration from the province or there is a resurgence in Catholic fertility, this projection pro-vides an estimate of the earliest date that a Catholic majority is likely to emerge.

Projection 2 is designed to illustrate the impact of Catholic fertility decline on the future population balance. In this instance, non-Catholic fertility rates are held constant at the levels given in Table 19.5 (equivalent to a TFR of 1.9), whereas Catholic rates are progressively reduced until equalisation is achieved in 2011. Mortality rates are again held constant. Under these assumptions a Catholic majority would never emerge. Rather, the two populations would move to stable states with the breakdown in the province eventually settling down at around 51.5 per cent non-Catholic and 48.5 per cent Catholic. By 2011 the Catholic proportion will have grown to 44.8 per cent of the total, increasing to 47.4 per cent by 2031 and so on to stability by 2071.

The significance of projection 2 lies not so much in the result but in the demonstration of the importance of differential fertility. The crucial factor is the speed at which Catholic and non-Catholic birth rates converge. If Catholic fertility decline continues at the rate estimated for the 1980s, it is quite plain that a Catholic majority will not emerge. But if the decline occurs at a slower rate than is assumed here, say convergence materialising only towards the end of the first quarter of the next century, then there could well be an eventual Catholic majority. At the moment, the balance of evidence would seem to support the notion of relatively rapid decline and convergence. Indeed, given the presumed drop in the Catholic birth rate since 1991, the projection could well understate the speed of this process. As the experience of the Irish Republic and elsewhere shows, once Catholic birth rates begin to slide, they can fall very rapidly indeed. It must be stressed, however, that even with rapid convergence, the future will still be radically different from now in the sense that Catholic and non-Catholic numbers will become much more evenly balanced. In other words, whatever the future actually holds, the current relative size of the non-Catholic majority is bound to shrink.

The projections so far have excluded any consideration of external migration, but it goes without saying that any significant differential in this respect will have a considerable impact on the future Catholic/non-Catholic balance. After all, if it were not for the substantially higher emigration rate of Catholics in the past, the Protestant population would already be in the minority. However, not only has net out migration fluctuated markedly over the last two decades or so but, as in the case of Scotland, the current recession has led to a reversal of the normal direction of net movement. On the question of the composition of the net inflow, the 1991 SAR suggests that two thirds of the gross inflow to Northern Ireland in the year preceding the census was composed of non-Catholics. Although this finding cannot be directly extrapolated to the current net inflow, it does suggest that anecdotal evidence that this is comprised mainly of Catholics is wrong. Given such instability, the estimation of how future migration may break down between Catholics and non-Catholics can be little more than subjective judgement.

Even so, notwithstanding the net inflow at the moment, it is probably safe to assume that the predominant direction of migration in future years will continue to be outwards — the 1991-based national projection makes this assumption; the economic fundamentals in which labour supply exceeds demand are unlikely to change quickly. It is probably also safe to assume that, in the medium term at least, Catholic labour migration will remain above the Protestant level due to higher natural growth in the Catholic labour force, though this will diminish once the effect of a lower Catholic birth rate begins to feed through. At the moment this is partly offset by greater Protestant student migration, but even here the evidence suggests that an increasing number of Catholics are attending courses in GB higher education institutes (Cormack et al.,1993). It is too early to make any judgement about the effect of a permanent peace settlement; but if anything, the short-term economic impacts could well be negative if peace leads to a cutback in government spending, and the rate of net outflow could even rise as a result.

In the light of these imponderables, the migration assumption is for Catholic and non-Catholic net outflow to continue at the same level as estimated for the intercensal period 1981–91 — that is a net loss of 36,600 non-Catholics and 33,000 Catholics. In view of the arguments above, this may well over-state the loss of non-Catholics relative to Catholics and, consequently, understate the future size of the non-Catholic population. The tendency to understate the future size of the non-Catholic population is compounded by the fact that migration loss is operationalised in terms of absolute numbers and not at a rate proportional to population size. Because below replace-ment fertility is already causing the non-Catholic population to decline, it is equivalent to assuming that the rate of non-Catholic outflow will actually rise in future. In other words, the migration assumption is probably overly pessimistic about future non-Catholic prospects.

The assumptions about net migration have been built into the constant fertility and mortality projection to produce projection 3. In fact, the out-come as far as future composition is concerned is comparatively minor. At the most it would bring forward the date of a simple Catholic majority by one or two years with a majority in the voting population by the mid-2040s. The manner in which the two populations change is radically different, however. Because non-Catholic fertility is already below replacement level, the assumption of migration loss, albeit comparatively modest, sends the non-Catholic population into quite rapid decline. As Catholic numbers are projected to continue to rise, the cross-over point occurs when each popula-tion reaches around 750,000 (Table 9.16).

Projection 4 combines the same migration assumption with the presumption of Catholic fertility decline (projection 2). In this scenario, although the Catholic population is projected to grow initially, it peaks around 2021 and then declines. But because fertility rates are assumed to converge, the eventual outcome of this scenario is governed by the small migration differential and is for an eventual Catholic majority sometime around 2050. To all intents and purposes, however, the two groups would have achieved numerical parity by 2036.

What may be concluded from these scenarios? In the event of the Catholic birth rate remaining above the non-Catholic rate indefinitely, a Catholic majority is virtually inevitable (only a return to strongly differentiated net out-migration could prevent it). The important point though is that even in these circumstances a Catholic majority is not imminent but is still some 30 to 40 years into the future. Moreover, in the event of a continuation of Catholic fertility decline, this time-scale is greatly extended. Indeed, if Catholic and non-Catholic birth rates converge rapidly, or if the Catholic rate were to fall below the non-Catholic rate, which is not impossible, a Catholic majority will never come about. The impact of migration will depend on the magnitude and direction of the differential. If Catholic net out-migration were to exceed the non-Catholic level in future years, the likelihood of a Catholic majority recedes even further into the future when coupled with fertility decline. On the other hand, a higher rate of non-Catholic migration loss increases the likelihood of a Catholic majority. What is certain, however, is that the size of the non-Catholic majority will continue to shrink for the foreseeable future; the in-built growth momentum of the Catholic population will ensure this even if the respective TFRs were equalised tomorrow.

In summary, the religious breakdown of the child population is already very finely balanced. It is consistent with the emergence of a Catholic majority within a generation or so. Indeed, extrapolating current birth and death rates by denomination produces a Catholic majority in around the year 2030. However, the actual situation is more subtle than this. The 1991 Census suggests that non-Catholic numbers have actually strengthened in the most recent birth cohorts. Although this may merely be the result of the uncertainties associated with non-statement, it is also consistent with the proposition that the Catholic birth rate is passing through a period of relative decline. If fertility convergence is rapid, a Catholic majority is unlikely to emerge. Indeed, with the collapse of the birth rate in the Irish Republic (down by over a third since 1980), this may well be the most likely scenario. It is difficult to gauge how migration will effect the situation. The scanty evidence that exists suggests that the level of Catholic net outflow was marginally lower over the last intercensal period as a whole, but in more recent years this may well have reverted to the more traditional pattern of lower non-Catholic migration loss. It is, of course, possible to postulate a wide range of plausible migration scenarios that would trigger either more Catholic or more non-Catholic migration loss. But what is certain is that the numerical gap between non-Catholics and Catholics will continue to narrow for the foreseeable future. It may well be that the situation will eventually settle down to a rough numerical equivalence in which neither group is in a clear majority or minority.

9.7 Conclusions

The ethnic group question in the 1991 Census does not capture the full heterogeneity of the UK population because it fails to disaggregate the category White into its component groups. As a consequence, investigating the demographic characteristics of the indigenous and other White minority groups can only be approached via birth-place data. By their very nature, however, birth-place data do not pick up second and higher generation members of minority populations and the sizes attached to the various groups examined in this chapter are therefore likely to be understatements. The problem is greatest for long-established minority populations, such as the Irish, where estimates based on birth-place seriously understate the size of such groups.

Regarding substantive findings, most of the foreign-born White minority populations have increased considerably in recent years. This not only applies to minority groups originating from EU countries, but also to the Old Commonwealth, the USA and Turkey. The only substantial decreases in size have been recorded by those originating mainly from the former communist countries of Central and Eastern Europe. Most White minority groups have a majority of females , primarily because foreign-born wives tend to reside in Britain with their husbands whereas British-born wives with foreign husbands are more likely to reside abroad. The age structures of these groups are also distorted, with children being particularly under-represented. Otherwise, the specific circumstances surrounding the settlement in this country of minority groups from Central and East Europe has produced profiles in which the bulk of the people concerned are now aged 50 and over.

The distributions of indigenous UK minority groups broadly reflect the patterns of long-term migration. Hence, more Scots and Northern Irish live in England than English live in Scotland or Northern Ireland, though within this the number of English in Scotland has been rising rapidly in recent decades. Roughly the same number of Welsh reside in England as English in Wales, though the Welsh population in England is on a sharply declining trend. The demographies of the different parts of the UK are less distinct now than in the past. The one exception to this is Northern Ireland, where the traditional disparities between the Catholic minority and Protestant majority in respect of fertility persist. This in turn produces differentials in natural increase which has fuelled a higher overall rate of population growth among Catholics and a rising proportion of Catholics in the Northern Ireland population. If this trend were to continue, Catholics could be expected to outnumber Protestants within two generations from now. However, close examination of census and other evidence suggests that Catholic and Protestant fertility levels are now converging and that a Catholic majority is by no means inevitable.

References

Annuario Pontificio (various years) The Vatican, Rome.

Breen, R. 1994) Over the horizon. *Fortnight*, February, 20–21.

Coleman, D. and Salt, J. (1992) *The British Population: Patterns, Trends and Processes*. Oxford: Oxford University Press.

Compton, P.A. (1993) Population censuses in Northern Ireland: 1926–1991. In: A. Dale and C. Marsh (eds), *The 1991 Census User's Guide.*London: HMSO, pp. 330–51.

Compton, P.A. (1995) *Northern Ireland: Demographic Review 1994*. Belfast: Northern Ireland Economic Council.

Compton, P.A. and Power, J. (1986) Estimates of the religious composition of the Northern Ireland local government districts in 1981 and change in the geographical pattern of religious composition between 1971 and 1981. *Economic and Social Review*, 17, 87–106.

Compton, P.A. and Coward, J. (1989) *Fertility and Family Planning in Northern Ireland*. Aldershot: Avebury.

Cormack, R., Obsorne, R. and Gallagher, A. (1993) Higher education participation of Northern Irish students. Paper presented to the Northern Ireland Higher Education Council.

Day, L. (1968) Natality and ethnocentrism: some relationships suggested by the analysis of Catholic-Protestant differentials. *Population Studies*, vol. XXI, 27–50.

Eversley, D. and Heer, V. (1984) *The Roman Catholic population of Northern Ireland in 1981*. Belfast: Fair Employment Agency.

Fitzgerald, G. (1993) The dubious arithmetic of 'outbreeding'. *Irish Times*, November 27.

General Register Office England. (1958) *Census 1951 England and Wales, General Report*, chapter V, Birthplace and Nationality. London: HMSO.

Jardine, E. (forthcoming) Demographic structure in Northern Ireland and its implications for constitutional preference. *Journal of the Social and Statistical Inquiry Society of Ireland*.

Kennedy, R. (1973) Minority group status and fertility: the Irish. *American Sociological Review*, 38, 85–96.

Macourt, M. (forthcoming). Using census data: religion as a key variable in studies in Northern Ireland. *Environment & Planning A*.

McKittrick, D. (1992) The numbers that matter. *Independent on Sunday*, November 1.

Morris, C. and Compton, P.A. (1985) 1981 Census of population in Northern Ireland. *Population Trends*, 40, 16–20.

Moxon-Browne, E. (1983) *Nation, Class and Creed in Northern Ireland*. Lower: Gower.

Northern Ireland General Register Office (1976) *Census of Population 1971 Religion Tables Northern Ireland*. Belfast: HMSO.

OPCS Immigrant Statistics Unit (1977) New Commonwealth and Pakistani population estimates. *Population Trends*, 9, 4–7.

OPCS (1993) *National Population Projections: 1991-based*. London: HMSO.

OPCS (1994) Internal migration: recorded movements between England, Wales, Scotland, Northern Ireland and standard regions of England, Table 20. *Population Trends*, 78, 69.

Spencer, A. (1979) The relative fertility of the two religious-ethnic communities in Northern Ireland, 1947–1977. In: A. Spencer (ed.), *Sociological Association of Ireland, Transactions 1977-78*. Department of Social Studies, Queen's University of Belfast, 122–31.

Waterman, S. and Kosmin, B. (1986) *British Jewry in the eighties: a statistical and geographical study*. London: Board of Deputies of British Jews.

Index

Page number in *italic* and **bold** indicate a figure and table respectively, appearing away from its text.
Abbreviation: LS = Longitudinal Study